APPLYING COGNITIVE SCIENCE TO EDUCATION

APPLYING COGNITIVE SCIENCE TO EDUCATION

Thinking and Learning in Scientific and Other Complex Domains

FREDERICK REIF, 1927-

A Bradford Book
The MIT Press
Cambridge, Massachusetts
London, England

© 2008 Massachusetts Institute of Technology

All rights reserved. No part of this book may be reproduced in any form by any electronic or mechanical means (including photocopying, recording, or information storage and retrieval) without permission in writing from the publisher.

MIT Press books may be purchased at special quantity discounts for business or sales promotional use. For information, please e-mail ⟨special_sales@mitpress .mit.edu⟩ or write to Special Sales Department, The MIT Press, 55 Hayward Street, Cambridge, MA 02142.

This book was set in Stone Serif and Stone Sans on 3B2 by Asco Typesetters, Hong Kong and was printed and bound in the United States of America.

Library of Congress Cataloging-in-Publication Data

Reif, F. (Frederick), 1927–
Applying cognitive science to education : thinking and learning in scientific and other complex domains / Frederick Reif.
    p. cm.
Includes bibliographical references and index.
ISBN 978-0-262-18263-8 (hardcover : alk. paper) 1. Cognitive learning.
2. Learning, Psychology of. 3. Cognitive science. 4. Education. I. Title.
LB1060.R423 2007
372.15′2—dc22   2007006486

10 9 8 7 6 5 4 3 2 1

In memory of Herbert A. Simon,
whose work I admired long before he became a personal friend,
and to Laura,
who was willing to rejoin me after I had left her

Contents

4   Specifying and Interpreting Concepts   43

5   Interpreting Scientific Concepts   61

6   Managing Memory   85

II-B   Effectiveness   101

7   Methods and Inferences   103

8   Describing Knowledge   119

9   Organizing Knowledge   137

23   Innovative Instructional Methods   417

24   Some Educational Challenges   439

Preface

FOSTERING A MORE SCIENTIFIC APPROACH TO EDUCATION

Unmet educational needs Since many people in our technological world need to acquire a knowledge of scientific subjects, numerous science courses are taught in high schools, colleges, universities, and professional schools. However, students often find it difficult to deal with the learning required in mathematics, physics, chemistry, biology, engineering, or similar such subjects. Furthermore, several investigations (such as Halloun and Hestenes, 1985) have revealed that students frequently emerge from such courses with significant misconceptions, with fragmented knowledge that they cannot reliably use, and without the problem-solving abilities needed to apply their acquired scientific knowledge.

Recent attempts to improve science education A greater awareness of such educational deficiencies has motivated some scientists to become more interested in improving science education and in applying a more scientific approach to such educational efforts. For example, physics education research has recently become a respected subfield of physics pursued in several universities. Indeed, some physics departments now offer Ph.D. degrees to physics students who are interested in pursuing careers in physics education. Furthermore, the *Physical Review* (the primary professional journal of American physicists) recently started a special online section of the journal devoted to research in physics education (PER, 2005).

Increasing interest in improving science instruction is also reflected in some recent scientific publications. For example, a guest editorial in the *American Journal of Physics* advocated more systematic efforts to foster physics education research (Heron and Meltzer, 2005). Similarly, eleven scientists from different fields recently published a joint article in *Science* (the journal of the American Association for the Advancement of Science) in which they call for more scientific approaches to teaching (Handelsman et al., 2004).

Limitations of such improvement efforts Attempts by university scientists to improve science education are certainly welcome and address important needs. But are these attempts sufficient—and to what extent are they really scientific? Most of them have tried to devise more effective teaching methods or to deal with students' scientific misconceptions. However, these attempts are unlike those used by scientists in their own scientific fields, where they aim to identify underlying mechanisms (processes and structures) responsible for observable phenomena and to achieve desired goals by building on an understanding of such mechanisms.

In science education the primary interest is not focused on the science itself, but on *students* who are trying to learn scientific knowledge and thinking. A truly scientific approach to education would thus need to strive for a better understanding of the underlying human thought processes and knowledge required for good performance in particular scientific domains. Such an approach would then deliberately exploit an understanding of these underlying mechanisms to help students learn.

Challenges of a genuinely scientific approach to science education The thinking needed for scientific work is often considerably more complex than that commonly required in everyday life. A fundamental difficulty is that science is largely an *artificial* domain—that is, one deliberately devised by special people ("scientists") who pursue the explicit goal of inventing knowledge where a few basic principles enable the prediction and explanation of many observable phenomena. Hence science is significantly different from the domain of everyday life where knowledge and thinking have historically evolved more naturalistically without the deliberate pursuit of any explicit goal.

Einstein was certainly correct when he wrote "the whole of science is nothing more than a refinement of everyday thinking" (Einstein, 1954, 290). However, this statement can be misleading because the refinement has been deliberately pursued for several centuries by some of the best minds in each generation. Hence the resulting refinement has been substantial and has resulted in scientific knowledge and thought processes that are often significantly different from those prevalent in everyday life. These differences need to be clearly understood since they can cause major difficulties for students' learning of science.

College or university science instructors are usually knowledgeable about their scientific discipline, but have ordinarily not studied psychological or educational issues. Thus they approach their educational activities largely on the basis of common sense, intuition, and personal experience. For example, they commonly teach in the way that they themselves have been taught—and try predominantly to transmit knowledge about important scientific facts and methods. They rarely think much about the underlying thought and learning processes that students need in order to use such factual knowledge and methods effectively. Furthermore, extensive experience in their scientific fields has led instructors to acquire knowledge that has become largely *tacit* (outside the range of their conscious awareness). Unless this important knowledge is elucidated, it is never explicitly communicated to students.

GOALS OF THE BOOK

This book aims to present a coherent introduction to some of the *cognitive* issues (issues concerning knowledge, thinking, and learning) that are important in scientific and other complex domains. In particular, I was motivated by the belief that a better understanding of the underlying knowledge and thinking useful in such domains can help to improve instruction and significantly facilitate students' learning.

The book's point of view is that of an *applied* cognitive science that is not as deeply theoretical as "pure" cognitive science, but is centrally interested in a level of analysis that is well suited for the design of practical applications (such as education or human-computer interaction). This level of analysis transcends the more empirical approach of most practitioners (such as teachers or textbook writers). An applied cognitive science thus strives to exploit insights identified by pure cognitive science (in the same way as the applied science of medicine exploits insights obtained by human biology).

As usual, there is a mutually beneficial interaction between pure and applied sciences. A pure science provides insights about underlying mechanisms and may suggest practical applications. Conversely, an applied science provides excellent opportunities for testing theoretical ideas and often reveals new phenomena that merit deeper investigation.

While I was a physics professor teaching at the University of California, my perception of the previously mentioned educational problems caused me, some thirty-five years ago, to shift my interests from research in physics to research dealing with the cognitive and educational issues involved in scientific domains. The present book is an outgrowth of my interests in these issues.

DESCRIPTION OF THE BOOK

The book attempts to present a coherent and readily accessible introduction to thinking, learning, and teaching in scientific domains (or in similar complex domains such as mathematics, engineering, or expository writing). The level of targeted complexity is that needed by high-school or college students, and is also a prerequisite for more demanding intellectual performance.

I have attempted to be judiciously selective by focusing on issues that I deemed most important and by trying to provide a framework that could help to explore other cognitive issues relevant to education.

In particular, the book examines the following questions: What kinds of knowledge and thought processes are needed for good performance? What are some of the difficulties faced by students, used to everyday thinking, when they need to deal with scientific domains? What instructional methods can help students to learn the kinds of knowledge and thinking skills required in such domains? How can such methods be implemented to provide practical instruction for many diverse students? The table of contents provides an outline of the topics explored to answer these questions.

Intended audience for the book   The following kinds of people may potentially be interested in the preceding questions: (1) Instructors (at high schools, colleges, universities, or professional schools) who are teaching scientific, mathematical, or similar demanding subjects. (2) College or university students studying such subjects and interested in improving their learning. (3) Students preparing for careers in teaching or educational research. (4) Authors of textbooks or other instructional materials. (5) Persons interested in cognitive processes or education. (6) People not motivated by specific professional concerns, but interested in ways of achieving good intellectual performance.

My own experience includes dealings with all such people. For example, I have for many years taught physics to undergraduate students and have authored several physics textbooks. I have also published research papers in cognitive-science journals—and taught courses on instructional design to graduate students preparing for careers in teaching or educational research. (I have even discussed cognitive issues in some courses for senior citizens and retirees.)

Attention to practical educational implications   While examining various cognitive issues, the book repeatedly points out their practical educational implications for learning, teaching, and instructional design.

Scope of the book   The following pages deal predominantly with knowledge and thinking skills of the kind needed for science or mathematics courses in high schools or colleges. Such knowledge and thinking skills are only moderately complex and might seem simple to some people. But they are essential prerequisites for more highly demanding intellectual performance. Deficiencies in such basic knowledge and thinking skills are also responsible for many students' difficulties or failures in science courses. Furthermore, the teaching of such knowledge and thinking skills is often inadequate.

Simplicity and comprehensibility   Although I have attempted to be fairly analytic, I have tried *not* to be excessively theoretical so that the ideas discussed here might be readily accessible to most teachers and to people unfamiliar with cognitive issues. In particular, I have tried to follow the advice, attributed to Einstein, that "everything should be made as simple as possible, but not simpler" (Calaprice, 2000, 314–315). Thus I have aimed to present a reasonably coherent framework of basic ideas, to illustrate abstract notions with homely examples, to avoid jargon, and to shun tedious prose where many words convey few significant ideas.

Form of presentation   The book emphasizes that effective knowledge and learning require as much attention to form (description and organization) as to content. To practice what I preach, I have tried to implement the following guidelines. (1) Explicate clearly the organization of the book since this makes it easier to assimilate, review, and retain the relevant information. (Thus I have used major titles to highlight the global structure of the book, and have used local titles to indicate the content of particular paragraphs.) (2) Emphasize central ideas by displaying subordinate comments or examples in a distinct smaller font. (This can help a reader to acquire a hierarchical knowledge organization where a few major ideas subsume more detailed information.) (3) Convey the same information in multiple forms of description (e.g., both words and pictures) since some particular forms may make it easier to perceive some relationships or to perform some tasks.

Since the book is largely intended for people who work or teach in scientific or technical domains, its style may perhaps be more similar to that of a book in the physical sciences than that of a typical book in education or psychology.

Kinds of examples   The illustrative examples used in the book often deal with basic physics or mathematics. There are good reasons for this (besides the fact that these subjects are familiar to me). (1) These subjects are prototypical of successful sciences, are commonly encountered by students early in their college careers, are prerequisites for many other courses (in physics, chemistry, biology, or engineering), and cause students difficulties that are similar to those encountered in more advanced science courses. (2) The chosen examples are likely to be comprehensible to most readers since these are probably familiar with elementary physics or mathematics. (3) The thought processes in physics or mathematics are complex, but the criteria of good performance are very clear. This is why even psychologists, who are not especially interested in these fields, have done substantial cognitive and educational research in these.

CONCLUDING REMARK

When I wrote my first book some forty years ago (Reif, 1965), I concluded the preface with the words "an author never finishes a book, he merely abandons it." This statement still seems equally applicable today. I realize that much in this book could be improved, that I may have failed to attain some of my intended goals, and that further revisions might result in a better product if my life expectancy were less limited. I can only hope that the book may (despite its deficiencies) be useful to some people—and may perhaps stimulate some others to do better.

ACKNOWLEDGMENTS

Chandralekha Singh and to Marsha C. Lovett deserve my thanks for their willingness to review the manuscript for the book. I am grateful for the useful comments made by the former and for some helpful suggestions made by the latter. I also want to express particular thanks to Tom Stone, the editor at the MIT Press, for his interest in publishing the book, his continuing support, and his willingness to respect my wishes despite some troublesome implementation difficulties.

I BASIC ISSUES

1 Performance, Learning, and Teaching

1.1 THINKING ABOUT THINKING

We spend most of our waking hours engaged in thinking, but rarely think much about thinking. Indeed, we are ordinarily not consciously aware of the thinking and knowledge that we commonly use. For example, we may speak our native language correctly, yet be unable to specify its underlying grammatical rules.

However, we may need to think more deeply about thinking when we want to engage in tasks that are more complex than those encountered in daily life. In particular, it is important to think more explicitly about the knowledge and thought processes needed for work in scientific domains, especially if one is interested in achieving good performance or in teaching students the skills and knowledge required for scientific work.

Einstein pointed out the need for a better understanding of human thought processes when he wrote

> The whole of science is nothing more than a refinement of everyday thinking. It is for this reason that the critical thinking of the physicist cannot possibly be restricted to the concepts of his own specific field. He cannot proceed without considering critically a much more difficult problem, the problem of analyzing the nature of everyday thinking. (Einstein, 1954, 290)

These words apply even more to the nature of *scientific* thinking since this has become increasingly complex as a result of refinements extending over several centuries of scientific progress.

Central question Such an interest in human *cognition* (in thought and learning processes and associated kinds of knowledge) leads naturally to the following question of primary concern in this book: *What kinds of knowledge and thought processes are needed for good performance in scientific or similar complex domains—and what instructional methods*

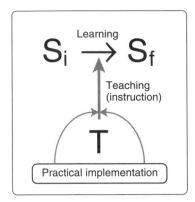

Figure 1.1
Learning and teaching.

can be devised to facilitate students' learning of such knowledge and thinking?

The following pages attempt to answer this general question because it is centrally important for all educational efforts in scientific or similar demanding fields.

1.2 BASIC ISSUES

The preceding general question about performance in complex domains requires a consideration of the following basic issues (schematically summarized in figure 1.1).

Initial performance What do we know about a student S (or other specified person) in an initial state S_i *before* the occurrence of new learning? For example, what kinds of things does S then do or is S able to do? What kinds of underlying knowledge and thought processes lead to this performance?

Final performance What do we know about a student S in the final state S_f *after* the occurrence of some learning? For example, what kinds of things does S then do or is S able to do? What kinds of underlying knowledge and thought processes lead to this final performance?

Learning and teaching *Learning* is the process (indicated by the horizontal arrow in figure 1.1) whereby a student S is changed from an initial state S_i to a final state S_f where the student can do things that the student could not do initially. Learning is thus an important transformation process that we would like to understand in greater detail.

Teaching (or *instruction*) is deliberate assistance provided to facilitate learning. (In figure 1.1 such teaching is indicated by the vertical gray arrow pointing to the learning process.)

Note that learning can also occur spontaneously *without* the aid of any deliberate assistance. (For example, most children learn their native language without any deliberate intervention, merely by being immersed in an environment where this language is spoken.) Conversely, teaching can occur *without* any learning (a situation unfortunately all too familiar in many classrooms).

The letter T in figure 1.1 indicates a *teacher* (tutor or instructor) who does the teaching. It may also denote a more complex teaching system consisting of a human teacher who may be supplemented by computers, books, and other teaching aids. Teaching can also be accomplished without an *external* human teacher if the learning is deliberately assisted by the student himself or herself. (In such *self-teaching* the student must also play the role of teacher by deliberately deciding what to read, what and when to practice, when to review, and so forth.)

Practical instructional implementation   There is a significant difference between instruction provided to an individual student by a good teacher and practical instruction whereby many diverse students can be effectively taught by various teachers in realistic situations. Hence we may also need to be concerned with issues involved in practical instructional implementation.

1.3   IMPORTANCE OF THESE ISSUES

Applicability to the design of any complex system   The basic issues mentioned in the preceding section are not only relevant when trying to achieve good human performance, but are generally important when trying to design or construct any complex functional system S (such as an airplane or a computer).

For example, in any such case one must deal with the following four basic issues: (1) One must know the components of the desired final system S_f and how these components interact to produce the desired functioning. (For example, one must know the needed components of an airplane and how these function to produce well-controlled flight).

(2) One must know the initial system S_i (for instance, the initially available components that might be assembled into an airplane). (3) One must know the processes by which this initial system can actually be transformed into the desired final system (such as the processes by which the initial components can be assembled into a functional airplane). (4) Finally, the construction of a few airplanes by excellent engineers and mechanics is far from sufficient to lead to the practical implementation of an airline transportation system like *United Airlines*.

Medical analogy Medicine is somewhat analogous to education since it too deals with human beings. Thus figure 1.1 (illustrating an educational process) is also applicable to medicine, which is centrally interested in the transformation of a person, from an initial state S_i where the person is sick, to a desired final state S_f where the person is in good health. Accordingly, medicine is concerned with the following four central issues: (1) A thorough understanding of the desired final state of good health (achieved by well-functioning anatomy, physiology, and biochemistry). (2) An understanding of possible initial states corresponding to various illnesses and their underlying causes. (3) A knowledge of the kinds of therapies that can help to cure sick persons so as to transform them into healthier ones. (4) The practical implementation of a health-care delivery system that can manufacture suitable drugs, provide sufficient hospitals and well-trained doctors, ensure patients' access to such medical facilities, and so on.

Note that each of the preceding issues is quite complex. Medical students spend many years trying to learn about the first three issues, and our society is desperately struggling with the problem of creating an adequate health-care delivery system. If they are seriously addressed, the corresponding educational issues (illustrated in figure 1.1) cannot be expected to be much simpler.

Importance of each issue The following example illustrates, in a simple and amusing case, that each of the basic issues listed in section 1.2 (and indicated in figure 1.1) is important, even in a seemingly trivial learning task. Each one requires even greater attention in more complex situations involving human learning or teaching.

A simple example: Learning to pronounce *R*

When I came to the United States from Austria at the age of 14, I was faced with the need to learn English. Although I found the learning task fairly simple, my main difficulty was English pronunciation. I gradually managed to learn most

English sounds, but could not learn how to pronounce the sound corresponding to the letter R. Instead, I produced the guttural R with which I was familiar from my native German tongue.

Lack of spontaneous learning   Although I was highly motivated to learn the proper pronunciation of this sound, and could hear people around me pronounce it correctly all the time, I was *not* able to learn it despite my best efforts.

I could hear that my pronunciation of the R-sound was wrong and believed that I sounded much like a caricature of Adolf Hitler. But even though I felt embarrassed by my faulty pronunciation and was highly motivated to do better, I could not learn to improve my performance. This example illustrates the following general lesson: *Although high motivation may help learning, it may not be sufficient.*

Every day I was surrounded by people who spoke good English, and was constantly exposed to examples of good pronunciations of the English R. But months of such exposure did not help me. This example illustrates a second general lesson: *Although exposure to examples of good performance may help learning, it may not be sufficient.*

Clarification of initial inadequacies   When I was in high school, an English teacher tried to help me learn the proper pronunciation of R. She first clarified my initial state S_i by pointing out that I was inappropriately trying to pronounce R by using my throat and that this was wrong. Thus I now knew what *not* to do. *But this did not help me to know what I actually should do.*

Explanation of good performance   How would *you* explain how to pronounce the letter R? If you are like most native English speakers, you can properly pronounce this sound, but probably cannot explain how you do this. For example, you might need to pronounce this sound, carefully observe what you are doing, and then try to describe your observations. (Your knowledge of the proper pronunciation is thus a good example of *tacit* knowledge—that is, of knowledge that you have without any conscious awareness).

My English teacher did, however, provide me with the following explanation of the desired final performance: I should *not* use my throat, but merely hold my tongue close to the roof of my palate (without touching it) and then blow a gentle steam of air over my tongue.

I tried to do this. *But despite repeated attempts, no correct sound emerged from my mouth.*

Suggestion of a learning process   Two more years elapsed without any progress on my part. The mere specifications of my initial state S_i of poor performance, and of the desired final state S_f of good performance, had been totally inadequate to help me learn since I did not know the process whereby I could go from my initial state to the desired final state.

By then I had entered college, where an English teacher suggested a helpful process. She advised that, when speaking, I should simply substitute the letter D for the letter R. (For example, instead of saying *rose*, I should say *doze*.) She also explained the rationale for doing this. When producing the sound for D, I could not possibly use my throat. Furthermore, my tongue would then be approximately in the right position (touching the roof of my palate, instead of being slightly away from it). I should then gradually, by successive approximations, be able to move my tongue further from my palate and thus obtain the proper English sound for R. *This seemed like very good advice.*

Implementation problems But I had difficulty in implementing this advice because the teacher had not considered the practical difficulties that I might have in following her suggestions. Could I, a busy college student struggling with many intellectually demanding courses, spare the time to engage in much deliberate pronunciation practice? And would it not be embarrassing for me in daily life to say *dead* when I meant *red*, to say *ditch* when I meant *rich*, or to ask a waiter for *dice* when I meant *rice*? The net result was that I did not engage in much practice—and that my awful pronunciation persisted.

But a few months later I was drafted into the United States Army and found myself in basic training in a Florida camp, surrounded by other soldiers almost exclusively from the South. Their Southern accent prevented me from understanding almost anything they said, and they probably could not understand anything that I said. Thus it occurred to me that it did not matter what I would say in this environment—so that I *could* comfortably substitute the letter D for the letter R. *After no more than one week, I thus learned how to pronounce an English R, a feat that I had not managed to accomplish in the preceding four years!*

Lessons from this example The preceding example illustrates, in a very simple case, the importance of all the four previously mentioned issues (which are even more important in more complex situations). Thus it is not sufficient to understand the desired kind of performance or a student's initial performance before instruction. It may not even be sufficient to understand the learning and teaching process by which the student may attain the desired final performance—unless one also thinks about practically realistic ways of implementing the instruction.

1.4 STRUCTURE OF THE BOOK

This first portion of the book consists of one more introductory chapter (chapter 2) dealing with intellectual performance. After that, the book is divided into the following four further parts, each dealing successively with one of the four basic issues mentioned in section 1.2.

Part II, Good Performance This longest part (chapters 3 through 15) identifies some essential characteristics of good intellectual performance (the kind of final performance ordinarily desired as a result of learning). To examine the kinds of knowledge and thinking enabling such good performance, it discusses important types of knowledge, how this knowledge can be specified and properly interpreted, how it can be usefully described and organized, how it can be flexibly applied by making judicious decisions and solving various problems, and how all such processes can be carried out effectively and efficiently.

This part of the book is centrally concerned with ways of achieving good performance, but also points out relevant educational implications. Thus it indicates what proficient performers do, what inexperienced students often do, what deficiencies exist in prevailing instructional approaches, and what improved instructional methods are suggested by an examination of relevant cognitive issues.

Part III, Prior Knowledge This part (chapters 16 and 17) examines the knowledge and thinking that are common in everyday life and prevalent among students before they try to learn about an unfamiliar scientific domain. It identifies some of the significant differences between the cognitive frameworks of science and of everyday life, points out how these differences lead to naive notions differing from more sophisticated scientific conceptions, and how these differences can cause appreciable learning difficulties.

Part IV, Learning and Teaching This part (chapters 18 through 21) focuses on the development of instruction that facilitates learning. Thus it discusses how to design an effective learning process—and how then to devise teaching methods that can provide the guidance, support, and feedback needed to ensure that students engage in effective learning.

Part V, Implementing Practical Instruction This last part (chapters 22 through 24) discusses how the preceding teaching methods can be extended to implement practical instruction for large numbers of diverse students. Lastly, this part ends by mentioning some unmet educational challenges that could be addressed with significant beneficial results.

2 Intellectual Performance

As the preceding chapter indicates, our ultimate interest is to devise instruction that is effective in improving students' performance to a level needed in scientific or similar complex domains. Hence we must try to understand better the desired kind of performance—and then compare it with the kind of performance commonly exhibited by inexperienced students.

Accordingly, the present chapter begins an examination of intellectual performance by addressing the following questions that are of primary concern throughout the book: (1) How can one adequately specify the desired performance? (2) What are some performance goals of central interest? (3) What are some of the main characteristics of desirable "good" performance? (4) How can one identify the underlying knowledge and thinking enabling such good performance?

This last question is the most complex and is explored at greater length in the following chapters.

2.1 DESCRIPTION OF PERFORMANCE

2.1.1 Specification needs

A clear specification of *desired* performance is particularly important because it determines what students try to learn, what instructors aim to teach, and how learning outcomes can be assessed.

To describe a person's performance, one must specify what the person does or can do under certain conditions. Such a specification must satisfy the following two requirements: (1) It must be *observable* (so that it focuses on what can actually be observed, without speculating about any knowledge or thought processes in the person's mind). (2) It must be *operational* (so that it specifies what one must actually *do* to determine whether the specified performance has been achieved).

Although the preceding two requirements may seem simple, they are often violated and can then lead to the kinds of difficulties described in the following paragraphs.

2.1.2 Common specification deficiencies

Excessively vague specifications It is easy enough to assert that students should *know* something, *appreciate* something, *understand* something, or have a *conceptual understanding* of something. But such words are so ill defined that they are almost meaningless. For example, what exactly would one have to do to assess whether a student *knows* calculus? Would one have to determine whether he has taken a course in calculus, whether he can state some theorems of calculus, whether he can calculate some derivatives, or whether he can solve physics problems by using the methods of calculus? Similarly, what would one have to do to assess whether a student *appreciates* the need to conserve natural resources? Would one have to determine whether the student can list various reasons why this is important, reads magazine articles about nature and wildlife, joins the Sierra Club, or recycles used glass bottles?

The difficulty with such vague specifications is that they don't adequately specify what tasks a student should actually be able to perform. Thus they don't provide adequate guidance about what a student should try to learn, what an instructor should try to teach, or what an instructor should do to ascertain whether a student has achieved the desired performance.

Ill-conceived specifications More severe and subtle difficulties arise when performance specifications don't reflect the actual instructional goals. For example, a few years ago some investigations (such as Halloun and Hestenes, 1985) revealed that students, emerging from introductory college physics courses, were unable to answer basic qualitative physics questions and exhibited gross misconceptions about the motions of objects. Yet, these students had ostensibly studied mechanics (where such motions had been discussed in considerable detail) and had also obtained good grades in their courses. Thus there was every expectation that these students would be able to answer simple qualitative questions of the kind used in these investigations.

Indeed, instructors thought that the ability to answer such qualitative questions was of central importance to demonstrate an understanding of basic physics. But in specifying their course goals, they had focused primarily on teaching fundamental physics principles and some mathematical techniques dealing with *quantitative* problems. They had merely *assumed* that such teaching would naturally lead to students' ability to answer important kinds of *qualitative* questions. This assumption was thus proven wrong by the discovery that students could not answer such questions.

The moral of this story should be clear. If the ultimate goal is to help students acquire the kind of understanding that allow them to answer basic *qualitative* questions, then the ability to answer such questions must be part of an explicit performance specification—and teaching efforts must deliberately aim to teach students such performance.

The following is an even more striking example of the discrepancy between ultimately desired goals and the performance specifications in actual courses.

Course goals versus real goals: Ph.D. qualifying examination

Graduate students in physics departments usually need to pass a qualifying examination before undertaking the research project that will ultimately lead to their Ph.D. degree. The oral part of this examination aims to assess whether students have learned to think somewhat like physicists (for example, whether they can generate qualitative predictions or explanations of the kind commonly used by practicing physicists). Remarkably often, however, the students' answers to such qualitative questions are disappointingly poor, despite the fact that the students received A grades in most of their prior physics courses.

The apparent paradox disappears if one examines how these prior courses have often been taught (even by the very same professors asking the questions in the oral qualifying examination). In these courses, the professors focused primarily on providing a clear logical exposition of basic physics principles and on teaching students the mathematical techniques useful for applying these principles to various problems. However, in their teaching many professors neglected to emphasize the qualitative thinking skills that students may ultimately need in research. It is then not too surprising that students often don't perform well on the oral qualifying examination or that they may later find it difficult to get used to the kind of thinking useful in actual research.

2.2 PERFORMANCE IN COMPLEX DOMAINS

Performance in scientific domains can be particularly demanding and is of primary interest throughout this book. These domains encompass the ones listed in the following paragraphs.

Purely scientific domains These include all basic sciences (such as physics, chemistry, biology, or psychology) that are characterized by the desire to attain knowledge with great predictive and explanatory power. The central goal of any such pure science is to *discover theoretical knowledge enabling the prediction or explanation of the maximum number of observable phenomena on the basis of a minimum number of basic principles*.

The preceding goal is clearly ambitious and difficult to attain without great amounts of thought and care. For example, accurate predictions require well-specified basic principles, an unambiguous use of language, and logically correct reasoning methods. They also require constant checking that all the knowledge, and all the inferences derived from it, do actually correspond to careful observations.

Related scientific domains These include all the applied sciences (such as engineering or medicine) whose goal is to exploit pure scientific knowledge for practical human purposes. Another related scientific domain is that of *pure mathematics*, which deals only with abstractly defined objects and relations. These can be perceived in our minds, but are not phenomena that are actually observable in the external world. Nevertheless, mathematics provides powerful intellectual tools that are widely useful in all the pure and applied sciences. Furthermore, *applied mathematics* deliberately strives to use these tools for practical purposes.

Science-like domains The relevance of the preceding scientific domains is actually far greater than the preceding comments might indicate. This is because scientific methods are widely useful. Furthermore, all of us are commonly concerned with performance that enables the prediction and explanation of observable phenomena. For example, such performance helps us to anticipate what is likely to happen, to foresee the consequences of our own actions, to prepare ourselves accordingly, and to design or construct various helpful artifacts (for example, buildings, machines, or social organizations). In short, such performance ensures that we can cope with our environment and survive in it.

Such science-like performance in our ordinary lives does not need to be as demanding as scientific performance because we are usually content with satisfactory predictions and explanations, without requiring the highly successful ones desired in scientific fields. However, *some* scientific kinds of performance and thinking are often needed in many situations, especially when theses are complex. Hence scientific abilities are of importance far beyond the range of actual sciences, despite the fact that they are *not* universally important in all domains (such as domains concerned with poetry, the arts, or religious beliefs).

2.3   CHARACTERISTICS OF GOOD PERFORMANCE

We are ordinarily interested in achieving desirable *good* performance. Such performance can also serve as a useful standard of comparison for assessing other kinds of performance. (For example, we judge performance as deficient when it differs significantly from such good performance.) Hence it is useful to specify some of the important characteristics of good performance.

The situation is somewhat analogous to that in medicine where *good health* is specified as a desirable situation of good physiological and mental functioning—and where departures from such good health are viewed as indications of disease. Therefore, it is medically important to identify some essential characteristics of good health—and to strive to achieve these when people suffer from disease.

2.3.1   Important requirements for good performance

Some widely important requirements for good performance are listed in figure 2.1 and described more fully in the following paragraphs.

Usability   Good performance should be *usable* for accomplishing significant tasks: it should involve actual accomplishments, rather than mere talk. For example, talking about cars (or describing how they can

Figure 2.1
Important requirements for good performance.

be built) is a purely verbal ability that is quite different from the performance abilities needed to construct or repair a car.

Effectiveness   Good performance should be *effective* in attaining desired goals. For example, we would like to undertake tasks that we can successfully complete and to write computer programs that produce the desired results.

Flexibility   Good performance should be *flexible*—that is, adequate performance should remain possible even under somewhat changed conditions. Even if the performance is then somewhat slower or less good, it should still be reasonably effective.

For example, an employee in a store may ordinarily be able to give you appropriate change when you pay for a purchase with a $50 dollar bill. But that employee's performance would *not* be flexible if he or she were unable to give you proper change if the computer happened to be temporarily out of order.

Efficiency   Performance should also be *efficient*—that is, it should be able to attain the desired goals with a relatively small expenditure of valuable resources (such as time, effort, or money).

Efficiency is not only important because of the obvious advantage of achieving desired ends with minimal costs. Adequate efficiency may also be an essential prerequisite for achieving *effective* performance. For example, young children perform reading tasks slowly and with much effort. If adult readers had not learned to perform such reading tasks much more efficiently, they would not be able to read scientific or other substantive articles. Indeed, they would then have to spend so much time and mental effort on the mere task of deciphering individual words that they would have no mental capacity left to understand the content of such articles.

Reliability   Finally, good performance should be *reliable* so that one can have confidence in the correctness of the results—and so that performance remains possible even after the lapse of some appreciable time.

2.3.2   Contrasts with deficient performance

The following common examples of deficient performance differ significantly from the kind of good performance described in the preceding paragraphs.

Usable versus nominal performance   There is an important distinction between performance that is *usable* (enabling the performance of significant tasks) and performance that is just *nominal* (enabling merely naming some things or talking about them).

For example, suppose that a student is asked the question "What is a triangle?" and responds by saying "A triangle is a three-side polygon". On the basis of the student's performance on this question, a naive teacher might well conclude that the student knows what a triangle is.

But suppose that the student is shown a sheet of paper displaying various geometric figures and is asked to point out which of them is a triangle. Or suppose that the student is asked to draw a triangle. If the student can perform neither of these tasks, would the teacher still say that the student has significant knowledge about triangles? In this case, the student's performance consists merely of his ability to *state* a verbal definition of a triangle. But if he cannot *use* this definition to do anything with it (for example, if he can neither recognize nor construct a triangle) then the student's knowledge is purely nominal rather than effectively usable.

Richard P. Feynman was a very bright and colorful physicist who died a few years ago. (He was a Nobel-Prize winner and also identified the cause of the *Challenger* spacecraft disaster.) In one of his books (Feynman, 1985), he describes vividly his experiences as a visitor in Brazil. When he asked doctoral students there questions about polarized light, he promptly received correct verbal answers. But when he then asked the students to look out the window to observe the phenomenon that they had described, they were unable to connect their words to the observable phenomena. Feynman (1985, 211) summarizes his experiences in the following words:

> After a lot of investigation, I finally figured out that the students had memorized everything, but they didn't know what anything meant. When they heard "light is reflected from a medium with an index," they didn't know that it meant a material such as water. They didn't know that the "direction of the light" is the direction in which you see something when you're looking at it. Everything was entirely memorized, yet nothing had been translated into meaningful words.

Indeed, the Brazilian educational system merely seemed to emphasize *nominal* knowledge that teachers taught, students memorized, and examinations assessed. But none of this knowledge was usable. Nobody seemed to know how to use this physics knowledge to predict or explain observable phenomena.

Flexible versus rote performance   Some years ago, a hospital technician wanted to obtain a drop of my blood so that it could be put onto a slide and examined under a microscope. To collect this blood, she asked me to let her prick the middle finger of my left hand. However, I requested her to prick the middle finger of my *right* hand. (I wanted to avoid a sore finger that might interfere with my violin playing.) But she insisted again that I let her prick the finger of my *left* hand. Once again, I reiterated my request that she prick the finger of my *right* hand. At this point, the technician seemed somewhat bewildered, stopped for almost a minute to ponder my request, and finally said hesitantly, "I suppose that's probably all right."

I remember this incident vividly as an example of *rote* performance —a performance so mindlessly remembered that it is carried out without significant thought and is thus utterly inflexible. The technician had probably learned a specific process of obtaining blood from the middle finger of a patient's left hand. Faced with slightly different circumstances where this process did not seem feasible, she did not know what to do. (Apparently, she lacked the basic knowledge that a person's blood is the *same*, whether collected from the left or the right hand.)

Such rote performance, involving a completely standardized way of performing a task, is inflexible because the task can then not be performed if conditions slightly change. Although such rote performance may be easy to learn, it is of limited utility in the real world where conditions are rarely exactly the same and where unforeseen events are all too common.

Yet students are often content to learn rote performance. For example, they may bitterly complain when confronted on an examination with a problem that is slightly different from one previously encountered in homework assignments.

2.4   ANALYSIS OF PERFORMANCE

How can we analyze performance to understand better what factors are responsible for observable performance or are necessary for good performance?

2.4.1   Kinds of analyses

Intellectual performance (like any other process) can be analyzed at different levels of detail. In particular, it is useful to distinguish between a phenomenological analysis and a theoretical analysis.

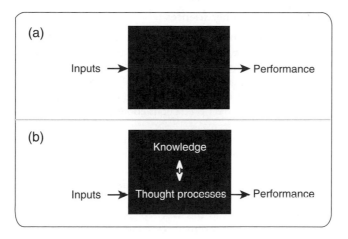

Figure 2.2
Alternative analyses of a person's observable performance.

Phenomenological analysis   A person's performance on various tasks may be examined by a *phenomenological* analysis—one that focuses solely on observable phenomena and does not speculate about any entities or processes within the person's head. Such an analysis, illustrated in figure 2.2a, looks upon a person as a *black box* whose inside is hidden from view, but whose inputs and outputs can be readily observed. (Behaviorist psychology, which was prevalent in the early part of the twentieth century, adopted such a point of view by focusing almost exclusively on input stimuli and output responses.)

Theoretical analysis   On the other hand, a *theoretical analysis* aims to identify the underlying mechanisms responsible for observable phenomena. To do this, it attempts to discover or invent theoretical concepts that describe hypothetical entities and processes inside a person. Such theoretical concepts are useful only to the extent that they help to predict and explain many observable phenomena. All these concepts must thus *ultimately* be clearly related to observable phenomena. (Although this relation may be indirect, it must be unambiguously specified.)

Such theoretical concepts are useful because they may allow much better predictions and explanations of observable phenomena than analyses focused solely on the phenomena themselves. Indeed, the following pages adopt such a theoretical point of view by talking about theoretical concepts such as *internal knowledge* or *thought processes*.

Theoretical concepts in other sciences

The introduction of hypothetical theoretical concepts is very common in the natural sciences. Indeed, such concepts have played an essential role in providing physics, chemistry, and biology with their highly successful predictive and explanatory power. For example, concepts such as *electron, magnetic field, wave function, gene,* or *virus* are theoretical and not directly observable. But they lead to so very many reliably correct predictions about the observable world that we may come to regard them as *real.*

Thus we cannot actually *see* an electron, but we can observe electrical or optical effects that can be consistently interpreted by introducing the concept of *electron.* Similarly, we cannot really *see* a virus, but we can observe holes formed in a bacterial layer within a dish—and can interpret these holes as being produced by something that we call a *virus.* Furthermore, we can consistently interpret other observations in this way. For example, after putting a sample into an electron microscope, we may see on its screen some shadows that we can also interpret as being due to viruses.

By contrast, another theoretical concept, called the *ether*, was introduced about a hundred years ago to describe a medium that fills all space and allows the propagation of light or other electromagnetic waves. However, after a while it became apparent that this concept did not have much predictive power and was even misleading. Hence this concept is no longer useful, and the ether is no longer presumed to exist.

2.4.2   Theoretical analysis of performance

A *functional* system is one that is able to perform various tasks. For example, a computer is a functional system because it can perform calculations, and an airplane is a functional system because it can fly. A human being is clearly also a functional system.

Instead of considering such a functional system as a black box (like that shown in figure 2.2a), one may analyze it more theoretically by trying to figure out what might be going on *inside* the black box. Thus one may *assume* that the observable performance is due to some internal processes that are enabled by some internal components. Figure 2.2b indicates that, in the case of a person, these assumed processes are *thought processes* and the internal components are components of *knowledge* (or *information*) embedded within a person's brain. The processes may also change the person's knowledge and thus affect the person's future performance—that is, the person can *learn.*

Figure 2.2b thus illustrates how we can analyze a person's performance on various intellectual tasks by trying to identify the underlying thought processes and kinds of knowledge that facilitate these processes.

Knowledge   A person's knowledge can be adequately specified without inquiring about the detailed biology of brain structure or neurons. For our purposes, it is sufficient to assume that the knowledge in a person's head consists of an assembly of interrelated *mental* entities (that is, entities about which one can think or talk). These mental entities, called *concepts*, may correspond to observable entities, to other concepts, or to relations among other concepts. This correspondence is highly useful because internal thought processes, performed on the basis of this knowledge, enable a person to make corresponding inferences about the surrounding world. Furthermore, extensive communication among persons ensures that the knowledge of different persons in a society is similar (although not identical).

Distinguishing observable and theoretical features

To avoid confusions, it is important to distinguish between observable performance and a theoretical interpretation of this performance in terms of hypothetical underlying knowledge and thought processes. For example, different persons might attribute the same observable performance to different underlying thought processes.

2.5   ANALYSIS OF GOOD PERFORMANCE

The performance of some tasks may be facilitated by certain kinds of underlying *cognition* (knowledge and thought processes) or may be hindered by other kinds. If we know the kinds of cognition that facilitate particular tasks and those that hinder them, we may then be in a better position to choose the facilitating ones and to avoid the others.

Figure 2.1 lists the previously discussed requirements important for achieving good performance. The following paragraphs now attempt to identify some of the cognitive needs that help to satisfy these requirements. These cognitive needs, outlined in figure 2.3, are elaborated and discussed in much greater detail in the following chapters.

Usability   A primary requirement for good performance is that it should be usable for doing significant tasks (that is, it should not just be nominal performance involving the mere ability to talk about such tasks). To ensure such usability, one needs some *important kinds* of knowledge (such as factual knowledge about various situations and knowledge about methods specifying possible actions).

Another essential requirement for the usability of any knowledge is that one can *specify* it well enough that its meaning is clear (so that

Performance and Cognitive Needs

Usability
Important kinds of knowledge 3
Specifying and interpreting concepts 4, 5
Managing memory 6

Effectiveness
Methods and inferences 7
Describing knowledge 8
Organizing knowledge 9

Flexibility
Making decisions 10
Solving problems 11, 12, 13

Efficiency
Efficiency and compiled knowledge 14

Reliability
Quality assurance 15

Figure 2.3
Performance requirements (in bold type) and cognitive needs. (The numbers correspond to chapters in this book.)

words or concepts refer unambiguously to clearly specified entities). One must also know how to *interpret* properly what such words or concepts mean in any specific instance. The unambiguous specification and interpretation of scientific concepts is particularly important. For how could one possibly hope to use ambiguous scientific concepts to achieve clearly specified predictions?

Lastly, all such knowledge must be adequately remembered so that it can be used whenever needed. Hence one must be able to *manage one's memory* effectively to incorporate new knowledge in it, to retain it there reliably for long periods of time, and to retrieve it appropriately when the need arises.

Effectiveness We already mentioned that performance should not merely be usable, but should also be effective for attaining desired goals. Hence one needs to know how to apply available knowledge by using appropriate *methods* and by *inferring* some of its important implications. The application of available knowledge can also be greatly facilitated if this knowledge is in a useful form, particularly if it is *described* and *organized* in useful ways.

Flexibility   Performance is flexible if it can be appropriately modified under somewhat changed conditions. Conversely, performance that merely follows a fixed process (where any action is always followed by another prescribed action) is *in*flexible and more reminiscent of machine-like behavior.

Flexible performance requires that a particular action may, depending on conditions, be followed by one of several possible alternative actions. But then it is necessary to decide which of the alternative possible actions should be chosen. Effective *decision making* is, therefore, an essential prerequisite for flexible performance.

More generally, flexible performance requires the ability to *solve problems* so as to figure out suitable means to attain any desired goal. Such problem solving is very important, but can be a demanding task requiring many judicious decisions.

Efficiency   Efficient performance is desirable because it allows one to attain desired goals rapidly and effortlessly. Such efficiency can often be achieved by using *compiled* knowledge (that is, knowledge that has been remembered as a result of previous use). For then one does not repeatedly need to figure out what to do, but may save time and effort by simply remembering what one has done before.

Efficiency is not only important because it can save time and energy, but also because adequate efficiency may be necessary for the *effective* performance of complex tasks.

Reliability   Lastly, performance should be reliably trustworthy. One must ensure that performance is of *good quality*—so as to be correct and free of defects. Furthermore, one must make sure that the ability to perform well can persist for a long time without deteriorating.

Figure 2.3 lists the preceding five requirements for good performance and indicates the cognitive needs that can help to satisfy them. These requirements serve as the basic themes that are elaborated in the following chapters where the needed knowledge and thought processes are discussed at much greater length.

2.6 COMPARISONS AND OVERVIEW

The preceding analysis of good performance provides a useful framework for examining some of the cognitive issues important in complex domains. It also suggests some useful comparisons and educationally significant issues which are discussed in the following chapters.

2.6.1   Comparisons with experts

It can be useful to compare an analysis of good performance with the observed performance of experts.

Expert performance versus good performance   Although experts may perform well in the domain of their expertise, they may *not* perform well in other domains. Indeed, experts may not even exhibit excellent performance in their domain of expertise. For example, experts in arithmetic, who were contemporaries of Julius Caesar, performed their calculations with Roman numerals. But we now know that the modern place-value representation of numbers provides a much better description of numbers and greatly facilitates calculations. If an ancient Roman had analyzed arithmetic tasks, and had thus invented such a place-value representation of numbers, he might then have achieved performance far better than that of existing experts.

Proficient experts versus presumed experts   Some experts do perform very proficiently in their field of expertise. But such proficient experts must be distinguished from people who are merely *presumed* to be expert, but whose actual proficiency has not been ascertained. For example, such presumed experts may be persons who have been socially designated as experts because of diplomas, positions, or titles (such as Ph.D. or M.D.). Although some such individuals may be proficient experts, some may well be much less competent—or may have become less competent because of the passage of time.

Other presumed experts may be individuals with long experience in a domain. However, long experience alone is *no* guarantee of superior competence. Indeed, sometimes it may merely lead to obsolescence and to a lack of familiarity with more recent developments in a field.

Expert performance versus good student performance   Good performance, of the kind attainable by a good student, can *not* be expected to be similar to that of a proficient expert. This is because actual experts have, through long experience, acquired large amounts of knowledge that they can use to recognize familiar situations and to apply without conscious effort. Inexperienced students (*novices*) can *not* reach such a level of proficiency in a limited time and must often perform deliberately tasks that experts perform subconsciously. Novice students may thus become quite competent, but without attaining expert-like proficiency.

Utility of comparisons with experts   Comparisons with experts may be informative if the preceding remarks are kept in mind. For example, comparisons with *proficient* experts may help to suggest or refine ideas about the requirements for good performance. Conversely, *deficiencies* observed in the performance of persons with long experience may help to identify skills that are *not* reliably learned and that must therefore be singled out for more explicit instruction.

2.6.2   Overview of part II

The following part II of the book (chapters 3 through 15) elaborates the issues indicated in figure 2.3 by considering the previously mentioned requirements for good performance and then discussing the cognitive needs that can help to satisfy these requirements.

Beginning of each chapter   Each chapter in part II starts by specifying the cognitive issues to be discussed and by outlining some of the pertinent questions to be considered. To indicate the educational relevance of these questions, it may also point out some of the behaviors or learning difficulties commonly exhibited by many students. These preliminary comments then pave the way for a detailed discussion of the chapter's topic.

End of each chapter   Before concluding with a final summary, the last section of each chapter points out some of the educational implications of the cognitive issues discussed in it. This section usually includes remarks about the following:

1. Comparisons with the performance of proficient experts   Such comparisons may help to identify some of the knowledge and thinking that students should acquire as a result of instruction.

2. Comparisons with the performance of novice students   Such comparisons can reveal commonly lacking or defective knowledge, identify knowledge or skills that must be explicitly taught, and help to discern expected learning difficulties.

3. Comparisons with prevailing instruction   Such comparisons may identify needed knowledge that is often not taught or faulty knowledge that is taught.

4. Instructional suggestions   These can become apparent since an analysis of good performance can help to identify what should be taught and may also suggest how it should be taught.

2.7 SUMMARY

• A useful specification of desired performance must be observable and operational so that it indicates what needs to be learned and how such learning can be assessed.

• Intellectual performance in scientific or related domains is particularly demanding. It is also generally important because the abilities to predict and explain are widely needed in all our lives.

• Important characteristics of good intellectual performance are its usability, effectiveness, flexibility, efficiency, and reliability.

• Observable human performance can be theoretically analyzed in terms of underlying knowledge and thought processes.

• Good performance can be facilitated by some of the following cognitive means: Usability is helped by careful specification and interpretation of all knowledge; effectiveness by suitably applying, describing, and organizing such knowledge; flexibility by judicious decisions and problem solving; efficiency by exploiting compiled knowledge; and reliability by ensuring good quality.

• The cognitive issues outlined in the preceding sections are elaborated in greater detail in the following chapters, which also explore some of their educational implications.

II GOOD PERFORMANCE

II-A Usability

3   Important Kinds of Knowledge

As indicated in figure 2.3, this portion of the book (chapters 3 through 6) deals with the *usability* of knowledge by examining what cognitive means help to ensure that knowledge can be used to perform significant tasks. Thus we shall discuss what kinds of basic knowledge are needed, how the concepts of this knowledge can be properly specified and interpreted, and how human memory can be managed to store and retrieve this knowledge.

In particular, this chapter examines two centrally important kinds of knowledge—a knowledge of facts needed to describe various situations, and a knowledge of methods needed to perform various actions. We shall then try to explore the following questions: What are the important characteristics of these kinds of knowledge? What are their distinctive advantages and disadvantages? Are both of them needed? Are they best used jointly or separately?

Educational relevance   Students or instructors often overemphasize one kind of knowledge at the expense of the other. For example, people who need to deal with a word-processing program often want to learn merely methods for performing specific tasks. However, they have little interest in knowing anything about the functioning of the computer or about the operations that can be invoked by clicking on various menus visible on the computer display. Similarly, inexperienced students tend to focus their attention predominantly on specific methods needed for tasks on homeworks or examinations. However, they have much less interest in learning general principles that they could apply more widely and that might allow them to deal with problems that are somewhat different from those previously encountered by them.

On the other hand, some instructors have the opposite tendency and may emphasize general theoretical knowledge without paying sufficient attention to the methods needed for applying it. For example, teachers in some mathematics courses often carefully discuss various abstract concepts and theorems and then ask students to prove some implied results—even though the teachers did not explicitly teach methods for constructing mathematical proofs.

3.1   DECLARATIVE AND PROCEDURAL KNOWLEDGE

Declarative knowledge   *Declarative knowledge* specifies factual knowledge about a situation by describing the relevant entities in the situation and the relations among them. Such declarative knowledge can be specified by one or more verbal statements or by alternative forms of description (for example, by diagrams or mathematical formulas).

Examples of declarative knowledge

Some examples of declarative knowledge are statements such as "Town A is 24 miles south of town B" or "John's car hit a lamppost."

Declarative geographical knowledge about some places may be described by statements such as "Town X is located 12 miles west from town Y." Alternatively, the same declarative knowledge may be described graphically in the form of a map indicating various towns like X and Y. These alternate forms of description are equivalent since they provide the same information (although a map may be more convenient for purposes of navigation).

Procedural knowledge   *Procedural knowledge* specifies methods or procedures (that is, sequences of actions describing *how* to perform particular tasks).

Example of procedural knowledge

Travel directions specify how to get from one place to another. For instance, "Drive to the next traffic light, turn right at the corner, and then drive another half mile until you see a church."

Common uses of these kinds of knowledge   To help a girlfriend find her way to your home, you might provide her with *declarative* information in the form of a *map*. Alternatively, you might provide her with *procedural* information in the form of detailed *verbal directions* specifying how to travel to your home. The knowledge contained within a computer's software consists of *declarative* information in the form of various data and of *procedural* information in the form of some algorithms.

The instructions manual accompanying a computer application commonly specifies detailed *procedures* for carrying out various tasks. However, the manual often has also a reference section that provides *declarative* information describing what the computer does when a user clicks on any of the menu items listed at the top of the screen.

3.2 COMPARATIVE ADVANTAGES AND DISADVANTAGES

Let us now examine some of the distinctive advantages and disadvantages of declarative and procedural knowledge. (The advantages and disadvantages listed in the following paragraph are well illustrated by the example of geographical information since this can be displayed either in the declarative form of a map, or in the procedural form of directions for traveling from one place to another.)

3.2.1 Declarative knowledge

Advantages Declarative knowledge has the following advantages:

• It can be flexibly used to devise methods for performing a large variety of tasks. (For example, a map can be used to figure out directions for traveling from any place to any other place.)
• It can be highly compact so that it can be easily stored and retrieved, yet it allows one to devise appropriate methods for performing many diverse tasks. (For example, the map of a region is much more compact than a whole sheaf of directions specifying how to travel between any two specific places indicated on this map.)

Disadvantage Declarative knowledge may require complex and time-consuming problem solving to figure out appropriate methods for reaching particular goals.

Limitations Declarative knowledge is meaningless if there is no possible way of determining its validity (that is, if one does not have *procedural* knowledge specifying what one would actually have to *do* to determine whether it is true or not).

3.2.2 Procedural knowledge

Advantages Procedural knowledge enables easy implementation of the processes that it specifies. Indeed, it allows people to carry out specified step-by-step directions without the need for any problem solving.

Disadvantages Procedural knowledge (without accompanying declarative knowledge) has the following disadvantages:

• Procedural knowledge is *inflexible* because it cannot readily be modified to deal with somewhat changed conditions. It also cannot be readily regenerated if it is partially forgotten. (If an obstacle prevents implementation of a specified procedure, a person may not have enough declarative knowledge to figure out what to do—and appropriate performance may become impossible.)

• Procedural knowledge cannot be checked for correctness if no declarative knowledge is available. (For example, how can you check whether you are still driving along a specified route if you don't know what to expect to see along the way?)

• Procedural knowledge is not economical because a sole reliance on procedural knowledge requires remembering, and then retrieving, very many procedures (one for each possible task of interest).

Limitations   It is impossible to specify procedural knowledge without also specifying some declarative knowledge. For example, declarative knowledge may be necessary to specify what to watch in executing a step in a procedure, to check correct implementation of each step, to determine whether the desired result of the procedure has been achieved, or to specify under what conditions a procedure is applicable.

3.3   USES OF DECLARATIVE AND PROCEDURAL KNOWLEDGE

3.3.1   Combined uses of both kinds of knowledge

Declarative and procedural knowledge are both commonly used and are often used jointly. For example, several sites on the Internet (such as ⟨*MapQuest*.com⟩) provide information that facilitates travel from one place to another. The requested information is provided in the form of a *procedure* giving step-by-step travel directions and also in the *declarative* form of a map displaying the specified route.

As another example, a proficient user of a computer program has *declarative* knowledge about what functions can be invoked by the menus displayed on the computer screen—and has also *procedural* knowledge about methods for carrying out commonly encountered tasks.

Judicious use of appropriate kinds of knowledge   An awareness of the advantages and disadvantages of each kind of knowledge allows people to choose the kind of knowledge that is most appropriate for a particular task.

Examples

Information about visiting a particular house   Suppose that you want to invite someone to visit your house in the city. It is then probably easiest to give the person specific directions indicating how to drive to your house. The person can then use this *procedural* knowledge by simply implementing these directions.

Information about visiting several houses   On the other hand, suppose that you want to ask somebody to visit a set of different houses in the city. You could then give the person many different directions, one for getting to each house. But it would probably be much easier if you merely gave the person a map on which you indicated the locations of all these houses. This single map would summarize all the needed information in a much more compact form—and the person could then fairly easily use this *declarative* information to find his or her way to every one of the houses.

Dangers of purely procedural travel information   After I relocated to Pittsburgh, a colleague gave me directions specifying a good route for driving home from the university where I worked. Every evening, I drove home by following this route, a trip that took about 20 minutes. But one evening, I encountered a terrible traffic jam (caused by some Christmas festivities in the city). Since I knew only my particular way for driving home, and had no other knowledge about the geography of the city, I felt unable to modify my usual route. Because I feared that any deviation from this route would get me irremediably lost, I felt compelled to persist in implementing my inflexible procedural knowledge. As a result, I arrived home only after some 90 minutes. By this time, I felt utterly frustrated and exhausted (but highly motivated to acquire more declarative knowledge about Pittsburgh's geography).

3.3.2   Practical implications

Different ways of preparing for examinations   Students often try to prepare themselves for a course examination by attempting to remember the particular methods that they used on all preceding homework problems in the course. But all this *procedural* knowledge (even if remembered) can make students quite inflexible and in great danger of not knowing what to do if a problem on the examination differs somewhat from a previously encountered problem. Hence the students would be much better prepared if they learned *declarative* knowledge about a few general principles applicable to all such problems.

Complementary use of both kinds of knowledge   The preceding comments about the advantages and disadvantages of declarative and procedural knowledge indicate that these kinds of knowledge are *complementary*. Thus, good performance ordinarily requires joint use of both. Each alone is inadequate without use of the other, and *both* are usually needed for good performance. In this way one can exploit the advantages of each while minimizing the disadvantages or limitations of the other.

Thus one can often deal efficiently with commonly occurring situations by using remembered *procedural* knowledge about how to act in such cases. On the other hand, one can then use *declarative* knowledge if one encounters obstacles that interfere with the implementation of familiar procedures or if one needs to deal with unfamiliar situations where known methods are not available.

Rules versus mental models To help a person deal with some device (such as an automobile or a computer), one can provide the person with a large set of procedures or rules specifying what to do in various situations. For instance, the rules might be of the form "If X is true, do Y." (Examples of such rules might be "If the car fails to respond when you press the accelerator pedal, check whether the gasoline gauge indicates empty" or "If you want to change your direction of travel, rotate the steering wheel").

Alternatively, it may be possible to provide a person with a model of the device. (A *model* is an approximate theory that specifies how a device functions.) Such a model provides *declarative* information about the components of the device and the processes that they perform to make the device work. This model is called a *mental model* if it is so simple that easy reasoning in one's mind can yield useful predictions or explanations.

For example, such a mental model of a car might specify knowledge that gasoline is burned to produce rotation of the wheels, that the steering wheel changes the orientation of the wheels and thus the travel direction of the car, and that the car contains a storage battery that helps to start the car and to light the headlights. Even a small amount of such simple declarative knowledge can help a person to figure out what to do or how to diagnose various difficulties. The person can then act flexibly without having to remember many special rules.

Hence it may often be preferable to learn simple mental models instead of a large number of rules. (Note that the mental model useful to a driver can be far simpler than the model needed by an automobile mechanic—and can be very much simpler than the complex model needed by an automotive engineer.)

3.4   CONDITION-DEPENDENT KNOWLEDGE

Any kind of knowledge may be accompanied by conditions specifying when it is appropriate. Such condition-dependent knowledge may be of the form "If condition C is true, statement S is true," where the statement S is an instance of *declarative* knowledge. (For example, "If the temperature is less than 32 degrees Fahrenheit, water assumes the solid form of ice").

Alternatively, such condition-dependent knowledge may be of the form "If condition C is true, perform action A," where action A is an instance of *procedural* knowledge. (For example, "If you want to shut off the water, turn the faucet clockwise.") Such condition-dependent procedural knowledge is also called a *rule*. Indeed, directions for performing many tasks (for example, for using devices or assembling equipment) are often specified in terms of such rules.

Applicability conditions   Since it is rare that some knowledge is *always* applicable, particular knowledge must be accompanied by applicability conditions specifying when it may be applied. Such applicability conditions are of two kinds:

• *Validity conditions* are especially important because they specify when it is correct to use the particular knowledge. Such validity conditions must always be heeded since a failure to do so would lead to faulty application of the knowledge.

• *Utility conditions* merely provide advice specifying when it may be useful to apply the particular knowledge. Although such advice may be ignored, it can be helpful in deciding whether the knowledge should be used in a specific case. (Note that, even if some knowledge *can* be validly applied, it may be more useful under some conditions than under others.)

Explicit *validity* conditions are particularly important in science since they specify the conditions under which particular concepts or principles can legitimately be used. (Indeed, many student mistakes are due to students' failures to heed the validity conditions associated with their acquired scientific knowledge.) *Utility* conditions are important for problem solving because they suggest which knowledge might usefully be retrieved to attain desired goals.

Examples of validity and utility conditions

Validity and utility conditions in everyday life   Both the Post Office and Federal Express can validly be used for sending a package across the United States.

But helpful utility conditions might specify that shipping by the Post Office is particularly useful if one is interested in low costs, and that shipping by Federal Express is particularly useful if one is interested in fast delivery.

Example from science Two basic mechanics principles are Newton's law (relating the acceleration of any object to the total force on it) and the energy law (relating kinetic and potential energies). Both laws are valid only if the motion of the object is described relative to an *inertial frame* (for example, approximately relative to the surface of the earth). But Newton's law is most useful if one wants to predict how the position or velocity of an object depends on the time, while the energy law is most useful if one wants to predict how the speed of an object depends on its position.

For instance suppose that a stone, initially at rest, is dropped from a specified height above the floor. If one wants to find out how long a time elapses before the stone hits the floor, the preceding utility conditions suggest that it would be best to solve the problem by applying Newton's law. But if one wants to find out with what speed the stone hits the floor, these conditions suggest that it would be best to apply the energy law.

3.5   EDUCATIONAL IMPLICATIONS

3.5.1   Proficient performers

Proficient performers usually have large amounts of *both* procedural knowledge and declarative knowledge. They ordinarily use their procedural knowledge by applying known methods to deal with commonly encountered tasks. On the other hand, they exploit their declarative knowledge to check their performance, to cope with emerging difficulties, and to deal with unfamiliar situations.

After long experience, experts become so familiar with the knowledge in their field that they use it spontaneously without deliberate thought. This knowledge has thus become *tacit* (so as to be usable without conscious awareness). Such lack of awareness can make it difficult for experts to transmit their knowledge to others, with the result that proficient performers may sometimes be poor teachers.

3.5.2   Inexperienced students

As mentioned at the beginning of this chapter, students often like to acquire procedural knowledge so as to learn methods that they can readily apply to homework assignments or examinations. They may thus avoid the kind of thinking or problem solving that is required for applying general declarative knowledge to specific situations. The ensuing danger is that such students may not acquire declarative knowledge that is more flexibly usable.

Students also often learn scientific knowledge without heeding restrictive validity conditions. Hence they also apply some of their knowledge in cases where this cannot legitimately be done.

3.5.3 Common instructional deficiencies

Excessive emphasis on procedural knowledge   Prevailing modes of instruction sometimes emphasize excessively procedural knowledge without adequate declarative knowledge. For example, you may recall the case (mentioned in section 2.3.2) where a technician did not know what to do when I requested that she take blood from my right hand rather than from my left hand. It then seemed fairly clear that the technician had merely been taught a standard procedure (taking blood from the left hand) without the declarative knowledge that the same blood flows through all of a person's blood vessels.

Many laboratory manuals specify detailed procedures for carrying out laboratory experiments. Students can then follow the specified directions in cookbook-like fashion without much thought—and may well complete an experiment without understanding why they performed the actions that they carried out. The amount of resulting student learning is then very questionable. Similarly, many instructional manuals accompanying computers or other systems provide step-by-step directions specifying what to do in various cases, but don't spell out the underlying system properties that provide the reasons for these particular steps. As a result, a user may often be perplexed when things don't quite work as expected or when some slight modifications are needed.

Example: Mystifying procedural advice

Recently I bought a device (a flash-memory drive) for my computer but could not make it work. When I finally called the supplier, a technician gave me a long series of mysterious step-by-step directions (such as "Erase this or that" or "Replace all the entries by zeros") all of which I faithfully executed like a brainless automaton. Lo and behold, after that the device suddenly worked! At this point, I finally dared to ask the technician about the purpose of this entire procedure. Only then did he tell me that the device needed to be reformatted to work with Macintosh (rather than Windows-based) computers.

If he had told me this in the first place, I would have understood the reasons for all these steps—and might even have been able to figure out what to do without the need for any outside help.

Excessive emphasis on declarative knowledge Conversely, some instructional methods emphasize predominantly declarative knowledge, without providing adequate procedural knowledge for using this declarative knowledge. For example, course syllabi often specify what *topics* students should know by the end of a course, but don't specify what students should actually be able to *do*.

As already mentioned at the beginning of this chapter, an excessive emphasis on declarative knowledge is sometimes also apparent in some mathematics or physics courses. These often focus mainly on important theorems or principles, but fail to adequately explicate the procedural knowledge needed for applying this knowledge to solve problems or to prove theorems.

3.5.4 Instructional suggestions

Teaching declarative knowledge together with interpretation procedures
Students often acquire nominal knowledge without knowing what it means. For example, they may blithely talk about "area," but may have no idea how to determine the surface area of an object (such as a statue)—or how to specify the numerical value of this area in units of square feet. In science, such nominal knowledge of a concept (like area) is completely inadequate.

Hence it is important to define declarative knowledge *operationally* by specifying the procedural knowledge that indicates what one must actually *do* to interpret the knowledge properly in any specific case. Only then is the declarative knowledge meaningful. Thus students need to learn what one actually needs to *do* to determine whether a concept has been properly applied or whether a statement involving the concept is true or false. The students can thereby acquire knowledge that is usable rather than just nominal.

Operationally specified knowledge is also important outside of science. It leads to less ambiguously specified meanings and can thus also help to avoid fruitless debates about the meanings of words such as *justice*, *democracy*, or other abstract concepts.

Teaching procedures together with associated declarative information
It may sometimes be useful to teach procedures for implementing particular tasks. But even then it can be helpful to include some kinds of associated declarative information. For instance, when specifying step-by-step directions for implementing a procedure, it is useful to include declarative information about the result expected after each step. Users

can then check whether the implementation of a step leads to the expected result and can thus verify whether they are still on the right track. Otherwise, a user may unwittingly make some mistakes and arrive at the end of the procedure completely off course.

3.6 SUMMARY

• Declarative knowledge is factual knowledge that specifies relevant entities and the relations among them. Procedural knowledge specifies methods that indicate how to perform various tasks.

• Declarative knowledge is compact and flexibly usable. But it requires reasoning or problem solving to figure out how it can be used for any particular task.

• Procedural knowledge can be easily used for an intended task. But extensive procedural knowledge is required for performing many diverse tasks. Furthermore, without adequate declarative knowledge, such procedural knowledge cannot be readily modified in case of need.

• Declarative and procedural knowledge are both needed for good performance since either one is inadequate without the other.

• Knowledge is often accompanied by applicability conditions indicating when it can be applied. Some of these are validity conditions that specify when it can legitimately be applied, while others are utility conditions that advise when it might usefully be applied.

4   Specifying and Interpreting Concepts

Concepts are the basic components of knowledge, the basic building blocks used to express statements or ideas. All such concepts need to have well-specified meanings so that we know what we are talking about and can communicate with other people. It is particularly important that the concepts used in scientific fields are unambiguously specified and can be properly interpreted in any specific instance. Otherwise, they could not be used to attain the central scientific goal of making definite predictions that can be clearly verified.

This chapter discusses the specification and interpretation of concepts, particularly the kinds of concepts used in scientific domains. It explores the following questions: What is a concept, and how is it related to the entities to which it refers? What are the commonly encountered types of concepts? What are some ways of specifying a concept, especially if it needs to be unambiguously interpreted in any particular instance? Why are such clear specifications important in scientific work?

Educational relevance   The concepts used in everyday life are ordinarily vaguely specified since ambiguities can often be tolerated or reduced by suitable negotiations. Such ambiguities become less acceptable in legal or financial domains, and are inappropriate in scientific fields. This need for adequately precise specifications is difficult for many students because they are used to everyday life. As a result, students are prone to many confusions or misinterpretations.

Students often get confused when the same word (for example, the word *acceleration*) is used to denote different concepts in science or in daily life. They frequently fail to discriminate between scientific concepts denoting related entities that are somewhat different (for example, to discriminate between *velocity* and *acceleration*, or between electric *current* and *potential*). They may interpret a scientific concept

properly in a simple case, but interpret it incorrectly in a more complicated case. Unfortunately, all such confusions or misinterpretations can
be disastrous when students need to apply their acquired scientific
knowledge to particular situations or problems. Indeed, when students
try to use their scientific knowledge, many of their difficulties can be
traced to failures in their interpretations of basic concepts.

The proper specification and interpretation of basic scientific concepts is an essential prerequisite for any scientific work. This prerequisite is more complex and difficult to satisfy than might be suspected.
Hence it also deserves more attention than it often receives in instructional efforts.

4.1 KNOWLEDGE AND CONCEPTS

Knowledge does not consist of meaningless words or symbols, but
is associated with corresponding entities to which it refers. (These are
called its *referents*.) If knowledge is to be meaningful, it must therefore
be clearly related to these referents.

The specification of the correspondence between knowledge and its
referents is crucially important. Indeed, this correspondence makes
knowledge useful because reasoning with this knowledge allows people
to make inferences about the actual world. The correspondence between scientific knowledge and its observable referents must be especially well specified since scientific knowledge strives to achieve
reliable predictions and explanations of observable phenomena.

Example: Meaningless words without underlying knowledge

A parrot might say the words "Coat is red." This is certainly an English statement that the parrot has learned to say. But the parrot's statement is meaningless because the parrot cannot identify the word *coat* with any particular object,
nor associate the word *red* with any particular color, nor judge whether the
statement is true or false.

Concepts The basic component of knowledge is a *concept*, namely
something that one can perceive, identify, or think about. (For example, *moon*, *dog*, and *walking* are words denoting particular concepts.)

Any meaningful concept must have well-specified referents. (For instance, the parrot may say words like *coat* or *red*, but these words have
no meaning for the bird.) The specification of a concept must thus be
sufficiently precise that its meaning is unambiguous (so that different
persons can communicate with each other by attributing the same
meaning to this concept).

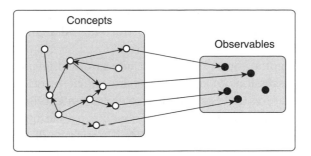

Figure 4.1
White circles schematically indicating various concepts. (The arrows point to their referents, either observable entities or other concepts.)

As indicated in figure 4.1, a concept can refer either to some observable entities or to other concepts. Furthermore, any concept can be denoted by a name (that is, labeled by a symbol) or by several alternative names. For example, the concept named *dog* in English is named *chien* in French, and *Hund* in German.

Concept specification and interpretation   A concept must be specified precisely enough that one can properly *interpret* this concept in any particular instance. The preceding specification requirement is essential in scientific domains and is sometimes also important in everyday life. For example, legislatures are careful to *specify* any law as precisely as they can, and then leave it to courts to *interpret* this law in any particular instance.

Knowledge   Knowledge consists of a set of interrelated concepts that correspond to observable entities, to other concepts, or to relations among these. Hence concepts are the basic building blocks of knowledge. The specification of some knowledge requires then the specification of all the concepts in it.

Knowledge is ultimately individual since it is contained in a particular person's mind. For example, when a person makes a new discovery, the knowledge acquired by the person is initially solely his or her own. But because of extensive communication among individuals, the knowledge usually becomes communal (so that it is shared among many people in a community or society).

Concepts in everyday life   The concepts used in everyday life are ordinarily only vaguely specified. Such imprecise (or *fuzzy*) specifications are usually adequate for most purposes. For example, what is a *chair*?

Is it a piece of furniture with a seat and four legs? Or is it any object on which one can sit? For instance, is a three-legged stool a chair? Is a beanbag a chair?

Such ambiguities don't ordinarily cause undue difficulties. If necessary, some discussions or negotiations are sufficient to lead people to an agreed meaning that is adequate in a given context. But vague specifications may also lead to situations where people attach different meanings to the same words, don't heed important distinctions, and fail to understand each other. The consequences can sometimes be disastrous, leading to persecutions or to deaths on battlefields.

Need for precise concept specifications   In scientific and other complex domains (such as in legal fields) adequately precise concept specifications are extremely important. For instance, reasoning with ill-specified knowledge cannot be used to arrive at trustworthy conclusions, and vaguely specified scientific knowledge cannot possibly lead to any accurate predictions. Acquiring knowledge with poorly specified concepts is thus quite dangerous—somewhat similar to building a house on a shaky foundation.

A satisfactory specification of a concept must make clear how the concept is related to its referents and how people can avoid possible confusions. The specification must also ensure that the concept is properly interpreted in any specific instance. To do this, it is helpful if the specification is *operational* so that it specifies a method indicating what one must actually *do* to interpret the concept properly in any specific case. In particular, it should help people to make all the discriminations needed to distinguish proper instances from non-instances—and thus to avoid confusions. Correspondingly, it should then also help people to determine whether specific statements involving the concept are true or false.

For example, the concept *triangle* is *not* well specified if it does not allow a person to recognize a picture of a triangle or to draw a triangle. Thus the Brazilian students (observed by Feynman as described in section 2.3) could talk about various physics concepts, but were not able to interpret them properly in specific situations observed by them.

Unambiguous and precise concept specifications may sometimes be difficult to achieve despite their importance. For example, consider the fundamental concept of time. My dictionary (*Webster's New World Dictionary*, 1999) defines *time* as an "indefinite unlimited duration in which things are considered as happening in the past, present, or future." This definition merely relates the word *time* to various other more or less equivalent words. But it does *not* specify how this word is related to any clearly observable entities—that is, it does not specify what one must actually *do* to determine a particular time or to measure some particular time interval.

Indeed, although *time* is a crucially important concept in all the sciences (and for centuries was used reasonably well in physics and astronomy), this concept had really never been well defined. It was only in 1905 that Einstein tried to specify a clearly measurable specification of time and was thereby also led to formulate his theory of relativity, which revolutionized physics and led to far-reaching scientific advances.

4.2 TYPES OF CONCEPTS

The meaning of *concept* can be more readily understood by examining several different types of concepts. The following paragraphs list and illustrate these types in order of increasing complexity.

4.2.1 Particular concepts

The simplest kind of concept is one denoting a single specified entity—such as *the sun, Boston,* or *George Washington.* A particular concept can also denote a specified *set* of entities. For example, *the solar system* denotes the set of entities consisting of the sun and all the planets revolving around it. (In mathematical language, a particular concept is called a *constant.*)

4.2.2 Generic concepts

A generic concept denotes any member (or instance) of a specified set of entities. Any such instance can be called a *value* of the generic concept. (In mathematical language, a generic concept is called a *variable.*)

Examples of generic concepts

- A *triangle* denotes any instance of the set of three-sided polygons.
- A *positive integer* denotes any one of the possible values 1, 2, 3, 4, ...
- A *parent* denotes any of the two possible values *father* or *mother.*
- A bird denotes any instance of the familiar set of flying animals. Possible instances (or values) of bird include pigeon, sparrow, and robin.

• A color denotes any of the possible values red, orange, yellow, green, blue, and so on.

In science, the set of possible values of a generic concept is well specified. But in everyday life, the possible values are often only vaguely specified (for example, by similarity judgments involving comparison with a prototypical instance). Thus a *bird* may well be considered as anything that *looks* somewhat like a robin—but this specification leaves it somewhat unclear whether an ostrich or a bat is an instance of a bird.

4.2.3 Relations

More complex concepts specify *relations* among other concepts. Thus, two generic concepts are *not* related if any value of one can be associated with the occurrence of any value of the other. On the other hand, two generic concepts *are* related if a value of one is associated with *only some* possible values of the other. In other words, a *relation* between generic concepts is a specified subset of corresponding values associated with each other.

Examples of simple relations

Figure 4.2 illustrates these notions in the very simple case of two concepts x and y (where x can assume only the values a and b, and y can assume only the values 1, 2, and 3). Figure 4.2a illustrates the case where these concepts are completely *un*related because any value of x can be associated with *any* value of y. On the other hand, figures 4.2b, 4.2c, and 4.2d illustrate three different relations between x and y. Indeed, in each of these cases, some values of x are associated with only *some* corresponding values of y. [A relation between x and y can be symbolically indicated by the abbreviation $R(x, y)$.]

Science is particularly interested in identifying the relations between various concepts. For example, there is a relation between the radius and the circumference of a circle, a relation between the volume and the weight of a particular liquid, and a relation between the length of a pendulum and the time required for one of its oscillations.

4.2.4 Properties

A special kind of relation is one where only *one* possible value of y is associated with every value of x. In this case, the concept y is said to be a *property* of x. (In mathematical language, y is called a *function* of x.)

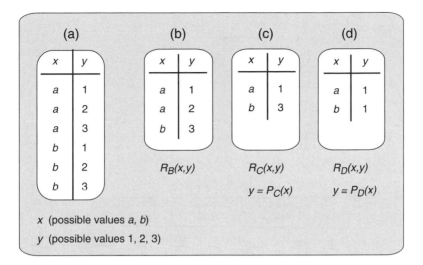

Figure 4.2
Relations and properties. (a) Unrelated concepts x and y. (b) A relation between x and y where y is *not* a property of x. (c, d) Two other relations between x and y, each specifying a different property of x.

For example, the relation R_B in figure 4.2b does *not* specify a property of x since the same value a of x is associated with *two* possible values of y. On the other hand, the relations R_C and R_D in figures 4.2c and 4.2d *do* specify properties of x since each value of x is associated with only one possible value of y. [One may write $y = P_C(x)$ and $y = P_D(x)$ to indicate that y is a property of x in each of these cases.]

Science is centrally interested in identifying the properties of various things—for example, properties such as the *weights* of various objects, the *volumes* of such objects, or the *speeds* of various moving objects.

More complex properties

One may also specify properties of more than a single independent variable. For example, the *area* A of a rectangle is a property of two independent variables, its length L and its height H. As another example, *velocity* is a property of three independent variables. Specifically, it is a property of some moving *object*, of the *time* at which the velocity is specified, and of the particular *reference frame* relative to which the velocity is described (since an object's velocity relative to the ground is different than the object's velocity relative to a moving train).

Lastly, one can also specify properties of other properties. For example, *color* is a property of an object. But a color can be further described by other properties (such as its *hue*, its *brightness*, and its *saturation*).

x	P(x)
a	T
b	F
c	F
d	T

Figure 4.3
A simple predicate.

x	y
a	1
a	2
b	1

R(x, y)

x	y	P(x,y)
a	1	T
a	2	T
a	3	F
b	1	T
b	2	F
b	3	F

Figure 4.4
A relation $R(x,y)$ indicated by the values T (*true*) of a predicate $P(x,y)$.

4.2.5 Two-valued properties (True or False)

A specially simple and important property is one that has only two possible values commonly denoted by T (*true*) or F (*false* or *not true*). Such a two-valued property is called a *predicate*. Figure 4.3 shows an example.

Any relation can be specified by labeling particular associated values as *True* (that is, by the *True* values of a particular predicate). Figure 4.4 shows an example. Indeed, all scientific principles are merely statements asserting that some general statements are true.

The equality predicate

A commonly encountered predicate is the equality predicate *Equality*(x, y), which has the value *True* when the value of x is the same as that of y, and has the value *False* otherwise. (In conventional algebraic notation this predicate can be expressed by the equation $x = y$.)

For instance, the predicate $Equality(v, u^2)$ (or equivalently, the equation $v = u^2$) expresses the fact that there is a relation between u and v that is true only if every value of u corresponds to a value of v that is the same as that of u^2.

4.3   KINDS OF CONCEPT SPECIFICATIONS

Concepts can be specified (or *defined*) in several different ways that differ in the precision of the specification.

4.3.1   Specification by prototype comparison

A concept can be specified by comparison with a prototypical case. Although this kind of specification is somewhat fuzzy (that is, not very precise), it can lead to fast and effortless recognition of a concept and is therefore often used in everyday life. For example, although we may have no explicit definition of *bird*, we commonly recognize a bird by comparison with a typical bird (like a pigeon or robin). Most of the time we then agree on which animals should be called *birds*, but sometimes the identification of a bird may become somewhat more problematic. For example, is it obvious that an ostrich *should* be called a bird, but that a bat should *not* be called a bird?

Even legal concepts may sometimes be defined by recognition processes. For example, Supreme Court Justice Potter Stewart once said that he might not be able to define hard-core pornography, "But I know it when I see it". Teachers and textbooks in science or mathematics sometimes also specify scientific concepts by prototypical situations. This instructional approach can help to make these concepts more concrete and facilitate their recognition. But the absence of more explicit concept specifications can also lead to ambiguities and student mistakes.

Examples: Concepts specified by typical cases

Angle between two vectors   A vector is a quantity (like velocity) that is characterized by a magnitude and a direction (for example, by 45 miles per hour south). Thus it can conveniently be represented by an arrow having the direction of the vector and a magnitude proportional to its length. (The positions of the arrow on the page are irrelevant.) The angle between any two such vectors **A** and **B** can then be specified by the angle θ illustrated in figure 4.5a.

Although this specification of the angle between two vectors seems clear, it is insufficient and can lead to misinterpretations. For example, when students are asked to specify the angle between the vectors **A** and **B** in figure 4.5b, many

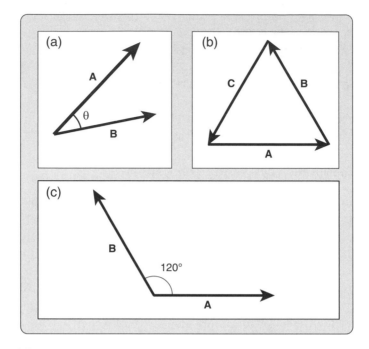

Figure 4.5
Angle between two vectors. (a) Prototype case. (b) Three vectors of equal magnitude. (c) Angle between the vectors **A** and **B** in part b of the figure.

say that this angle is 60 degrees (since this is the magnitude of every angle in an equilateral triangle). But this answer is *not* correct. (A more careful specification of the angle, mentioned later, will indicate why.)

 Resistors in parallel Simple electric circuits consist of batteries and *resistors* (which are circuit elements resisting the flow of electric current). Such circuits can be conveniently represented by circuit diagrams that indicate the circuit elements and the connections among them. These connections are represented by lines indicating resistance-less wires. (Small black circles are used to represent terminals where different wires can be connected.)

 Two resistors are said to be connected *in parallel* when they are connected in the way illustrated in figure 4.6a. This is a visually clear specification of a parallel connection, but is again insufficient and can lead to misinterpretations. For example, when students are asked whether the two resistors in figure 4.6b are connected in parallel between the terminals A and B, quite a few claim that they are *not* (because they don't look like the resistors in figure 4.6a). Similarly, when they are asked whether the two resistors in figure 4.6c are connected in parallel between the terminals A and B, quite a few claim that they *are* (because they look similar to those in figure 4.6a). But *none* of these answers are correct. (More careful specifications, mentioned later, will again indicate why.)

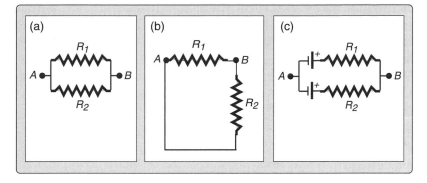

Figure 4.6
Two connected resistors. (a) Prototype of two resistors connected in parallel.
(b) Two resistors in a circuit. (c) Two resistors in a circuit with two batteries.

4.3.2   Declarative specification

A concept can be specified by a declarative statement that summarizes its distinctive characteristics. Such a specification can be concise and thus readily remembered. With sufficient care and ancillary knowledge, it can also be elaborated in greater detail.

Examples of declarative specifications

Angle between two vectors   The angle between two vectors can be explicitly defined by the statement that this is the angle between their representing arrows emanating from the same point. Careful attention to this specification makes clear that the arrows representing the vectors *A* and *B* in figure 4.5b do not emanate from the same point—so that the angle between them is *not* 60 degrees. However, when these arrows are drawn so as to emanate from the same point (as shown in figure 4.5c), it is apparent that the angle between these two vectors is actually 120 degrees.

Resistors in parallel   Such a parallel connection between two terminals can be specified by the statement that the resistors are connected so that one end of each resistor is connected to one terminal, and the other end of each is connected to the other terminal. Careful attention to this specification makes clear that the two resistors in figure 4.6b *are* connected in parallel between the indicated terminals. However, the two resistors in figure 4.6c are *not* connected in parallel because of the intervening batteries.

4.3.3   Procedural specification

A *procedural* (or *operational*) specification of a concept specifies a procedure that indicates what one must actually *do* to recognize or exhibit any instance of the concept. Indeed, this is the most detailed and unambiguous way of specifying a concept since it describes a clear *method* indicating how to interpret the concept in any particular case. (The actual interpretation of the concept requires also the proper implementation of this method.)

Examples of procedural specifications

Angle between two vectors   The angle between two vectors can be explicitly defined by the following method:

1. Draw the arrows representing the two vectors so that both of them start from the same point.
2. Identify the angle (less than 180 degrees) between these arrows. This is the relevant angle.

Note that this method is highly explicit in specifying that the two arrows must be drawn from the same point. Hence it also prevents any misinterpretations of the kind suggested by figure 4.5b.

Resistors in parallel   Similarly, a parallel connection between two resistors can be specified by the following method:

1. Verify that one terminal of one resistor is connected to one terminal of the other resistor.
2. Verify that the other terminal of one of these resistors is connected to the other terminal of the other resistor.
3. The resistors are connected in parallel if both of these conditions are true.

Note that this method is sufficiently explicit that identification mistakes (like those indicated in figures 4.6b or 4.6c) are very unlikely.

Such procedural specifications can help students to avoid many common mistakes and misconceptions. (The next chapter provides some concrete illustrations.) They can also help people in everyday life to overcome their disagreements about the meanings of words used in argumentative discussions.

4.4   SCIENTIFIC IMPORTANCE OF CONCEPT SPECIFICATIONS

Science aims to use a small amount of basic knowledge to predict a large number of observable phenomena. To ensure adequate generality, scientific concepts are often abstract so that they can encompass many particular cases. Such abstractness is a common source of difficulty since human beings find it much easier to think about familiar concrete and readily visualized situations than about abstractly specified concepts or purely logical reasoning (Wason and Johnson-Laird, 1972).

However, mere abstractness is *not* the main reason why scientific concepts are often difficult to learn and use. After all, in everyday life we also commonly use many abstract concepts (such as *justice, love, honesty*, and *democracy*).

The main difficulty is that in science one must be able to interpret concepts unambiguously in any particular instance—and this is a requirement usually *not* necessary in everyday life. For example, we may well tolerate differing opinions about whether a particular relationship is an instance of *true love*. But in science, the concept of *energy* needs to be sufficiently well specified that its meaning is clear and that people agree about the amount of electrical energy supplied to their homes.

Since scientific knowledge aims to achieve predictions that can be as accurate as desired, all the concepts in this knowledge must be precisely enough specified. This is why *procedural* specifications (or *operational* definitions) have proved useful, forcing scientists to be very careful in their specification of scientific concepts. In particular, scientists have had to specify concepts not by mere words, but by what people must actually *do* to relate scientific concepts to observable phenomena. Indeed, the twentieth century witnessed two major scientific revolutions (the theory of relativity and quantum mechanics) that were closely tied to more careful procedural specifications of some commonly used concepts. The following examples indicate how reexaminations of two seemingly simple concepts have led to such far-reaching implications.

Example 1: Specification of the concept of time

Although *time* is a very important and much-used concept, it had not been clearly specified. A specification that involves more than mere words must relate time to a suitable measuring instrument (called a *clock*). Such a clock consists of some repeating device (such as an oscillating pendulum or the light emitted by atoms in an atomic clock). An elapsed time can then be determined by counting the number of repetitions of the clock (for example., the oscillations of the pendulum or the frequency of the emitted light).

By using such a clock, one can readily measure the time elapsed between two events observed at the *same* place. But measuring the time elapsed between two events observed at two *different* places A and B requires *two* clocks, one at A and the other at B. Furthermore, these clocks must be properly synchronized (for example, when one of them indicates 3 o'clock, the other one must also indicate 3 o'clock).

But how can one synchronize these clocks? One might send out a light signal from A at 3 o'clock and, when this signal arrives at B, set the clock there also to 3 o'clock. But since the signal required some time to travel from A to B, it actually arrived at B slightly after 3 o'clock. [The travel time is actually very short, since the speed of light is very large (about 300,000 kilometers per second). But if one is interested in high precision, this travel time cannot be ignored.]

This travel time could be calculated if one knows the distance from A to B and the value of the speed of light. But to determine the speed of light, one has to measure the time required for light to traverse a known distance between two points—and this again requires two properly synchronized clocks at these two points. Thus we are now going around in logical circles. We are unable to synchronize accurately two distant clocks without knowing the speed of light—and we are unable to determine accurately the speed of light without properly synchronized distant clocks.

Hence this (and other) proposed methods for specifying the times at different places are all inadequate. One is thus led to the conclusion that nobody had ever clearly specified how to compare the times at two different places. This left Einstein free to propose such a specification himself. Accordingly, he introduced the bold hypothesis that the speed of light is a universal constant (the same everywhere and in all directions) and that this *same* speed would be measured by all observers even if they move relative to each other. This hypothesis leads to a precise specification of time by allowing distant clocks to be synchronized with light signals.

This hypothesis is the basis of Einstein's *theory of relativity* and provides a perfectly self-consistent description of nature. However, some of its conclusions seem paradoxical from the perspective of prior notions based on inadequate specifications of time. For example, the theory predicts that two different observers, moving relative to each other, will *not* agree on whether two events observed by them occur at the same time or not; will *not* agree on the time elapsed between two different events occurring at different places; and will *not* agree on the lengths of objects moving relative to them.

These seemingly strange conclusions merely indicate that statements made by different observers depend on their particular points of view. (Furthermore, each observer knows how the same situation would be described from the other's point of view.) These conclusions do *not* lead to directly observable consequences in everyday life where extremely high precision is not needed and where objects move with speeds very much less than the speed of light. But with modern technology, very high precision can readily be attained; furthermore, objects of atomic size (such as electrons or atomic nuclei) can readily be made to move with speeds very close to the speed of light. Thus, the theory of relativity has resulted in profound modifications of classical mechanics, made many correct predictions, and led to various practical applications (for example, in navigation and the global positioning system).

Example 2: Specification of the path of a moving object

We commonly talk about the paths traversed by moving objects. But what would one actually have to *do* to specify the path of such an object, that is, to specify the successive points traversed by the object? At first blush, the answer seems clear: simply observe the object. But to *observe* an object, one needs light (or something similar) bouncing off the object. Ordinarily, this does not cause any difficulties. But if the object is very small (for example, an atomic particle), then light bouncing off the object would cause it to recoil in unpredictable ways. Hence we would *not* be able to clearly determine the path of the particle.

Thus it is *not* really possible to specify the path of an object when the object is of atomic size. Classical mechanics, the theory of motion of large-scale objects, is therefore *not* applicable in the realm of atomic particles. This conclusion led, around 1926, to the formulation of *quantum mechanics* applicable even to very small objects. In this theory, the motion of objects is described only probabilistically. Indeed, the *Heisenberg uncertainty principle* asserts that the position and momentum (or velocity) of an object cannot simultaneously be determined with unlimited precision. When one is dealing with objects much larger than atomic size, this limitation is utterly negligible. But in the realm of atomic particles (that is, when dealing with atoms, molecules, or the detailed properties of matter) it is of utmost importance. It has led to a profound restructuring of our ideas about the world, led to innumerable correct predictions, and also to many practical applications.

4.5 EDUCATIONAL IMPLICATIONS

4.5.1 Proficient performers and inexperienced students

Expert scientists specify carefully the concepts that they use and ordinarily interpret them properly in any specific case.

By contrast, inexperienced students often deal with scientific concepts in ways similar to those that they use with everyday concepts—without great care to ensure a clear connection between these concepts and their referents. Thus they may talk about *area* without having any idea about how to determine the area of a surface. They may seemingly know the concept of acceleration when they say that "acceleration is the rate of change of velocity"—but may be unable specify whether the acceleration of an object, moving in a particular way, is zero or not. Similarly, they may have learned Newton's basic mechanics law $F = ma$ and can quote it like a mantra ("F equals $m\ a$"). But they may not know how the mass m of an object can be determined, may not realize that the pertinent acceleration a must be specified relative to a special (*inertial*) reference frame, may forget that the force F denotes the vector sum of all individual forces on the object, and may talk about the acceleration a of one object while mistakenly considering the force F on some other object.

Students also commonly fail to distinguish properly between different scientific concepts. For example, they may indiscriminately use words like *force, momentum, power,* and *energy* as if these meant the same thing.

Such deficiencies of concept specification help to account for the observations that students often emerge from their science courses (even after receiving good grades) unable to interpret correctly the concepts and principles that they ostensibly learned (Halloun and Hestenes, 1985). These deficiencies can persist for a long time and may also hinder students' abilities to deal with more advanced science courses.

4.5.2   Common instructional deficiencies

Many instructors underestimate the difficulties experienced by students who are faced with the need to learn basic scientific concepts. Thus they commonly spend insufficient time and care teaching how to specify and interpret such concepts. They may also ask students to solve substantial problems before the students have learned to interpret reliably the needed scientific concepts. As a result, many student mistakes in problem solving are due to faulty misinterpretations of such concepts, rather than to deficiencies in more sophisticated problem-solving skills (Heller and Reif, 1984).

4.5.3   Instructional suggestions

Introductory courses often introduce one new concept after another in quick succession, without elaborating any of these at greater length. Unfamiliar concepts may then be too difficult to assimilate and may remain largely meaningless. This is one reason why introductory courses may sometimes be more difficult than more advanced courses that discuss fewer concepts in much greater depth.

It may sometimes be appropriate to introduce a new concept by using examples or prototypical cases. But at some point, it becomes necessary to define such a concept more operationally by a clearly specified method. Students should then learn how to implement this method in a variety of particular instances. Merely *demonstrating* such interpretations in class or in textbooks is almost useless. Instead, students themselves must implement this method, perhaps with a little help from an instructor. In this way, students can actually learn to apply the concept in various situations likely to be encountered in the future. They can thereby also become familiar with some important properties of the concept and learn to pay attention to some important discriminations.

4.6 SUMMARY

• If knowledge is to be reliably usable, its concepts must be adequately specified so as to be clearly related to their referents. This is particularly true for scientific concepts needed to achieve unambiguous predictions and explanations.

• The simplest types of concepts are particular or generic concepts. More complex concepts specify relations among generic concepts (for example, a property relates each value of a concept to a single corresponding value of the property concept). Furthermore, any relation can be expressed by the *true* value of a two-valued property.

• A concept can be specified by comparison with a prototype or, more precisely, by a declarative specification. However, the most precise specification can be achieved by means of an *operational* (or *procedural*) specification that provides a method specifying what one must actually *do* to relate the concept to its referents. The proper implementation of this method then allows the concept to be properly interpreted in any particular instance.

• Operational specifications are very useful in scientific domains and have led to some revolutionary scientific advances.

• Inexperienced students often find it difficult to correctly specify and interpret scientific concepts. The next chapter examines these difficulties at greater length by discussing a particular example.

5   Interpreting Scientific Concepts

The preceding chapter discussed the importance of adequately specifying and interpreting scientific concepts—and also indicated some ways whereby this can be done. To make the relevant cognitive and educational issues more concrete, this chapter illustrates these issues in the case of the particular scientific concept *acceleration*. This basic and important concept is usually studied within the first two weeks of any introductory college physics course and is then used repeatedly thereafter. This concept is also typical of many more advanced concepts that are encountered in science or mathematics courses.

How well do students learn such a basic scientific concept when it has been taught to them? This chapter reviews some experimental investigations designed to answer this question. Such investigations have shown that, even after students have studied and used such a concept for a couple of months, they make many mistakes in interpreting it properly. Indeed, even after students have been studying physics for a few *years*, their ability to interpret such a basic concept is still remarkably poor.

Observations of this kind lead us to explore the following questions: How can a concept like acceleration be sufficiently well specified that its proper interpretation is clear? What are students' common interpretation difficulties and the underlying reasons for them? Why are these difficulties so persistent and hard to overcome? How might scientific concepts be taught more effectively? These questions, examined here in the particular case of acceleration, are actually much more widely relevant to students' learning of all scientific concepts.

5.1 STUDENTS' INTERPRETATION OF THE CONCEPT *ACCELERATION*

5.1.1 Reasons for focusing on acceleration

The scientific concept *acceleration* is useful for describing the motion of objects. The specification of this concept is seemingly quite simple and is provided by the following declarative statement:

Definition of *acceleration* The acceleration of an object
is the rate of change of its velocity with time.   (5.1)

There are several reasons why it seems useful to focus attention on this particular concept.

• The concept *acceleration* is crucially important in Newtonian mechanics, the highly successful theory of motion that has been responsible for the great advances in physics and astronomy since the seventeenth century.

• The concept is typical of many other concepts that are encountered in the physical sciences, mathematics, and engineering.

• Because a great deal can be learned by examining students' difficulties in interpreting this concept, several experimental investigations have dealt with students' abilities to interpret it properly.

• This concept is sufficiently simple that a prior knowledge of physics is *not* needed to understand the issues involved in interpreting the concept. Hence even an unsophisticated reader should find it possible to understand these general issues and to appreciate their importance.

The next few paragraphs describe the results of two experimental investigations that examined how well various students, who are familiar with the concept *acceleration*, can interpret this concept appropriately.

5.1.2 Detailed small-scale investigation

Description of the investigation One such investigation, carried out by one of my colleagues and myself (Reif and Allen, 1992), observed individually five students and five physics experts at the University of California in Berkeley. The students were all enrolled in an introductory physics course where they had studied the concept *acceleration* two months previously and had used this concept repeatedly since then. The "experts" were professors who had been engaged in physics research for many years and who had also recently taught basic physics courses dealing with acceleration.

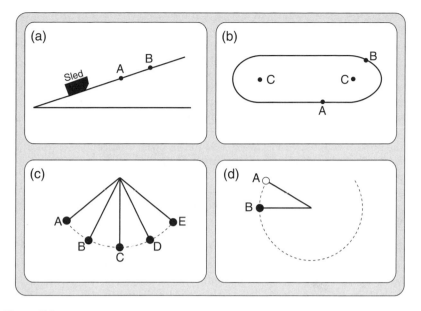

Figure 5.1
Motions of different objects. (a) A sled sliding up along a hill after an initial push. (b) A car traveling around a racetrack. (c) A pendulum bob swinging back and forth. (d) A pendulum bob moving along a circular arc after being released from point A.

Each person was individually presented with 15 different situations, some of which are illustrated in figure 5.1. Each situation involved a moving object and was accompanied by the following question: "What is the acceleration of the object at the instant when it is at the indicated position? (To answer, specify whether its acceleration is zero or not. If it is not zero, draw an arrow indicating its direction.)"

The preceding question requires merely *qualitative* determinations of the acceleration in some particular cases (and thus request no numerical answers). In principle, each such questions can be answered merely by remembering and properly interpreting the definition (5.1) of acceleration.

Examples of specific interpretation questions

The following interpretation questions were asked about the situations illustrated in figure 5.1:

• Figure 5.1a shows a sled that, after being given a push, slides up along a straight hill, passes point A, comes momentarily to rest at point B, and then slides down again along the hill. What is the acceleration of the sled at A? What is its acceleration at point B?

• Figure 5.1b shows a car traveling with constant speed around a racetrack, first passing point A and then passing point B. What is the acceleration of the car at point A? What is its acceleration at point B?

• Figure 5.1c shows a pendulum swinging back and forth. The pendulum bob is momentarily at rest at the extreme point A, passes the point B while descending with increasing speed along the circular arc, reaches its maximum speed at the lowest point C where the string of the pendulum is vertical, passes the point D with decreasing speed, and then is again momentarily at rest at the extreme point E. What is the acceleration of the bob at point A? What is it at point B? What is it at point C?

• Figure 5.1d shows another pendulum whose bob was initially released from rest at point A and which then descends along a circular arc. What is the acceleration of the bob at point B?

Each person was asked to talk out loud about his or her thinking (and was tape-recorded) while trying to answer each question. After answering all 15 questions, each person was asked to review his or her previous answers to all the questions and to modify these answers if necessary. (The aim was to give each person sufficient time and opportunities to arrive at well-considered answers to all the questions.)

Results of the investigation   Figure 5.2 shows the results of the investigation by indicating how many of the 15 questions were correctly answered by each of the persons (after *two* opportunities to think about each question).

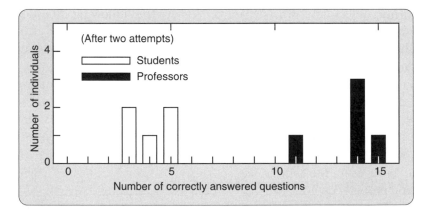

Figure 5.2
Performance of students and professors on questions assessing their ability to interpret the concept *acceleration*.

The students answered correctly only about 25 percent of the questions. Only two of the students could answer correctly as many as 5 of the 15 questions. The students in this physics class thus displayed a surprisingly poor ability to interpret properly the concept *acceleration* that they had ostensibly learned and then repeatedly used for about two months.

The performance of the physics experts (the professors) was obviously much better. For instance, one of the experts answered correctly all 15 questions. But the experts did *not* all perform perfectly since three of them answered one of the questions *in*correctly—and since one of them answered incorrectly as many as 4 of the questions.

5.1.3   Larger-scale investigation

The results of the previous investigation, dealing with students' interpretation of the concept *acceleration*, might possibly be misleading since it involved only a small number of students who might not be representative of larger numbers of individuals. However, a much larger (although less detailed) investigation was later performed at the University of Washington in Seattle (Shaffer and McDermott, 1994, 2005).

In this investigation, physics students (of varying degrees of sophistication) were shown the pendulum situation displayed in figure 5.1c. The students were then asked to determine qualitatively the acceleration of the pendulum bob at the indicated points in that figure. [A correct interpretation of the definition 5.1 would yield the answers indicated in figure 5.3.]

The investigation was carried out on 124 students enrolled in an introductory physics course, 22 physics graduate students acting as teaching assistants in that course, and 11 advanced graduate students taking the qualifying examination needed to proceed toward the Ph.D. degree in physics. The results of this investigation are summarized in figure 5.4.

These results indicate again surprisingly poor performance by all these students. Indeed, *none* of the introductory physics students (who had been using the concept *acceleration* in this course for many weeks) could properly determine the pendulum bob's acceleration at all points. Only 15 percent of the teaching assistants (who were physics graduate students charged with helping the introductory students learn the concept *acceleration*) were able to determine correctly the bob's acceleration in this problem. Lastly, only 20 percent of the *advanced* graduate

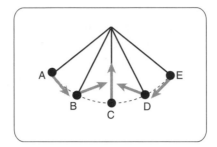

Figure 5.3
Solution of the pendulum problem of figure 5.1c. The acceleration of the bob is nowhere zero, and its acceleration at the different points is indicated by the gray arrows.

	Number	Correct answers
First-year students	124	0%
Teaching assistants	22	15%
Ph.D. candidates	11	20%

Figure 5.4
Number of tested students and percentage of these giving correct answers for the acceleration of the pendulum bob at the points indicated in figure 5.1c.

students, about to start their Ph.D. research in physics, could determine this acceleration.

These data are consistent with those obtained in the previously mentioned small-scale investigation. They also indicate that the interpretation of a scientific concept (even one as elementary as acceleration) can be remarkably difficult, even for persons who have been familiar with it for a long time.

5.2 MOTION AND THE CONCEPT OF ACCELERATION

The preceding investigations reveal that the proper interpretation of a scientific concept (even one as relatively simple as acceleration) can be remarkably difficult for students and can lead to mistakes that persist for a long time. Let us then examine more carefully how the concept

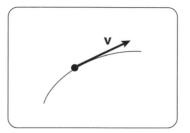

Figure 5.5
Path of a moving object and its velocity **v** at the indicated instant.

acceleration can be adequately specified. We shall then see that the definition 5.1 is correct, but that its seeming simplicity is deceptive and hides subtle complexities. Thus it will become apparent that the students' interpretation difficulties are not unduly surprising.

Path of a moving object   A useful description of motion is of central importance in physics, astronomy, and engineering. The simplest motion is that of an object that is small enough that its position can be adequately described by that of a single point. When such an object moves, it then traverses a particular path consisting of the successive positions of the object.

Velocity   To describe how rapidly an object moves, it is convenient to introduce the concept *velocity* which describes the *rate of change* of the object's position with time. This velocity is a *vector* (that is, a quantity specified jointly by its magnitude and its direction). The *magnitude* of the velocity is the object's speed (for example, measured in units of miles per hour). The *direction* of the velocity is the direction of the object's motion along its path. The velocity can be indicated pictorially by an arrow that has a length proportional to the magnitude of the velocity (that is, to its speed) and that has the same direction as the velocity. This velocity can be denoted by the letter **v** (in boldface to indicate that it is a vector) and is illustrated in figure 5.5.

Acceleration   When an object moves, its velocity can change. Hence one may want to describe how *rapidly* this velocity is changing at any instant. This *rate of change* of the velocity with time is called the *acceleration* of the object.

In daily life the word *acceleration* is used to describe the rate of change of an object's *speed*. In science, the same word is used to describe a more general concept, namely the rate of change of an object's *velocity*. This conception of acceleration is more general because a change of velocity can involve a change of its magnitude (or *speed*), a change of its direction, or a change of both. Hence the acceleration (as defined in science) is zero only if neither the magnitude nor the direction of the velocity is changing.

Example: Everyday and scientific meanings of acceleration

If a car travels around a curve at a *constant* speed of 20 miles per hour, an ordinary driver would say that the car is *not* accelerating. But a scientist would say that it *is* accelerating (since the direction of the car's velocity is changing).

Importance of the scientific specification of acceleration   This seemingly minor change in the specification of acceleration has had the following far-reaching scientific consequences.

• It revealed the underlying similarity of several apparently different kinds of motion (such as the motion of a vertically falling object, of a baseball moving along a curved trajectory, and of the moon orbiting around the earth). Indeed, in all these cases the objects' accelerations are similar because they are all directed toward the center of the earth. (The major difference is that, in the first case, the velocity changes only in its magnitude; in the second case, it changes both in magnitude and direction; and in the last case, it changes only in direction).

• The recognition of this similarity led Newton to the profound insight that the moon, as well as all objects near the surface of the earth, are similarly influenced by their gravitational interaction with the earth.

• An object interacting with nothing else (for example, one in outer space very far from any other objects) moves simply with *constant* velocity—that is, with zero acceleration. What then is an object's acceleration when it *does* interact with other objects? This question led Newton to focus on acceleration as a key concept in his theory of motion. The central scientific question then became that of specifying *how* an object's acceleration depends on its interactions with other objects (for example, how it depends on the object's distance from other objects and on the properties of all these objects). Newton summarized all these considerations in his famous law $m\mathbf{a} = \mathbf{F}_{tot}$ which specifies how an object's acceleration $\mathbf{a}$ (which describes its motion) is related to the total force $\mathbf{F}_{tot}$ on the object (where this total force describes the object's interactions with all other objects).

5.3   SPECIFICATION OF ACCELERATION

The preceding qualitative comments about the scientific concept *acceleration* have prepared us to specify this concept more precisely. We shall then see how a seemingly simple specification, like that provided by the definition 5.1, can lead to many interpretation difficulties.

5.3.1   Specification of a change of velocity

How is the change of a velocity $\mathbf{v}$ (or of any other vector) specified when this change can be due to both a change of magnitude and a change of direction? Such a change is equal to the difference between the new velocity $\mathbf{v}'$ and the original velocity $\mathbf{v}$. (In figure 5.6a, both of these velocities are indicated by arrows drawn from the same point.) In particular, such a *small* velocity change $d\mathbf{v} = \mathbf{v}' - \mathbf{v}$ (where the letter d indicates a small difference) is defined as the small vector $d\mathbf{v}$ indicated in figure 5.6a (that is, as the small vector drawn from the tip of the original velocity $\mathbf{v}$ to the tip of the new velocity $\mathbf{v}'$).

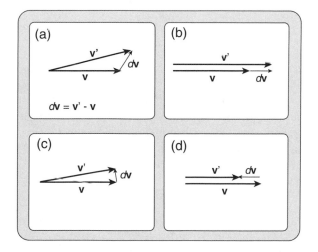

Figure 5.6
Small change of a velocity from $\mathbf{v}$ to $\mathbf{v}'$. (a) General case. (b) The velocities $\mathbf{v}'$ and $\mathbf{v}$ have the same direction, but $\mathbf{v}'$ is slightly larger. (c) The velocities have the same magnitude but slightly different directions. (d) The velocities have opposite directions, but $\mathbf{v}'$ is slightly smaller.

Relation between new and original velocities

Note that $\mathbf{v}' = \mathbf{v} + d\mathbf{v}$, so that the new velocity is equal to the original veloc-ity plus its change. (This is clear from figure 5.6a since vectors are added like successive displacements.)

Figure 5.6 also illustrates small changes of velocity in some special cases. Thus figure 5.6b shows that, if the new velocity $\mathbf{v}'$ has the same direction as the original velocity $\mathbf{v}$ but a slightly *larger* magnitude, then the velocity change $d\mathbf{v}$ has the same direction as $\mathbf{v}$. Figure 5.6c shows that, if the new velocity $\mathbf{v}'$ has the *same* magnitude as the original ve-locity $\mathbf{v}$ but a slightly different direction, then the velocity change $d\mathbf{v}$ is approximately perpendicular to $\mathbf{v}$. Finally, 5.6d shows that, if the new velocity $\mathbf{v}'$ has the same direction as the original velocity $\mathbf{v}$ but a slightly *smaller* magnitude, then the velocity change $d\mathbf{v}$ has a direction opposite to $\mathbf{v}$.

5.3.2   Declarative specification of acceleration

As already mentioned in section 5.1, the concept *acceleration* can be defined by the statement that *"Acceleration is the rate of change of velocity with time."* This statement can be summarized even more compactly by the equation

$$\mathbf{a} = \frac{d\mathbf{v}}{dt} \tag{5.2}$$

where $\mathbf{a}$ denotes the acceleration, $\mathbf{v}$ the velocity, and t the time. Here the symbol d denotes a slight (or *infinitesimal*) difference (one so small that a smaller one would negligibly affect the calculated acceleration). Furthermore, any vector quantity (characterized jointly by a magnitude and a direction) is denoted by a boldface letter.

5.3.3   Procedural specification of acceleration

The equation 5.2 (or that in figure 5.7a) provides a very compact specification of acceleration. But its proper interpretation is made much clearer by its procedural specification. As illustrated in figure 5.7b, this procedural specification can be achieved by a method involv-ing the following five steps:

1. Identify the object's velocity $\mathbf{v}$ at the time t of interest. (This step is illustrated in the left part of figure 5.7b.)

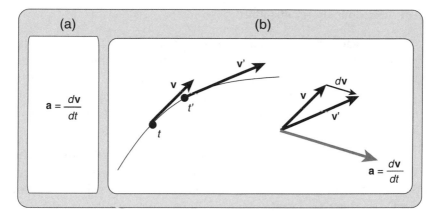

Figure 5.7
Specifications of the concept *acceleration*. (a) Declarative specification. (b) Steps
of the method describing a procedural specification.

2. For the sake of comparison, identify the velocity $\mathbf{v}'$ at a slightly
later time t'. (This step is also illustrated in the left part of figure 5.7b.)

3. Find the small change of velocity $d\mathbf{v}$ during the slight time interval $dt = t' - t$. (This step is illustrated in the right part of figure 5.7b.)

4. Calculate the ratio $d\mathbf{v}/dt$. (This ratio has the same direction as $d\mathbf{v}$,
but has a much larger magnitude since dt is very small.)

5. Consider the limiting case where the time interval dt has been
chosen sufficiently small (that is, where the time t' has been chosen
sufficiently close to t) that a smaller choice would have negligible effect
on the ratio $d\mathbf{v}/dt$. This is then the desired acceleration $\mathbf{a}$ (indicated in
the right part of figure 5.7b).

5.4 CAUSES OF INTERPRETATION DEFICIENCIES

Now that the preceding section has clarified the specification of
an acceleration, we can try to answer the following questions: Why
are many students unable to properly interpret a rather elementary scientific concept that they have studied? What kinds of interpretation
deficiencies do they exhibit? What are the reasons why such deficiencies occur? These questions, examined in the following paragraphs, are
particularly important because answers to them provide valuable
insights that can be used to help students deal with many scientific
concepts.

5.4.1 Discrimination difficulties

Work in scientific or similar domains often requires fine discriminations between closely related entities. Indeed, an inability to distinguish significant features can lead to many confusions.

Discrimination difficulties commonly occur whenever two concepts specify somewhat differing aspects of similar things. The concept *acceleration*, discussed in the preceding sections, provides many such examples.

Confusing scientific and everyday meanings   It is easy to confuse the scientific meaning of the word *acceleration* with the everyday meaning of the same word. For instance, students commonly claim that an object's acceleration is zero when it is moving with constant speed around a curved path. (This would clearly be correct in everyday language, where the word *acceleration* pays no attention to a changing direction of the velocity.)

Confusing velocity and speed   Students often confuse the word *velocity* and the word *speed* (which denotes the *magnitude* of the velocity). For example, they may wrongly say that a car moves with constant *velocity* when it is moving around a curve with constant *speed*. Or they may wrongly claim that an object's *speed* must change if its *velocity* changes. (Of course, in everyday life the words *velocity* and *speed* are often used interchangeably.)

Confusing velocity and acceleration   The concepts *velocity* and *acceleration* both describe motion, but describe different aspects of motion. Velocity describes a change of *position*, but acceleration describes a change of *velocity*.

The neglect of the preceding distinction leads many students to claim that, if an object's velocity is zero, then its acceleration must also be zero. They may even misleadingly elaborate this claim by saying "If an object's velocity is zero, it does not move. Hence its acceleration must be zero". Of course, this statement is wrong. Even if an object's velocity is zero at some instant, it may be somewhat different slightly later (that is, its velocity may be changing).

Confusing vectors and numbers   A vector quantity, characterized by a magnitude and a direction, is conventionally denoted by a boldface letter. The same letter, without any boldface, is then used to denote the numerical *magnitude* of this vector. For instance, a vector velocity is denoted by the boldface letter $\mathbf{v}$, but the magnitude of this velocity (that is, its speed) is denoted simply by the plain letter v.

Students often ignore this distinction. For instance, they may write the definition of acceleration in the form $a = dv/dt$ (instead of using the correct form shown in equation 5.2 where all vector quantities are properly indicated by boldface letters). Such indiscriminate or careless use of symbols can lead them to the erroneous conclusion that acceleration is the rate of change of *speed*. Furthermore, it may also lead them to confuse *the magnitude of the rate of change of the velocity* with *the rate of change of the magnitude of the velocity* (two very similarly sounding phrases with completely different meanings).

5.4.2 Defective interpretations of an invoked definition

Students sometimes invoke explicitly a correct definition of a concept, but then go awry because they don't interpret it properly. For example, when asked about the acceleration of the pendulum bob at the extreme point A in figure 5.1c, a student said the following:

> *"The velocity is zero, so the acceleration has to be zero—because acceleration equals the change in velocity over the change in time....I mean, acceleration is the derivative of the velocity over time. And the derivative of velocity is zero."*

Here the student stated correctly the definition of acceleration. He even went on to express it in the formal mathematical language of the calculus (where the word *derivative* is used to denote a rate of change). But then he completely misinterpreted this definition by claiming that it implies that the acceleration is zero. (The student fell into the previously mentioned trap of believing that, if an object's velocity is zero, it cannot be changing—so that the change of velocity (and thus the acceleration) must also be zero.

This is a good example of the difference between *nominal* knowledge (involving the ability to say the correct words) and *usable* knowledge (involving the ability to use knowledge appropriately.)

5.4.3 Erroneous use of compiled knowledge

After using a concept for some time, people may remember commonly occurring special cases of this concept. (For example, they may remember that the acceleration of an object, moving with constant speed around a circle, is directed toward the center of the circle.) Indeed, remembering such accumulated (or *compiled*) special-case knowledge is efficient because one can then merely recall this knowledge

without needing to go back to infer conclusions from the general specification of the concept. But reliance on such compiled knowledge can
also be dangerous because one needs then to remember (and subsequently also to recall) the validity conditions under which such compiled special-case knowledge is actually correct.

Students often remember much special-case knowledge, but don't
adequately heed its validity conditions. Indeed, many students' errors
are due to their faulty invocation of such special-case knowledge. This
statement can be illustrated by the following words of a student
observed while he confronted the task of determining the acceleration
of the pendulum bob at the point B in figure 5.1d.

> *If it's moving, it has a velocity,...maybe a constant velocity or increasing
> velocity,...and you'll always have acceleration in a circular path. It's not the
> change in velocity, it's just v^2/r. And it's always directed toward the center of
> the circle.*

Here the student invoked his previously acquired knowledge that
the acceleration of an object, moving with a speed v around a circle of
radius r, is directed toward the center and has a magnitude v^2/r. However, the student failed to heed the validity condition that this result is
true only if the speed v is *constant* (and this is *not* true in the situation
of figure 5.1d).

5.4.4   Fragmented knowledge

The dangers of compiled case-specific knowledge become particularly apparent if a person's knowledge consists merely of various tidbits
of special-case knowledge, but does *not* include more general knowledge from which such special cases can be inferred. The various knowledge elements (especially if faulty) may then be mutually inconsistent
and may lead to apparent paradoxes that cannot be resolved (because
more coherent general knowledge, which could help to identify the difficulties, is not available).

Unsophisticated students are particularly prone to accumulate various bits of knowledge without much concern for their validity conditions or for the coherent organization of their acquired knowledge. As
a result, such students encounter frequent paradoxes that they cannot
resolve.

Paradox encountered in the pendulum problem   The preceding remarks are well illustrated by the observations of a student who was
considering the situation in figure 5.1c and tried to identify the accel-

eration of the pendulum bob at the extreme point A of its path. The following is an actual transcript of the student's words while he was engaged in this task:

> *"Acceleration is zero because it's not moving, so I'm sure of that. There's no acceleration on a non-moving object."*
>
> *"Just because velocity at that point is zero, that doesn't mean that there's no change in it. It's got to go from one direction to another."*
>
> . . .
>
> *"Well, I'm stuck. There's two ways to think about it, and I don't know which way to think about it."*
>
> *"I can think, 'It's not moving, so it's not accelerating.'"*
>
> *"Or I can think, 'It moved to this point, and it's immediately moving away from it with a different direction . . . so the velocity had to change.'"*
>
> . . .
>
> *"Wait a minute. . . . There's no velocity here, so there's no direction."*
>
> *"Wait, I'm really messed up. . . . It gets harder and harder to think the longer I think about it."*
>
> *"It's not even moving at point A, it stops. . . . Is there an acceleration when the velocity is zero? I don't know. I don't know any more. I can't answer."*

In this case, the poor struggling student encountered a paradox that he could not resolve and finally just gave up. (His main difficulty was the mistaken belief that the acceleration must be zero if the velocity is zero.)

Examples of other student paradoxes   Many students run into similar irresolvable paradoxes because they rely predominantly on bits of accumulated special-case knowledge, but lack the more coherent general knowledge upon which their special-case knowledge is based. Other examples of such paradoxes, encountered by students when trying to identify the acceleration in the situations shown in figure 5.1, are illustrated by the following kinds of incompatible statements made by some students.

Students' contradictory statements

   • *Sled moving along straight hill (at point A in figure 5.1a)*

   1. Decreasing speed implies that the sled's acceleration has a direction opposite to its velocity.

   2. The presence of gravity implies that the sled's acceleration is directed downward.

   (The second statement is wrong because the sled does not merely interact gravitationally with the earth, but interacts also with the surface of the hill with which it is in contact.)

• *Car moving around a racetrack (at point B in figure 5.1b)*

1. The acceleration is zero because the car is moving with constant velocity.
2. The acceleration is *not* zero because the car is moving around a circular path.

(The first statement is wrong because the car moves around a curve so that the *direction* of its velocity is changing.)

• *Horizontal pendulum (at point B in figure 5.1d)*

1. The bob's circular motion implies that its acceleration is directed toward the center.
2. The bob's increasing speed implies that its acceleration is directed along its velocity.

(The first statement is wrong because the bob does not move with constant speed. The second statement is wrong because the bob does not move along a straight line.)

In all of the preceding situations, and many others, the students were unable to deal with the apparent contradictions of their conclusions and thus became irremediably stuck.

Another example of students' incoherent knowledge   The following observation, in a different context, involved a senior undergraduate physics major who was asked to solve a problem involving an object moving with constant speed around a circle. The student first claimed that the object's acceleration was directed along its velocity. Then he quickly corrected himself, concluding (rightly) that the acceleration around this circle must be directed toward its center. But then he added, "Although I could never understand why."

It was clear that the student had simply remembered a particular fact about the acceleration in the case of circular motion. But this fact made no sense to him and seemed unconnected to any general knowledge about acceleration.

5.4.5   Correct concept interpretations of experts

Figure 5.2 indicates that most expert physicists were proficient (although not perfect) in interpreting the concept *acceleration*. To do this, they often invoked remembered special-case knowledge about the concept when such knowledge was properly applicable. But they also used the general definition of the concept.

Equivalently, they sometimes used the fact that the acceleration can be viewed as the sum of two component vectors. The definition of *ac-*

celeration then implies that one of these vectors (*along* the direction of motion) specifies how rapidly the *magnitude* of the velocity changes. The other one (*perpendicular* to the direction of motion and toward the inside of the object's curved path) specifies how rapidly the *direction* of the velocity changes.

5.4.6 Faulty concept interpretations of an expert

Figure 5.2 indicates that the performance of one of the expert physicists was surprisingly poor. Why did this individual have so much difficulty in interpreting the concept of acceleration? After all, acceleration is a very basic physics concept. Furthermore, this expert was an experienced research physicist who had recently taught introductory courses dealing with acceleration.

His major difficulty seemed to be that he used an unduly mathematical and routinized approach (rather than more qualitative thinking). For example, when trying to determine the acceleration of the pendulum bob at point A in figure 5.1c, and that of the sled at point B in figure 5.1a, he spent much time writing and manipulating many equations. Yet all this work did *not* lead him to the correct answer for the acceleration of the pendulum bob.

This individual seemed aware of the reasons for his difficulties, and he himself afterward articulated these reasons in the following words:

> *I could probably have solved it [the problem] just using the physics without the equations if I had stopped and thought more about it. Whew! Hard work! ...If I had stopped and thought about it longer before starting the systematic procedure, I could have done it in a tenth less time.*

> *My tendency in seeing a new problem ... is to fall back on what I am most sure of ... usually, Newton's second law.... If I were better at physical insight, ... I think that I could have answered all these questions, or a lot of it, based on physical insight.... In other words, not setting up the laws of motion and solving them, and getting the answer out of that—but working qualitatively.*

5.5 REQUIREMENTS FOR USABLE CONCEPT KNOWLEDGE

Although the preceding discussion focused on the particular concept of acceleration, the resulting insights are general and equally applicable to other scientific concepts (such as *force, work, potential energy, angular momentum,* or *electric field*).

It is clear that *nominal* knowledge about a scientific concept (mere knowledge about its name and a few remembered facts about it) is *not* sufficient to interpret and apply the concept appropriately. Hence we are led to ask the following question: What basic knowledge is required to make a scientific concept *usable*? The answer to this question can help to clarify what students need to learn about the concepts taught in their science classes.

5.5.1   Useful knowledge about a property concept

As mentioned in section 4.2.4, a property concept (like acceleration) has values that are associated with those of the independent variables described by it. The following then summarizes the basic knowledge required to make such a concept effectively usable.

Concept specification and interpretation   To define the meaning of the concept, one must specify how the concept is related to its referents and how the concept can be properly interpreted in any specific case. A *declarative* specification is useful because it is compact and easily remembered. But a *procedural* (or *operational*) specification is necessary to indicate what one must actually *do* to elaborate the declarative specification and to interpret the concept properly in any specific instance. (For example, section 5.3 provides such specifications for the concept *acceleration*.)

Characteristics of the concept   It is helpful to know the characteristics of the concept so that it can be used appropriately. Important characteristics include the following:

• *Name of the concept*   (For example, *acceleration*.)
• *Type of concept*   Is it a number or a vector? If it is a number, is it positive, negative, or either? (For example, acceleration is a vector described by a magnitude and a direction.)
• *Units*   What units are used to describe the concept? [For example, if velocity is described in terms of the units meter/second, acceleration is described in terms of the units meter/(second)^2.]
• *Symbolic descriptions*   (For example, an acceleration, like any other vector, can be symbolically described by a boldface letter or graphically by an arrow.)
• *Independent variables needed for specification*   (For example, an acceleration must be specified by its dependence on the following three

things: a particular object, a particular time, and a particular reference frame relative to which the object's motion is described.)

• *Validity conditions*   (For example, the concept *acceleration* can be applied only to describe the motion of a particular point. Thus it can *not* adequately describe the complicated motion of an entire twirling baton flying through the air.)

Important discriminations   One must know important discriminations to avoid ambiguities or confusions—and must heed these discriminations in any application of the concept. (For example, in the case of acceleration one must know how to distinguish a scientific acceleration from an everyday acceleration—and how to distinguish a change of velocity from a change of speed.)

Special-case knowledge   To achieve efficient performance, it is useful to remember important special cases of the concept and to pay careful attention to their validity conditions. (For example, it is helpful to remember that, if an object moves along a curved path with constant speed, its acceleration has a direction perpendicular to its path.)

Simple inferences   It is also useful to know how to infer simple implications of the concept specification (for example, how to use a knowledge of an object's acceleration to find its change of velocity during a short time).

Connections to other knowledge   Finally, it is desirable to know how the concept is connected to other relevant concepts or principles. (For example, after one knows something about forces, one should also know how the acceleration of an object is related to the total force acting on it.)

5.5.2   Useful knowledge about a principle

A *principle* is a complex concept that describes a relationship between two or more previously defined concepts. The specification of a principle is more complex than the specification of a property concept because one must properly specify not only each of the related concepts, but also the *relation* between them.

For example, Newton's famous mechanics principle $m\mathbf{a} = \mathbf{F}_{tot}$ relates the mass m of any object, the acceleration $\mathbf{a}$ of this object, and the total force $\mathbf{F}_{tot}$ on this object. This principle is important because it specifies an equality relation between two very different quantities—between the quantity $m\mathbf{a}$ (which depends only on the properties of the considered object) and the total force $\mathbf{F}_{tot}$ (which depends on the distances of this object from all other objects and on the properties of all the interacting objects).

5.5.3 Complexity of scientific concepts and principles

The preceding paragraphs indicate explicitly that a large amount of knowledge is required to apply properly a scientific concept or principle. None of the needed knowledge listed in section 5.5.1 is superfluous. Indeed, inadequacies in any of this knowledge lead to many of the mistakes commonly observed among students who try to use scientific concepts. For example, we already discussed (and illustrated in the case of acceleration) that many of the mistakes are caused by failing to consider needed discriminations, by incorrectly interpreting the general specification of a concept in particular cases, and by relying on special-case knowledge without heeding restrictive validity conditions. Other mistakes occur also because of a lack of attention to the essential characteristics of a concept. For example, students often describe vector concepts by mere numbers (forgetting about their directions), describe concepts in terms of incorrect units, or pay no attention to the independent variables required to specify a property (thus forgetting that an acceleration must be specified relative to some particular reference frame).

The proper application of scientific concepts or principles thus requires much greater care than that needed for dealing with everyday concepts. Hence it is not surprising that inexperienced students make many mistakes in using scientific concepts or principles—and that they require a considerable amount of time before they can learn to use such concepts or principles appropriately.

5.6 EDUCATIONAL IMPLICATIONS

5.6.1 Proficient performers

Good scientists (such as professors in scientific or engineering fields) ordinarily apply scientific concepts properly. However, not all such scientists are highly proficient. Indeed, some presumed experts (despite doctoral titles and experience in research or teaching) may perform more poorly than expected. Thus it is also of interest to elucidate *why* some highly experienced people sometimes perform poorly. For example, the resulting insights may reveal some poor habits or may indicate that some skills are *not* readily learned (and thus may deserve more explicit attention in instruction).

5.6.2 Inexperienced students

Students' poor performance Many students, who have ostensibly studied a scientific concept and used it for months or even years, may still be unable to interpret it properly—even in fairly simple situations. For example, in the previously described investigations, students were able to answer correctly only about 25 percent of qualitative questions about acceleration. These results are consistent with other investigations of students' conceptual knowledge. For instance, one such investigation (Halloun and Hestenes, 1985) found that college students, in the top 10 percent of their basic physics class, scored no better than 75 percent on a diagnostic test of their conceptual knowledge of elementary mechanics.

Students' performance is often equally unsatisfactory when dealing with other concepts in basic or more advanced physics courses (for example, with concepts such as *force*, *work*, *energy*, or *torque*). Furthermore, students have similar difficulties dealing with many concepts in mathematics, chemistry, engineering, and other scientific fields.

Reasons for students' deficiencies Even if students are able to state the definition of a concept, they may interpret it incorrectly in particular situations. They often fail to make important discriminations and thus get confused. They rely excessively on remembered special-case knowledge that is often faulty because of failures to heed restrictive validity conditions. Because students' accumulated knowledge about various special cases is not integrated into a coherent knowledge structure, it may lead to inconsistencies and paradoxes that students cannot resolve by resorting to more fundamental knowledge. As a result, students may also be unable to deal with somewhat unfamiliar situations.

5.6.3 Common instructional deficiencies

Many instructors, who have used scientific concepts or principles for many years, are no longer consciously aware of how much knowledge is required to apply them properly—and thus spend too little time teaching them adequately. As a result, many students are left with largely nominal or fragmented knowledge—a house of cards that does not provide sound support for students' further learning. Indeed, when students are later asked to perform various problem-solving tasks, many of their mistakes are traceable to misapplications of basic concepts that they had inadequately learned at earlier times.

Newly introduced concepts are sometimes not sufficiently well specified. Examples or analogies sometimes take the place of more explicit specifications. Furthermore, declarative statements may provide definitions that students cannot properly interpret without more procedural knowledge. Even when operational definitions (procedural specifications) are mentioned or illustrated, the students themselves rarely get enough practice in implementing them.

Lastly, attempts to teach and practice important discriminations from preexisting knowledge (or from other recently acquired scientific knowledge) are usually inadequate.

5.6.4 Instructional suggestions

The previous pages lead to the following suggestions for teaching scientific concepts so that students may learn to use them effectively.

When introducing a new concept (or principle), specify this concept explicitly—especially by a method indicating how this concept can be properly interpreted in any particular instance. Then let the students *themselves* use such a procedural specification to actively practice interpreting the concept in diverse instances.

During this process, help the students to compile some useful special-case knowledge, accompanied by explicit validity conditions. (Such accumulated special-case knowledge becomes more meaningful and memorable when the students have generated it themselves).

When a scientific concept is denoted by the same word as a scientific concept, help students to distinguish these concepts by giving them (at least initially) distinct names. For example, the names *scientific acceleration* and *everyday acceleration* can be used to distinguish the distinct meanings of acceleration in science and in everyday life.

More generally, give students specific discrimination tasks to help them detect, diagnose, and correct likely confusions between somewhat similar concepts.

Examples of discrimination tasks

Distinguishing related concepts The following are discrimination tasks that can help students to recognize that velocity and acceleration are distinct concepts and thus help them to avoid confusions between them: (1) If an object's velocity is zero, can its acceleration be nonzero? If yes, give a specific example. If no, explain why not. (2) If an object's acceleration is zero, can its velocity be nonzero? If yes, give a specific example. If no, explain why not.

Distinguishing correct and incorrect concept interpretations Present students with the problem of interpreting a concept in a specific situation—and give them also a purported solution to this problem. Then ask the students whether this solution is correct. If students claim that it is not correct, ask them (1) to explain why it is not correct, (2) to diagnose what mistakes were made and why they were probably made, and (3) to produce a correct solution to the problem.

Such instructional guidelines were implemented in an investigation dealing with the concept of acceleration (Labudde, Reif, and Quinn, 1988). This investigation showed that students' ability to properly interpret this concept was thereby increased from 40 percent to about 90 percent. These guidelines have also proved practically effective when teaching actual physics classes.

Lastly, students need to be given enough time and practice in interpreting a scientific concept or principle in relatively simple situations—so that they can achieve reasonable competence. (They can then achieve more proficient performance later when asked to undertake more complex problem-solving tasks.) But do *not* require them to deal with complex tasks prematurely because they may then face excessive learning difficulties and are likely to be plagued by many recurring mistakes of concept interpretation.

5.7 SUMMARY

• Investigations of students' abilities to interpret scientific concepts (such as the concept *acceleration*) reveal that even fairly experienced students make numerous mistakes, fail to make crucial discriminations, and are led to inconsistencies and irresolvable paradoxes. Such deficient concept interpretations can persist for a long time and are exhibited even by more advanced students.

• Students' difficulties are predominantly due to inadequate discriminations, to defective interpretations of basic definitions, to faulty bits of remembered knowledge, and to fragmented conceptual knowledge leading to irresolvable paradoxes.

• Such investigations make clear that considerable amounts of knowledge and care are required to interpret scientific concepts or principles properly in specific cases—and that the required knowledge and skills are not easily acquired.

• Commonly prevailing teaching practices are often inadequate to endow students with sufficient competence in dealing with scientific concepts or principles. It is possible to identify the major reasons for students' observed deficiencies and to suggest some improved instructional methods.

6   Managing Memory

Any acquired knowledge must be stored in memory until it is used. Indeed, all learning depends on the ability of human memory to store such knowledge. To examine some of the basic properties of human memory, this chapter explores the following questions: How can new knowledge be effectively incorporated in human memory? How can it be retained there for long periods of time? How can any specific knowledge be appropriately retrieved when the need arises?

These questions have been extensively investigated by psychology researchers. Here we want to discuss them only briefly by examining some of the basic memory processes that are involved in learning and in performing complex tasks.

Educational relevance   The preceding questions are clearly important for learning and all educational efforts. For example, most of us tend to forget all too quickly many of the things that we once learned. Many students are even less able to retain and use their acquired knowledge because they ordinarily have less well-developed learning skills. For example, it is rarely possible to rely on the prerequisite knowledge that students were supposed to have acquired in prior courses. Much of this knowledge has often been forgotten and can no longer be retrieved or used.

Students commonly don't allow enough time to practice and consolidate their knowledge, but cram shortly before their examinations. The knowledge thus acquired is then often quickly forgotten. Furthermore, many students tend to rely mostly on brute memorizing, without making efforts to change the relevant knowledge into a form that can be more easily remembered. They also don't carefully examine newly acquired knowledge to ensure that they make appropriate distinctions and are aware of restrictive validity conditions. As a result, they may remember facts or words that they use indiscriminately—and can easily get confused.

The preceding comments suggest that it would be useful to help students to learn more effectively by managing their memories more carefully.

6.1 PROPERTIES OF HUMAN MEMORY

6.1.1 Working memory and long-term memory

Human memory consists of *working memory* and *long-term memory*, two parts which have quite different characteristics.

Working memory   *Working memory* allows only short-time storage of small amounts of knowledge—that is, of not more than about seven items of information (Miller, 1956). For example, we are unable to remember, even briefly, an unfamiliar number consisting of more than about seven digits.

Despite its limitations, working memory is essential for processing the information needed to perform various tasks. For example, it allows a person to focus attention briefly on a few information items in order to compare or manipulate them in useful ways. (Some such information items may be composite items consisting of a combination of other items.)

Long-term memory   After some processing in working memory, information can be incorporated in *long-term memory*. The information-storage capacity of this memory appears to be practically unlimited and the information stored there can be retained for a very long time.

All learning depends on these properties of long-term memory. Furthermore, the apparent capacity of short-term memory can be enhanced by associating information in it with knowledge stored in long-term memory.

The remainder of this chapter deals mainly with long-term memory.

6.1.2 Memory assessment methods

Several different methods can be used to assess how well a person remembers some acquired knowledge.

Free recall The method of *free recall* merely asks a person to recall some previously acquired information (for example, to recall eight musical composers who died before 1900.)

Cued recall The method of *cued recall* uses a memory task that is somewhat easier than free recall. Here a person is asked to recall some previously acquired information when the person is also given some helpful *cues* that specify some other information associated with the information to be recalled. (For example, the person might be asked to recall the name of the composer who wrote the *Messiah* oratorio that is commonly performed at Easter time.)

Recognition A memory task involving mere *recognition* is appreciably easier than free recall since it merely asks a person to *recognize* some previously remembered information. [For example, the person might be given a list of several composers (such as Mozart, Beethoven, Verdi, and Puccini) and then be asked to identify which one of these composers wrote the opera *Fidelio*.]

Relearning time A method that assesses the *time needed for relearning* is particularly useful to determine what a person still remembers after a long time when the person may seem to have forgotten much of what he or she originally had known.

Suppose that the person, after spending some time T to learn some knowledge, has at some time t_1 achieved a good performance level in recalling this knowledge. At an appreciably later time t_2 the person may then seem to remember only little of what he or she knew originally.

To assess how much the person actually still remembers at the time t_2, one may ask the person to relearn what the person knew at the original time t_1 (so as to attain the *same* performance level as that achieved at this earlier time). If the person still remembers something at the later time t_2, the time T' required for relearning should then be *less* than the time T required for the original learning. The time saving $(T - T')$ provides then a good measure of what the individual still remembers at the later time t_2.

6.1.3 Measures of memory performance

The following performance measures can be used in conjunction with some of the preceding memory tasks.

Number of recall errors   One can determine the *accuracy* of recall by counting the number of errors committed by the individual doing the recall task. (These errors can be either items omitted because of forgetting or items incorrectly recalled.) Fewer such errors indicate a better memory performance.

Time required for recall   One can measure the *reaction time* required before the information is recalled. A shorter required time indicates better memory performance.

6.2   BASIC MEMORY PROCESSES

Memory allows people to recall information acquired at an earlier time. The process leading to such recall can usefully be decomposed into the following three subprocesses:

1. The initial *encoding* of the acquired information in a form allowing it to be properly incorporated in long-term memory.

2. The retention (or storage) of this information so that it remains available for recall at a later time.

3. The subsequent retrieval of any specifically desired information.

The following is a simplified discussion of these processes. A more detailed and careful discussion can be found in the book by Anderson (Anderson, 2000).

6.2.1   Encoding

Strength of a memory record   When new information is acquired, it must be properly encoded in a form that allows it to be readily stored and retrieved. It is convenient to characterize the resulting memory record by its *strength S*, a property describing how firmly this memory record has been encoded and linked to preexisting knowledge. This strength can be assessed by the previously mentioned memory tasks (such as free recall, cued recall, recognition, or time for relearning). A greater strength implies a better memory performance (that is, greater resistance to forgetting). Thus the strength is presumed to be *inversely* proportional to the number of errors, or to the needed retrieval time, observed in these memory tasks.

Dependence of strength on practice   More practice (involving more rehearsal by more repetitions) increases the strength S of the encoded memory record. Experimental studies indicate that the strength of the

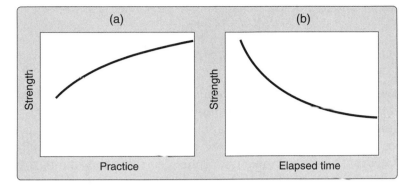

Figure 6.1
Strength of memory record. (a) Increase with amount of practice. (b) Decrease with elapsed time.

memory record increases with practice, *but at an ever-decreasing rate.* (Thus increasing practice helps, but with diminishing returns.)

More precisely, a small *fractional increase* in the amount of practice leads to a corresponding small *fractional increase* in the strength of the memory record. This statement implies that a small amount of additional practice, after long practice, produces a *smaller* increase in memory strength than this same amount of practice produces after shorter practice. (This is so because the same amount of additional practice represents a smaller *fractional* increase in practice after the long practice). Figure 6.1a shows a graph illustrating this relationship between practice and resulting memory strength.

Quantitative dependence of memory strength on practice

The previous statement, relating the fractional increase of practice to the fractional increase of strength, can be expressed more quantitatively by introducing a few convenient symbols. Let P denote the amount of practice and S the resulting strength of the memory record. Correspondingly, let dP denote a small *change* in the amount of practice and dS the corresponding small *change* in the strength of the memory record.

The preceding statement can then be expressed in terms of these symbols by the relation

$$dS/S = b \, (dP/P) \tag{6.1}$$

where dP/P denotes the fractional increase in the amount of practice, dS/S is the corresponding fractional increase in the strength, and b is some positive constant. A basic knowledge of calculus then implies that

$$d(\ln S) = b \, d(\ln P) \quad \text{so that} \quad \ln S = b \ln P + constant,$$

(where *In* denotes the natural logarithm). This implies the proportionality

$$S \propto P^b \tag{6.2}$$

This relation is called the *power law of practice*. (The graph in figure 6.1a illustrates this power law.)

Creating more connections by elaborate processing   Remembering is facilitated not only by mere repetition (that increases the strength of a particular memory record), but also by active processing that creates more connections linking memory records. Hence remembering can be increased by the elaborateness of the processing done during acquisition of new information. Such processing associates this information with other existing knowledge in memory and thus provides more connections (or *retrieval paths*) by which the new information can be accessed.

Elaboration during the acquisition process can be achieved in some of the following ways (all of which connect the new information to preexisting knowledge):

• *Using the new information to perform some tasks* (such as asking or answering questions about the new information, or solving some problems with the new information).

• *Describing the new information in different forms*   (Describing it in visual form can be particularly effective since pictorial information tends to be more resistant to forgetting.)

• *Organizing the new information* so that it is meaningfully incorporated in a coherent knowledge structure.

• *Generating the new information by oneself* is particularly helpful since it requires much active processing and thus results in many available retrieval paths. It also leads to the encoding of procedural knowledge that is useful for regenerating the new information if it has been partially forgotten—or for modifying the information to adapt it for other needs.

6.2.2   Retention

Retention is the storage of acquired knowledge over significant periods of time. Such storage is not permanent but may gradually decay. Thus we tend to forget some of the knowledge initially acquired by us

Retention and elapsed time   Forgetting is initially fast, but becomes increasingly slow later. The strength of a memory record thus decreases rapidly at first, but decreases at an increasingly less rapid rate as time goes on. (The graph in figure 6.1b illustrates this behavior.)

More precisely, a small *fractional increase* in the elapsed time leads to a corresponding small *fractional decrease* in the strength of the memory record. This statement implies that a small increase in the elapsed time after a long elapsed time produces a *smaller* decrease in strength than this same increase of elapsed time produces after a shorter elapsed time. (This is so because the same increase in elapsed time represents a smaller *fractional* increase in elapsed time after the longer elapsed time).

Quantitative dependence of memory strength on elapsed time

The previous statement, relating the fractional increase of elapsed time to the fractional decrease of memory strength, can again be expressed more quantitatively by introducing some convenient symbols. Let T denote the elapsed time and S the strength of the memory record. Correspondingly, let dT denoted a small *change* in the elapsed time and dS the corresponding small *change* in the strength of the memory record.

The previous statement can then be expressed in terms of these symbols by the relation

$$dS/S = -c(dT/T) \qquad (6.3)$$

where c is some positive constant and the minus sign merely indicates that an increase in the elapsed time produces a *decrease* in the strength. An argument completely similar to that leading to equation 6.2 then leads to the proportionality

$$S \propto T^{-c} \qquad (6.4)$$

This relation is called the *power law of forgetting*. (The graph in figure 6.1b illustrates this power law.)

Retention and the spacing of learning Since the strength of remembered knowledge decays with time, it is reasonable to refresh this strength by further practice. But the spacing between practice sessions can have an appreciable effect on the subsequent retention of the acquired knowledge.

For example, so-called *massed practice* involves *short* time intervals between practice sessions. Such massed practice leads to little forgetting between practice sessions and to little forgetting during short elapsed times thereafter. But it also leads to rapid forgetting after the massed practice.

On the other hand, so-called *distributed practice* involves *longer* time intervals between practice sessions. Such distributed practice results in repeated refreshing of the memory record that has been partially forgotten between practice sessions. Hence it also leads to much slower forgetting during appreciable elapsed times after the distributed practice.

Practical implication for learning

The preceding remarks have the following important implication: *Last-minute cramming for an examination may help performance on the examination, but will lead to rapid forgetting afterward.* Hence such cramming leads ordinarily to *no* appreciable long-term benefits.

Interference effects   The learning of some information may interfere with the learning and retention of other information. This is because newly formed associations may compete with previous associations. In other words, the learning of new information creates additional retrieval paths that can impede access to the desired information.

This is particularly true if the new information and the old information share some common elements. In this case, there are more possible retrieval paths connecting different memory records. The resulting ambiguity about the choice of proper retrieval path then can hinder the retrieval process. For example, if a person learns some information involving items A and B, and subsequently learns some information involving items A and C, attention focused on A makes it more difficult to remember the previously learned information—and also more difficult to remember the subsequently learned information.

Everyday examples of interference

Spellings in different languages   For many years, and even now, I cannot quite remember how to write words like *address* or *apartment*—and often misspell them. The reason is that I learned French as a boy before I knew any English. It so happens that the French word for address is *adresse* (spelled with a single *d*) and that the French word for apartment is *appartement* (spelled with two *p*'s). These slightly different spellings are confusing and thus result in appreciable interference.

Inconsistent prefix usage   The word *parasol* denotes a device protecting against the sun and the word *parachute* denotes a device protecting against a fall. (The same words are also used in French. Indeed, *chute* is the French word for fall.) Quite logically, the French then use the word *parapluie* to denote a device used against rain (since *pluie* is the French word for *rain*).

As a result, I have had consistent difficulties retrieving the English word for the device protecting against rain—because I start retrieving the prefix *para* and am then stymied because the word *pararain* does not exist in English. It has taken me years to overcome this interference effect so that I can now usually retrieve the proper word *umbrella* used in English.

If previously learned information has been thoroughly consolidated so that retrieval paths to it have become firmly established, such interference effects become less pronounced. This is why experts are usually not much bothered by interference from newly learned knowledge.

Interference effects in introductory courses

The situation is different for students—particularly in introductory courses, where many new concepts are often introduced in quick succession without much intervening time for the consolidation of the newly acquired knowledge. In this case, interference effects between such concepts can become more pronounced, leading to confusions and learning difficulties.

6.2.3 Retrieval

The previous comments already mentioned the importance of retrieval. Indeed, much forgetting is due to retrieval difficulties. Although indiscriminate retrieval may sometimes be useful, the more difficult task is the *selective* retrieval of some specifically desired information.

Dependence on prior encoding   Appropriate retrieval of some information depends crucially on the prior encoding of this information. For example, the retrieval of some information can be much facilitated by its useful initial description and by its proper place in a more comprehensive knowledge organization.

Recognition versus generation   Retrieval by recognition is easier than recognition by generation—that is, *recognizing* some desired information is easier than *generating* this information when it is needed. Retrieval is also facilitated if the retrieval process is similar to the processes used during encoding (because one can then exploit previously used connecting paths).

Retrieval of appropriate information by generation can often be accomplished by searching for potential candidates and then recognizing the appropriate one.

Retrieval by inference   Retrieval of some particular information can sometimes be accomplished by *inferring* this information from other available information. This can be a useful way of retrieving information that has been partially forgotten.

Partially remembered information can thus be used to make various inferences so as to reconstruct an entire memory record. Such reconstructive memory may lead to *false* recalls since one may erroneously infer information that was *not* actually acquired. For example, witnesses in a trial may sometimes honestly claim that they remember things that never actually happened.

6.3 PRACTICAL MEMORY MANAGEMENT

Good performance requires the appropriate retrieval of information stored in memory. As the preceding paragraphs indicate, such retrieval depends crucially on how this information has previously been encoded and retained in memory. Hence one arrives at the following seemingly obvious, but important conclusion: Effective retrieval of information requires careful attention at *much earlier times*—that is, at the time of its acquisition and during the subsequent storage time in memory.

The discussion of the preceding section then leads to the following practical suggestions for managing one's memory effectively.

6.3.1 Effective knowledge acquisition

To ensure that knowledge is well remembered, it is helpful to do appropriate *active processing* when the knowledge is initially acquired. Such active processing can be achieved by engaging in some of the following kinds of activities.

Properly timed practice   Sufficient practice helps to consolidate any newly acquired knowledge. To facilitate the long-term retention of the knowledge, this practice should be *distributed*—that is, suitably spaced so that some forgetting occurs between practice sessions. Otherwise, if all practice is performed during a short time, the acquired knowledge may be quickly forgotten. Cramming does thus *not* lead to the acquisition of significantly useful knowledge.

Elaborating acquired knowledge   It is important to elaborate acquired knowledge so as to create more connections to it. For example, one may redescribe this knowledge in different ways or perform some tasks with it. (Of course, such elaboration requires sufficient time and freedom from competing distractions.)

For example, teaching is a very effective way of learning because it forces one to elaborate relevant knowledge much more fully than students ordinarily do when passively sitting in a classroom.

Using new knowledge   Actually *using* any newly acquired knowledge is a very good way of elaborating it. For instance, one can use it to ask or answer some questions, to solve some problems, or to perform some other relevant tasks.

For example, one learns very little if one merely reads an instruction manual accompanying a computer or some software. It is much better to implement each instruction immediately after one has read it (or even while still reading it).

Examining important discriminations Whenever one acquires new knowledge, one must identify important discriminations that can help to avoid confusions. Thus one should examine the similarities and differences between things that need to be carefully distinguished—and should generate particular examples illustrating these distinctions.

Such discriminations help to avoid future confusions and mistakes. They can also help to reduce interference effects that may hinder the appropriate retrieval of this knowledge.

Example: Indiscriminate use of words in everyday life

In everyday life, words like *force, momentum, power,* and *energy* are often used indiscriminately (and may be so used in advertisements seen in newspapers or on television). However, these words have distinct scientific meanings. If the scientific concepts denoted by these words are not carefully discriminated at the time that these concepts are learned, the ensuing confusions and mistakes are almost endless.

Attaining facility Knowledge is usually first acquired by dint of significant effort and deliberate thought. But some of this knowledge, especially if it is likely to be frequently relevant, needs to become more efficiently usable with much less needed time and effort. Thus one must engage in sufficient practice so that this knowledge becomes encoded in a form where it becomes readily and rapidly usable (so that easy recognition processes and familiar habits can replace more cumbersome thinking). Only after one has reached this level of facility does this knowledge becomes a tool that is usable for accomplishing complex tasks.

6.3.2   Encoding knowledge in useful forms

Redescribing knowledge A helpful way of elaborating involves describing or redescribing acquired knowledge in a form that make the knowledge easy to remember and to use. Pictorial forms of description (visual encoding) may be particularly useful.

Example of visual encoding

While teaching thermodynamics to college seniors, who were well trained in mathematics and physics, I pointed out that a particular quantity F (the *free*

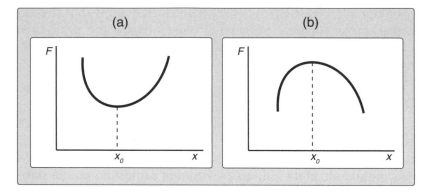

Figure 6.2
(a) Minimum of a quantity. (b) Maximum of a quantity.

energy) had to be a minimum in a state of equilibrium. Then I mentioned that the second derivative of this quantity must therefore be positive. This last statement elicited blank stares on the faces of about half of the students. Why was this statement, which was so obvious to me, puzzling to them?

The students had all taken previous courses in calculus and had thus learned about the properties of *derivatives*. Had they merely memorized these properties as miscellaneous facts? If so, it was not surprising that they had quickly forgotten these facts and were unable to apply the knowledge that they had ostensibly learned.

On the other hand, I had encoded my own knowledge about derivatives in a different visual way. I know that a *derivative* indicates the rate of change of a quantity—and is therefore positive if this quantity increases and negative if this quantity decreases. When a quantity depends on some parameter x so that it has a minimum, I see in my mind a curve like that in figure 6.2a. Then it is obvious to me that, when the quantity *decreases* to the left of its minimum at x_0, its derivative must be negative; when the quantity *increases* to the right of this minimum, its derivative must be positive; and when the quantity is *at its minimum*, it neither increases nor decreases (so that its derivative must then be *zero*). Furthermore, this derivative itself constantly increases from negative values to the left of x_0 to positive values to the right of x_0. Hence the rate of change of this derivative (the so-called *second derivative*) must be *positive*.

Note that this visual encoding of information about derivatives does *not* require one to remember any miscellaneous facts about the properties of derivatives near minima or maxima. Instead, these properties are obvious from the shape of the visualized curve. For instance, analogously to the case of a minimum, merely visualizing a *maximum* (like that illustrated in figure 6.2b) makes it apparent that the derivative must be *zero* at the maximum and that the second derivative (the rate of change of the derivative itself) must there be *negative*.

Organizing knowledge coherently It is also helpful to organize one's knowledge so that newly acquired information is systematically related

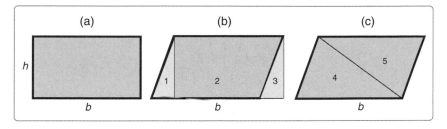

Figure 6.3
(a) A rectangle. (b) A parallelogram related to a rectangle. (c) A parallelogram related to two triangles.

to other knowledge in a coherent knowledge structure. The newly
acquired knowledge becomes then easier to retrieve and to regenerate
if it is partially forgotten. The following are some illustrative examples.

Areas of geometric figures

Many students' knowledge about the areas of geometric figures is fragmented and consists mostly of disconnected formulas. Thus these students
simply remember that the area of a rectangle = length × width; that the area
of a parallelogram = base × height; and that the area of a triangle = $(1/2)$
(base × height).

A better way of organizing this knowledge (so that it can be reliably remembered and easily regenerated if forgotten) is illustrated in figure 6.3 which con-
nects all the relevant information in a coherent visual form. The following are
some examples.

Area of a parallelogram   The parallelogram in figure 6.3b can be imagined
decomposed into the parts 1 and 2. If the triangular part 1 is moved into the
position 3, this parallelogram is transformed into the rectangle consisting of
the parts 2 and 3 (that is, into the rectangle of figure 6.3a). Thus the area of
the parallelogram is the same as the area of this rectangle. Hence parallelogram
area = (base b) × (height h).

Area of a triangle   The parallelogram in figure 6.3c can be decomposed into
the two equal triangles 4 and 5. Hence the area of each triangle is just equal to
half the area of the parallelogram. Thus it is apparent that the area of a triangle
= $(1/2)$(base × height).

Area of a circle   Figure 6.4 shows an easy way whereby the area of a circle
can be related to other known areas—and can thus be encoded in a way that is
almost impossible to forget. As illustrated in the figure, the circle can be sub-
divided into many equal small triangles (somewhat like the slices of a pie). Each
triangle has a base b and, if it is imagined to be very small, has a height equal to
the circle's radius r. The area of each triangle is thus $(1/2)br$. Furthermore, the
number of such triangles is equal to the length $2\pi r$ of its circumference, divided
by the very small base length b of a single triangle. In other words, the number

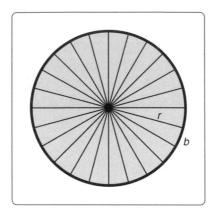

Figure 6.4
Area of a circle.

of such triangles is $2\pi r/b$. Hence the area A of the entire circle can be obtained by multiplying the area of a single triangle by the number of such triangles so that

$$A = (br/2) \times (2\pi r/b) = \pi r^2.$$

This is the familiar result that most students remember merely as a piece of disconnected factual knowledge.

Note that the preceding simple argument requires the knowledge that π is the number specifying the ratio of the circumference of a circle to its diameter $2r$. But if students merely know that the value of π is approximately 3.14, then their knowledge is so extremely shallow as to be almost useless.

6.3.3 Ensuring retention

All of the preceding activities are helpful for encoding and also aid the retention of knowledge. However, one must avoid the delusion that acquired knowledge will be retained indefinitely. Indeed, knowledge that is *not* commonly used can easily be forgotten. Hence it is important to engage in frequent (adequately spaced) reviews and active uses of any initially acquired knowledge.

6.4 EDUCATIONAL IMPLICATIONS

6.4.1 Proficient performers

When trying to remember newly acquired information, proficient performers pay deliberate attention to how it can be effectively stored and subsequently retrieved. Accordingly, they try to encode and describe the information carefully, using adequate practice and elaboration. They also periodically engage in subsequent reviews.

Good performers use, in complementary ways, both their *internal* memories (the information stored in their heads) and *external* memories (information stored on paper or in computers). For example, internal memory alone is often inadequate to carry out a calculation or to solve a problem. Hence good performers deliberately supplement their internal memories by writing down on paper some results of their mental processing.

Similarly, good performers often find it useful to make written notes because they don't have confidence in their ability to remember useful knowledge over extended periods of time. For instance, they may make written notes in order to remember knowledge needed to resolve some difficulty (for example, knowledge needed to overcome a previous mistake or misconception). In the long run, the time required to write such notes can often *save* time for two reasons: (1) Writing the notes involves appreciable elaboration, thus strengthening the memory and helping to remember the relevant knowledge. (2) If something is nevertheless forgotten, a glance at the notes facilitates prompt recall of the knowledge without a need to figure it out all over again.

6.4.2 Inexperienced students

By contrast, inexperienced students often suffer from the delusion that merely listening to a lecture, or reading a chapter in a book, will lead them to acquire usable knowledge. Thus they commonly devote inadequate time and insufficient processing to the useful encoding of newly acquired knowledge. As a result, their knowledge is often left in poorly encoded and inadequately organized form.

Students also tend to have excessive confidence in the persistence of their acquired knowledge. Hence they often fail to refresh their knowledge by adequate review and reexamination. As a result, students' newly acquired knowledge is often readily forgotten and not easily regenerated when the need arises.

6.4.3 Common instructional deficiencies

Instructional efforts often don't provide students with sufficient well-designed practice, and opportunities for elaboration, to ensure reliable learning. Hence many students acquire inert knowledge that they cannot readily use or remember—and often cannot rely on knowledge presumably acquired in prerequisite courses.

6.4.4 Instructional suggestions

The preceding sections suggest the following instructional guidelines:

• Present knowledge in a form facilitating effective encoding and incorporated in a coherent knowledge structure.

• Provide well-structured practice opportunities where students can actively use any newly acquired knowledge. It is important that the students *themselves* engage in such activities. Very little is learned if a teacher merely illustrates or demonstrates them.

• Lastly, provide frequent reviews and other opportunities for integrating any newly acquired knowledge—so that it can be used jointly with preexisting knowledge.

6.5 SUMMARY

• The ability to remember some knowledge can be assessed by tasks such as free recall, cued recall, recognition, and time needed for relearning.

• Basic memory processes involve the initial encoding of acquired information, its subsequent retention, and its final retrieval.

• Effective encoding is helped by repeated practice and by elaborative processing of the acquired knowledge. Practice should be properly spaced since massed practice leads to rapid forgetting.

• The resulting stored knowledge gradually decays with time, but can be refreshed by reviews and further practice. However, care is needed to reduce interference effects between successively learned knowledge.

• An important practical implication of these findings is that effective learning requires active processing by the learner.

• Memory can be managed more effectively by adequate practicing, by elaborating and using newly acquired knowledge, by deliberately examining important discriminations, by redescribing and organizing this knowledge in useful forms, and by repeatedly reviewing previously acquired knowledge.

II-B   Effectiveness

7 Methods and Inferences

The preceding chapters examined some basic cognitive needs to ensure that knowledge is actually usable. However, we are ordinarily not content if our knowledge and performance are merely sensible and correct, but also want them to be *effective* in achieving desired goals. As indicated in figure 2.3, this portion of the book (chapters 7 through 9) therefore discusses how effective performance can be achieved. Thus it examines some useful methods, helpful ways of describing available knowledge, and effective ways of organizing it.

This chapter deals with the first of these issues by examining the following questions: (1) What kinds of methods facilitate the effective use of knowledge? (2) How can such methods be usefully specified? (3) What kinds of inferences facilitate more extensive applications of available knowledge?

Educational relevance Most students are interested in effective performance. But they often try to achieve it by resorting to previously learned procedures that specify sequences of steps useful for performing various tasks. (For example, students may prepare themselves for examinations by trying to memorize procedures that they saw demonstrated or that they used in past homework exercises.) However, these procedures are often not in a form that can be readily adapted to deal with slightly different conditions or with somewhat unfamiliar tasks.

Students also frequently lack the ability to extend their knowledge by appropriate inferences from it. They may jump to unjustified conclusions, engage in faulty reasoning leading to wrong conclusions, or occasionally use misleading analogies. It is true that *plausible* inferences can be very useful in science for formulating hypotheses or making discoveries. But students sometimes don't realize that such inferences should not be trusted unless they can be verified by more rigorous reasoning or by experimental evidence.

7.1 METHODS AND PROCEDURES

Methods The application of knowledge is facilitated by suitable methods that specify the steps needed for performing particular tasks. Each such step consists ordinarily of the following actions: (1) deciding what to do, (2) implementing the decision, and (3) assessing whether the implementation has been satisfactory.

It is essential to implement each action in order to accomplish the task. The decisions and assessments may, however, be done without conscious awareness or may sometimes be omitted.

Example: Performance of a familiar simple task

Writing one's signature is a task that most of us perform by a highly familiar method. To carry it out, we decide (mostly unconsciously) how to move our hand and fingers—and then implement these actions. We also spontaneously assess whether our signature has been properly affixed (for example, we ordinarily notice any defects in our signature and promptly correct them.)

Procedures Some methods may involve complex decisions and actions. But the simplest kind of method is a *procedure*, a method that clearly specifies all needed successive steps (decisions or actions). For instance, such a procedure may merely specify which particular next step should be started after the preceding one has been completed, or it may specify several alternative next steps and a particular rule for choosing among them.

A procedure thus specifies a sequence of well-defined successive steps to be performed while dealing with some system (such as some available knowledge). As schematically illustrated in figure 7.1, the implementation of these steps then leads from some initial state A to some definite final state F of the system.

Examples of familiar procedures

The following are examples of procedures that are commonly encountered in everyday life. (1) To help a person reach a particular destination, we commonly provide the person with a procedure that specifies detailed directions for driving there. (2) The recipes in a cookbook specify procedures for preparing various dishes. (3) Unassembled furniture is usually accompanied by directions specifying a procedure for putting it together. (4) Income-tax forms are accompanied by complicated directions that specify a procedure for filling out these forms.

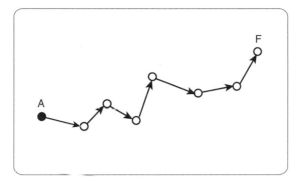

Figure 7.1
Schematic illustration of a procedure. The successive steps are indicated by arrows, and the resulting states by small circles.

Reliable implementation of a procedure   To ensure the reliable implementation of a procedure, each step must be carried out correctly in appropriate sequence, no step may be omitted, and no extraneous steps must be included. A correct implementation must also include adequate monitoring—that is, repeated assessments verifying that all these requirements are met.

Mistakes in implementing a procedure can arise because the procedure is not clearly specified, because it is faulty, or because a correct procedure is improperly executed. For example, faulty decisions may lead to the performance of some inappropriate steps, appropriate steps may be omitted or incorrectly implemented, or careless assessments may result in undetected errors.

Human beings (more so than computers) can be quite unreliable, even when performing seemingly simple procedural tasks. They can easily get distracted (especially if they are interrupted), their attention may drift, or they may be careless in reading or following specified directions. For example, people may sometimes forget to implement some steps. They may believe that they performed a step, when they actually merely *intended* to perform it. (This is a great danger in the use of checklists, such as those designed to ensure that all parts of an airplane or other device get properly inspected.) Persons may fail to implement a step or implement it haphazardly. They may not monitor adequately their own performance and thus fail to detect various errors. Indeed, there are many reasons why human beings commit errors (Reason, 1990).

Routine implementation of procedures   The implementation of a procedure may become much less deliberate after a person has become
highly experienced in its use and acquired much relevant knowledge.
Indeed, the acquisition of such accumulated (or *compiled*) knowledge
can make the person more efficient. He or she may then save time and
effort by performing with less need for deliberate thought, may take
shortcuts by bypassing some steps, and may make some decisions by
simply recognizing the appropriate choice.

Such routine performance can be faster and *may* also be quite reliable. But such reliability can *not* be assured. Although good performance may rely on compiled knowledge or well-developed intuition,
it must always include careful checks to assess that the performance
has been satisfactory.

7.2   SPECIFICATION OF PROCEDURES

Although the specification of a procedure is seemingly straightforward, some specifications can be more useful than others, especially
when they are intended for human use.

7.2.1   Appropriate level of detail

A procedure should be specified at a level of detail that is well
adapted to the intended users. Although a procedure consists merely
of a sequence of successive steps, might it be better to specify it by
a few large steps or by a larger number of small steps? In fact, both
extremes may be undesirable. Thus, a procedure may be difficult or
impossible to implement either because it is described in insufficient
detail or because it is described in excessive detail.

Examples: Procedures specified with inappropriate detail

Excessively coarse description   Suppose that one wants to give a person
directions specifying how to find the radiology department in a hospital. One
might then tell the person to go to the fourth floor, to turn left after leaving the
elevators, and then to follow the large passageway. These directions might be
adequate for a person who is familiar with the hospital. But they might be insufficient for a stranger who could easily get lost in the maze of hospital corridors.

Excessively detailed description   On the other hand, suppose that one gave
this person directions by telling him to lift his left foot by 3 inches, then to move
it forward by 13 inches, then to put it down on the floor again, then to lift his
right foot by 3 inches, and so on. Such directions would be ridiculously detailed

and hopelessly confusing to a normal person who knows how to walk. (Indeed, imagine telling a centipede how to move its legs!)

In short, the specification of a procedure should be well adapted to the prior knowledge of the intended users. For example, procedures that may be inadequately specified for novices in a domain, may be sufficient for persons who have acquired more experience as a result of prior learning.

7.2.2   Useful ancillary information

Specification of the final result   It is *not* necessary to specify the final result attained by implementing a procedure because the correct implementation of all the successive steps guarantees the attainment of a specific result.

This final result may sometimes even come as a surprise to the implementer of a procedure. For example, procedures in *origami* (the Japanese art of paper folding) sometimes specify a long sequence of complicated foldings of a sheet of paper. After many seemingly unmotivated foldings have been made, there may then suddenly appear a bird able to flap its wings.

Specification of the final result of a procedure provides, however, several advantages. (1) It makes the procedure more motivating than a mere sequence of steps without any apparent purpose. (2) It makes it somewhat easier to remember the steps. (3) It helps one to verify that the procedure has been correctly implemented (since one can then check whether the actual outcome of the procedure properly agrees with the expected result). (4) If one forgets some steps, one may be able to regenerate them by problem solving designed to attain the desired known goal.

Declarative information about individual steps   It can also be helpful to provide declarative information about the result of *each* step or about features observable during a step. Persons can then use this information to check whether they are properly implementing the procedure. Otherwise they might arrive at the end of an implemented procedure, notice that they did not attain the expected final result, and have no idea about where mistakes might have occurred. (For example, travel directions may not only direct one to turn right at a particular intersection, but might also indicate that a McDonald's restaurant should be visible at that street corner.)

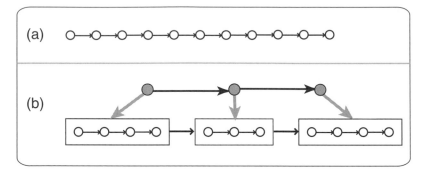

Figure 7.2
Schematic illustration of different descriptions of the same procedure. (a) Linear
description. (b) Hierarchical description.

Applicability conditions   Finally, it is helpful to specify the conditions under which a procedure is applicable. Such conditions include
validity conditions that specify when the procedure can legitimately be
applied, and *utility conditions* that specify when the procedure is likely
to be useful.

7.2.3   Helpful descriptions

Graphical aids   A procedure can be readily described by a list of
printed directions (such as a checklist). Pictorial descriptions (such as a
flow chart) can also be very useful.

Hierarchical description of a procedure   A procedure may be described
by a linear sequence of small steps (as schematically illustrated in figure
7.2a). Alternatively, the same procedure may be described *hierarchically*
by a few major steps that are elaborated into more detailed subordinate
steps (as illustrated in figure 7.2b).

Example of linear and hierarchical descriptions of a procedure

Linear description   The following detailed steps specify a procedure for traveling from a particular school to the public library: (1) After leaving the school,
turn left. (2) Drive straight until the third traffic light. (3) At this light, turn right.
(4) Drive two blocks until you come to the entrance of the park. (5) Enter the
park and drive until you come to a pond. (The directions then continuee until
the last step which terminates at the library.)

Hierarchical description   A hierarchical description of the same procedure
might simply specify the following three *major* steps: (1) Leave the school and

drive to the entrance of the park. (2) Cross the park and leave it at its West gate. (3) Drive on to the library next to the city hall.

Each of these steps can then be further elaborated. For example, the first major step can be specified in grater detail by the following four directions: (1) After leaving the school, turn left. (2) Drive straight until the third traffic light. (3) At this light, turn right. (4) Drive two blocks until you come to the entrance of the park.

The second and third major steps can be similarly elaborated into more detailed steps.

Advantages of a hierarchical description   A hierarchical description of a procedure has the following advantages: (1) It is easier to remember a few major steps than a long series of detailed steps. Once a major step is recalled, it is then also fairly easy to elaborate it into the few detailed steps subsumed by it. (2) It is easier to detect a mistake because one may first try to locate it in one of the few major steps, and one can then look within this step to locate the particular subordinate step where the error occurred. (This is much easier than trying to locate a mistake somewhere in a long series of small steps.) (3) It is easier to modify a procedure if necessary. (For example, if one realizes that a modification is needed only in the last major step, one can merely focus on this step and leave all the preceding major steps unchanged.) (4) A prior knowledge of the major steps provides a context within which the more detailed minor steps become more meaningful. (Thus one is not just forced to act like a robot who is merely asked to execute a seemingly unmotivated sequence of detailed steps.)

Experimental assessment of these different descriptions   An experimental investigation (Eylon and Reif, 1984) confirmed some of these advantages of hierarchical descriptions. In this investigation students learned a particular problem-solving procedure that was described either in a linear way (as in figure 7.2a) or in a hierarchical way (as in figure 7.2b). Subsequent tests then showed that, compared to students who had learned the linearly described procedure, the students who had learned the hierarchically described procedure were significantly better at remembering the procedure, modifying it, or detecting mistakes in its implementation.

7.3 MAKING INFERENCES

A useful way of applying some available knowledge beyond its specified domain of applicability is by *inferring* other knowledge that is

implied by it. In some cases such inferences may be *plausible* (so that
they are probably correct, although not necessarily so). However, in
other cases the inferences may be *strict* (or *deductive*) so that the implied
knowledge is necessarily true.

7.3.1 Plausible inferences

Limited knowledge can often permit one to infer conclusions that
are probably (although not necessarily) true. Such *plausible* inferences
are common in everyday life. They can also be very useful in science
to formulate hypotheses, to propose possible explanations, to discover
new scientific principles, or to diagnose likely reasons for encountered
difficulties.

Plausible inferences can be useful in *suggesting* new knowledge, provided that the actual validity of this knowledge is subsequently
checked or that its limits of validity are carefully specified. However,
unless suitably verified, plausible inferences may also be dangerous
because they can lead to unwarranted generalizations and to false
conclusions.

Plausible inferences can be made in some of the following ways.

Induction Inferring by induction involves using knowledge of a few
special cases to arrive at plausible general conclusions. (These conclusions may be suggestive, but may not necessarily be true.)

Examples of inductive inference

• Experiences with people in government positions may lead one to the conclusion that all politicians are greedy and dishonest. (This conclusion is not universally true.)

• Our familiarity with many metals may lead us to the conclusion that all
metals are hard and shiny solids. (This is usually true, but not always. For example, mercury is a metal that is a liquid at room temperature.)

• A limited knowledge of physics can lead to the conclusion that all liquids
become solids if they are cooled to sufficiently low temperatures. (This is not universally true. For instance, liquid helium remains a liquid even when cooled to
the lowest-possible temperatures.)

Analogy Inferring by analogy involves noticing that two systems
have some similar features—and then concluding that other properties
of the two systems are probably also similar. Such a conclusion may be
suggestive, but is again not necessarily true. The following are examples
of some such analogies.

Examples of analogies

- The human mind is like a computer. (To some extent this is true, but there are also significant differences).
- Blood flow in the human vascular system is similar to water flow in a plumbing system. (The two systems do have some common properties, but this analogy cannot be pushed too far.)
- The electrons moving around the nucleus of an atom behave like the planets revolving around the sun. (This is a historically important analogy, but needs to be greatly modified because atomic particles must be described by quantum mechanics.)
- The protons and neutrons within an atomic nucleus behave somewhat like the molecules in a liquid. (Indeed, this so-called *liquid-drop model* of the nucleus did historically suggest some useful ways of analyzing the behavior of the strongly interacting particles within an atomic nucleus.)

7.3.2   Strict inferences

Strict (or *deductive*) inferences are implemented by careful logical reasoning and lead to reliably correct conclusions (if the starting premises are true).

Utility of deductive inferences   Deductive inferences are commonly used in mathematics and science, but have also much wider utility. For example, by using deductive inferences one can store (or remember) only a small amount of knowledge—and then use it to reliably infer a much larger amount of knowledge. Thus one's knowledge can be made much more consistent and coherent than that provided by disparate nuggets of special-case knowledge.

Examples of deductive inference

- The knowledge that all birds lay eggs allows one to infer that pigeons lay eggs.
- A memorized knowledge of the multiplication table tells us that $7 \times 8 = 56$. An obvious deductive inference then leads to the conclusion that $56/8 = 7$.
- Suppose that one remembers that π is defined as the ratio of the circumference C of a circle compared to its diameter D (that is, $\pi = C/D$). Then a simple deductive inference leads to the conclusion that $C = \pi D$ so that the circumference of a circle can be found by multiplying its diameter by π. Similarly, another such inference leads to the conclusion that $D = C/\pi$ (so that the diameter of a circle can be found by dividing its circumference by π). Note that it would be foolish to remember these conclusions as separate facts when they can be immediately inferred from the mere definition of π.

Predictions and explanations   Science is centrally interested in predicting or explaining many phenomena on the basis of relatively few

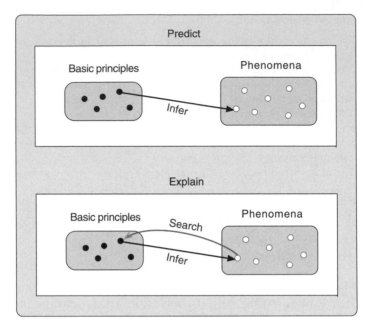

Figure 7.3
Predicting and explaining.

basic premises (such as scientific principles). Deductive inferences are therefore very important in all the sciences.

When one is trying to *predict*, one starts from some basic scientific principles to infer corresponding conclusions about various phenomena. On the other hand, when one is trying to *explain* some observable phenomena, one starts from these phenomena and searches for basic principles that might explain them. Then one completes the task by actually showing how these principles can be used to infer these phenomena. (Figure 7.3 schematically illustrates these processes of prediction and explanation.)

Contrast between science and everyday life Long inference chains (involving successive inferences) are more common in science than in everyday life. Indeed, since science aims to predict numerous observations on the basis of very few basic principles, long reasoning chains are often required. On the other hand, people in everyday life don't have similar goals. Hence they usually do much less reasoning, but rely mostly on large amounts of case-specific knowledge accumulated over their lifetimes. Although such knowledge is somewhat incoherent, it often allows efficient daily-life functioning without much intellectual effort.

7.4   EDUCATIONAL IMPLICATIONS

7.4.1   Proficient performers

People are frequently asked to specify procedures for carrying out di verse tasks. For example, in everyday life policemen or other people are often asked for directions that specify how to reach a particular destination—and cooks are often asked for recipes that specify how to prepare good dishes. Similarly, scientists often need to specify the procedures for proposed experiments, or the procedures used in the experiments leading to their reported results.

Many people thus become fairly good at specifying procedures (although they don't always specify these in the most easily comprehensible form).

7.4.2   Inexperienced students

As already mentioned at the beginning of this chapter, students tend to like procedures that help them to perform various tasks. However, their procedures sometimes resemble poorly organized laundry lists (without any of the useful features mentioned in section 7.2). Inexperienced students also have a tendency to make plausible inferences and then to assume their correctness without checking their validity. Needless to say, such inferences can easily lead to mistakes and unjustified conclusions.

7.4.3   Common instructional deficiencies

Procedures are fairly often used in teaching efforts, but are sometimes used rather inappropriately. The major difficulties arise from *mindless* procedures that students use (like robots) without any understanding of how or why they work. Such mindless performance is often encountered, but can lead to difficulties of the kind illustrated in the following examples.

Examples: Disadvantages of mindless procedures

Teaching arithmetic   When young students are first introduced to arithmetic operations, they are ordinarily taught standard procedures for multiplying or dividing two many-digit numbers. Even as adults, they may remember and use these procedures, but still have no idea why they work.

Nowadays it may be less necessary to perform such operations oneself, since one may rely on electronic calculators and the mysterious algorithms incorporated in them. But should one be utterly helpless if the calculator is not available or happens to break down? Does it not seem bizarre that some college science students, when needing to divide 10^8 by 10^5, mindlessly punch these numbers into their electronic calculators (instead of finding the result 10^3 more quickly by mentally subtracting 5 from 8)?

Training of technicians   Section 2.3.2 mentioned the example of a medical technician who did not know what to do when a patient requested that she take blood from a finger of his *right* hand rather than from a finger of his *left* hand. Her difficulty was clearly traceable to prior training that had merely taught her standard procedures that she could apply mindlessly without any basic understanding of elementary biology. As a result, she was ill prepared to deal with an even slightly unusual situation.

Directions for assembling furniture   Many stores sell compactly packaged furniture that is accompanied by directions specifying how it is to be assembled. These directions specify a step-by-step assembly procedure that is designed to be sufficiently simple to be implementable by any person. But actual users can easily misinterpret some steps or be confused about the exact way that one part is supposed to match another part.

Such users often find it more helpful to be given a clear *diagram* illustrating how all the parts fit together to form the complete piece of furniture. Then the steps of the assembly procedure can make much more sense. Indeed, such a diagram alone, *without* any specified procedure, may be sufficient to allow someone to figure out how to assemble the furniture.

Laboratory manuals   Laboratory manuals, of the kind used in basic science courses, often specify the procedures to be used for carrying out various experiments. Many students use these procedures mindlessly to finish their laboratory work. (This is why some students call these "*cookbook labs*".) However, students often learn little from such laboratory work.

Indeed, when students are afterward asked about what they did during a laboratory period, they may tell you that they used a meter stick to measure a particular length or a stopwatch to measure some time interval. But they may *not* be able to tell you why they did these things—and may not be able to describe the purpose of the experiment carried out by them.

Qualitative analysis in chemistry   When I was a freshman in college, I took a chemistry course that was accompanied by a laboratory in qualitative chemical analysis. I received a grade of A in the course, but did I really learn anything?

I do remember a textbook that specified a long procedure for systematically identifying the various chemicals present in a solution. I also remember that, by faithfully following this procedure and tolerating the foul smell of hydrogen sulfide, specific kinds of ions could be made to precipitate out of solution. But did I learn more than that?

Indeed, I recall a couple of times when we were given unknown solutions with the additional information that these did *not* contain some particular chemicals. I then thought that I could use this information to omit a few particular steps in the standard procedure. But this never worked! These experiences convinced me that I really did *not* understand anything. They also made me dislike learning mindless procedures and (unfortunately) also instilled in me a general dislike of chemistry.

Possibilities of fatal mistakes   When I was drafted into the United States Army at age 18 and sent to basic training, we soldiers were supposed to learn how to use rifle grenades. Such a grenade is affixed to a rifle's muzzle, and the rifle is loaded with blank ammunition that contains no actual bullet. When the rifle is fired, the expanding gases from the explosion then propel the grenade so that it travels an appreciable distance.

Our company was divided into small groups, each of which was supposed to learn some part of the relevant knowledge. For example, one such group was taught how such a grenade functions and another group was taught how to launch such a grenade.

It so happened that one group was taught the launching procedure before it had the opportunity to learn about the functioning of a rifle grenade. Not knowing any better, one of the soldiers in that group loaded his rifle with a real bullet (instead of a blank). This bullet then struck the grenade at his rifle's muzzle and caused it to explode there, killing one soldier and wounding several others.

7.4.4   Instructional suggestions

Judicious use of procedures   Procedures can be very useful in some situations, particularly in emergencies or other situations where rapid performance is required. But in many other cases, it is better not to teach mere procedures or to teach them only with proper care.

If procedures are taught, they should be accompanied by relevant declarative knowledge. Thus students should know the goals of such procedures, the underlying knowledge exploited by them, and possible ways that they can be modified in case of need. Furthermore, procedures can be used more reliably if they are expressed in useful forms (such as those suggested in section 7.2).

Problem solving instead of procedures   It is often preferable to emphasize problem solving rather than mere procedures. Even quite simple problem solving (more elementary than that discussed in chapter 12) can be sufficient. For example, such problem solving, together with some simple mental models (of the kind mentioned in section 3.3.2), can sometimes be more useful than mere procedures.

There is also no intrinsic reason why laboratory manuals should predominantly specify procedures for carrying out certain experiments.

For example, they could indicate the goals of experiments to be performed, describe the kinds of equipment available for performing these, and then ask students to design and carry out experiments for attaining the specified goals. The students' laboratory work would then resemble more closely the kinds of experiments performed in actual scientific work. Furthermore, students would then also have to apply flexibly their acquired scientific knowledge and to think more actively about what they are doing. The use of such an approach can, in fact, prove quite advantageous (Reif and St. John, 1979; Etkina, Murthy, and Zou, 2006).

A greater reliance on problem solving, rather than on mere procedures, has the following advantages: (1) It is more motivating to students. (2) It engages students in more active and productive learning. (3) It makes it easier for them to recall what they learned. (4) It also helps them to acquire knowledge that can be more readily modified or generalized to deal with somewhat different situations.

Exploiting inferences   One should make sure that students can do sufficient deductive reasoning to infer some simple implications. For example, they should know enough algebra that, when faced with a simple relation among quantities, they can readily find any one of these quantities from a knowledge of the others.

A teacher can then exploit the students' reasoning abilities to reduce the amount of disparate knowledge to be taught—and can thereby also make the students' knowledge more coherent. For example, chemistry or physics instructors sometimes discuss ideal gases by first teaching Boyle's law (asserting that the pressure p of a gas is inversely proportional to its volume V), and then teaching Charles's law (or the law of Gay Lussac) which asserts that the pressure p of such a gas is proportional to its absolute temperature T. More economical and coherent knowledge can be achieved if the student can ultimately just remember the ideal-gas law $pV = nRT$ (where n is the number of moles of gas and R the *gas constant*) since this law can easily be used to infer all the previously mentioned laws and some other useful results.

7.5   SUMMARY

• A procedure is a method that specifies explicitly the successive steps needed to perform some task.

• Although procedures may seem rather simple, human beings can be unreliable in implementing them and can thus easily make mistakes.

• Procedures can be specified in useful ways that help to facilitate their implementation. For instance, they should be described at a level of detail appropriate for their intended users, should be accompanied by declarative information useful for checking their proper implementation, and may usefully be described in a hierarchical form where major steps are elaborated in subordinate steps.

• Plausible inferences are useful for discovering new knowledge and generating hypotheses, but deductive inferences from a few scientific principles are needed to yield reliable predictions and explanations.

• Although procedures are often used in teaching and in everyday life, mindlessly used procedures can result in little learning and may lead to inflexible or inappropriate performance.

8 Describing Knowledge

The ability to use knowledge effectively depends not only on its content, but also on its *form* (that is, on its description and organization). This chapter discusses some alternative ways of describing knowledge. Some of these descriptions may be more useful for performing some tasks than other tasks—or may make it easier to perceive important relationships than some other descriptions do. Hence one can apply knowledge effectively by deliberately choosing a form of description that is most appropriate for an intended task.

This chapter explores some of the following questions: (1) What are some commonly useful kinds of descriptions? (2) What are some of their distinctive advantages and disadvantages? (3) How can one use alternative descriptions in complementary ways? (4) What kinds of descriptions are useful in scientific work?

Educational relevance   Inexperienced students often work by relying mostly on some particular descriptions (such as verbal or mathematical descriptions). For example, in some basic science courses, students find it most congenial to use words, but have difficulties translating verbally expressed relationships into mathematical form. But in college or high-school science or mathematics courses (such as those dealing with physics or engineering), students often have a predilection for learning and remembering many formulas as if these were the keys to all relevant knowledge. Yet many of these students have difficulties translating the meaning of a formula into words. (For example, when some students look at a formula like $F = x/y$, they may not be able to tell whether F increases or decreases when y increases.)

The ability to use various different kinds of descriptions can be very helpful for coping with the kinds of tasks encountered in scientific or other complex domains. Hence instructional efforts are well advised to make students aware of multiple kinds of descriptions and to help them learn to use these appropriately.

8.1 DESCRIPTIONS AND THEIR REFERENTS

A *description* consists of entities and relations that correspond, in specified ways, to the entities and relations of a situation that one wishes to describe (the *referent situation*). A given situation may thus be described in many alternative ways, but some of these may be more useful for certain tasks than for others.

Since the features of a description correspond to those of the referent situation, one can say that the description *represents* the referent situation. A description can therefore also be called a *representation*.

8.1.1 Correspondence between descriptions and referents

The correspondence between a description and its referent situation must be carefully specified. This correspondence may, however, only be partial. For example, only *some* features of the description may correspond to features of the referent situation, while there may be no correspondence between some other features. Furthermore, different descriptions may be used to describe the same situation.

Examples of descriptions and their referents

Maps   Ordinary maps indicate the relative horizontal positions of objects, but *not* their relative heights above sea level. Someone looking at a map of the city of Pittsburgh might thus be led to believe that some well-known restaurants are located adjacent to some railroad tracks. However, they are actually located on top of a cliff, and the seemingly adjacent railroad tracks are some 800 feet below.

Vectors   A *vector* is a quantity characterized jointly by a magnitude (some positive number) and a direction. [An example of such a vector is a car's velocity (for instance, 60 miles per hour south).] Any vector can be described by an *arrow* whose length is proportional to the magnitude of the vector and whose direction is the same as that of the vector.

Note that a vector is characterized entirely by its magnitude and direction. On the other hand, an arrow is characterized by its length, its direction, and its *position*. The position of an arrow drawn on a page corresponds, therefore, to *no* existing property of a vector. Hence *several* different arrows with the same length and direction, but different positions, may all describe the *same* vector (as illustrated in figure 8.1a). Accordingly, one can feel free to describe a vector by an arrow drawn at *any* convenient position.

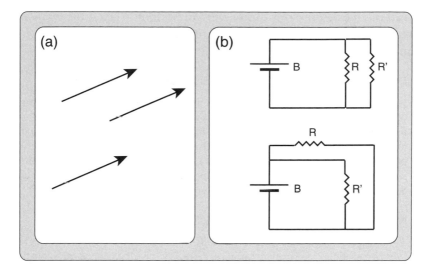

Figure 8.1
(a) Three arrows describing the same vector. (b) Two circuit diagrams describing the same circuit consisting of a battery B and two resistors R and R'.

> *Circuit diagrams* A conventional diagram describing an electric circuit in-dicates how all the elements in this circuit are interconnected, but does *not* indicate their positions in space. Hence the same circuit may be described by diagrams whose elements are drawn at different places on a page, as long as these elements are connected in the same way (see figure 8.1b). Accordingly, one can feel free to describe a circuit by a diagram laid out on a page in any convenient way.

Proficient performers often exploit the previously mentioned free-doms of choice by selecting particular forms of description that are most convenient for particular tasks. But inexperienced students some-times find it confusing that different descriptions can refer to the same situation.

8.1.2 Importance of alternative descriptions

Although different descriptions of the same situation may seem equivalent, they may be functionally quite different. For example, rela-tionships apparent in one description may be difficult or impossible to be perceived in another description. Similarly, a task that can be easily accomplished with the aid of one description may be difficult or impos-sible to be handled with another description.

Alternative descriptions can be very important in scientific work and have historically led to major scientific advances. The following are some examples.

Copernicus and alternative descriptions of planetary motions

Copernicus's great discovery was the insight that the motion of the planets could be described relative to the sun as legitimately as relative to the earth, but that the former description is much simpler and thus also much better suited for astronomical predictions. This mere change of description led to far-reaching progress in astronomy. It also profoundly changed people's conceptions of the world, although it was at the time so controversial that people like Galileo, who adopted this point of view, were in danger of being burned as heretics.

Newton and the changed description of acceleration

As discussed in chapter 5, the scientific description of *acceleration* is different from its everyday description because it focuses on *any* change of velocity— irrespective of whether this change of velocity involves a change in its magnitude or in its direction. This seemingly innocent change of description led Newton to some of the insights mentioned in section 5.2. Thus it helped to reveal that seemingly very different motions near the surface of the earth (for example, the motion of a vertically falling object or that of a baseball flying through the air) are all characterized by an acceleration toward the center of the earth; that the circular motion of the moon around the earth is similarly characterized by an acceleration toward the center of the earth; and that all such objects are therefore similarly affected by a gravitational force exerted by the earth.

8.2 ALTERNATIVE DESCRIPTIONS

The following paragraphs discuss some different kinds of descriptions and their distinguishing characteristics.

Different descriptive concepts   The same situation can be described by means of different descriptive concepts. For example, one can describe the position of a town B relative to another town A by stating that town B is located 10 miles away from town A, at an angle of $37°$ degrees north from east (see figure 8.2). Alternatively, one can state that town B is located 8 miles east and 6 miles north from town A. The first of these descriptions specifies the location of town B by one distance and one angle; the second one specifies it by two different distances. But the information provided by both descriptions is the same.

This example also illustrates two alternative ways of describing a vector in two dimensions. Any such vector can be described by a magnitude (a positive number) and a direction specified by some angle.

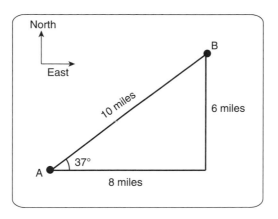

Figure 8.2
Different descriptions of the location of town B relative to another town A.

Alternatively, it can be described by its two components which are two (positive or negative) numbers.

Another example is provided by alternative ways of describing a color. One such way involves the specification of the three quantities *hue*, *saturation*, and *brightness*. Another way involves the specification of the relative amounts of the three basic colors *red*, *green*, and *blue*. These descriptions (commonly used to specify colors on a computer screen) are largely equivalent so that one can convert one of these descriptions to the other.

Different symbolic representations   A description can frequently be expressed in different *symbolic* forms (for example, verbally in the form of words, visually in the form of a drawing, or more abstractly in the form of mathematical symbolism).

Example: Descriptions in different symbolic forms

If an object is dropped from rest, the distance that it falls during various amounts of time can be described in words by saying that "the traversed distance increases with increasing time." Alternatively, the same information can be described in a visual form by a graph like that in figure 8.3a; in the form of numbers like those in the table in figure 8.3b; or mathematically in the form of an equation like that in figure 8.3c.

Although such alternative descriptions are largely equivalent, they have distinctive advantages or limitations. Thus, verbal descriptions tend to be lengthy and somewhat vague. Visual descriptions (like graphs, bar charts, or pie charts) are useful because they portray

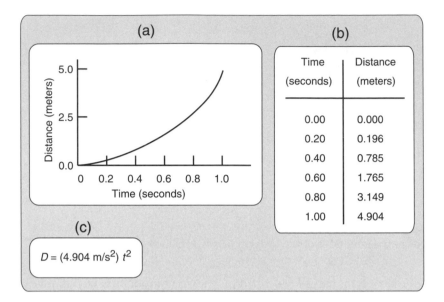

Figure 8.3
Alternative descriptions of the distance D traversed by a falling object after some elapsed time t. (a) Graph. (b) Table. (c) Equation.

information (such as temporal behavior) in a graphical form that can be perceived at a glance. Similar information summarized by numbers (or tables of such numbers) can be specified more precisely, but in ways that make it more difficult to perceive any trends. Not all information can be described in the form of mathematical equations; but when this is possible, such equations provide a compact and precise way of summarizing the relevant information.

Figure 8.4 illustrates how a visual description (a graph) describes the rapid growth of the world's population much more strikingly than any verbal description or mathematical equation could.

Different points of view The same situation can sometimes be described from different points of view. For example, the motion of the planets can be described from the point of view of an observer on the earth or from the point of a hypothetical observer on the sun. As already mentioned, this second point of view led Copernicus to a much simpler description and thus resulted in major advances in astronomy.

Similarly, useful insights in physics can often be obtained by describing the same motion from the point of view of an observer at

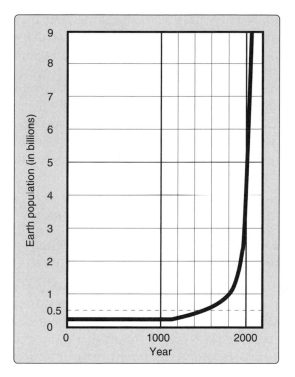

Figure 8.4
Growth of the world population.

rest on the earth or of another observer located on a vehicle moving relative to the earth. In particular, Einstein developed his important theory of relativity by examining how phenomena, involving the propagation of light, would be described from the points of view of different observers moving relative to each other.

In everyday life and in the social sciences, it can also often be difficult, but instructive, to describe the same situation from the points of view of different people (for example, from the point of view of a wealthy person or a poor worker, of an established citizen or an immigrant, of a typical American or a Moslem).

External and internal representations It is important to distinguish between *external* representations (forms of description in papers or computers located outside a person) and *internal* representations (forms of description inside a person's mind). The external representations may be readily visible, but the internal representations are not. These two representations may have some similarities, but they need *not* be the same. For example, someone may write down *words* listing the parts of a machine, but may do this by internally visualizing a *picture* displaying the parts of such a machine.

The internal and external representations are complementary (since both are often used simultaneously and assist each other). But our thought processes rely predominantly on our *internal* representations. The external representations may sometimes be given to us by others in books or on blackboards. But our *internal* representations are ultimately constructed by ourselves.

8.3 CHARACTERISTICS OF DIFFERENT DESCRIPTIONS

Descriptions can differ in some of the following general characteristics so that they may be useful for different kinds of tasks.

Detailed versus coarse   Descriptions may be *detailed* or may be *coarse* (or *sketchy*). A detailed description specifies many features in a situation and thus provides rather complete information about it. However, the amount of detail may be so overwhelming that it causes difficulties for a person trying to cope with all the information and to focus on its centrally important aspects without being distracted by the details. (Thus the person "may fail to see the forest because of all the trees").

Coarse descriptions may be useful when detailed ones are not available. They can also be useful for planning, designing, or troubleshooting (that is, for tasks where detailed information may be irrelevant or distracting). Hence coarse descriptions can serve as good starting points for methods of successive approximations that are designed to attain more detailed information by progressive refinements.

Explicit versus implicit   An *explicit* description specifically indicates the relevant features of a situation, whereas an *implicit* description does not. Thus, a verbal description or a drawing can explicitly focus attention on the important features in a situation; but a photograph of this situation reveals all its features implicitly.

For example, a map of a city specifies explicitly the various streets in the city, but an aerial photograph indicates these only more implicitly. Accordingly, a map is more helpful than such a photograph when one wants to find one's way in a strange city. Similarly, it is easier to learn the components of a biological cell from drawings of such a cell than from photographs of it. As a last example, it may take many months of repeated observations to learn how to determine the sex of one-day-old chicks; but explicit descriptions can help people to perform the same task in a very much shorter time (Biederman and Shiffrar, 1987).

Since an *explicit* description of a situation can deliberately highlight significant or theoretically important features, it may sometimes help persons' learning more effectively than direct observations of the actual situation. For example, a student can easily observe a current-carrying wire by connecting it to a battery—and may also measure the magnitude of the resultant electric current by observing an ammeter inserted in the circuit. But these observations do not reveal the electric and magnetic fields surrounding the wire, fields that might be explicitly indicated by a drawing of the situation.

Displays on a computer screen can provide explicit descriptions that are even more effective and dynamic. For example, computer simulations may dynamically portray the electrons that move through the wire to produce the electric current. Similarly, such simulations may display the moving electric and magnetic fields that are responsible for radio waves propagating through space. Indeed, computer simulations may sometimes be more conducive to learning than actual laboratory experiments (or may usefully supplement such experiments) because they can explicitly display useful descriptions and can also be readily modified.

On the other hand, *implicit* descriptions (like photographs) may not only provide more complete information than words or more abstract drawings, but may also help fast and effortless recognition. For instance, to help the apprehension of a criminal, the published photograph of this criminal may be much more useful than a verbal description of the person.

Precise versus imprecise A description is *precise* if it allows fine discriminations between significant features. It is *imprecise* (*approximate* or *vague*) if it does not allow such fine distinctions.

High precision may be necessary for some tasks but not for others. Indeed, it would be wasteful to be precise when precision is not necessary. For example, it may be useful to specify dimensions to the nearest thousandth of an inch when talking to a machinist who is working with metal. But such precision would be pointless when talking to a carpenter since wood cannot be fabricated to such precise dimensions.

Vague or qualitative descriptions may be very useful for some tasks, such as planning or searching. They allow one to make major preliminary decisions without being encumbered by needless precision, and these decisions can later be elaborated into more precise form. This is why qualitative reasoning can often be quite helpful in precise domains like mathematics or physics.

Although more detailed descriptions are often more precise than coarser ones, this is not always the case because precision may depend on which particular details are specified. For example, a description is certainly *not* detailed if it merely specifies that a particular man has a red scar on his left cheek. On the other hand, this description may be very precise if it allows this man to be easily distinguished from other men in a room.

Specific versus general   A description is *specific* if it refers to a particular case or instance. It is *general* if it subsumes many such special cases. For example, a description specifying that hens lay eggs is more specific than one specifying that birds lay eggs.

General descriptions are particularly useful in science since the central scientific goal is to predict or explain the largest number of phenomena on the basis of the fewest number of basic premises. Hence scientific concepts or principles are usually described in highly general forms. However, one must then be able to interpret them properly in any specific instance.

It is often far easier to remember some general knowledge rather than many more special cases of it. For example, in chemistry or physics, it is easier to remember the general ideal-gas law $pV = nRT$ (relating the pressure p, volume V, and absolute temperature T of n moles of an ideal gas) than to remember separately Boyle's law (relating p and V) and the law of Charles or Gay-Lussac (relating p and T, or V and T).

Similarly, Ohm's general law $V = RI$ relates the voltage drop V across a circuit element to its resistance R and to the electric current I flowing through it. Yet some electrical engineering books introduce *three* separate Ohm's laws (namely, $V = RI$, $R = V/I$, and $I = V/R$). It seems unnecessary to remember *three* such separate laws when all of these are easily inferred special cases of the single general relation $V = RI$.

General descriptions, that encompass many specific cases, can often be imprecise or qualitative. But this is *not* necessarily so. For example, some highly general concepts (such as energy or entropy) are very precisely defined so that their quantitative numerical values can be specified in any particular case.

Is it better to remember general or case-specific knowledge?

The answer to this question is a trade-off. Storing general knowledge requires one to remember less, but to do more thinking in order to apply this general knowledge in a particular instance. On the other hand, storing knowledge about many special cases requires more remembering, but less thinking since knowledge about any such case can then be immediately applied whenever it is relevant.

Knowledge about any special case also requires associated knowledge about the conditions under which it is valid. One needs thus not only to store case-specific knowledge, but also to store (and then to retrieve) its associated validity conditions. Indeed, failure to store properly such validity conditions (or to consider them properly when retrieving case-specific knowledge) is a common cause of mistakes. Hence it is usually preferable to remember general knowledge (unless it requires much effort to apply it in specific cases).

For example, students in basic physics are often taught that, if an object is at rest, the total force $\mathbf{F}_{tot}$ on the object is zero. On the other hand, it is far preferable simply to remember Newton's general law $\mathbf{F}_{tot} = m\mathbf{a}$ which relates the total force on an object to its mass m and its acceleration $\mathbf{a}$. It is then trivial to infer that the acceleration $\mathbf{a}$, and hence total force $\mathbf{F}_{tot}$, must be zero if an object is at rest. Furthermore, students are then less likely to be led into the temptation of claiming that the force $\mathbf{F}_{tot}$ is always zero, even in some situations where an object is *not* at rest.

8.4   COMPLEMENTARY USE OF DIFFERENT DESCRIPTIONS

Good performance can be facilitated by the complementary use of alternative descriptions. In this way one can deliberately choose descriptions helpful for performing particular tasks of interest, and avoid descriptions that may hinder the performance of these tasks.

Even when different descriptions of the same situation are *logically* equivalent, they may be *psychologically* different. For example, one particular description of a problem may suggest a useful way for solving it, but another description of this problem may not. Indeed, the careful choice of a particular *form of description* can be crucial in determining whether a task can be readily performed or not. For example, the description may determine how easily some knowledge can be remembered, how well it can be used to solve problems, or how readily it can lead to new discoveries.

The availability of alternative descriptions can thus be very useful. For example, some descriptions may make apparent relationships that are far less evident in other descriptions. Some descriptions may facilitate tasks that are more difficult to perform with the aid of other descriptions. Different descriptions may also require different thought processes for their use (Larkin and Simon, 1987).

8.4.1 Consistency of alternative descriptions

Alternative descriptions of the same situation require that these descriptions should be neither inconsistent nor misleading—so that implications inferred from one description do not contradict those inferred from another. The following example illustrates that even seemingly slight differences in wording may sometimes violate this consistency requirement.

Seemingly equivalent descriptions: Different interpretations of zero

Seemingly equivalent wordings can sometimes lead to major student difficulties. For example, the phrase "This object has no velocity" seems to mean the same as the phrase "The velocity of this object is zero." However, when saying that "*an object has no velocity*," some students are led to the conclusion that the object's velocity cannot change—so that its acceleration is zero. After all, if something does not exist, how can it possibly change? On the other hand, asserting that "*an object's velocity is zero*" is not very different from saying that its velocity is small. Most students then readily believe that such a small velocity *can* change (so that the acceleration may *not* be zero).

The apparent difficulty is that the first description leads students to interpret the word *zero* as meaning non-existence, whereas the second description leads them to interpret *zero* properly as just one particular value among many other possible values. (An analogous distinction might perhaps be that between having *no* bank account, or having a bank account with a current balance of *zero* dollars.)

8.4.2 Translating between alternative descriptions

Since the complementary use of alternative descriptions can be very useful, it is often exploited in scientific work. (For example, it is useful to be able to describe the same situation in words, in graphs, or in mathematical equations.) Hence it is important that students acquire the ability to translate between different descriptions of the same situation.

Indeed, some recent reform movements in calculus instruction (such as the one sponsored by the Calculus Consortium based at Harvard University) have specifically stressed the abilities to describe mathematical knowledge interchangeably in graphical, numerical, and symbolic forms (Hughes-Hallett, Gleason, and McCallum, 2003).

8.4.3 Precise and approximate descriptions in science

Explicit mathematical descriptions are highly useful in science for the following main reasons: (1) They allow precise quantitative specifications of important relationships. (2) By using well-defined symbols and well-specified rules, they enable correct long reasoning chains that are needed to predict or explain many phenomena.

On the other hand, science requires also many other important tasks. For example, scientists must be able to search for different kinds of possible explanations, discover new phenomena or principles, design experiments and the apparatus needed for them, diagnose the underlying reasons for faulty predictions or unsuccessful experiments, troubleshoot equipment when it fails to work properly, and so on. But formal mathematical descriptions are usually *not* particularly useful for carrying out such tasks like searching, discovering, designing, diagnosing, or troubleshooting. Approximate qualitative descriptions can then be much more appropriate.

Hence good scientists often use *both* precise quantitative descriptions as well as approximate qualitative descriptions. For example, Albert Einstein was a very good theoretical physicist who used mathematics to great effect. For example, his papers on the theory of general relativity bristle with the complex mathematics of tensor analysis. He also wrote that the physicist's work "demands the highest possible standard of rigorous precision in the description of relations, such as only the use of mathematical language can give" (Einstein, 1954, 225). On the other hand, some of his own thinking was also vague and nonmathematical. For example, in a letter sent to the mathematician Hadamard he wrote:

> The words of the language ... do not seem to play any role in my mechanisms of thought. The psychical entities which seem to serve as elements of thought are certain signs and more or less clear images which can be "voluntarily" reproduced and combined ... before there is any connection with logical construction in words or other kinds of signs which can be communicated to others. The above-mentioned elements are, in my case, of visual and some muscular type. Conventional words or other signs have to be sought for laboriously only in a secondary stage, when the mentioned associative play is sufficiently established and can be reproduced at will. (Hadamard, 1954, 142)

One might naively believe that theoretical physicists, who use mathematics extensively in their work, would predominantly think in mathematical language. But just as in the case of Einstein, this is often not true. Good theoretical physicists often use also qualitative and pictorial reasoning. For example, Hans Bethe, another well-known theoretical physicist, says the following when recalling how he learned to use such reasoning from Enrico Fermi (famous for his work in nuclear physics and for building the first nuclear reactor in 1942):

> *From Fermi I learned lightness of approach; that is, to look at things qualitatively first and understand the problem physically before putting a lot of formulas on paper.... Fermi was as much an experimenter as a theorist, and the mathematical solution was for him more a confirmation of his understanding of a problem than the basis of it.* (Bethe, quoted in Bernstein 1979, 84)

The famous theoretical physicist Richard Feynman (perhaps best known for his innovative work in quantum electrodynamics) is even more vivid in describing his way of thinking:

> *What I am really trying to do is bring birth to clarity, which is really a half-assedly thought-out pictorial semi-vision thing.... It's all visual. It's hard to explain.... Ordinarily, I try to get the pictures clearer, but in the end the mathematics can take over and be more efficient in communicating the idea of the picture.... In certain particular problems that I have done it was necessary to continue the development of the picture as the method before the mathematics could be really done.* (Gleick, 1992, 244)

Furthermore, in the lecture that Feynman gave when receiving the Nobel Prize, he said the following:

> *Physical [i.e., qualitative] reasoning does help some people to generate suggestions as to how the unknown may be related to the known. Theories of the known, which are described by different physical ideas, may be equivalent in all their predictions and are hence scientifically indistinguishable. However, they are not psychologically identical when trying to move from that base into the unknown.... I, therefore, think that a good theoretical physicist today might find it useful to have a wide range of physical viewpoints and mathematical expressions of the same theory... available to him.* (Feynman, 1965)

Indeed, Feynman himself also invented particular kinds of visual representations (called *Feynman diagrams*) that have proven widely useful for describing the interactions between atomic particles and for facilitating the highly complex calculations needed for the quantitative analysis of such interactions (Kane, 2005; Kaiser, 2005).

8.5 EDUCATIONAL IMPLICATIONS

8.5.1 Proficient performers

Expert scientists   Expert scientists commonly achieve much of their proficient performance by relying on multiple descriptions that they can flexibly use wherever these are most advantageous. For example, mathematical equations are often embedded in qualitative knowledge. The preceding paragraphs illustrated how good physicists use both qualitative and quantitative mathematical description in complementary ways. Furthermore, the following comments indicate how different descriptions were historically important in the work of the key scientists responsible for our modern understanding of electromagnetism.

Faraday and Maxwell: Outstanding scientists using different descriptions

Michael Faraday and James Clerk Maxwell, living in Great Britain in the nineteenth century, were the preeminent scientists whose work led to our present-day understanding of electricity and magnetism. These two scientists were very different. Faraday had very little education and was apprenticed as a bookbinder before turning his attention to science. He knew scarcely any mathematics, but became an excellent experimenter by relying on qualitative reasoning and highly visual concepts to understand the electromagnetic phenomena that he was studying. On the other hand, Maxwell was very well trained in theoretical physics and, building on Faraday's work, used his mathematical skills to develop a highly unified electromagnetic theory culminating (around 1870) in the four famous Maxwell equations. Maxwell was thereby also able to predict the existence of electromagnetic waves (encompassing radio waves, radar, visible light, X-rays, and so on).

Despite their different qualitative and mathematical approaches, each of these scientists greatly respected the other. Furthermore, the combined contributions of both are responsible for much of the technology permeating our present age.

In other fields that exploit mathematics, scientists also commonly use qualitative and visual descriptions. For instance, chemists use diagrams of molecular structure or atomic orbitals and use phase diagrams showing the temperatures and pressures under which a substance is in solid, liquid, or gaseous form. Economists use graphs of demand and supply. Engineers commonly use many graphs and diagrams. Indeed, even pure mathematicians use visual descriptions. For example, Michel Loève (a professor of mathematics and statistics at the University of California at Berkeley) wished that his graduate students could have been present at several of his conversations with Norbert Wiener (Loève, personal communication). Indeed, they might have seen that the famous mathematician (despite his formal mathematical papers) was actually thinking qualitatively while drawing all kinds of diagrams on the blackboard.

Experts in other fields   On the other hand, some fields traditionally rely almost exclusively on verbal descriptions. Thus, lawyers seem to use only words, words, and more words. As a result, legal documents are often remarkably hard to understand. For example, a will consists of a set of complex instructions specifying how wealth is to be passed on after a person's death under various possible subsequent conditions (each specified by statements of the form "if ..., then ..."). One may well wonder whether such instructions could not be specified much more clearly in the visual form of a flow chart (similar to the ones used to specify computer programs).

Similarly, historians almost always convey their thoughts in the form of prose (except for some occasional photographs). But could some such historical knowledge not be conveyed more clearly in the visual form of a time line indicating a specific sequence of events and distinct time periods? Or could several such parallel time lines not help to indicate more clearly what particular developments in one field (such as politics, economics, technology, music, or painting) occurred at the same time as developments in another one?

The preceding comments are not meant to denigrate common practices of experts in these fields. But they suggest that the forms of description prevalent in a domain may sometimes be determined largely by tradition, rather than by deliberate analyses of the kinds of description that are likely to be most useful.

8.5.2 Inexperienced students

As mentioned at the beginning of this chapter, students tend to rely predominantly on only some particular forms of description—and have difficulties translating from one form of description to another. Hence they also lack the ability to perform as effectively and flexibly as most proficient experts.

8.5.3 Common instructional deficiencies

Teaching deficiencies can occur at all levels. For example, at lower levels (in high schools or below) science teaching is mostly qualitative so that students never appreciate why mathematical descriptions are very useful in the quantitative sciences. At higher levels (in colleges or graduate schools) the opposite situation often prevails. There instruction in physics or mathematics may be rather formal, stressing the logical exposition of fundamental principles and the mathematical techniques for working with them. In the process, qualitative descriptions and qualitative reasoning are often largely ignored. Section 2.1 mentioned some of the deleterious consequences of such excessively formal instruction that often does not prepare students well for actual scientific work.

Sometimes teaching practices may even encourage students' simple-minded tendency to focus on formulas. For example, one commonly used textbook on basic college physics (Ohanian, 1985) includes a two-page appendix entitled "Formula Sheets" that merely lists some 140 miscellaneous formulas mentioned within the book. Furthermore, an early page in the book gives students the following advice:

Advice on Solving Problems

The solving of problems is an art; there is no simple recipe for obtaining the solutions. Most of the problems in this and the following chapters are applications of the formulas derived in the text. If you find it difficult to decide what formula to use, begin by looking at formulas that are valid under the given physical conditions of the problem and make a list of known and unknown quantities. Then try to spot a formula that expresses the unknowns in terms of the known quantities. . . . Be discriminating in your selection of formulas—sometimes a formula will tempt you because it displays all the desired quantities, but it will be an invalid formula if the assumptions that went into its derivation are not satisfied in your problem. You will often find that you seem to have too many unknowns and too few equations. Then ask yourself the following questions: Are there any extra mathematical relationships that the conditions of the problem impose on the unknowns? Can you combine several equations to eliminate some of the unknowns? Are there any quantities that you can calculate from the known quantities? Do these calculated quantities bring you nearer to the answer? (Ohanian, 1985, 39)

This recommended approach to problem solving seems entirely centered on formulas and the manipulation of equations. Such a formula-centered approach may possibly help students to pass the tests given by some instructors. But this approach differs significantly from the problem solving done by good physicists and is also not helpful for gaining a useful understanding of physics.

8.5.4   Instructional suggestions

To avoid the kinds of teaching deficiencies mentioned in the preceding paragraphs, it is helpful to teach students multiple descriptions (both qualitative and quantitative), how to use them appropriately, and how to translate between them.

As mentioned in section 2.1, investigations of students' learning in basic physics courses have revealed some of the deficiencies caused by an excessive emphasis on mathematical descriptions. As a result, there have been recent attempts to remedy the situation by paying greater attention to more qualitative descriptions and reasoning skills (Hestenes and Wells, 1992; Hestenes, Wells, and Swackhamer, 1992; Mazur, 1997).

The utility of multiple descriptions can also be fruitfully exploited in non-scientific domains. For example, when trying to teach students writing skills, one might be tempted to focus on purely verbal descriptions. But although the ultimately desired product is good prose, the *process* of generating such prose can greatly profit from more visual descriptions (such as diagrams and outlines at successively more detailed levels). Such descriptions can help students to decide what effect they wish to have on their intended audience (for example, which essential ideas they wish to convey, which of these are central or subsidiary, and how these ideas can be effectively organized). The students can then perform all these important thinking tasks without *simultaneously* needing to worry about grammar or style. The writing task can thus be appreciably simplified because it becomes a process of progressive refinement where the essential issues are addressed first and are used afterwards to deal with more minor issues.

8.6 SUMMARY

• A description of a situation specifies entities and relations corresponding, in specified ways, to the entities and relations in the situation.

• The same situation may be described in many different ways, but a particular task can sometimes be performed more easily with the aid of a well-chosen description.

• Descriptions may differ in their level of detail, explicitness, precision, and specificity.

• Good performance can be greatly enhanced by the availability of multiple descriptions so that appropriate descriptions can be chosen for the tasks for which they are best suited. For example, good scientists (even in highly quantitative fields) often use *both* qualitative and precise mathematical descriptions.

• The use of multiple descriptions also requires the ability to translate between them so that the same situation can be described in alternative ways.

9 Organizing Knowledge

As indicated in figure 2.3, the *organization* of some knowledge (that is, the specified relationships among its component elements) can greatly influence how effectively this knowledge can be used. For example, it can determine how readily the knowledge can be remembered, retrieved, regenerated if partially forgotten, checked for consistency, generalized, and extended by further learning.

The same knowledge may be organized in different ways. But a particular form of organization may help the performance of some tasks and hinder the performance of some others. This chapter examines the following questions: (1) What are some different ways of organizing knowledge? (2) What are some of their advantages and disadvantages? (3) What forms of organization are useful for dealing effectively with large amounts of knowledge?

Educational relevance Students' knowledge is often poorly organized and may remain so for a long time. For example, as discussed in section 5.4.4, students' knowledge about acceleration seems to consist largely of various bits of knowledge that are sometimes inconsistent with each other, don't form a coherent knowledge structure, and may thus lead to irresolvable paradoxes. Similarly, students' knowledge about some physics topic (like mechanics) often consists mostly of various memorized equations that are not clearly related to each other and not embedded in more comprehensive knowledge. It is thus not surprising that, when students make notes to prepare themselves for an examination, these notes often consist merely of a laundry list of miscellaneous facts and formulas.

As mentioned in chapter 6, poorly organized knowledge cannot readily be remembered or used. But students often don't know how to organize their knowledge effectively and don't realize that learning can be greatly facilitated by good knowledge organization. Hence instructional efforts need to focus more deliberate attention on the organization of students' acquired knowledge.

9.1 IMPORTANCE OF KNOWLEDGE ORGANIZATION

As the preceding comments indicate, the organization of one's knowledge can be highly important to ensure that it is effectively usable. This importance can be illustrated by the following analogy familiar from everyday life. Imagine that you have a file cabinet containing many file folders with valuable information. Suppose now that, as a result of the passage of time and neglect on your part, the folders have become disorganized and haphazardly arranged. Although the same information would then be still *available*, it would no longer be readily *accessible* (because its disorganized form would make it difficult to retrieve any specific information of interest to you). Hence the information in your file cabinet would have become almost worthless.

Organization and size The organization of knowledge becomes particularly important if the amount of knowledge is large because *selective retrieval* (the retrieval of some particular information) can then become increasingly difficult. For example, there is a familiar saying that some task is as difficult as "finding a needle in a haystack." But the task of finding a needle in a *large* haystack is even more difficult than that of finding the same needle in a smaller haystack.

External versus internal knowledge organization It is important to distinguish between external and internal forms of knowledge organization. The *external* knowledge organization may be manifest in notebooks, file cabinets, and computers. The *internal* knowledge organization in a person's head is much less apparent, yet most significant for the person's thinking. But both forms of organization are important and mutually affect each other.

Importance of knowledge organization in science The central goal of science is to use a small number of fundamental principles to predict or explain a large number of observable phenomena. The effective organization of scientific knowledge is, therefore, particularly important. As the famous mathematician and scientist Henri Poincaré once wrote (Poincaré, 1902):

> The scientist must organize. One makes a science with facts in the way that one makes a house with stones. But an accumulation of facts is no more a science than a pile of stones is a house.

More generally, a person's knowledge does not consist of a miscellaneous collection of knowledge elements, but is a knowledge *structure* (an organized assembly of knowledge components). In particular, scientists strive to organize their knowledge in highly systematic and careful ways.

Expert versus student perceptions of physics knowledge

Some expert physicists proudly claim that the beauty of physics (unlike organic chemistry) is that there is rather little to remember. On the other hand, physics students often complain about the need to remember many formulas.

This apparent paradox can be largely explained by noting that expert physicists have their knowledge tightly organized around relatively few major principles. On the other hand, students' physics knowledge often consists predominantly of a collection of miscellaneous facts and equations.

9.2 SOME FORMS OF KNOWLEDGE ORGANIZATION

The following are examples of some commonly encountered forms of knowledge organization.

Nearly random organization The organization, schematically illustrated in figure 9.1, is an extreme case. It is so disorganized that it consists of a nearly random collection of unrelated knowledge elements. (As mentioned in section 5.4.4, some students' knowledge about acceleration resembles this form of organization because it seems to consist of a haphazard collection of unconnected facts.)

List A familiar form of organization is a *list* consisting of a well-ordered sequence of knowledge elements (as illustrated in figure 9.2). Such a list is certainly more orderly than the organization shown in figure 9.1 and is particularly useful for retrieving a particular sequence of items. For example, it is suitable for specifying the successive steps of a

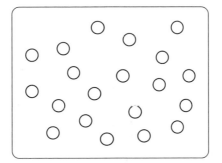

Figure 9.1
A nearly random organization.

Figure 9.2
A list.

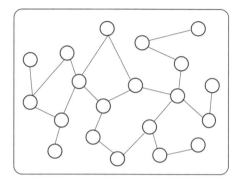

Figure 9.3
A network.

procedure or the successive items in a checklist (such as a laundry list or an alphabetical list). But it is *not* useful for indicating richly interrelated concepts or ideas.

   Network   A frequently encountered form of knowledge organization is a *network* of interrelated knowledge elements (as illustrated in figure 9.3). Any knowledge element is here associated with some other knowledge elements. Knowledge in the form of such an *associative network* is thus fairly coherent since its knowledge elements are greatly interconnected.

   The everyday knowledge possessed by most of us is predominantly organized in such an associative network. Our nervous system then allows us to retrieve particular information by exploiting the connections among the knowledge elements stored in our minds.

   When students learn new concepts, they may find it helpful to draw *concept maps* which are network diagrams (similar to figure 9.3) that visually display these concepts and the relationships among them. Some teachers advocate the use of such concept maps because they may help students to perceive the relationships among newly learned concepts and may thus help them to acquire more coherent knowledge.

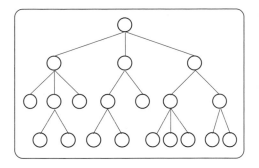

Figure 9.4
A hierarchy.

However, associative networks (and concept maps) have some limitations: (1) The retrieval of specific information in a network may be difficult, especially if the network contains a large amount of information. This is because one then encounters a veritable jungle of interconnections, without any clearly indicated path for retrieving specific information. (2) The existence of local connections does not ensure the consistency of the entire knowledge. For example, if knowledge element A is consistent with knowledge element B and is also consistent with knowledge element C, there is no guarantee that B and C are mutually consistent.

Hierarchy A hierarchy is a special case of a network in which elements are more systematically connected in tree-like fashion. Such an inverted tree, with branches progressively fanning out from its root at the top, is illustrated in figure 9.4.

The systematic relationships specified in such a hierarchy of knowledge elements make the entire knowledge highly coherent. In particular, this organization allows specification of an efficient retrieval method whereby specific information can be found by starting from the top knowledge (the root of the tree) and successively fanning out from there along the branches of the tree. Since only a few branches emanate from any encountered branch point, it is fairly easy to decide which particular branch to choose next. In this way, only relatively few successive decisions are needed to locate any particular information at any level within the hierarchy.

Indeed, hierarchical organizations are commonly used because they facilitate information retrieval. For example, the files in a computer are ordinarily organized in hierarchical fashion.

9.3 DEALING WITH LARGE AMOUNTS OF KNOWLEDGE

How can one effectively deal with large amounts of knowledge? In other words, how can one retrieve and flexibly use some selected part of a large amount of knowledge—despite the fact that human beings have quite limited information-processing capacity?

These are clearly important questions since the amount of knowledge in our world (and in any science) is very large and rapidly growing. Part of the answer can be provided by describing and organizing this knowledge in useful ways.

9.3.1 An inadequate simplistic solution

If the amount of knowledge is so large that it is difficult to manage, a seemingly obvious solution might be to partition this knowledge into smaller parts. For then one might be able to perform a task by successively dealing with each of these smaller parts separately.

Although this answer is not entirely wrong, it is too simplistic. A more useful example, familiar from everyday life, is provided by geographical knowledge and its use for navigational tasks.

Example of geographical knowledge Geographical knowledge about the United States might be provided in the form of a large map (20 feet by 10 feet in size) that is printed in black color and displays all the cities, towns, roads, and rivers in the country. In keeping with our previous suggestion, the knowledge contained in this huge map might then be partitioned into more manageable parts by cutting the map into 200 smaller maps (each 1 foot by 1 foot in size).

However, it would be very difficult to use all these smaller maps to plan a trip from some town in California to some town in Virginia. The many separate maps would provide no awareness of the country as a whole—and the amount of detail would be so overwhelming that it would be very hard to relate the information in one small map to the information in any other such map.

9.3.2 A better solution

All of us know that we don't deal with geographical knowledge in this way, but partition the knowledge into smaller parts in a very different manner. Thus all the geographical knowledge about the United States is usually summarized in the form of a coarse map that summarizes, with few details, only the major features of the country (for example, the major cities, roads, and rivers). This map is then elaborated into more detailed maps of the western, the midwestern, and the eastern parts of the country. Each of these maps is then further elaborated into more detailed maps (for example, the map of the western United States is elaborated into more detailed maps of Washington, Oregon, and California). This process is then continued by providing maps that are progressively elaborated in greater detail (even down to street maps of particular towns.)

By using a set of maps constructed in this way, we can easily navigate from any place to any other place in the country. Furthermore, even when dealing with detailed knowledge, we still remain aware of coarse knowledge about the entire United States. Thus we can also readily determine how detailed knowledge about one part of the country is connected to detailed knowledge about some other part.

9.4 KNOWLEDGE ELABORATION

The preceding geographical example illustrates the utility of systematic knowledge elaborations. In particular, knowledge can be *elaborated* by specifying additional knowledge that is associated with it. This elaborated knowledge may be called *subordinate* (or *subsumed*) knowledge relative to the original knowledge. Conversely, the original knowledge may be called *more central* (or *superordinate*) knowledge relative to the subordinate knowledge.

Elaboration can facilitate retrieval because access to some central knowledge then makes it easy to access the subordinate knowledge associated with it. Figure 9.5 illustrates schematically the elaboration

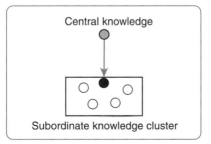

Figure 9.5
Elaboration of some central knowledge into subordinate knowledge.

of some central knowledge or *topic* (indicated by the small gray circle) into a cluster of associated subordinate knowledge elements (indicated by the small white circles in the cluster within the rectangle). This cluster can be given a name (indicated by the small black circle) referring to the elaborated topic. For example, if the small gray circle denotes some mention of Oregon, the rectangle might represent a map, named *Oregon*, in which the small white circles represent elaborated information about the state of Oregon.)

9.4.1   Special kinds of elaboration

Knowledge can be elaborated in different ways, depending on what kind of associated knowledge is specified. The following are some examples of knowledge elaboration.

- *Coarse → detailed   Coarse* (or roughly described) knowledge may be elaborated into *more detailed* (or more refined) knowledge.
- *Vague → precise   Vague* (or approximate) knowledge may be elaborated into more *precise* knowledge allowing finer discriminations.
- *Important → subsidiary   Important* knowledge may be elaborated into less important *subsidiary* knowledge.
- *Whole → parts   Knowledge* about some *whole* entity may be elaborated into knowledge about its *parts* (or components).
- *General → specific   General* (or abstract) knowledge may be elaborated into more *specific* (or more particular) knowledge.
- *Primary → implied   Primary* knowledge may be elaborated into *implied* (or derivable) knowledge. (Derivation is thus a special case of elaboration.)

The previous kinds of elaborations are not mutually exclusive. For example, elaboration of some general knowledge may lead to subordinate knowledge that is both more specific and less important.

9.4.2   Successive elaborations

Knowledge may be successively elaborated by elaborating some of this knowledge, then further elaborating some of this elaborated knowledge, then further elaborating some this elaborated knowledge, and so on. As illustrated in the previous geographical example, a small amount of knowledge can thus be used to subsume a much larger amount of subordinate knowledge.

The utility of such successive elaborations is apparent. By remembering only a small amount of central knowledge, a person can systematically retrieve much larger amounts of subordinate knowledge. In this way it becomes easier to remember and use large amounts of knowledge.

9.5 HIERARCHICAL KNOWLEDGE ORGANIZATION

The previous example of progressively more detailed maps can be generalized to suggest how successive elaborations can be used to organize knowledge so as to facilitate the retrieval of specific information.

9.5.1 Hierarchically clustered organization

A large amount of knowledge can be hierarchically partitioned into knowledge clusters. This can be done by starting with the most central knowledge cluster (indicated at the top of figure 9.6) and elaborating some of its knowledge elements into clusters of subordinate knowledge elements. In turn, some knowledge elements in each such cluster can then be elaborated into further subordinate knowledge clusters. This process can then be successively continued. The result of these successive elaborations is a hierarchical knowledge organization of the kind schematically illustrated in figure 9.6.

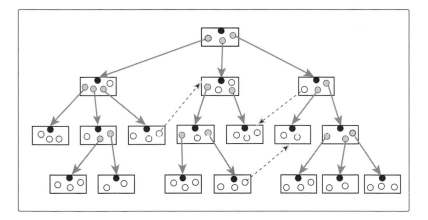

Figure 9.6
Hierarchically clustered knowledge organization.

For example, in the case of geographical information about the United States, the central knowledge cluster at the top of this figure might indicate a coarse map of the entire country. In this map, selected parts (indicated by the gray circles) are then elaborated into subordinate clusters representing more detailed maps. In this way, the entire geographical knowledge about the country is partitioned into progressively more detailed maps.

9.5.2 Auxiliary features

The following features can enhance the utility of a hierarchically clustered knowledge organization like that in figure 9.6.

Useful size of a cluster   Each knowledge cluster should be small enough that a person can easily deal with the knowledge contained in it. However, it should not be so small that the total number of clusters, needed to accommodate the entire knowledge, is so large that it becomes difficult to relate the knowledge distributed over many small clusters.

Internal organization of a cluster   It is helpful if the knowledge *within* each cluster is also organized in an easily manageable way. (For example, it might be organized hierarchically in some clusters, or organized in different useful ways in some other clusters.)

Overlapping clusters   It may help if some of the knowledge in a cluster is also contained in another cluster. (The boundary of a knowledge cluster may thus be fuzzy rather than sharply defined.) Such partly overlapping knowledge can be useful to relate the knowledge in different clusters.

For example, it is helpful if a map of the state of New York also indicates a small portion of the neighboring state of Connecticut. Drivers then will not become disoriented when crossing the border between the two states, but can readily see how a road shown in a map of one state continues into the next state.

Cross-references   Lastly, it may be helpful to include occasional *cross-references* (or *cross-links*) to clusters *not* interconnected by elaborating links. (Such cross-references are indicated by the dashed black arrows in figure 9.6.) These cross-references allow one to short-circuit the usual retrieval process that starts from the most central knowledge and proceeds along elaborating links. Instead, such a cross-reference allows one to go from a knowledge element in a branch to a knowledge cluster in another branch *without* the need to follow elaborating links only. (However, too many cross-references may hinder information retrieval because they convert the hierarchical structure of figure 9.6 into a network containing a jungle of indiscriminately many links.)

As a simple example, a map of Illinois is an elaboration of a map of the *midwestern* United States. Since this map shows the Ohio River emptying into the Mississippi River, it may include a cross-reference to the origin of the Ohio River in Pennsylvania (although Pennsylvania is an elaboration of a map of the *eastern* United States).

9.5.3 Task adaptation

A hierarchical knowledge organization, like that shown in figure 9.6, should be well adapted for retrieving the knowledge needed to perform the tasks of interest. Hence the most central knowledge should be chosen to be knowledge that is most *important* for the intended kinds of tasks. The elaborated subordinate knowledge clusters are then of correspondingly lesser importance for the relevant tasks. (In general, something is considered *important* to the extent that it helps, or that its absence hinders, the attainment of desired goals.)

The preceding comments imply that the knowledge about a domain should be organized differently depending on the particular kinds of tasks of interest. For example, knowledge about high-energy physics should be organized differently depending on whether one's main interest is in the fundamental physics principles or in the historical development of these principles.

Evidence for the benefits of a task-adapted knowledge organization

An experimental investigation (Eylon and Reif, 1984) showed that knowledge, when organized according to principles, facilitates the application of the knowledge; however, it does *not* facilitate the recall of the historical development of this knowledge. Conversely knowledge, when organized according to the historical development of the ideas, facilitates the recall of the intellectual history; however, it does *not* significantly help the application of these ideas.

9.5.4 Advantages of a hierarchically clustered organization

A knowledge organization, like that illustrated in figure 9.6, provides the following advantages.

Compact knowledge storage   It is relatively easy to remember hierarchically organized knowledge because all knowledge is then clearly embedded in more central knowledge. Remembering the knowledge in a few central knowledge clusters helps one then to elaborate this knowledge so as to access all subordinate knowledge.

Facilitation of selective retrieval   Specific information can be retrieved by a search process that starts with the most central knowledge and proceeds to subordinate clusters by successively deciding which links to follow. A decision at each branch point requires only a choice among a few options, and earlier decisions restrict the range of choices that need to be considered in subsequent decisions. Thus only relatively few decisions are needed to find any specific information.

High coherence   The knowledge organization of figure 9.6 allows one to accommodate any amount of detailed knowledge without losing sight of the global knowledge structure. Thus one can work locally, paying attention to all the necessary details, while remaining clearly aware of the global context. (For example, one can navigate through the streets of a particular city while still remaining fully aware of one's location within the United States or within a particular region of this country.)

Modifiability   When acquiring changed or additional knowledge about a topic, it is usually fairly easy to modify the preexisting knowledge organization to incorporate the new knowledge in it. (For example, one may merely have to add new knowledge that can also be subsumed by some preexisting more central knowledge.)

9.5.5   Coexistence of different knowledge organizations

Different organizations of the same knowledge may coexist without confusion if each one is used appropriately for the tasks for which it is most suited.

Examples of coexisting knowledge organizations

The files in a computer are ordinarily organized logically according to the kinds of content that they contain. But they may also be organized alphabetically according to their names or may be organized sequentially according to their dates of creation.

An atlas contains geographical information in the form of maps organized according to locations. However, it usually also contains an index where this information is organized in the form of an alphabetical list of place names.

A logical hierarchical organization of scientific knowledge may coexist with a simple associative network organization of knowledge about the same topic.

9.5.6   Using or creating a knowledge organization

After a knowledge organization (like that shown in figure 9.6) has been created, it can be effectively used to store information or to perform various tasks requiring the retrieval of specific information. As already mentioned, such tasks are usually best performed by starting from more central (higher-level) knowledge clusters and elaborating these to obtain more subordinate (lower-level) knowledge.

Creating an effective organization of some knowledge is a much more complex task than that of using such an organization. Thus one may not immediately know how to select the most central knowledge or how best to elaborate it. In this case, one may have to create the desired knowledge organization by a process of successive approximations. For example, one may sometimes proceed top-down by elaborating some central knowledge into subordinate knowledge. But at other times, one may proceed bottom-up by condensing some knowledge elements into more central knowledge from which they can be elaborated. In this way one may gradually create a useful hierarchical knowledge organization of the form indicated in figure 9.6.

The preceding comments illustrate the following general insights: (1) It is usually much more difficult to create a product than to use an existing one. (2) A particular product can be created by many different processes, but the examination of a product may reveal very little about the process whereby it was created.

Analogy: Using maps versus creating maps

Many people know how to use maps of a region and these can be very useful. However, it is much more difficult to *create* such maps. Indeed, the *creation* of a map involves a complex process of assembling and systematically organizing extensive information obtained from direct observations, from aerial photographs, and from survey measurements.

9.6   EXAMPLES OF HIERARCHICAL KNOWLEDGE ORGANIZATIONS

9.6.1   Geographical maps

As already mentioned, maps displaying geographical knowledge at different levels of detail (at different scales) represent a common example of hierarchically organized knowledge. Indeed, this example of maps can serve as a prototype illustrating useful aspects of *any* hierarchically organized knowledge.

9.6.2   Plans for a house

The plans, used by architects to design a house, provide a familiar example of hierarchically organized knowledge. Indeed, such plans commonly start with a sketchy drawing of the entire house. This drawing is then elaborated into more detailed drawings showing the different parts and rooms of the house. In turn, these drawings are elaborated further into even more detailed *blueprints* that also specify all relevant dimensions.

The construction workers, who actually build the house, rely heavily on these blueprints since these specify all the details that need to be implemented. But the sketchy drawings are still useful because they provide the workers with some awareness of the ultimate goal of their work. For example, they can help workers to detect whether some actions might be incompatible with the overall design. (Small incompatibilities can readily arise in a complex construction project since it may be difficult to foresee the consequences of all planned actions.) Even after a house has been built, all these plans may still be useful for its future maintenance. For example, they may help one to locate the origin of a water leak detected in some part of the house.

9.6.3   Hierarchical organization of sequential information

A particularly simple kind of knowledge describes a sequence of successive events (for example, a sequence of historical events or a sequence of successive steps in a procedure). As illustrated in figure 7.2, such a sequence can be described hierarchically as a series of major events that can be elaborated into more subordinate events. Indeed, as discussed in section 7.2.3, it can be helpful to specify a lengthy procedure by organizing it hierarchically as a sequence of major steps consisting of more minor steps.

9.6.4   Applications to public speaking

There are many occasions when one may need to speak to a group of people, to give a lecture, to talk about one's work, or to make some other oral presentation. Some people prepare themselves by writing

down everything that they plan to say and then simply read their prepared text to the audience. Although some individuals can do such
reading better than some others, the effect on the audience is often life-
less and boring. (There are good reasons why reading to children at
bedtime is a good way of lulling them to sleep.)

It is usually far preferable to *speak* to an audience rather than to read
to it. Speakers can then be more lively and spontaneous, pay more attention to the audience and its reactions, and adjust their behavior accordingly. But how can a speaker remember all that he or she wanted
to say?

It is useful to keep in mind the following points: (1) Speakers needs
to remember only the relevant ideas, but *not* any exact words (since
they are not trying to recite a poem or a Shakespeare play). (2) Persons
listening to a talk are likely to carry away only very few basic ideas,
even from a very long presentation. Thus a speaker must make sure
that the ideas that are taken away are actually the ones that the speaker
intended to convey.

Accordingly, a speaker can organize as talk in hierarchical fashion by
focusing only on the sequence of central ideas and on the ways that
these can be elaborated. These central ideas then provide a simple
framework than can be easily remembered—and that can then be elaborated during the talk with a spontaneity similar to that common during ordinary conversations. Furthermore, this kind of hierarchical
organization helps the speaker to emphasize only a *few* central ideas—
and these may then actually have a chance of being remembered by
the audience.

9.6.5 Hierarchical organization of some scientific knowledge

It is often useful to organize scientific knowledge in hierarchical
form. For purposes of illustration, the following paragraphs indicate
a useful hierarchical organization of basic mechanics (the science
of motion), an important topic in most physics courses. This mechanics knowledge is also fairly typical of other kinds of knowledge encountered in physics, mathematics, engineering, or other scientific
fields.

The following paragraphs illustrate an effective organization of a
substantial field of scientific knowledge (mechanics), but do *not* expect
a reader to have any prior knowledge about this field or to learn usable
physics knowledge about it. They merely indicate how such complex

knowledge can be organized in a hierarchical fashion far different from the "formula sheets" (mentioned in section 8.5.3) where mere lists of equations are used to summarize this knowledge in the appendix of a typical physics textbook (Ohanian, 1985). The illustrated hierarchical knowledge organization also contains a few equations that express some important relationships in precise form. But these equations are embedded in a more meaningful qualitative framework that reveals the underlying structure of the knowledge—and thus makes all this knowledge easier to remember and to use.

For the sake of simplicity, the following mechanics knowledge deals only with the motion of relatively small objects ("particles"). But this knowledge can readily be extended to larger objects and, although it is then slightly more complex, it is essentially of the same form.

Central knowledge about mechanics   As indicated in figure 9.7, the most central knowledge about mechanics consists of the following three parts.

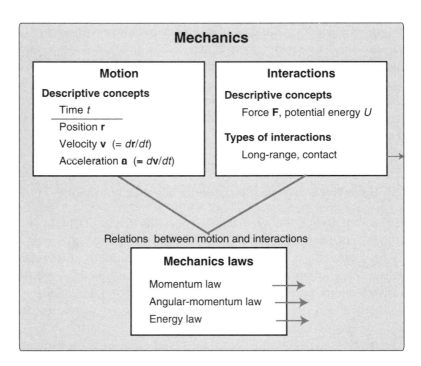

Figure 9.7
Central knowledge about mechanics.

1. Knowledge about motion This specifies how motion can be described by concepts such as *position, velocity* (the rate of change of position with time), and *acceleration* (the rate of change of velocity with time).

2. Knowledge about interactions This specifies that interactions between objects can be described by the concept *force* or the concept *potential energy.* It also specifies that interactions can be of two types— either *long-range interactions* (interactions, such as gravitational interactions, that can be appreciable even when two objects are far apart) or *contact interactions* (interactions that are appreciable only when two object are so close that they "touch" each other).

3. Knowledge about the relation between motion and interactions This is the most crucially important knowledge since it allows useful predictions and explanations about many observable phenomena. (For example, a knowledge of the interactions between objects allows one to predict how they will move. Conversely, a knowledge of the motions of objects allows one to determine how they interact with each other.) As indicated in figure 9.7, this knowledge about the relation between motion and interactions can usefully be expressed in terms of three interrelated principles (*mechanics laws*).

Elaborations of the central mechanics knowledge Figure 9.7 indicates (by the gray arrows) that the knowledge about interactions can be elaborated by more detailed subordinate knowledge. This knowledge (not displayed here) specifies precisely how the interaction between two objects depends on their properties and on the distance between them.

Figure 9.7 also indicates that each of the basic mechanics laws can be quantitatively elaborated. (Only two of these three elaborated knowledge clusters are displayed in figure 9.8.) Each of these laws relates motion and interactions, but describes these in different ways. For example, the momentum law in figure 9.8 describes motion by the concept *momentum* and describes interactions by the concept *force*. On the other hand, the energy law in figure 9.8 describes motion by the concept *kinetic energy* and describes interactions by the concepts *potential energy* and *work*. (The work W_{oth} is work done by forces *other* than those included in the potential energy U.) Figure 9.8 also indicates that, although each of these mechanics laws is valid under similar conditions, each is more useful under some conditions than under others.

Advantages of this knowledge organization This organization of mechanics knowledge reveals its underlying simplicity. In particular, it

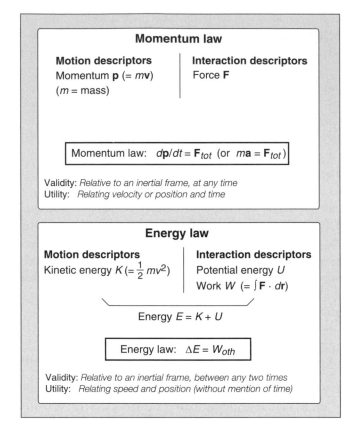

Figure 9.8
Elaborations of the momentum and energy laws.

indicates that this entire knowledge is centrally concerned with the relation between motion and interactions. Each of the three mechanics laws merely introduces a few convenient definitions to express this relation in a somewhat different form. These three laws have an impressive amount of predictive power (illustrated by their wide-ranging applications in physics and engineering). Indeed, the study of these laws can easily require more than a semester course.

Note that this mechanics knowledge is *not* organized around formulas (although some equations embedded in the knowledge are used to express important relationships compactly in precise form). Indeed, when the solution of a mechanics problem requires various decisions, the main decisions can usually be made on the basis of *qualitative* considerations. For example, unless one is merely interested in relating different descriptions of motion or different descriptions of interaction, one simply needs to invoke one of the three mechanics laws relating motion and interaction. Not only is it then rather easy to decide among these three alternatives, but accompanying *utility conditions* (indicated in figure 9.8) provide helpful advice about when a particular law is likely to be useful.

A coherent knowledge organization, like that illustrated in the preceding paragraphs, has many advantages. (1) It is easily elaborated in much greater detail so that it can be applied to solve diverse mechanics problems. (2) It can readily be generalized to deal with systems consisting of many particles (for example, to deal with the motions of rigid bodies) and its basic structure then remains very similar. (3) It can even be extended to more advanced (graduate-school) mechanics by introducing other descriptors of motion and interaction (such as so-called *Lagrangian* and *Hamiltonian* functions). (4) This organization makes apparent a highly coherent knowledge structure that makes learning appreciably easier.

9.7 EDUCATIONAL IMPLICATIONS

9.7.1 Proficient performers

The knowledge of expert scientists is usually highly coherent and often organized in hierarchical fashion. For example, physicists' knowledge of mechanics or electromagnetism is subsumed by a few well-identified unifying principles that the scientists can elaborate in much greater detail. Such an organization helps to ensure the consistency of the entire knowledge and greatly facilitates the ease with which the knowledge can be remembered and appropriately retrieved.

Example of scientists' knowledge organization

One of my colleagues (Jill Larkin) once investigated how expert scientists would deal with problems that they had not encountered for a long time. Hence she gave several physics professors a specific problem involving the "Doppler effect" (the effect describing how the perceived pitch of a sound changes if the observer is moving through the air relative to the source of sound). She carefully chose professors who were *not* engaged in research where the Doppler effect is relevant and who had recently *not* taught any physics course involving a discussion of this effect.

All of the experts qualitatively recognized that this problem involved the Doppler effect, but *none* remembered the formula specifying how the change of pitch depends on the speed of the observer relative to the source. But *all* of them could use their central knowledge about wave propagation to figure out an equation relating the relative speed to the resultant change of pitch—and could thus solve the problem.

However, there were significant individual differences in the way that the experts elaborated their central knowledge to obtain the needed equation. Some of them made a drawing of a propagating wave and then used it to ascertain how the motion affects the spacing between successive crests of the detected wave. But some other experts proceeded purely quantitatively by writing down an equation describing a propagating wave, writing another equation describing the relative motion, and then combining these equations.

9.7.2   Inexperienced students

As mentioned at the beginning of this chapter, the knowledge of inexperienced students is often rather fragmentary and poorly organized, consisting of concepts and ideas only loosely related to each other. For example, most students' knowledge of mechanics consists mostly of various equations. (Very few students have their knowledge coherently organized around motion and interactions in a form resembling that outlined in section 9.6.5.) Their fragmented knowledge can easily lead students to misapplications and is also not readily remembered after significant periods of time.

Example: Students' fragmented knowledge about area

Fragmented knowledge is common among many students. For example, science or engineering students in college courses have often only a fragmentary knowledge of the concept of area that they learned back in elementary school. For instance, when asked about the meaning of area, many students simply say that it is "length times width" (a memorized formula which is only applicable to a rectangle). But most students are mystified when asked how they would apply their knowledge to find the surface area of a bronze statue of a man on horseback. Indeed, what then is the relevant length and width? In fact, many students don't seem to have a general conception of the area of a surface. By the same token, they also have no idea how to answer the following question: "How much larger would be the surface area of this statue if the statue were twice as large (that is, twice as wide, twice as deep, and twice as tall)?"

Most students know formulas for finding the areas of some simple figures (like rectangles, parallelograms, and triangles), but often don't know how these areas are interrelated or how to find the area of one from a knowledge of the area of another. College students may remember that the area A of a circle of radius r can be found by using the formula $A = \pi r^2$, but may have no idea about how to find this area if they forget this formula. Furthermore, when asked "What is π?," most students say that "π is 3.14." But when asked "What is the *meaning* of π?," quite a few students cannot tell that π denotes the ratio of the circumference of a circle to its diameter.

9.7.3 Common instructional deficiencies

Most instructors or textbooks pay much more attention to the content of conveyed knowledge than to its organization. Even when knowledge is locally well organized in a lecture or chapter, there is little effort to organize the entire knowledge globally. Thus the task of organizing a student's *entire* acquired knowledge is left largely to the student. This is often a rather difficult task. (Even highly experienced individuals may find it difficult to organize a complex body of knowledge in a coherent and easily remembered form.) The net result is that many students' acquired knowledge often remains poorly organized.

We often suffer from the delusion that knowledge transmitted to another person is actually communicated to that person. The situation is well illustrated by the cartoon in figure 9.9 which shows a policeman giving directions to a pedestrian. Because the policeman's knowledge is embedded in a well-organized framework, he can easily recall relevant information and transmit it to the pedestrian. But all this new information largely overwhelms the pedestrian. Thus the information actually communicated to him consists mostly of a jumble of unfamiliar facts that cannot be readily incorporated within a coherent knowledge organization. Hence the pedestrian is left largely bewildered and is likely to need further information after he takes a few more steps.

The cartoon of figure 9.9 should serve as a warning that even well organized knowledge, transmitted by a teacher, can easily result in highly fragmented knowledge in a student's mind.

Instructors themselves may sometimes convey knowledge in a poorly organized form and thus contribute to students' difficulties. For example, section 8.5.3 already mentioned a textbook's inordinate emphasis on formulas and its summarization of physics knowledge in the form of long formula lists.

9.7.4 Communication and knowledge organization

The cartoon in figure 9.9 illustrates the following important lesson: *transmitting information is not the same as communicating.* Indeed, there are several reasons why human communication can be deficient and may easily be unreliable or faulty.

Figure 9.9
Cartoon showing a policeman giving directions to a pedestrian. (© The New Yorker Collection 1976 James Stevenson from cartoonbank.com. All rights reserved.)

A person's knowledge structure consists of an organized assembly of knowledge components. Communicating information to some other person (or teaching something to another person) thus requires that one modifies the other person's knowledge structure appropriately so that this person can behave in some new kinds of ways.

Analysis of a communication process Communication involves a *transmitter* of information (for example, a teacher or the policeman in the cartoon of figure 9.9) and a *receiver* of that information (for example, a student or the pedestrian in the cartoon). The *transmitter* of the information must have a well-organized knowledge structure from which he or she can retrieve some relevant parts to transmit to the receiver. Conversely, the *receiver* must have some preexisting knowledge structure which can be suitably modified.

Common communication difficulties The following kinds of communication difficulties may then easily arise, either because of deficiencies due to the transmitter, due to the receiver, or due to both of them.

Transmitter does not convey well-structured information. The transmitter (even when his or her own knowledge is well organized) may not convey information that is sufficiently well organized to facilitate the receiver's acquisition of this information. (For example, the transmitter may merely ramble or verbalize whatever comes to mind.) Furthermore, the transmitter may have little of no knowledge of the receiver's knowledge structure and may thus not know how to adapt the conveyed information appropriately to the receiver.

Transmitter fails to convey some relevant information. The transmitter may fail to convey some relevant information because it seems "obvious" (so familiar that it has become tacit knowledge outside the range of the transmitter's conscious awareness).

Transmitter erroneously believes that he has communicated all relevant information. The transmitter unjustifiably *assumes* (without checking) that he or she has conveyed all the needed information—and that the receiver has understood it properly.

Receiver pays inadequate attention. The receiver may pay insufficient attention to the transmitted information and may thus fail to notice important features of it. (For example, the receiver may fail to notice some validity conditions or qualifying adjectives attached to the information.)

Receiver has no relevant preexisting knowledge structure. The receiver may have no preexisting knowledge structure to which the received information can be readily connected. Thus this new information cannot be encoded in a form that can be effectively retained. Hence the receiver (for example, the pedestrian in the cartoon) remembers only very little of the transmitted information and may soon need to acquire it again.

Receiver's knowledge structure is incompatible with the transmitted information. The receiver's preexisting knowledge structure may be ill-adapted to, or even incompatible with, the conveyed information. (For example, the receiver may have beliefs or ideologies conflicting with this information.) The received information may then not be acquired, but may be rejected or distorted.

Receiver may misinterpret or misunderstand some of the transmitted information. In this case the receiver's knowledge is not modified in the intended ways—so that the communication has been unsuccessful.

Need for communication checks   The preceding list of possible communication deficiencies should be sufficient to indicate why human communication is often fallible. Hence it is always important to check explicitly whether any communicated information has actually been acquired by the receiver. For example, this can be done by asking the receiver to repeat the conveyed information in his or her own words— or by asking the receiver to answer some probing questions about this information.

9.7.5 Instructional suggestions

As much attention must be paid to the organization of knowledge as to its content. When trying to convey a body of knowledge, teachers should attempt to develop explicitly, and then gradually expand, a well-organized knowledge structure that students can actively use. In this way, a student's knowledge can be well organized at every stage— and can be gradually reorganized as more knowledge is acquired. The student can then begin to appreciate the advantages of well-organized knowledge and can consistently practice using such knowledge. This way of proceeding is much better than letting students acquire new knowledge in piecemeal fashion—so that they are afterward left with the need to reorganize all this knowledge at the end.

It is advisable to teach successively the following increasingly so-phisticated skills of knowledge organization:

1. Teach the utility of good organization Demonstrate the utility of a good knowledge organization and explain why such an organization can be very helpful.

2. Teach how to use a good knowledge organization When introducing new knowledge, summarize this knowledge in an explicit well-organized form of important definitions and principles (described qual-itatively and quantitatively). Then demonstrate how this knowledge can be effectively used for various tasks. Finally, ask students to answer all questions, solve all problems, and justify all their arguments by al-ways starting from this summary of well-organized knowledge (rather than by appealing to miscellaneous results or formulas retrieved from a textbook).

3. Teach how to generate a good knowledge organization Organizing originally poorly structured knowledge can be a difficult task that tran-scends the abilities of most students in introductory courses. However, the task *can* be accomplished if the students are properly assisted so that they become active participants in the process. For example, such teaching can be effectively done as a part of problem solving (Bagno and Eylon, 1997).

9.8   SUMMARY

• The organization of knowledge is very important since it determines how readily the knowledge can be remembered, appropriately retrieved, kept consistent, communicated to others, and extended beyond its original scope.

• Knowledge can be elaborated in various ways by specifying additional knowledge associated with it. A hierarchical knowledge organization displays knowledge in the form of successive elaborations.

• Hierarchical forms of knowledge organization are particularly useful (especially in science) for organizing large amounts of knowledge in a compact, coherent, and readily elaborated form that facilitates the retrieval of specific information. (A familiar example is the organization of geographical knowledge in the form of maps elaborated at increasing levels of detail.)

• The organization of knowledge must be well adapted for the performance of the intended kinds of tasks.

• Instructional efforts need to pay as much attention to the organization of acquired knowledge as to its content.

II-C Flexibility

10   Making Decisions

The preceding chapters discussed ways of achieving effective performance by using methods, descriptions, and organizations that are appropriate for particular tasks. But although such performance may be effective, it may be quite inflexible. For example, if conditions slightly change or unforeseen difficulties arise, a known method may no longer be applicable. How then can one figure out what to do? Or how can one devise methods for dealing with previously unfamiliar tasks?

As indicated in figure 2.3, this portion of the book (chapters 10 through 13) discusses how it is possible to achieve greater flexibility. Thus it examines how one can make appropriate decisions and how such decisions help to deal with problems of various complexity. Indeed, problem solving is of great importance in all the sciences as well as in everyday life.

When a task is performed by implementing a procedure, every specified action is followed by another prescribed action. More flexible performance can clearly be achieved if an action may be followed by one of *several* possible actions. But then one needs to *decide* which particular action to choose among several alternative options.

Since some options may be more useful than others, it is important to make decisions leading to desirable results. Such decisions may be difficult since they may require a consideration of many competing factors and may have consequences that cannot be readily foreseen. The challenge then is to make good decisions ensuring desirable outcomes—and to avoid poor decisions leading to detrimental results. Such decision making is clearly necessary to achieve flexible performance. It is also highly important for dealing with many situations arising in everyday life and with many tasks encountered in scientific or other complex domains.

The present chapter discusses some ways of making sensible decisions. In particular, it examines the following questions: (1) How do simple decisions differ from complex decisions that require an identification and careful evaluation of potential options? (2) What is a systematic decision process that can help to ensure that no significant issues are ignored? (3) What are common decision deficiencies, and how can some of these be avoided? (4) How can one efficiently make the many practical decisions commonly encountered in everyday life and in scientific work?

Educational relevance   Decision making is widely important. For example, students often need to make decisions with far-reaching implications for their lives. They may have to decide which particular college or graduate school to attend, which career to pursue, which field to choose as a major, which courses to select, how to obtain the money to sustain themselves during their studies, and how to make many other decisions in their personal lives. In quite a few of these cases, students' decisions are made somewhat haphazardly rather than with systematic care.

Many other student decisions are less consequential, but important for their work and learning. For example, students may have to decide which method to choose to solve a problem or to perform an experiment—or what to study to remedy detected deficiencies in their knowledge. In such cases, students often fail to identify some available options, don't adequately examine their probable consequences, make poorly considered choices, or get stuck not knowing what to do. Hence it is clearly desirable that students learn to make decisions in better ways.

10.1   IMPORTANCE OF DECISION MAKING

10.1.1   Wide prevalence of decision making

All of us repeatedly need to choose among alternative possible actions. Thus we are constantly making decisions and are constantly affected by the decisions made by other people. These decisions can lead to successes or failures, to beneficial consequences or to irremediable harm. Hence it is important to make thoughtful decisions and to be aware of their possible consequences. (Even a decision to do nothing is a decision—a choice to ignore all possible alternatives.)

Decisions and their consequences   Many of our decisions have only minor consequences, but some may have far-reaching implications. For example, they may determine the work projects that we pursue, the ideas that we adopt or discard, or the choice of our career and of our spouse.

Our decisions can also have important effects on other persons. For example, they can help them or hurt them—or ignore them while we attend to our own narrow interests. Furthermore, all of us are affected by the decisions made by many other people. For example, we are affected by the decisions made by our parents early in our lives, by the decisions of schools to admit us, by the decisions of employers to hire us, or by the decisions of politicians to engage in wars that may cause the deaths of millions of people.

10.1.2   Decision making as an important cognitive skill

Decision making is not only important in everyday life, in work, and in politics. It is also crucially important in all scientific or engineering fields since these require good problem-solving abilities and since decision making is essential for all problem solving.

Since decision making is such a widely important cognitive skill, it is useful to gain a better understanding of it. For example, what are the underlying thought processes involved in decision making? How can one make decisions systematically to ensure outcomes that are more desirable than those attainable by haphazard approaches? How can one avoid mistakes leading to poor decisions?

The answers to such questions may help one to improve decision making and thereby achieve better performance in problem solving, in scientific work, and also in everyday life. The rest of this chapter is, therefore, devoted to a discussion of decision processes.

10.1.3   Basic decision process

Any decision implies the existence of two or more *options* (alternative possible actions) among which one needs to choose a particular one. Accordingly, one must (1) identify the available options, (2) assess the options according to some specified criteria, and (3) choose a selected option. After that, it is necessary to implement this option.

Figure 10.1
Basic decision process.

This basic decision process is summarized in figure 10.1. The complexity of such a decision process can, however, differ widely depending on the difficulties of identifying and assessing the available options. Thus it is useful to distinguish simple decisions from more complex decisions requiring careful thought.

10.2   KINDS OF DECISIONS

10.2.1   Simple decisions

Some commonly occurring decisions are simple because the available options are clear and the choice criteria are well specified by definite rules. The decision process is then straightforward and yields some uniquely determined choice. One can then also clearly assess whether such a decision is right or wrong.

Examples of simple decisions

Deciding what to do at an intersection   When coming to an intersection with a traffic light, a driver has three clearly specified options—continue driving, slow down, or stop. The choice criteria involve the following well-known rules that depend on the color of the traffic light: If the light is green, go on; if it is yellow, slow down; and if it is red, stop.

Hence the driver merely needs to assess the prevailing color of the traffic light and to follow the directions specified by these rules. The result is then a clear choice.

Deciding where to go for an examination   Students have been given written directions specifying the location of their final examination, which is to be given either in room 203 or in room 207. These directions also specify that students, whose last names start with a letter between *A* and *L*, should go to room 203—and that students, whose last names start with a letter between *M* and *Z*, should go to room 207.

The two pertinent options are thus clear and the choice criteria are well specified. A student then merely needs to assess in which range the starting letter of his or her last name belongs—and can then make the corresponding choice.

10.2.2 Complex decisions

Complex (or *judicious*) decisions are those that require careful judgments because neither the available options nor the choice criteria may be explicitly specified. (Only the goal of the decision may be reasonably clear.)

Hence such complex decisions may require appreciable thought. For example, the available options may need to be identified, and the choice criteria may require judgments depending on personal knowledge and individual preferences. Correspondingly, there is also no uniquely *right* decision (for example, different persons facing the same situation may reasonably make different decisions).

Such complex decisions can be much more difficult than simple rule-based decisions, but they are the most common and most important decisions needed in everyday life, in scientific work, and in most other fields of endeavor. The following example illustrates that even a seemingly simple decision may be complex and involve delicate judgments.

Simple example of a complex decision: Choosing a restaurant

Suppose that the time is getting close to noon and you need to decide where to eat lunch. What are your options for possible restaurants? Since these options have not been specified, you yourself need to identify some sensible options.

You certainly could not consider *all* possible restaurants listed in the telephone book. (The required amount of time and effort would be prohibitive and would not be justified by the resulting benefits.) Thus you would probably be quite content to identify only two or three seemingly sensible restaurant options.

How then would you select a particular one of these? Although you have no prescribed criteria, the following guideline is helpful: Assess how useful each of the few identified options would be to you, and then choose the seemingly most useful of these options. Accordingly, you would proceed to assess these options, using your judgment to consider their anticipated advantages and disadvantages (such as cost, quality of food, and waiting time). After weighing these relative advantages and disadvantages, you would then arrive at a choice of the restaurant that seems best to you.

There are several reasons why the decision process used in the preceding example is considerably more complex than that used in a simple decision. (1) The relevant options have *not* been specified, so that one must identify these by searching for potentially useful options. (2) These options must then be carefully assessed according to some sensible choice criteria (such as selecting the seemingly best of the assessed options). (3) This assessment needs to consider factual information about anticipated consequences, as well as purely personal preferences. (4) The assessment needs to weigh the relative advantages and disadvantages of all the considered options.

The preceding assessment is far from straightforward since it may require uncertain predictions about expected consequences and somewhat uncertain judgments about individual preferences. Hence such a decision does *not* lead to a uniquely right choice (although some choices may, in retrospect, be judged better than others). Furthermore, different people, faced with the same decision, may well arrive at different choices.

Note also that this kind of complex decision cannot realistically aim to make the *best possible* choice. Indeed, that would be impossible for human beings with limited time and limited mental abilities. Instead, the aim is rather to achieve a sufficiently *satisfactory* choice. In other words, such a decision process does not aim to optimize, but to *satisfice*. (This verb, first introduced by Herbert Simon in 1956, has by now become sufficiently common to be listed in some dictionaries, such as *Webster's New World Dictionary*.)

10.3   MAKING COMPLEX DECISIONS

Careful decisions require systematic thought. Since complex decisions deal with options and choice criteria that are only loosely specified, a generally useful decision process can *not* be described by a completely specified decision method (that is, by an *algorithm* that guarantees a good choice). But one can specify a decision *strategy* that is *heuristic* (so that it offers useful advice increasing the likelihood of making a good choice.)

10.3.1   Analytic decision strategy

The decision strategy summarized in figure 10.2 elaborates the basic decision process of figure 10.1 so as to facilitate complex decisions. This strategy is analytic since it specifies explicit thinking about all relevant issues. However, it does *not* aim to achieve the unrealistic goal of obtaining the best possible choice, but merely aims to achieve a *satisfactory* choice. Correspondingly, it does *not* make unrealistic demands of identifying all possible options, of predicting their consequences with certitude, or of assessing purely personal values and preferences with complete reliability.

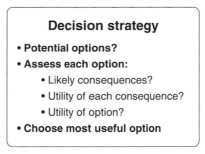

Figure 10.2
Analytic decision strategy.

As outlined in figure 10.2, this decision strategy involves three major steps—identifying potential options, assessing these carefully, and then choosing the seemingly most useful of them. These steps are described more fully in the following paragraphs.

1. Identifying potential options If potential options are not already known, one must search to find suitable ones—particularly, options that are likely to help attain desired goals. (Alternatively, one may identify obstacles that hinder the attainment of such desirable goals—and then try to find options that help to overcome these obstacles.)

It is sufficient to identify only a *few* such potential options. (One cannot realistically identify *all* possible options). The subsequent assessment of these few options then helps one to select the seemingly most useful among them.

2. Assessing each option One needs to assess each option to determine its expected utility. This assessment involves the following subsidiary steps:

· *Likely consequences* Try to predict the important consequences likely to ensue as a result of implementing each option.

· *Utility of each consequence* Assess the expected *utility* of each such consequence. This utility is merely an estimate of how useful this consequence seems to one—and may involve the decision maker's purely personal judgments or preferences. (Utilities provide thus a way whereby nonrational or emotional factors can be incorporated in a rational decision process.)

The utility U of a consequence may be specified numerically according to some convenient scale (like the one indicated in figure 10.3). Useful consequences can be described by a positive utility, and harmful

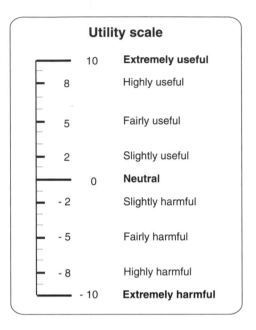

Figure 10.3
Convenient specification of utilities.

consequences by a negative utility. The utility may thus range all the way from extremely useful ($U = 10$) down to extremely harmful ($U = -10$). A neutral utility ($U = 0$) then is neither useful nor harmful. Figure 10.3 also indicates verbal descriptions of intermediate values of the utility.

Other utilities can also be described by words. For example, $U = 9$ denotes a utility that is *very highly* useful (since it is considered larger than highly useful, but smaller than extremely useful). Similarly, $U = 7$ denotes a utility that is somewhat less than highly useful.

Specifying utilities by numbers, rather than by descriptive words, makes it easier to compare relative utilities. However, the use of numbers should *not* convey a misleading sense of precision or obscure the fact that utilities are merely rough estimates of personal judgments. Hence there is also no need for unduly precise estimates of utilities.

· *Utility of an option*   The utility of an *option* is simply equal to the sum of the utilities of all its expected consequences.

3. Choosing the most useful option   To arrive at a sensible decision, one needs then merely to choose the most useful of all the assessed options.

Options	Consequences	Utility	Option utility
College A	Very good education	8	4
	Somewhat expensive	- 4	
College B	Fairly good education	5	7
	Close to home	2	

Figure 10.4
John's college decision.

10.3.2 Example: Deciding between two colleges

To illustrate the preceding decision process, consider the simple example of John who is trying to decide which of two colleges he should attend. His considerations are summarized in the table of figure 10.4. Thus John believes that attending college A would provide him with a very good education (a consequence that he rates to have a utility $U = 8$). But this option A would also be somewhat expensive (a somewhat undesirable consequence that he rates to have a negative utility $U = -4$).

John's other option, attending college B, would probably provide him with a somewhat less useful education (one that he rates to have a utility $U = 5$). On the other hand, this option B would have the slight advantage of his being closer to home (a consequence that he rates to have a utility $U = 2$).

All of John's considerations are summarized in figure 10.4. By considering each option and adding the utilities of all its consequences, John finds that the utility of option B is somewhat larger than that of option A. Hence he concludes that it would be more sensible to attend college B than to attend college A.

10.4 MORE REFINED OPTION ASSESSMENTS

The preceding section implicitly assumed that all expected consequences are equally likely. However, when some consequences are more probable than others, one needs to pay more attention to those likely to occur more frequently than to those occurring only rarely.

10.4.1   Important distinctions

Utility and desirability   When a consequence is certain to occur, its utility is the same as its desirability. But more generally, the utility of a consequence depends also on its probability of occurrence. For example, winning ten million dollars in a lottery is a consequence of extremely high *desirability*. But the probability of winning is so small that the *utility* of this consequence is actually very small.

Conversely, it is highly undesirable to die in an airplane crash (that is, the *desirability* of this consequence is negative and has a very large magnitude). But the probability of a crash is so small that the *utility* of this consequence is only slightly negative (and thus easily surpassed by the positive utilities associated with all the other advantages of airplane travel).

Specification of desirability   The desirability D of a consequence can, like the utility U, be specified numerically on a scale like that indicated in figure 10.5. Thus this scale extends from $D = 10$ (extremely desirable) down to $D = -10$ (extremely undesirable), while $D = 0$ indicates a desirability which is neutral (i.e., neither desirable nor undesirable).

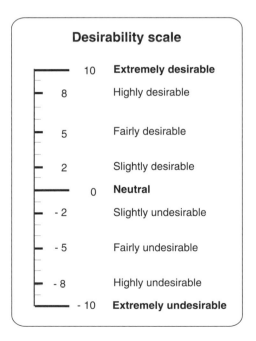

Figure 10.5
Convenient specification of desirabilities.

Specification of probability The probability of occurrence of some event is conventionally specified on a scale like that indicated in figure 10.6. Thus this probability ranges from $P = 1$ (extremely probable or almost certain) down to $P = 0$ (extremely improbable or almost never occurring).

General specification of utility The utility U of a consequence can then be defined as its desirability multiplied by its probability: $U = D \times P$ or

$$\text{Utility} = \text{Desirability} \times \text{Probability}.$$

For example, one might believe that winning ten million dollars in a lottery is exceedingly desirable (for example, that its *desirability* is even larger than 10). But the probability of winning is so small that the *utility* of this consequence would actually be very small.

As pointed out in section 10.3.1, the utility of an option depends on the utilities of all its expected consequences. More careful assessments of the utility of each consequence thus lead to correspondingly improved assessments of the utility of every option.

10.4.2 Example: Deciding how to get a car

Mary needs a car and must decide how she can get one. She can think of the following options: buy a new car, buy a used car, or get her father's old car as a gift if he buys himself a new one. She assesses

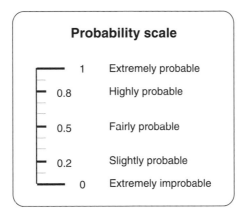

Figure 10.6
Specification of probabilities.

Options	Consequences	Desirability D	Probability P	Utility $= D \times P$ U	Option utility U_{op}
Buy new car	Have a reliably good car	8	1	8	3.2
	Lack money for next year	- 6	0.8	- 4.8	
Buy old car	Have an adequate car	5	1	5	5
Get gift of car	Have good car at no cost	8	0.5	4	4

Figure 10.7
Mary's car decision.

these three options in the ways described in the following paragraphs and summarized in figure 10.7.

• *Buying a new car* In this case Mary is certain $(P = 1)$ that she would have a reliably good car, something that she considers highly desirable $(D = 8)$. On the other hand, it is then highly probable $(P = 0.8)$ that she would lack money to live comfortably next year, a consequence that she considers more than fairly undesirable $(D = -6)$. The utility of this option would then be $U = D \times P = -4.8$.

• *Buying a used car* Mary is quite certain $(P = 1)$ that she could buy such a used car at a reasonable cost. She would then have an adequate car with possible maintenance problems, a situation that she considers only fairly desirable $(D = 5)$.

• *Getting the car as a gift from her father* This option would, of course, be highly desirable $(D = 8)$ since Mary would then get a well-maintained car at no cost. On the other hand, there is only a 50 percent probability $(P = 0.5)$ that her father would soon buy a new car for himself and give her his old one. The utility of this option would then be $U = D \times P = 8 \times (0.5) = 4$.

As illustrated in figure 10.7, the utility of each of Mary's options can be obtained by adding the utilities of all of its consequences. It is then clear that the second option has the highest utility. Thus Mary's most sensible decision would be to buy a used car.

10.5 LIMITATIONS OF ANALYTIC DECISIONS

An analytic decision process, based on a careful analysis of available options, increases the likelihood of making a sensible choice, but does *not* necessarily lead to a good decision. In particular, such a decision process has some intrinsic limitations and may also suffer from deficiencies that can be reduced by sufficient care.

10.5.1 Intrinsic limitations of decision making

Even the most careful decision processes have some of the following intrinsic limitations.

Limited ability to identify all potential options A person cannot be sure to identify *all* potentially useful options. For example, some available options may be missed simply because one fails to think of them. This may be particularly true if some imagination is required to identify possible options that are unconventional or have not been considered in the past.

Limited predictive power None of us is able to predict future consequences with great certainty. We may try to exploit all our available knowledge, try to imagine what is likely to happen, or try to mentally simulate a sequence of expected events. Yet we may easily fail to anticipate some consequences or misjudge their likelihoods. Unintended consequences are thus likely to occur and may sometimes even vitiate our original intent. [This is what Tenner (1997) calls *the revenge of unintended consequences.*]

Limited ability to judge desirabilities Judgments of desirabilities are subjective. Individuals may not be able to assess them properly because they are not fully aware of their own personal values and preferences. Indeed, such personal values may sometimes become clearer only in retrospect. Furthermore, desirabilities may also be context-dependent (so that they may be assessed differently in the current context than in the context prevailing after a decision).

10.5.2 Avoidable decision deficiencies

On the other hand, the following are some common decision deficiencies that *can* be reduced with sufficient care.

Thoughtless decisions   Decisions, made with little or no thought, can easily result in undesirable consequences. The following are some examples.

• Haphazard decisions leading to nearly random choices.

• Intuitive decisions merely based on gut feelings, without any further thought.

• Decisions stemming from blind imitation (so that one simply does what others do and just follows the crowd).

• Decisions based on mindless persistence or inertia—so that one merely continues to do what one has been doing. (A decision to do *nothing* is also a significant decision since it automatically eliminates any other alternatives.)

Ill-considered decisions   Decisions can be made with some thought, but without properly considering some important issues. Examples of such decision deficiencies include the following:

• Failure to identify some potential options.

• Inadequate effort to predict the consequences of a decision or the probabilities of their occurrence.

• Inadequate assessment of the expected utilities of these consequences.

• Incorrect determination of the relative utilities of identified options.

Biased or faulty judgments   Inadequate thought can lead to faulty judgments that are biased because some relevant situations are more salient or more easily imagined. The following are some common examples (Plous, 1993; Kahneman, Slovic, and Tversky, 1982).

• *Representativeness*   A particular set of cases may be viewed as representative of *all* cases. (1) For example, if a coin is thrown 10 times, this sample of 10 throws may be viewed as representative of very many throws. This may lead to the naive (but wrong) belief that heads should be shown by five of the ten coins. If the first nine successive throws show heads, one may then be led to expect that the tenth throw will show tails. (This erroneous conclusion is called the *gambler's fallacy*.) (2) More generally, specific situations are naively viewed as more likely than more abstract general situations because they are more representative of the way that we imagine particular situations.

• *Availability*   People commonly pay undue attention to situations that are easily imagined or that have been recently encountered). (1)

Doctors may wrongly diagnose a particular illness as a case of the flu because they have recently seen many patients suffering from the flu. (2) Because fires, floods, earthquakes, or murders are often reported in newspapers, they are more often feared as causes of death than a disease like diabetes. (3) Case histories are often more persuasive than more abstract statistical information.

• *Anchoring* When making decisions, people preferentially tend to use the information that they encounter first—and then latch on to it without much further thought. (1) For example, after a doctor arrives at a diagnosis, he or she often tends to confirm it rather than to explore possible alternatives. (This is called *confirmation bias.*) (2) After having been shown expensive houses first, a buyer considers other houses reasonably priced; but after having seen cheaper houses first, a buyer tends to think that other houses are unduly expensive.

• *Attribution* People's decisions may be affected by the causes that they attribute to observed phenomena. (1) For example, if a man is shabbily dressed, a doctor may be inclined to believe that he is an alcoholic and probably suffering from kidney damage. (2) A teacher who believes that a student's difficulties are due to situational factors will try to modify the situation. But one who believes that the difficulties are due to the student's lack of motivation or diligence will try to modify the student's attitudes and behaviors.

• *Personal or emotional factors* (1) Factual assessments can easily be affected by personal hopes or preferences. For example, undue optimism can lead people to overestimate the probabilities of desirable consequences and to underestimate the probabilities of undesirable consequences. (2) Similarly, overconfidence can cause people to consider demanding options while ignoring some that might be more easily implemented.

Decisions misguided by misconceptions or prejudices Even well-considered decisions can be made with inappropriate thinking leading to poor judgments. The following are some examples.

• Ill-founded beliefs or ideologies can easily obscure or distort factual information.

• Preconceptions or prejudices may unjustifiably rule out some available options or cause inappropriate judgments of their consequences.

• The importance of purely personal beliefs or preferences may be underestimated because these are subjective rather than "objective."

However, it is useful to remember the following wise remark, made by the sociologist William Thomas (Thomas and Thomas, 1928): "If men define situations as real, they are real in their consequences." (For example, when people thought that some woman was a witch, she was burned at a stake—irrespective of whether she was actually a witch or not.)

10.6 PRACTICAL DECISION MAKING

The preceding paragraphs have clarified the basic issues involved in decision making. Hence we now examine how one can reduce the time and effort needed to make decisions in practical contexts. To this end, it is useful to keep in mind that the time and effort involved in making a decision should be commensurate with its importance. Thus it may be worthwhile to spend much time and thought on a decision with far-reaching implications, but it makes little sense to spend a lot of time on a decision entailing only minor consequences. The following paragraphs discuss some practical ways of dealing with decisions of various degrees of importance.

10.6.1 Important real-life decisions

Some decisions are very important because they can have far-reaching consequences. Examples include decisions about a wise choice of college or graduate school, decisions about one's choice of a career or profession, decisions about alternative job possibilities, decisions about engaging in long-term work projects, or decisions about very expensive purchases. In such cases, it is wise to make careful decisions guided by a systematic decision strategy like that discussed in section 10.4. It may then be well worth the time and effort to identify the potentially useful options, to assess their expected consequences and utilities, and thus to arrive at a well-considered choice that may not be regretted afterward.

Such an analytic decision process ensures that one will have thought about many of the significant issues, but it does *not* automatically guarantee a wise decision. The major difficulty, beyond that of predicting all likely consequences, is that of judging their desirabilities because these are so highly subjective. Thus one may not be fully aware of one's own values and preferences, nor of the relative importance of these preferences.

Elucidating personal preferences To overcome these difficulties, one may simulate the decision by trying to imagine what it would be like to live with its consequences. Thus one can *pretend* to have actually made the decision and then observe how one *feels* about it. For example, one can spend a couple of days pretending to have made one choice and observing whether one feels comfortable or anxious about it. Then one can spend another couple of days pretending to have made another choice and again observing one's reactions. The feelings elicited by these simulated situations can help to reveal a fair amount about things that one really considers desirable or important.

Indeed, there is some experimental evidence that, in the case of complex decisions depending on many factors, too much thought may obscure one's spontaneous reactions and thus lead to less satisfactory decisions (Dijksterhuis et al., 2006).

Even if a systematic decision process (like that illustrated in figure 10.7) does not lead to a clear-cut choice, it may still lead to a useful clarification of one's own values and preferences. Thus one can better ensure that some important priorities are not forgotten and that the consequences of the decision will evoke fewer regrets.

Example: Reexamining assumed utilities

Many years ago, I was faced with the decision of choosing between possible professorship positions at two different universities. Since this was a difficult decision for me, I tried to be systematic by using an analytic decision process like that shown in figure 10.7. When I came to the end of it, the process led to a "most useful choice" that just did not *feel* right to me. Thus I began to reexamine my indicated utilities and discovered that there was one desirable consequence that was so important to me that its utility overwhelmed everything else. (What I considered so highly important was a position that would offer many diverse possible opportunities.) Hence I readjusted my estimated utilities, thereby brought my systematic decision in line with my feelings, and never regretted the resulting choice during the ensuing thirty years.

10.6.2 Efficient decisions

Many of our decisions are only moderately important since they are unlikely to lead to any long-term repercussions or irremediable consequences. (For example, we may merely have to decide where to go for lunch or which particular principle to invoke to solve a problem.) It is neither possible nor worthwhile to expend much effort on such minor decisions, especially if the available time is limited. We are then primarily interested in making such decisions quickly and efficiently, even if our choices might be less good. (It is sensible to be content with sufficiently satisfactory decisions, even if they are not the best possible ones.)

One way of making decisions more efficient (faster and more effortless) is by simplifying the analytic decision process discussed in sections 10.3 and 10.4. This can be done in some of the following ways.

Limited search for options   One can often be satisfied with identifying only one or two potential options, without searching for any others.

Rough estimates of parameters   (1) Desirabilities may be only roughly estimated (and not even expressed in numerical form). (2) Probabilities may be only roughly estimated—or even ignored if different consequences seem equally likely. (3) In this last case there is also no need to distinguish utilities from desirabilities. (4) The utility of an option may only be crudely estimated, without any actual calculation, by merely comparing the *relative* utilities of its various consequences.

Cost-effective assessments   It is not sensible to continue the comparative assessment of options beyond the point where the costs (time and effort) involved in assessing them exceed the anticipated benefits.

Sequential assessment of options   One may identify and assess potential options sequentially, immediately discard each one that does not seem satisfactory, simply select the first one that seems sufficiently satisfactory, and then stop further assessments. This is a simple way of identifying an option that is good enough, without comparing all of them against each other. (Note that the selected option may then depend on the order in which the options were considered.)

10.6.3   Heuristic choice guidelines

Instead of analyzing alternative options, one can merely rely on some heuristic choice guidelines (that is, on simple rules of thumb that provide useful advice about how to make sensible choices under various conditions). Such guidelines can then be rapidly and easily implemented without much thought. They can also frequently lead to sensible decisions, particularly in familiar situations (Gigerenzer, 2007; Gigerenzer et al., 1999). However, sometimes they may also lead to very poor decisions.

The following are some examples of such heuristic choice guidelines:

• Choose what seems best as a result of your prior experience. (This may often be good advice, but it may be inappropriate because circumstances have changed or because newer options have become available.)

• Choose what other people are choosing. (This advice does not encourage originality, but relies on the seeming experience of other people.)

• If you are interested in high quality, choose the most expensive item. (This advice may often be valid, but may occasionally also be quite misleading.)

10.6.4 Experience-based decisions

People highly experienced in a particular domain often make decisions rapidly and effectively by relying on large amounts of accumulated knowledge. Instead of deliberately analyzing alternative options, such people immediately *recognize* a familiar or analogous situation, remember the actions that are appropriate in this context, and also recall warnings to avoid past mistakes. Sometimes the recognition of such familiar situations may even be intuitive or almost automatic, without any conscious thought. Such decisions can thus be made very rapidly— and most of the time (although not always) the resulting choices are also appropriate (Klein, 1998). If some deliberation is needed, experienced people can also easily use their accumulated past knowledge to imagine what is likely to happen in some situation—and can thus readily foresee the consequences of any contemplated action.

As a result of their past experience, such people can often make quick and good decisions by relying on perceptual recognition processes (rather than on more lengthy and effortful analyses of alternative options). Needless to say, such good and rapid decision-making skills lead to efficient performance and are particularly important for dealing with emergency situations. Hence they are invaluable for people like firemen, paramedics, or nurses in intensive-care units.

10.7 DECISIONS IN SCIENTIFIC DOMAINS

The following are some examples of practical decisions that commonly arise in scientific or similar domains.

10.7.1 Choice of method

When one is faced with the task of solving a problem or performing an experiment, it is necessary to choose an appropriate method that is likely to achieve the desired goals. Since a poor choice can easily lead to much wasted time and effort, it is then important to make well considered decisions.

Example: Choice of method by an expert

An expert physics professor was asked to solve a fairly simple physics problem. He was asked to talk out loud about his thinking and was tape-recorded. (The problem involved a frame consisting of four equal steel rods hinged at their ends so as to form a parallelogram. If the frame is hanging at rest when suspended from one of its corners, and this corner is tied by a string to the opposite corner so that the frame assumes the shape of a square, what is the force that must be exerted by this string?)

The expert first remarked that the simplest way of solving the problem would probably be to use the fact that the work done, during a hypothetical small distortion of the frame, would then have to be zero. But then he said that he did not feel confident in his ability to calculate this work correctly. Hence he thought that it would be better to use a more straightforward (although longer method) that exploits the fact that the total force on each rod would then have to be zero.

The following two facts are interesting about this example: (1) The expert was very deliberate in deciding on a useful method for approaching this problem, despite the fact that this problem was fairly simple. (2) In making his decision, he also used his *metacognitive* knowledge (that is, his knowledge about his own knowledge and its limitations). This actually led him to prefer a less efficient method rather than one about which he felt less confident.

10.7.2 Avoiding unsuitable familiar methods

It is possible to rely routinely on a familiar method instead of deciding that another method might be more appropriate. A good example is provided in section 5.4.6 where an "expert" physicist tried to determine the accelerations of objects moving along some simple paths.

As this individual himself subsequently remarked, he routinely tried to approach every mechanics problems by writing down equations expressing Newton's law. But in the cases presented to him, he was only asked to provide *qualitative* information about the acceleration.

Hence the routine application of his standard mathematical method was inappropriate, led to long calculations and wrong conclusions, and was more characteristic of novice rather than expert behavior. Even a slight attempt to decide on an appropriate method for answering these questions would have convinced him that his approach was far too complex—and that mere recall of the definition of acceleration should be sufficient to answer all questions.

10.7.3   Diagnosing performance defects

It is all too common that performance leads to deficient results. One must then decide which underlying defects are responsible for the observed results (so that these defects may be properly corrected).

The needed decision process is then somewhat similar to that outlined in figure 10.2. Thus one must try to identify various possible options (that is, possible defects) and attempt to predict their likely consequences. The defect most likely to be responsible for the observed deficiencies is then the one whose consequences lead to the observed deficiencies.

After this defect has been removed, the resulting performance may still be deficient in some respects. In this case, one must repeat the preceding process to identify (and then properly correct) any further defects.

10.8   EDUCATIONAL IMPLICATIONS

10.8.1   Proficient performers

People with long experience in a domain have considerable advantages in decision making. As a result of their experience, they often have much knowledge about potentially useful options. Their accumulated knowledge also makes it much easier for them to predict the likely consequences of such options and to assess their relative utilities.

Because their long experience allows such people simply to *recognize* appropriate choices in familiar situations, they can often make good decisions very quickly. It is only when such people encounter less familiar situations that they may need to engage in lengthy examinations of alternative options.

10.8.2 Inexperienced students

People inexperienced in a domain (such as novice students) don't have the preceding advantages. They may have to spend appreciable time searching for suitable options and may sometimes fail to consider some potentially useful ones. Furthermore, their assessment of identified options may be haphazard or superficial. As a result, inexperienced people can easily make inappropriate decisions or get stuck not knowing what to choose.

10.8.3 Common instructional deficiencies

Decision making is ordinarily *not* explicitly taught to students in high schools, colleges, or beyond. (However, it may sometimes be discussed, from a more advanced or theoretical point of view, in some courses in economics, operations research, or psychology.) Yet, as pointed out at the beginning of this chapter, students often have to make many decisions. For instance, many decisions are necessary for solving problems in mathematics or science, or for designing or performing experiments. Furthermore, students have to make important decisions about their choice of college, graduate school, and profession.

The decision-making skills acquired by many students are usually merely picked up as a result of their own personal experience. As a result, students' decision-making skills may remain primitive or haphazard—and may lead to ill-considered choices and undesirable consequences.

Given the wide-ranging importance of decision making, one may well ask: Why is decision making not more deliberately addressed at various levels of our educational system?

10.8.4 Instructional suggestions

Explicit teaching of decision making   It should be possible to teach decision making more explicitly, even to fairly young students. At least, it should be possible to teach a somewhat more systematic and thoughtful approach than haphazard choices or guessing. Even a few simple guidelines, if actually followed, could lead students to significantly better choices.

Any such teaching would have to involve more than some miscellaneous comments, but would require that students apply a few simple ideas repeatedly in contexts of differing complexity. As discussed in the next chapter, decision making is important in all problem solving (whether in mathematics, physics, chemistry, engineering, or other scientific fields). Hence better decision-making skills need certainly to be taught more explicitly in these domains. Furthermore, it would be useful to provide students with some realistic opportunities for deliberate decision making (for example, in deciding what method to use for carrying out an experiment or solving a moderately complex problem). Decision-making skills, practiced in such situations, could then also be extended to more significant contexts of the kind encountered in real life.

Needless to say, one cannot expect students in a limited time to acquire decision-making skills similar to those of proficient experts in a domain. But they might be taught to become somewhat more competent novices who are able to identify sensible options, to examine their relative utilities, and to make deliberate choices based on such considerations.

Possible applications to the study of history Human history is largely an account of human decisions and their consequences. Thus one can gain a better understanding of history by focusing on the following kinds of questions: Who made significant decisions? How did they make them? What were their resultant choices, and how did they arrive at these? What were the consequences of these choices? Were these initially foreseen by the decision makers? If not, why not? In what respects were these decisions ultimately beneficial or detrimental?

A focus on the decision-making processes of various significant individuals might lead to a more engaging and illuminating study of history. (It could also be instructive to let students play the roles of some historically important decision makers.) Such an approach to the study of history might not only get students more actively engaged in studying history and thus achieve a deeper understanding of historical events. It might also help them to learn more about the decision-making processes required in their own lives.

10.9 SUMMARY

- Any decision requires identifying alternative options and choosing among them according to some criteria.
- Decisions are simple if the available options and choice criteria are well specified. Otherwise, decisions are more complex because they require appreciable thought and careful judgments.

• An analytic and heuristically useful decision strategy involves the following main steps: (1) Identifying some potentially useful options. (2) Assessing these options by predicting their likely consequences, assessing their utilities, and determining the utility of each option. (3) Choosing the most useful of these options.

• The utility of a consequence can be assessed by estimating its desirability D and its probability P of occurrence. The utility U of the consequence is then related to its desirability so that $U = DP$.

• An analytic decision strategy (like that outlined in figure 10.2 and illustrated in figure 10.7) is helpful for making important decisions, but is limited by inadequate abilities to predict anticipated consequences and to specify subjective individual preferences. It can, however, help to avoid thoughtless or ill-considered decisions.

• Sufficiently satisfactory decisions can often be made efficiently by simplifying the decision process. For example, one may identify only few potential options, make only rough estimates of their relative utilities, and not assess options more carefully than seems cost-effective.

• People who are highly experienced in a domain can often make appropriate decisions very quickly by relying on the recognition of past situations that are familiar to them.

• Since decision making is so widely important, it appears useful and possible to teach some helpful decision-making processes explicitly to more students.

11 Introduction to Problem Solving

The preceding discussion of decision making has prepared us to deal with the more general question of problem solving. To be specific, a problem is a task requiring one to devise a sequence of actions that lead to some desired goal. *Solving* such a problem (actually devising such a sequence of actions) can be difficult since it may necessitate many judicious decisions of the kind discussed in the preceding chapter. On the other hand, problem solving is very important in everyday life as well as in all fields that require the flexible use of knowledge to achieve various goals. In particular, problem soving in science is an essential tool for predicting and explaining many diverse phenomena.

The present chapter aims to identify and clarify some of the important issues involved in problem solving. Thus we shall examine some of the following questions: (1) How does problem solving differ from other kinds of tasks that can be performed by implementing some specific method? (2) How does the solution of a problem differ from the answer to a problem? (3) What are the central difficulties of problem solving? (4) Why are some common ways of teaching problem solving often inadequate? (5) What would be needed to do better? The consideration of these issues will prepare us for chapters 12 and 13 which present a more extensive discussion of methods useful for solving problems of various complexity.

Educational relevance Problem solving is an essential prerequisite for flexible performance, is widely needed, and is particularly important in scientific or other complex domains. It is also of paramount importance in education, especially since problem solving can be quite difficult. Many students, even at the college level, have only poorly developed problem-solving abilities and often approach problems in haphazard ways that are unlikely to lead to good solutions. Furthermore,

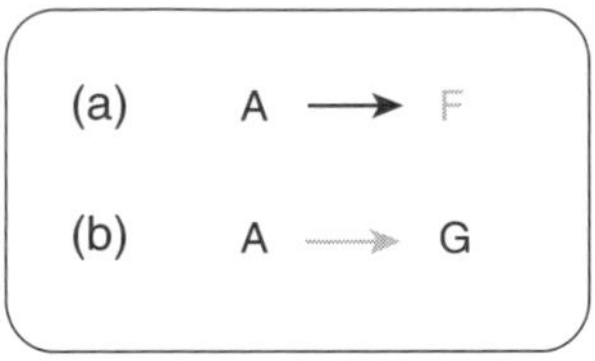

Figure 11.1
Contrasting specifications. (a) Procedure. (b) Problem. (Specified entities are indicated in black, unspecified ones in gray.)

efforts to improve students' problem-solving abilities are often inadequate. Accordingly, it is a challenge to understand better some of the thought processes needed for good problem solving and to develop instructional methods whereby these might be more effectively taught.

11.1 PROBLEM CHARACTERISTICS

11.1.1 Procedures and problems

Procedure   As discussed in chapter 7, a *procedure* specifies a sequence of actions, starting from some particular initial state. The specification of such a procedure is indicated schematically in figure 11.1a where *A* indicates the initial state and the arrow indicates the sequence of actions. (The finally attained state *F* does *not* need to be specified.) The task of implementing such a procedure requires then merely the execution of the specified actions.

Problem   On the other hand, a problem consists of the specification of an initial state and of some final state (called the *goal*)—together with the request to implement a sequence of actions leading from this initial state to the goal. The specification of such a problem is indicated schematically in figure 11.1b where *A* indicates the initial state and *G* indicates the goal. The task of *solving* such a problem then requires devising and implementing some procedure (indicated by the gray arrow) leading from the initial state *A* to the goal *G*.

Central difficulty of problem solving   The task of solving a problem is much more demanding than that of implementing a procedure because one must first discover or invent a useful procedure for attaining the goal.

Any problem deals with some system that can be in any one of a large number of possible states (such as possible states of knowledge).

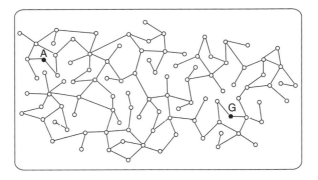

Figure 11.2
Problem states and possible actions.

In figure 11.2 the small circles indicate schematically the possible states of a system, and the lines indicate possible actions leading from one state to another. To solve a problem, starting from the initial state *A*, one must then make many judicious decisions so as to select, out of a large number of possible sequences of actions leading to nowhere, the one (or very few) that lead to the desired goal *G*. The fundamental difficulty of problem solving is thus decision making. Once successful decisions have been made, the result is a problem-solving procedure that can ordinarily be implemented without much further difficulty.

Analogy to a maze Figure 11.2 illustrates that the task of solving a problem is analogous to the task of navigating through a maze if one is initially at some position *A* and wants to get to some specified goal *G* (such as an exit from the maze). In this case the difficulty is also that of making careful decisions to find a particular path leading to the desired goal.

Examples comparing procedures and problems

Baking a pie Suppose that you are asked to perform one of the following two tasks.

• *Task 1* You are supplied with various ingredients and given a recipe for baking a pie. This task requires you to implement a procedure. Indeed, by merely following the recipe step by step, you would end up with a particular kind of pie.

• *Task 2* You are supplied with various ingredients and asked to bake a lemon meringue pie. This task requires you to figure out how to bake such a pie and then actually to bake it. This second task is a problem and is clearly a much more difficult task than the first one.

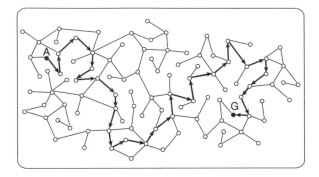

Figure 11.3
A solution of the problem indicated in figure 11.2.

> ***Driving to the airport***   Suppose that somebody gives you directions specify-
> ing how to drive to the airport in a city unfamiliar to you. (In this case, you
> would have been given a procedure.) Alternatively you might be left on your
> own to find your way to the airport. (In this case, you would be facing a prob-
> lem.) You would probably prefer the first alternative since it would be much
> easier for you. Note that the difficulty of the second alternative is *not* the driving.
> (You already know very well how to drive.) The main difficulty is deciding what
> particular route to follow in order to get to the airport.

11.1.2   Important definitions and distinctions

Solution of a problem   A *solution* of a problem consists of the specification and implementation of a procedure leading to the desired goal
(together with a description of this goal). For example, the successive
thick arrows in figure 11.3 indicate schematically the procedure (or
method) representing a solution of the problem illustrated in figure
11.2. (A proper solution must be comprehensible so that it can be
checked by other people.)

Answer versus solution   An *answer* to a problem is a description of the
attained goal. The *answer* to a problem must be clearly distinguished
from the *solution* of the problem. For example, the answer to a problem
may be correct, although its solution may be wrong. Figure 11.4 shows
some examples.

Failures to distinguish problem answers and solutions

> In figure 11.4a the student obtained the correct answer 4 by using the digit 6
> in the numerator to cancel the same digit in the denominator. The student made
> a similar mistake in figure 11.4b. Such a "cancellation" of individual digits is not

$$\text{(a)} \quad \frac{6\,4}{1\,6} = \frac{\cancel{6}4}{1\cancel{6}} = \frac{4}{1} = 4$$

$$\text{(b)} \quad \frac{2\,6}{6\,5} = \frac{2\cancel{6}}{\cancel{6}5} = \frac{2}{5}$$

Figure 11.4
Right answers, but wrong solutions.

a legitimate mathematical operation (it is *not* a division of the numerator and denominator by the same number). In these cases, the student thus arrived at the correct answers by sheer accident.

Most reasonably educated students would probably not make as primitive a mistake as that illustrated in figure 11.4. But even college students often complain that a problem on an examination was unfairly graded because the students had obtained the correct *answer*. It is often very difficult to convince such students that their poor grade is well deserved (despite the correct answer) because their *reasoning* was wrong.

Answers without solutions can be useless

It is not only students who may confuse answers and solutions. For example, artificial intelligence (AI) is a challenging field of endeavor that aims to design computer programs performing tasks that would be deemed to require human intelligence. Workers in the early days of this field (around 1980) tried to build computer programs that could display medical expertise similar to that of human physicians. After such a computer program was given information about a patient's symptoms and about the results of various laboratory tests, it was then asked to diagnose the particular disease and to recommend appropriate treatments for it.

The performance of some such programs was quite good and comparable to that of human medical experts. Why then were actual physicians reluctant to use these seemingly helpful programs? The reason is actually apparent. If you were a physician, would you simply trust the answers provided by some computer? Would you want to be responsible for any mistakes or errors that the computer might have made in arriving at its answers? Would you not want to make sure that any advice given to a patient is appropriate and unlikely to do harm? What doctors really wanted was a computer that would provide not only the *answer* to a medical problem, but its *solution*. Then the doctor would be able to assess whether the solution is correct on the basis of proper factual knowledge and reasoning. Hence the AI investigators learned to modify their programs so that they would not only give *answers*, but also display their *solution methods* in a form that could be checked by human physicians.

The central goal of science is to discover basic concepts and principles enabling one to predict and explain many observable phenomena.

Science is thus interested in solutions, not just answers. In other words, it is *not* interested in answers that might be guessed or proclaimed by some soothsayer, but in problem solutions that show *how* proper reasoning from a few basic principles can lead to correct predictions and explanations.

Solution versus solution process   The solution of a problem is the *product* generated by some solution process. Such a solution can be displayed and checked for correctness, but it provides only very limited information about the *process* used to produce it. (1) A solution does *not* reveal how much time or effort was spent to devise it, how decisions were made to choose particular actions rather than some others, how useless alternatives were avoided or impasses overcome (so that one did not get stuck without knowing what to do next). (2) A solution also does *not* provide information about strategies used to make wise decisions leading to an efficient search for a solution, or about how to solve unfamiliar problems that one might encounter. (3) Lastly, a problem solution presented in a textbook or a lecture exhibits only *one* possible path to the desired goal.

Analogy to maze problems

The preceding comments are fairly obvious if one remembers that solving a problem is somewhat analogous to finding one's way out of a maze. For example, suppose that you are given maps of ten different mazes, where each map indicates a path leading out of the maze. Would all this information provide you much help in finding your way out of a *different* maze?

Indeed, it would do you no good to have memorized the paths through the ten known mazes (the solutions of the first ten maze problems). What you really need to know is some general *method* for navigating through *unfamiliar* mazes.

11.1.3   Routine and demanding problems

If a person starts in an initial state and performs random actions, it is extremely unlikely that the person will reach the desired goal of a problem. Indeed, the main difficulty of problem solving involves the need to make wise decisions so as to choose, out of a great number of possible actions, a particular sequence of actions (a *procedure*) that leads to the desired goal. Once such a procedure is known, the solution of the problem requires merely the implementation of its specified steps. The problem has then been reduced to a simple implementation task so that it has become a *routine* problem (that is, a task not requiring much deliberate thought). But, if a solution procedure is *not* known, a problem can be *demanding* since careful thought and judicious decisions are then required to find an appropriate solution method.

Perceived problem difficulty   Note that the same problem can be routine or demanding, depending on the knowledge and prior experience of the person trying to solve it. For example, an expert (who has seen and solved many similar problems in the past) may already know a solution method for the problem and may thus consider the problem an easy routine problem. But a novice, who does not have all this knowledge and experience, may consider this same problem quite demanding.

Similarly, an *unfamiliar* problem encountered by a person may be demanding, requiring much time and effort for its solution. However, if this person encounters the same (or a similar) problem again, he or she may remember *how* to solve it and may then believe that the problem is just an easy routine problem. The perceived difficulty of a problem is thus subjective, depending on the particular person faced with the problem. For example, a complex problem may seem easy to an expert with much experience in solving such problems. But a simple problem may seem difficult to an inexperienced student unfamiliar with such problems.

Contrast with everyday notion of a problem

In section 11.1.1 we defined a *problem* as a particular kind of task, irrespective of the kind of person confronting this task. By contrast, In everyday life something is called *a problem* only if it seems difficult (that is, only demanding problems are called problems, but routine problems are not).

For example, according to our definition, a problem stated at the end of a chapter in a textbook remains the same problem after it has been solved. However, it may be perceived as a difficult problem beforehand, and may be considered easy at a later time after its solution method is known.

Familiar and unfamiliar problems   It is useful to be familiar with a repertoire of problems that can be readily solved by implementing known solution methods. Such familiar problems can serve as basic building blocks for solving more complex problems. They can sometimes also help to solve somewhat similar problems. But one certainly can *not* solve all problems by merely relying on analogous remembered problems because one would then be incapable of dealing with most problems encountered in realistic situations.

The ability to solve *unfamiliar* problems is essential if one needs to deal flexibly with diverse situations, including those not encountered previously. The ability to solve unfamiliar problems is particularly important in scientific fields in order to make predictions, provide explanations, or design practical applications.

Efforts to teach problem solving should, therefore, *not* merely deal with routine problems or with problems closely analogous to familiar problems. Furthermore, such efforts need to avoid the danger of subdividing complex problems into so many simpler parts that there is no further need for any significant decision making.

Example of excessive problem simplification

When I was teaching one of the two sections of a large introductory physics course, the other instructor and I agreed to give the same final examination in both sections. I proposed for this examination a particular problem dealing with two stars (of known masses and initially at rest a large distance apart) that approach each other as a result of their mutual gravitational interaction. The goal specified in this problem was: "Find the speed of each star when the stars are a distance D apart."

When I saw the other instructor's examination, the goal was specified in the following words: "*Use the principles of energy and momentum* to find the speed of each star when the stars are a distance D apart." By this seemingly slight change in wording, the other instructor had totally changed the difficulty of the problem. Indeed, his wording no longer required students to make the crucially important decisions about which principles to invoke.

11.2   CHALLENGES OF IMPROVING PROBLEM SOLVING

Since problem solving can be difficult and is widely important (and since many students have poor problem-solving skills), there is a need to improve many individuals' problem-solving abilities. The preceding introductory comments are sufficient to indicate some of the relevant difficulties and needs.

11.2.1   Prevailing instructional inadequacies

Teaching by examples and practice   Problem solving is most commonly taught by means of examples and practice. This teaching process usually involves the following major steps: (1) Teaching students the basic knowledge and principles needed for solving problems in a particular domain. (2) Providing students with a few examples of typical problem solutions (either solutions presented in a textbook, or solutions worked out by an instructor on a blackboard in front of a class). (3) Letting students practice by asking them to solve somewhat similar problems given as homework.

Deficiencies of this instructional approach The preceding approach has the following main deficiencies.

Solutions reveal little about the solution process. The solution examples shown to students are *products* and (as already discussed) reveal little about the solution *process*. They can be checked for correctness, but don't indicate *how* to make wise decisions, *how* to recover from impasses if one gets stuck, or *how* to pursue a systematic approach likely to lead to success. Yet this is precisely the kind of knowledge that students need to acquire if they are to learn how they themselves can independently deal with *unfamiliar* problems.

There is a misleading similarity between product and process. Examples of solutions may suggest a misleading similarity between the *product* (the final solution) and the *process* used to obtain such a solution. In fact, a useful solution process may be quite different from that suggested by the orderly arrangement of the successive steps in a solution.

For example, an essay or other piece of prose consists of a sequence of sentences (the second sentence following the first one, the third sentence following the second one, and so forth). But this does *not* mean that an essay is best produced by first writing the first sentence, then the second sentence, then the third sentence, and so on. Indeed, good writers do *not* ordinarily write in this way. Instead, they may start by making a sketchy outline, then refining this into more detailed outlines, then writing a crude first draft of actual text, and then reorganizing and rewriting this draft repeatedly until they obtain the desired final product. This writing *process* is really a process of progressive refinements, and not at all the purely linear process suggested by the successive sentences in the final product.

Similar comments can be made about the performance of most complex tasks. For example, constructing a computer program involves a special kind of problem solving, and a completed program consists of successive lines of code. But no sane programmer would construct such a program by first writing line 1 of code, then line 2, then line 3, and so forth. Once again, the actual process of writing such a program is a process of progressive refinements and quite unlike the process that might be suggested by the neat sequence of lines of code exhibited in the final program.

Dangers of inappropriate practice. Practice is certainly necessary to learn problem solving, but it must be *right kind* of practice. Indeed, inappropriate practice can be dysfunctional, leading to poor or deleterious habits that can be hard to break.

When students practice, they commonly work at home or in other unsupervised settings and often fail to practice recommended methods. Instead, they frequently revert to familiar unsystematic ways of behaving—and thus merely reinforce poor ways of approaching problems. Furthermore, students in such settings often spend much of their time floundering and may thus mostly learn floundering (hardly a useful skill). In short, when students practice problem solving at home (or in schools where individual supervision is almost nonexistent), such practice may sometimes do more harm than good.

Evidence for inefficacy In view of the preceding comments, it is perhaps not too surprising that many students' problem-solving skills remain rather poor, even after attempts at instruction. For example, Don Woods, a professor of chemical engineering who has been much interested in problem-solving instruction, reached the following conclusion:

> *During the four-year undergraduate engineering program studied, 1974–1978, the students had worked over 3000 homework problems, they had observed about 1000 sample solutions being worked on the board by either the teacher or by peers, and they had worked many open-ended problems. . . . They showed no improvement in problem solving skills despite the best intentions of their instructors.* (Woods et al., 1997)

11.2.2   Achieving effective problem solving

Inappropriate simplistic approaches Problem solving is not an easy task since many careful decisions are required to attain a desired goal. Could one not avoid such decisions by simply trying *all* possible sequences of action until one finds the appropriate one? Except in the case of extremely simple problems, such an approach would be practically impossible since the number of possible actions (for example, the number of possible paths in a maze) is enormously large.

Alternatively, could one not try to select possible courses of action in random fashion and thus hope, sooner or later, to find the appropriate one? This approach too would be practically impossible since the probability of finding the appropriate path by chance is extremely small. Thus one clearly needs a more deliberate approach.

Using a systematic approach One may be able to specify a particular method for solving a specific problem. But one can*not* specify a well-defined method for solving many diverse problems since these may differ in far too many respects. However, it may be possible to specify a less well-defined general method that is *heuristic* (that is, a method that provides helpful *advice* for solving most problems, but does not guarantee their solution). Despite its limitations, such a general method (called a *strategy*) can be quite useful, is certainly much better than a haphazard approach, can facilitate appropriate decisions, and may also be used in conjunction with other more specific methods.

Important needs It is thus apparent that an effective approach to problem solving requires the following two essential ingredients:

1. A problem-solving strategy suggesting a systematic approach facilitating the solution of many problems.

2. Well-organized knowledge about the relevant domain (such as mechanics, organic chemistry, or electrical engineering) in a form facilitating the retrieval of helpful information.

Chapter 9 already dealt with the useful organization of knowledge. The following chapter discusses a general problem-solving strategy that can help a person to deal with many kinds of problems.

11.3   EDUCATIONAL IMPLICATIONS

11.3.1   Proficient performers

Proficient problem solvers usually approach problems systematically. They commonly describe and analyze a problem before attempting to construct its solution, and they check its solution carefully afterward. Their decisions are made judiciously so that they are rarely faulty.

Most experts have much experience working in their domain of expertise and have solved many problems in it. Their accumulated knowledge often allows them to recognize familiar problems and to recall their solutions without the need for making new decisions. This kind of knowledge provides them with a considerable advantage. (On the other hand, when such experts are faced with a difficult *unfamiliar* problem, they may sometimes be so persistent as to spend hours or days attempting to solve it.)

11.3.2   Inexperienced students

Novice students tend to approach problems in fairly haphazard ways. They often fail to analyze problems adequately before trying to solve them, and they commonly fail to check their solutions adequately to ensure that they are correct. Their unsystematic approach also leads them frequently to faulty decisions—or causes them to get stuck without knowing what to do. (Inexperienced students also have often the unjustified belief that any problem should be solvable in no more than about five minutes.)

11.3.3   Common instructional deficiencies

As already mentioned, many attempts to teach problem solving rely mostly on providing examples and practice, but don't explicitly teach how to make appropriate decisions or how to implement a systematic approach. As a result, many students' problem-solving skills remain quite poor.

11.3.4   Instructional suggestions

It seems useful to focus explicitly on the decision processes needed for problem solving and to teach these deliberately within the framework of a systematic strategy for solving problems. The next couple of chapters discuss such an approach.

11.4   SUMMARY

• A problem is a task requiring one to devise a sequence of actions that lead to some desired goal.

• The solution of a problem is the implemented procedure that specifies this sequence of actions. The result of this procedure is the answer to the problem. A solution must be distinguished from the process needed to generate this solution.

• The central difficulty of problem solving is judicious decision making required to choose, out of many possible sequences of actions leading nowhere, the one (or the very few) leading to the desired goal.

• Such decision-making requires a systematic approach that is guided by a problem-solving strategy (of the kind discussed in the next chapter) and that is aided by well-organized knowledge about the relevant domain.

12   Systematic Problem Solving

Since problem solving can be difficult and may require many careful decisions, this chapter discusses a strategy helpful for constructing the solutions of many problems.

Any task requires adequate preparation beforehand and adequate review after its implementation. A useful problem-solving strategy needs therefore to address the following questions: (1) How can one describe and analyze a problem so as to bring it into a form facilitating it subsequent solution? (2) How can one make all the appropriate decisions that are necessary to construct this solution? (3) How can one assess whether this solution is correct and exploit the knowledge gained from it?

The following sections attempt to answer these questions by suggesting an explicit strategy useful for solving many problems. No such strategy can *guarantee* correct solutions of all problems, but it can provide a systematic approach that can greatly facilitate their solutions.

Educational relevance   As previously mentioned, many students have poor problem-solving skills. They often approach problems haphazardly, make various mistakes, or get stuck not knowing how to arrive at a solution. On the other hand, problem solving facilitates the flexible use of knowledge and is, therefore, very important in all scientific and similar fields. Hence an effective problem-solving strategy can help students to apply their acquired knowledge, to think more deeply about the requirements needed to deal with problems, and to learn better problem-solving abilities.

12.1   A USEFUL PROBLEM-SOLVING STRATEGY

12.1.1   General guidelines

The suggested problem-solving strategy abides by the following two general guidelines which are useful for performing most complex tasks.

Decomposing tasks (divide and conquer)   Any complex task can be more readily performed if it is decomposed into more manageable parts. Thus it is helpful to decompose a problem into simpler *subproblems*. (A *subproblem* is any problem whose solution facilitates the solution of the original problem).

This decomposition process can be repeated. Thus one may decompose an original problem into some subproblems, may decompose these subproblems into further subproblems, may decompose these further, and so forth.

Successive approximations   It is often difficult to attain a goal as a result of a single major effort. Instead, a problem may be approached more gradually by a process of successive approximations (where each such approximation brings one progressively closer to the desired goal). Each such approximation process can then be relatively simple. As one approaches the goal more closely, it may also become clearer what needs to be done next.

12.1.2   Basic problem-solving strategy

The suggested problem-solving strategy, outlined in figure 12.1, decomposes the solution process into several successive *phases* (major subproblems). The following paragraphs briefly describe these phases, which are then discussed much more fully in the subsequent sections.

Describing the problem   This initial phase of the strategy aims to produce a clear description of the problem. Thus it should clearly describe the situation contemplated in the problem and the goal specified by it.

Although this initial phase of the strategy is relatively simple, it is an essential prerequisite for all later phases. Indeed, any deficiencies in this initial phase can be fatal and ruin all subsequent work on a problem.

Analyzing the problem   This second phase of the strategy aims to put the problem into a form facilitating the subsequent construction of its solution. Accordingly, this phase tries to identify the knowledge useful for solving the problem, then analyzes the problem more theoretically (by using available specialized knowledge), and finally provides a more analytic description of the problem.

Constructing the solution   This central phase is the most important and complex one since it attempts to construct the actual solution of the problem. To this end, it suggests appropriate decisions leading to the decomposition of the problem into carefully chosen subproblems.

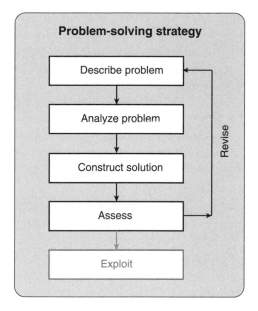

Figure 12.1
Basic problem-solving strategy.

These may then be successively solved so as to lead to the solution of the original problem.

Assessing the solution   This final phase of the strategy aims to assess whether the solution obtained in the preceding phase is correct and useful. Accordingly, it provides some general criteria for checking the solution. If the solution is in some ways unsatisfactory, the problem solver must then go back to revise it appropriately.

This assessment phase is very important since it is readily possible to fool oneself into believing that a carefully constructed solution must be correct. Unfortunately, this is often not the case since errors of omission or commission can be all too common. A final critical assessment of one's work is thus *always* essential.

Exploiting the solution   This phase of the strategy is *not* necessary for the solution of a particular problem (and is therefore indicated in a lighter color in figure 12.1). However, one ordinarily has ulterior goals beyond a particular problem. For example, one usually wants to gain further useful knowledge and to improve one's abilities to solve future problems. Thus it would be foolish to spend time and effort working on a particular problem—and then simply to forget all about it.

Hence this supplementary phase suggests reflecting about the problem so as to exploit one's work for future purposes. For example, it suggests identifying and correcting detected deficiencies in one's knowledge—and remembering any new methods discovered while doing working on the problem.

Sequence of the problem-solving phases

Occasionally, one may deviate somewhat from the indicated sequence of the problem-solving phases. For example, if one encounters some difficulties in solving a problem, one may find it useful to go back and reanalyze the problem more carefully.

The preceding overview of the problem-solving strategy of figure 12.1 allows us to examine its phases more fully in the following sections.

12.2   DESCRIBING A PROBLEM

12.2.1   General remarks

Figure 12.2 indicates the main ingredients of a clear problem description. As shown there, one needs to summarize the information about the problem situation, the goal of the problem, and any conditions imposed on its solution.

Situation   One must clearly specify the relevant entities in the problem and their important properties. If the problem involves some time-dependent processes, one also needs to specify important times or time intervals.

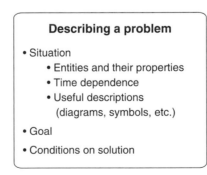

Describing a problem

- Situation
    - Entities and their properties
    - Time dependence
    - Useful descriptions
      (diagrams, symbols, etc.)
- Goal
- Conditions on solution

Figure 12.2
Clear initial description of a problem.

It is helpful to describe available information in visual forms (such as diagrams or tables) and to denote significant quantities by conveniently chosen symbols.

Goal   The goal of the problem (the ultimately wanted information) needs to be clearly specified.

Conditions on solution   One also needs to specify any special conditions that must be heeded in solving the problem. For example, there may be *constraints* that impose restrictions on what can be done in solving the problem—or there may be special *resources* available for solving the problem.

Examples of special problem conditions

Constraints   (1) The goal might be to go to Paris for a week without spending more than 2000 dollars. (2) The goal might be to solve a mathematics problem without using any calculus.

Special resources   (1) The goal might be to go to Paris for a week with permission to stay at a friend's apartment. (2) The goal might be to solve a mathematics problem with the availability of an electronic calculator.

Common errors in problem description   Although the initial description of a problem is relatively simple, one must be careful to avoid common errors, such as ignoring relevant information or making unwarranted assumptions. (Both of these errors can be fatal.)

12.2.2   Illustrative example: Dome problem

General remarks about the strategy are likely to become more meaningful if they are illustrated in the case of a specific problem. Hence we shall throughout this chapter focus on a particular problem (the "dome problem") because it is very concrete and illustrates many important aspects of problem solving in a relatively simple case. Although this problem deals with physics, *no* special knowledge of physics is required to understand the problem-solving issues illustrated by it. (Indeed, an undue preoccupation with the physics may merely distract attention from the relevant problem-solving issues.)

Figure 12.3 shows the original statement of this dome problem. An application of the problem-solving strategy then yields the clear description of this problem illustrated in figure 12.4. The following are some explanatory comments.

Statement of the dome problem

A worker sits at the top of a smooth hemispherical dome, of radius R, which covers a factory on horizontal ground. If the worker loses his hold and starts sliding, at what vertical height above the ground will he slide off the dome?

Figure 12.3
Verbal specification of the dome problem.

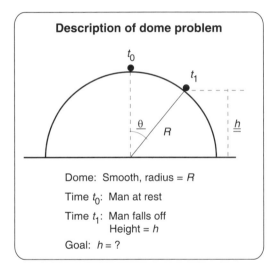

Description of dome problem

Dome: Smooth, radius = R

Time t_0: Man at rest

Time t_1: Man falls off
          Height = h

Goal: $h = ?$

Figure 12.4
Clear description of the dome problem.

Description of the dome problem

The purely verbal specification of the problem, stated in figure 12.3, has in figure 12.4 been converted into a diagram of the situation and a summary of the relevant information. The diagram shows the man (indicated by the small black circle) at the time t_0 just before he starts sliding down along the surface of the dome—and at the later time t_1 when he slides off the dome. The letter h has been introduced to indicate the man's height above the ground at this instant. The diagram also indicates the radius R of the dome and the man's angular displacement while sliding along the dome. (This angular displacement has been labeled by the Greek letter θ.)

The summary specifies the properties of the dome (that it is smooth and has a radius R) and indicates the man's sliding process between the times t_0 and t_1. Finally, it specifies that the goal of the problem is to find the value of the height h.

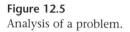

Analyzing a problem

- Useful knowledge?
- Analyze theoretically
- Describe analytically

Figure 12.5
Analysis of a problem.

> To help distinguish different kinds of symbols, it is sometimes useful to underline *once* any symbol whose value is unknown, and to underline *twice* any symbol (like *h*) whose value is unknown and needs to be found. Symbols without any underlines then denote *known* quantities (like the specified radius *R* of the dome).

Note that the problem description of figure 12.4 is much easier to understand than the original problem statement of figure 12.3. Words have been replaced by a diagram that helps one to visualize what is going on. Furthermore, the relevant quantities have been clearly identified and labeled. Indeed, the dome problem would be significantly easier for students if it were given to them in the form of figure 12.4 rather than in the form of figure 12.3.

Common student difficulties Some students start working on a problem, like that stated in figure 12.3, without ever drawing a diagram illustrating the situation. Although such students may believe that they thereby save some time, they find it harder to visualize the situation and are likely to find the problem much more difficult.

12.3 ANALYZING A PROBLEM

12.3.1 General remarks

The strategy of figure 12.1 specifies that, after a problem has been clearly described, it should be carefully analyzed so as to facilitate the problem's subsequent solution. The main ingredients of such an analysis are outlined in figure 12.5 and described more fully below.

Identifying useful knowledge The strategy suggests first to identify theoretical or other special knowledge useful for solving the problem. (For example, if a problem deals with motion, useful theoretical knowledge about this problem would be knowledge about mechanics, the topic dealing with motions and interactions). Special knowledge may also include knowledge about somewhat similar problems that have been solved in the past.

Analyzing theoretically The problem can now be analyzed by exploiting the available specialized or theoretical knowledge about the domain. For example, one can use such knowledge to identify important qualitative implications; one may examine symmetry properties and explore what would happen in special or extreme cases; and one may try to decompose the problem into separable parts.

Analytic description Finally, one can exploit all the preceding information to obtain a more analytic description of the problem. The initial clear description of the problem can thereby be augmented by identifying theoretically important systems, properties, and times—and by reformulating the problem in terms of theoretical concepts or principles important in the relevant domain. The result is then an analytic problem description that incorporates specialized or theoretical knowledge and thus facilitates constructing the solution of the problem.

12.3.2 Illustrative example: Dome problem

Such an analysis transforms the previous clear description of the dome problem of figure 12.4 into an analytic description like that in figure 12.6. Once again, there is no need to understand the details of the physics. But it is helpful to appreciate how much theoretical knowledge may be incorporated in an analytic problem description.

> The diagram in figure 12.6 shows the man at some particular instant of time while he is sliding down along the surface of the dome. Since the analysis has recognized that mechanics knowledge is relevant to understand the man's motion, all relevant concepts of mechanics have been exploited. Thus the man's mass m is explicitly included in the diagram (although it is an unknown quantity). Furthermore, the diagram uses familiar mechanics concepts (like velocity and acceleration) to describe the man's motion and indicates various forces to describe the man's interactions with other objects.
>
> At the instant when the man starts sliding, his velocity is still negligible. But as the man slides down along the dome because of gravity, the magnitude of his velocity keeps increasing. The man's acceleration (the rate of change of his velocity) can conveniently be considered to consist of two components. One of these components is directed along the velocity (along the surface) and indicates that the *magnitude* of the man's velocity along the dome's surface is increasing. The other component is directed toward the center of the man's circular path and indicates that the *direction* of the man's velocity is changing as he moves along his circular path. (Knowledge of mechanics is used to specify that that magnitude a_c of this component is related to the radius R, and to the magnitude v of the man's speed, according to the equation listed in figure 12.6.)

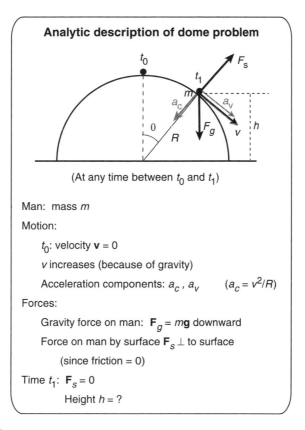

Figure 12.6
Analytic description of the dome problem described in figure 12.4.

This figure also indicates that one of the forces acting on the man is the downward gravitational force F_g exerted by the earth. (As indicated in the diagram, this force is related to the man's mass m and to the quantity g specifying the strength of the gravitational interaction.) The other force F_s is that exerted on the man by the touching surface of the dome. Since the dome is smooth, this force has no frictional component directed along the surface. Hence the force exerted on the man by the dome is entirely perpendicular to its surface (as indicated in the diagram).

At the instant t_1 when the man slides off the dome, the man loses contact with the surface of the dome. Hence the force exerted on the man by the dome then becomes zero.

Note that the analysis of this problem has led to an analytic description that incorporates much theoretical knowledge about the domain of mechanics. Accordingly, the analytic problem description of figure 12.6 differs considerably from the earlier problem description of figure 12.4 and provides much more useful information for solving the problem. It even reformulates the description of the problem's goal. Whereas the originally stated problem asked to find the man's height above the ground *when he slides off the surface of the dome*, the redescribed problem asks one to find the man's height *when the force on the man by the dome becomes zero*.

Common student difficulties   Students often get stuck in this problem because they don't know how to interpret the condition that the man slides off the dome. The preceding analysis resolves this difficulty by considering the relevant forces and thus revealing that this condition implies that the force exerted on the man by the dome is then zero.

More generally, the analysis of a problem in any domain is likely to incorporate more specialized knowledge about this domain, to lead to a more useful analytic description of the problem, and to lead to a reformulation of the problem's goals. All of these things can greatly facilitate the subsequent construction of a problem's solution.

12.4   CONSTRUCTING A SOLUTION

The strategy outlined in figure 12.1 suggests that, after a problem has been analyzed, one should turn to the construction of its solution. This central phase of the strategy is ordinarily the most difficult since it may require many judicious decisions.

12.4.1   General approach

Decomposition into subproblems   A useful guideline for dealing with any complex task is to *divide and conquer*. Hence the strategy aims to construct a solution by decomposing a problem into subproblems. (A *subproblem* is any problem whose solution facilitates the solution of the original problem.) Such subproblems are usually simpler and can then be handled separately. These subproblems can also be decomposed into further subproblems until one obtains subproblems that can readily be solved.

Useful choice of subproblems   How can helpful subproblems be identified? Start by identifying subproblem options that are likely to help attain the specified goal. If such options are not obvious, search for them deliberately by identifying obstacles hindering the attainment of the goal—and then identify corresponding needs to overcome these obstacles.

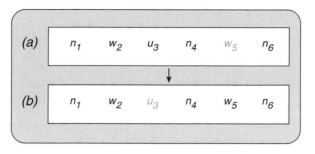

Figure 12.7
(a) Wanted and unwanted features in a problem situation. (b) Situation after elimination of the obstacles. (Present features are indicated in black, absent features in gray.)

By repeatedly identifying the obstacles encountered in the original problem and in all subproblems, and by eliminating all these obstacles, one should then ultimately be able to overcome *all* obstacles hindering the solution of the original problem. The original problem would then be solved.

Kinds of obstacles   Figure 12.7a illustrates schematically various features in a problem situation. Some features (labeled by w) are *wanted* because they can help the solution of the problem, while other features (labeled by u) are *unwanted* because they hinder the solution of the problem. Features labeled by n are *neutral* (neither wanted nor unwanted) and thus of no particular interest.

Obstacles arise if some wanted feature (like w_5) is absent or lacking, or if some unwanted feature (like u_3) is present. Such obstacles can then be eliminated by trying to obtain such wanted features, and by trying to remove such unwanted features. Figure 12.7b indicates the resulting situation after these two kinds of obstacles have been eliminated.

Obstacles and needs   Figure 12.8 summarizes the preceding comments by indicating that each kind of identified obstacle suggests a corresponding *need* to eliminate this obstacle. (A *need* is a subgoal that aims to attain some ulterior goal—and thus specifies a subproblem aiming to address this need.) For example, if a wanted feature is absent, there is a corresponding need to *obtain* this feature. Similarly, if an unwanted feature is present, there is a corresponding need to *remove* this feature.

An attempt to solve subproblems addressing such needs may reveal further obstacles and thus further needs to address these obstacles—

Obstacle	Need
Wanted feature absent	Obtain wanted feature
Unwanted feature present	Remove unwanted feature

Figure 12.8
Obstacles and corresponding needs for eliminating them.

and so forth. Thus one may be led to an entire sequence of successive subproblems—until one arrives at some that can actually be solved.

Examples of common obstacles or needs

The kinds of obstacles or needs mentioned in figure 12.8 can encompass a great variety of special cases, such as the following:

Absence of wanted features (1) Absence (or lack) of some important knowledge—and a corresponding need to obtain such knowledge. (This need might be addressed by applying some general principle to some particular system.) (2) A lack of potentially useful comparative knowledge—and a corresponding need to obtain such knowledge. (This need might be addressed by recalling knowledge about a familiar analogous problem or by considering a somewhat simpler similar problem.) (3) Absence of progress in trying to solve a problem—and a corresponding need for greater progress. (This need might be addressed by backtracking and making some alternative choices.)

Presence of unwanted features (1) The presence of some unwanted *kind* of information—and a corresponding need to remove this information. (For example, this kind of information might be an unwanted unknown quantity in an equation—and the need might be addressed by combining equations to remove this quantity). (2) The presence of an unwanted *form* of information—and a corresponding need to remove this unwanted form. (For example, the unwanted form might be an unduly complex formula—and the corresponding need might be addressed by simplifying this formula by some algebraic operations.) (3) The presence of an excessively vague goal specification—and the corresponding need for a more precise specification. (For example, the original vague goal might be "find more information relating motion and interaction"—and the need for more precision might be met by the more precise specification "apply Newton's law to some specific object".)

12.4.2   Process of constructing a solution

The preceding general approach for constructing a solution can be implemented by using a solution strategy (like that outlined in figure 12.9) that keeps on repeating the following three major steps:

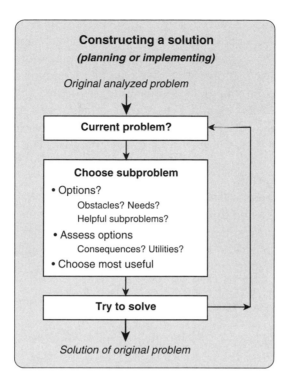

Figure 12.9
Strategy for constructing the solution of a problem.

1. Identifying the current problem At the beginning, this is the original analyzed problem. (At a later stage, this is the current problem resulting after this original problem has been modified by all the additional information acquired during the problem-solving process.)

2. Choosing a helpful subproblem This requires a decision process (like that discussed in chapter 10) in which one first identifies the potentially useful options by searching for subproblems addressing existing needs, then assesses these options by considering their consequences and utilities, and finally chooses the seemingly most useful of these options.

3. Trying to solve the chosen subproblem If this subproblem can be solved, then the original problem might thereby also be solved. Otherwise, the next current problem becomes the original problem modified by all the newly acquired information. (If the chosen subproblem cann*not* be solved, then the current problem remains the previously considered problem. One must then go back to choose another subproblem that might be more readily solved.)

The preceding cycle of choosing and solving a subproblem can be repeated until the original problem has been solved (or until one can make no further progress and gives up with an admission of failure).

Note that the solution strategy of figure 12.9 involves a sequence of successive approximations approaching the desired solution. To this end, it repeatedly identifies existing obstacles and corresponding needs—and tries to solve subproblems addressing these needs. This solution process is thus driven by a needs analysis. (This is sometimes called a *means-ends analysis* since a need is just a means designed to attain a specified end.)

It must be emphasized that any problem solution, obtained as a result of the preceding solution strategy, should be considered *provisional* because it might contain various errors or other deficiencies. It can be regarded as a final solution only after it has been properly assessed in the next phase of the problem-solving strategy of figure 12.1.

12.5   EXAMPLES OF SOLUTION CONSTRUCTIONS

The following examples illustrate the preceding process of constructing a solution.

12.5.1   Mailing a photograph

Although the solution process of figure 12.9 may seem complex, the following simple example indicates that it explicates what people commonly do in everyday life.

Lisa's problem

Lisa wanted to send a photograph to her boyfriend in England. She realized that this photograph was awkwardly large and would look better if it were properly cropped. Thus she needed to crop it. But how could she do this? The simplest and most desirable option might be to use a pair of scissors. But then the resulting cuts would probably be somewhat uneven. Another option, likely to yield straighter cuts, was to use a knife guided by a ruler. Since this option seemed more useful, she chose to use this one.

But to implement this choice, Lisa needed a sufficiently sharp knife, which she did not have. However. she could overcome this obstacle by using a box-cutter equipped with a razor blade. But then she would also need a surface on which she could place the photograph to cut it. How could she obtain such a surface? One option was to place the photograph on her wooden dining-room table. But that risked making some very undesirable cuts in her nice table. A better option was to place the photograph on a vinyl cutting mat suitable for such cutting tasks. But she had no such cutting mat. Thus she came up with a third option—placing the photograph on an old newspaper. This option seemed the best since it would be adequate and since injuries to the old newspaper would not matter.

Now Lisa had to confront a second major need: What kind of envelope should she use to mail the photograph? One option would be a large manila envelope. But this might allow the photograph to be bent in the mailing process. Another option would be a cardboard box stiff enough to prevent bending. But such a box would also be heavy and more expensive to mail. Lisa then thought of a third option—using an envelope with the photograph backed by a stiff piece of cardboard. Since this seemed the best option, Lisa decided to choose this one. This left a third major need—determining the required amount of postage for this envelope. Lisa knew that this would depend on the weight of the envelope and had a scale whereby she could determine this weight. She also had various stamps. But how could she find out the applicable postage rates? One option was to go to the post office, but this seemed much too time-consuming. Another option was to telephone the post office. A third option was to look up the postage rates on the Internet. This option seemed the most useful since Lisa could access the Internet by using her computer.

Comments about Lisa's solution process   Lisa solved her original problem by doing all the preceding things spontaneously. (The whole process took her probably less time than that required to describe it). Yet she identified many obstacles and corresponding needs, considered several subproblem options to address each need, and in every case chose the seemingly most useful one.

Note also how much everyday knowledge Lisa invoked to solve her problem. For example, she knew about scissors and knives, the things that can be done with these tools, and the advantages and disadvantages of these tools. She knew about various kinds of envelopes, about cardboard boxes, and about the stiffness of cardboard. She knew that postage rates depend on weight, that information about these rates could be obtained from the post office, and that such information can also be retrieved from the Internet. All this knowledge seems very familiar to us who have grown up in our present society. But to a person from a very different or more primitive culture, this knowledge would be unfamiliar and thus *not* available when trying to identify potential options. A seemingly simple problem, like that faced by Lisa, would thus be quite difficult for such a person.

Knowledge required for problem solving   The preceding example illustrates that problem solving often requires appreciable knowledge rather than mere cleverness. [This is less true in the case of puzzles (like those about the *tower of Hanoi* or *missionaries and cannibals*) of the kind often used in psychological investigations (Newell and Simon, 1972).] Similarly, problems in mathematics, physics, biology, or engineering

(a)	$5x + 4 = 20 - 3x$
(b)	$5x = 16 - 3x$
(c)	$8x = 16$
(d)	$x = 2$

Figure 12.10
Solution of an algebraic equation.

require for their solution much knowledge about the particular domain. Indeed, problems in any such domain become much easier after
one can use the knowledge about this domain with as much facility as
one uses one's knowledge about everyday life.

12.5.2 Solving a simple algebra problem

Description of the problem An *algebraic equation* is an equation relating two algebraic expressions containing an unknown quantity (often
denoted by x). The goal of the algebra problem is to find the particular
value of x that satisfies this equation. For example, figure 12.10a shows
such a simple equation. The goal of this problem is then to transform
this equation into the desired form $x = K$ (where K is some known
quantity).

Any such problem can be solved by applying the solution strategy of
figure 12.9 in order to transform the original equation into the desired
form. To do this, one merely needs to identify an unwanted feature in
an existing equation—and then to remove this obstacle by performing
the *same* appropriate operation on both sides of the equation. (Such an
operation does not destroy the equality of both sides). By repeatedly
identifying and removing such unwanted features, one can then decompose the original problem into easier subproblems whose solutions
lead to the solution of the original problem.

Solution of the algebra problem

The following illustrates my solution of the equation in figure 12.10a. As
already mentioned, my goal was to transform this equation so that only x itself
would be on the left side and only a known quantity would be on the right side.
One obstacle hindering this goal was the unwanted number 4 on the left side.

But I could remove this unwanted feature by subtracting 4 from both sides of the equation. The result was then the simpler equation in figure 12.10b.

This equation was still not in the wanted form where x alone would be on the left side. One obstacle was the unwanted term $-3x$ on the right side. But I could remove this obstacle by simply adding $3x$ to both sides of the equation. The result was then the simpler equation in figure 12.10c.

This equation was still not in the wanted form because the x on the left side was multiplied by 8. But I could remove this unwanted feature by simply dividing both sides of the equation by 8. The result was then the equation in figure 12.10d and this final result yielded the wanted value $x = 2$.

Most of the equations commonly encountered in a basic algebra course can be solved in a similar way by merely identifying an unwanted feature in an equation—and then removing it by an appropriate operation performed on both sides of the equation. Successive repetitions of this process then yield the desired solution.

12.5.3 Solution of the dome problem

A more realistically complex example is shown in figures 12.11a and 12.11b which illustrate how the solution strategy of figure 12.9 can be used to find the solution of the dome problem stated in figure 12.3 and analyzed in figure 12.6. Once again, it is *not* necessary to know all the relevant physics or to follow the mathematics used to implement the steps of this solution. But it is instructive to note how obstacles or needs are identified, how subproblems are chosen to address them, and how all such decisions are made in conjunction with the relevant general knowledge about mechanics.

First major subproblem

The problem clearly involves motion and interactions. Hence it requires a knowledge of mechanics (knowledge previously summarized in well-organized hierarchical form in figures 9.7 and 9.8). The first obstacle (indicated within parentheses in figure 12.11a) is then obviously a lack of sufficient information relating motion and interactions—particularly at the crucial time t_1 when the man slides off the surface of the dome. This obstacle might be overcome by applying one of the two basic mechanics principles indicated in figure 9.8. Because of the present interest in a particular instant of time, the utility conditions accompanying these principles lead to a clear choice—namely, to Newton's law. The decision is then to apply Newton's law [equation (1) in figure 12.11a] to the man at the instant when he is leaving the surface of the dome.

To implement this decision, one needs to modify the analytic description of figure 12.6 so as to describe the man's motion and interactions at the particular

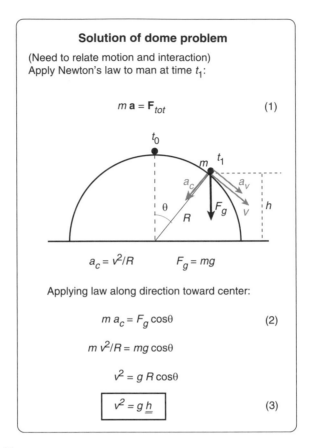

Figure 12.11a
Initial part of the solution of the dome problem stated in figure 12.3 and analytically described in figure 12.6. (Identified obstacles or needs are indicated within parentheses.)

time t_1 when he slides off the dome (so that the force $\mathbf{F}_s$ on the man by the dome's surface has become zero). The result is indicated in the diagram of figure 12.11a. By applying equation (1) along the direction toward the center of the dome, one then obtains equation (2) and, after a little algebra, equation (3). This equation relates the man's speed v to the man's height h above the ground at the instant when he slides off the dome.

Second major subproblem

The speed v in equation (3) is still an unknown quantity and thus needs to be removed if one wants to find the desired height h. To do this, one could combine equation (3) with additional information about the speed v. But such

$$v^2 = g\,\underline{h} \qquad (3)$$

(v is unwanted unknown) Remove $v \rightarrow$
Combine with other information about $v \rightarrow$
(Lack such info) $\rightarrow$
Find more info relating motion and interaction $\rightarrow$
Apply energy law to man between t_0 and t_1:

$$\Delta E = W_{oth} \qquad (4)$$

$$\Delta K + \Delta U_g = W_s \qquad (5)$$

$$(\tfrac{1}{2}mv^2 - 0) + (mgh - mgR) = 0 \qquad (6)$$

$$\underline{v}^2 = 2g\,(R - \underline{h}) \qquad (7)$$

(v is unwanted unknown) Remove $v \rightarrow$
Combine equations (3) and (7):

$$g\,h = 2g\,(R - h) \qquad (8)$$

$$3g\,h = 2g\,R$$

$$\underline{h} = \tfrac{2}{3}R \qquad (9)$$

Figure 12.11b
Final part of the solution of the dome problem. (The initial part of this solution
is shown in figure 12.11a.)

additional information is lacking. Hence one can address the subproblem of
obtaining additional information about v by exploiting the relation between the
man's motion and his interactions during the entire time between t_0 and t_1. The
choice between the two relevant laws in figure 5.8 is again clear since the energy
law is useful between any *two* times. Thus one is led to apply this law, as indicated in equation (4) of figure 12.11b.

The implementation of this decision is now straightforward. The change of
the man's energy E consists of the change of his kinetic energy K and change
of his gravitational potential energy U. One also knows how K depends on the
man's speed v and how U depends on the man's height. Furthermore, the work
W_{oth} done by all forces (other than gravity) is zero since the force $\mathbf{F}_s$ on the man
by the surface has no component along this surface. All this knowledge is incorporated in the Equations (5) and (6) of figure 12.11b—and then leads to
equation (7) which provides additional information relating the speed v and the
height h.

Third major subproblem

At this point, one is still left with the obstacle that v is an unwanted unknown quantity. But now there are available *two* different equations relating v and h—namely equations (3) and (7). To remove v, one can then combine these two equations—thus obtaining equation (8) and finally, after a little more algebra, equation (9).

After all this labor, one has now obtained the desired answer $h = (2/3)R$ which asserts that the man slides off the dome at a height equal to two-thirds of the dome's radius.

Important issues illustrated by this example   This solution illustrates how much the solution of problems in any particular domain is facilitated by the knowledge about this domain.

1. In this example the relevant knowledge is theoretical knowledge about mechanics. This knowledge makes clear that the central need in mechanics is adequate information relating motion and interactions—and it also provides well-organized mechanics knowledge helpful for addressing this need. Hence it is apparent that the solution of the problem is best started by using this domain-specific theoretical knowledge.

By contrast, inexperienced students (unlike experts) often try to work backward from the desired goal (Chi, Feltovich, and Glaser, 1981). For instance, in the present example, they might start by asking themselves, "What do I know about the height h?" This is a very poor starting point. Even an expert could not answer this question. Indeed, only when the problem is addressed with theoretical mechanics knowledge, does it become clear how this height enters the solution of the problem.

2. As indicated in section 9.6.5, the available knowledge about mechanics is so well organized that one needs to choose only among very few relevant principles. Furthermore, this choice can be made on the basis of *qualitative* knowledge about the kind of information provided by each such principle and about the conditions under which the principle might be useful. These qualitative considerations then lead to the choice of a particular principle and some specific equations associated with it. (Note that the choice of a useful principle does *not* involve a mere search through a list of formulas.)

3. The knowledge about the relevant domain of mechanics also leads one to introduce the man's mass m as a theoretically useful quantity, despite the fact that information about this mass is *not* specified. (Inexperienced students are often reluctant to introduce symbols denoting such unknown quantities.) In fact, it turns out that the final

answer to the problem does *not* involve the man's mass m and also does *not* involve the strength g of the gravitational interaction. Hence the solution of the problem actually does *not* require a knowledge of either one of these unknown quantities.

4. Some needed subproblems (such as applying Newton's law or the energy law in particular cases) should be routinely solvable by people with some experience in mechanics. Indeed, it is important that the mere interpretations of important concepts and principles have become so familiar that they are routine tasks. Otherwise a person would not have enough mental capacity to deal with all the decisions required for solving complex problems.

12.6 ASSESSING A SOLUTION

The problem-solving strategy of figure 12.1 indicates that the construction of a solution does *not* complete the solution of a problem since the resulting solution might still contain various defects. Hence the following paragraphs discuss the assessment of a solution.

12.6.1 Assessment criteria

Figure 12.12 indicates some useful criteria for assessing a solution. These criteria are listed in order of increasing stringency (so that later criteria are less readily satisfied than earlier ones). If some of these criteria are *not* satisfied, the solution certainly has some defects. However, even if *all* of these criteria are satisfied, the solution may still have some defects.

> **Assessing a solution**
>
> • Goals achieved?
>
> • Clearly specified?
>
> • Internally satisfactory?
>
> • Externally consistent?
>
> • Optimal?

Figure 12.12
Criteria for assessing a solution.

Note that these criteria may also be applied to assess another person's solution of a problem, even if one does not know how to solve the problem oneself. For example, if a solution does *not* satisfy all these criteria, one can be sure that it is somehow defective.

Indeed, such a solution is *worse* than wrong. It is *nonsensical* because some simple checks would clearly indicate that it cannot be correct. (To get students into the habit of checking their problem solutions, it may be useful to penalize them more for nonsensical solutions than for solutions that are merely wrong.)

Let us now examine the criteria of figure 12.12 and elaborate them at slightly greater length.

Goals achieved?

- Have all goals been achieved? Has all desired information been obtained?
- Have all asked questions been answered?

Clearly specified?

- Have all answers been expressed in terms of known quantities and well–defined symbols?
- Have all relevant units been specified? (For example, the statement *length* = 5 is meaningless. Is this length 5 inches or 5 feet?).
- Has every vector been specified by its magnitude and its direction?
- Have numerical answers been specified with an appropriate number of significant figures to indicate their estimated precision?

Internally satisfactory?

- Is the solution free of internal defects?
- Is the solution self-consistent? (Are the units on both sides of every equation consistent?)

Externally consistent?

- Is the solution consistent with information beyond that considered in this particular problem?
- Are the answers of reasonable magnitude?
- Are answers consistent with knowledge about simple or extreme cases?

(For example, is the calculated acceleration of a cart rolling down along a ramp consistent with the fact that it must be zero if the ramp is horizontal?)

- Are answers consistent with the expected dependence on parameters?

(For example, does the calculated speed of a falling object agree with the expectation that it would be larger if the fallen distance were larger?)

- Is the solution consistent with one obtained by different reasoning?

Optimal?

- Is the solution as simple as possible?
- Are the results expressed in the simplest and most easily interpretable form?

12.6.2 Revising a solution

When the assessment of a problem solution reveals some defects, it is necessary to revise the solution appropriately. (Indeed, it is useful to revise a solution even when no defects are apparent since a solution can almost always be improved.) Revisions may aim merely to correct any detected defects. However, it is also often useful to go again through the entire problem (its analysis, solution, and assessment) so as to make sure that everything is clear and correct. Indeed, it may well be necessary to undertake several successive revisions until one arrives at a solution that is deemed satisfactory.

12.7 EXPLOITING A SOLUTION

It is foolish to spend much time and effort on a problem if one does not afterward reflect about it so as to profit from the experience. Thus it is wise to exploit the solution of a problem in order to improve one's knowledge and capabilities for dealing with future problems. As indicated in figure 12.13, it is useful to explore the following issues.

Improving prior knowledge While solving a problem, one may make various mistakes or realize that one's previous knowledge was somewhat faulty. Thus it is useful to identify the detected deficiencies in one's prior knowledge, to diagnose the reasons why they occurred, and to devise ways to avoid similar deficiencies in the future.

Identifying new knowledge In the process of solving a problem, one is likely to learn some new factual knowledge or new methods. Hence it is useful to identify clearly the new knowledge that one has acquired and to make sure that one could use it in the future.

> **Exploiting a solution**
>
> • Improve prior knowledge
>
> • Identify new knowledge
>
> • Integrate entire knowledge
>
> • Extend knowledge

Figure 12.13
Exploiting the solution of a problem.

Integrating one's entire knowledge At this point it is useful to summarize and organize one's *entire* knowledge (previous knowledge and newly acquired knowledge) so that it is coherent and can be used jointly.

Extending one's knowledge Finally, one can extend one's knowledge by exploring some implications of the knowledge gained from solving the problem. For example, are there related or somewhat different problems that one can now solve? Does one now have better methods for solving some previously encountered problems?

12.8 EDUCATIONAL IMPLICATIONS

12.8.1 Proficient performers

As already mentioned in the preceding chapter, proficient problem solvers usually solve problems systematically. In particular, they spend significant time describing and analyzing a problem before trying to construct its solution. They also are careful to check their solutions afterward and try to learn from them.

In constructing a solution, such problem solvers make decisions largely driven by assessing perceived needs and exploiting their theoretical knowledge about the domain. Thus, they often start by applying some basic principles and then work forward toward the intended goal. Most of the time they also arrive at correct answers.

12.8.2 Inexperienced students

By contrast, inexperienced students focus most of their attention on the actual construction of a problem's solution, but spend little prior time on carefully describing and analyzing a problem. (They probably suffer from the naive belief that such preliminary activities are unnecessary and merely take time away from the central task of constructing the solution.) As a result, such students often try to construct the solution of a problem while they are ill-prepared and not aware of some knowledge useful for the problem-solving task. Many of these students are also overconfident and thus fail to check their solutions with adequate care.

In trying to construct the solution of a problem, students often proceed somewhat haphazardly, trying to grab miscellaneous formulas or other remembered bits of knowledge. They usually do not make well-considered decisions or engage in a strategic approach. Thus they often get stuck without knowing what to do. Furthermore, students often rely predominantly on their accumulated knowledge of previously encountered similar problems, rather than on reasoning based on a few general concepts and principles.

Many student mistakes in problem solving arise from deficiencies in their basic knowledge (for example, from erroneous interpretations of basic concepts and principles that they were supposed to have learned long ago). Students often don't approach problems in systematic ways. Furthermore, they may lack simpler required knowledge that should have become routine, but that is still defective.

Example of students' problem-solving difficulties

In one investigation (Heller and Reif, 1984) students who had completed a basic mechanics course with grades of B or better were given problems similar to the ones that they had previously encountered in that course. It was found that the students described incorrectly about 50 percent of these problems (for example, specified incorrectly the motion of relevant objects or the forces acting on such objects). Such deficiencies alone caused them to produce incorrect solutions. But since some students also made mistakes after correct initial descriptions, the net result was that the students could solve correctly only about 35 percent of the problems. (Such results certainly do not inspire confidence in the efficacy of usual methods of teaching problem-solving.)

12.8.3   Common instructional deficiencies

Problem solving is most commonly taught by means of examples and practice. As already mentioned in section 11.2.1, this instructional method has severe deficiencies. When instructors do teach problem-solving strategies, they rarely emphasize the important decision processes needed for problem solving (that is, how to search for potentially useful options and how to make sensible choices among these).

Even if attention is paid to such issues, students rarely engage in the consistent supervised practice needed to learn good problem-solving skills—and thus don't acquire skills that they can reliably implement and spontaneously use. (Of course, such supervised practice is difficult to achieve with the low faculty-to-student ratio prevailing in most schools.)

12.8.4 Instructional suggestions

Teachers should explain to students why a systematic approach to problem solving is important—and introduce them to a problem-solving strategy like the one discussed in this chapter. This strategy should then be demonstrated in various problems and explicitly taught so as to help students apply it consistently to a large range of problems.

Such instruction might well start by teaching parts of the strategy *separately* before asking students to use them jointly. For example, one may teach students how to describe and analyze problems—and ask them to construct solutions only after they have become reasonably proficient at these somewhat simpler tasks. Similarly, one may give them separate practice in merely assessing solutions (including solutions ostensibly constructed by other people).

Students must be given adequate practice in applying such a strategy to diverse problems, but this practice must be under conditions where the students' actions can be closely monitored (preferably by well-trained instructors, or possibly by student peers in small-group settings).

Learning from advice or from one's own experience A strategy (like the one discussed in this chapter) can provide useful advice for improving problem-solving skills. However, students tend *not* to heed such advice (just as motorcycle riders often don't heed the advice to wear protective helmets). In all these cases people often believe that it is cumbersome to follow the advice, that it is more trouble than it is worth, and that they themselves don't need it (although other less careful people may).

It is quite difficult to overcome such beliefs, in education as well as in many other spheres of human life. People are generally more prone to learn from their own experiences than from sage advice (for example, motorcycle riders are much more likely to wear a helmet after they have suffered a near-fatal accident). Students are no exception.

Thus it may be useful to let students fail in their problem-solving attempts—and then repeatedly point out to them that the use of the strategy could have helped them to prevent some of their mistakes or to avoid getting stuck. It is even better to convince students that *they themselves* are facing a challenging personal problem—namely, figuring out how *they* can avoid mistakes and how *they* can devise reliably successful ways of solving the kinds of problems encountered in scientific or similar complex fields. The problem-solving strategy of this chapter is thus merely an aid suggested to help them solve their *own* personal problem—but this personal problem is really the one deserving most of their systematic thought.

12.9 SUMMARY

• Successful problem solving can be facilitated by a systematic approach that can be guided by a strategy providing helpful advice.

• A useful strategy subdivides the problem-solving process into successive phases that involve an initial clear description of the problem, its analysis aided by domain-specific knowledge, the actual construction of the solution, the subsequent assessment and revisions of this solution, and the exploitation of this solution for ulterior goals.

• The process of constructing the solution is helped by systematically decomposing a problem into simpler subproblems. These subproblems can be chosen by repeatedly identifying needs to overcome obstacles that hinder the solution of the problem, and then choosing subproblems designed to address these needs.

• It is important to assess any solution to ensure that it is free of defects. Such an assessment can be facilitated by checking the solution with the aid of some simple criteria and then revising the solution if it exhibits any defects.

13 Dealing with Complex Problems

The strategy discussed in the preceding chapter is useful for solving many problems. To indicate how it can be refined and applied to deal with somewhat more complex problems, this chapter explores the following questions: (1) How can planning be used to facilitate the many decisions needed to cope with complex problems? (2) How can one effectively manage all the information required for such problems? (3) How can one deal with both quantitative and qualitative problems, and are there significant differences between these kinds of problems? (4) Can the previously discussed problem-solving strategy also be applied to the seemingly very different problem of writing articles, reports, or other documents?

Educational relevance   All these questions are highly pertinent in education. Planning is important for many tasks and students are often not good at planning their work or their other activities. As pointed out in section 8.4.3, both quantitative and qualitative problems are needed in scientific work (although teachers often overemphasize problems of one kind at the expense of those of the other). Lastly, writing is a complex task often inadequately performed by many students and other people. Yet, writing is not only essential to succeed in school, but is also generally needed to produce reports, grant or job applications, publishable articles, and many other documents.

An exploration of the preceding questions is thus educationally important and may also help to persuade students that problem solving is widely relevant.

13.1 MANAGING COMPLEXITY BY TASK DECOMPOSITION

Problem solving and other tasks become increasingly complex when one needs to deal with many relevant features. Indeed, paying attention to many such features can become so difficult as to transcend human capabilities. How can one cope with such situations?

Simplistic decomposition of a task   One useful way of dealing with such complexity is to "divide and conquer" by decomposing a complex task into distinct parts (*subtasks*) that are smaller and thus more manageable. Then one can address each of these parts separately and thereby deal with only a limited number of features at any one time.

This suggested approach is unduly simplistic because not all ways of subdividing a task into separable parts are equally helpful. The difficulty is that the selected parts of a task are ordinarily not independent, but are related so that they affect each other. The performance of one part of a task may thus either help or hinder the performance of other parts of the task. How then can one decompose a complex task in such a way that the interactions between component tasks are helpful rather than harmful?

Example: Simplistic way of painting a portrait

Suppose that a man wants to paint the portrait of a woman. One way that he might decompose this complex task is by subdividing his canvas into small squares (each one inch on a side) and then successively painting each square in detail. The contents of these squares are, however, interrelated. Even when painting the first small square in the uppermost left corner of the canvas, the man needs to do this with an awareness of the other parts of the painting (for example, an awareness of the shape of the woman's entire head). Indeed, his completed painting of this first small square might interfere with the proper placement of the woman's eyes and nose—and would provide little information facilitating the rest of the contemplated painting.

Needless to say, no sensible person would ever paint a portrait in this way.

Decomposition by progressive refinements   A far better way of decomposing a complex task is by dealing first with the most important features (those that affect the largest number of other features) and then progressively dealing with less important ones. Thus one can first deal with major features that have widespread effects on the entire task, before one addresses minor features of more limited significance.

Indeed, this is what portrait painters commonly do. They first deal with major features, such as the person's shape, before worrying about more minor features such as coloring. (The person's shape will crucially affect the placement of all colors, but coloring will be of little importance for drawing the person's shape.) Thus painters commonly first indicate the painting coarsely, without much detail, by making a rough sketch of the entire person. Then they refine this first sketch so as to obtain a more detailed sketch including more minor features (such as lips and eyebrows). Finally, they add further details and colors to complete the painting.

In this way, painters can use earlier coarse sketches as guides for constructing more detailed features of a painting. They can then deal with many details while always maintaining an awareness of the entire context. Furthermore, their local actions in one part of the canvas are then much more likely to be compatible with their local actions in other parts of the canvas.

These increasingly refined sketches made by a painter represent an example of *planning*, a general process discussed more fully in the next section.

13.2 PLANNING

13.2.1 Planning in problem solving

Planning is a very useful strategy facilitating the solution of complex problems. Such planning involves solving a problem in a coarsely described form (without attention to many details) and then using this schematic solution as a guide for constructing a more detailed solution.

Planning strategy   A systematic planning strategy involves the following major steps.

• To reduce the need to deal simultaneously with excessively many features, redescribe the problem at a coarse level that omits detailed features of lesser importance. (The retained features are then the most important because they are likely to affect many other detailed features.)

• Solve the problem at this coarse level where the task is simpler because one does not need to be concerned with too many details.

• Use this solution as a guide to help solve the problem at the next more detailed level of description. (The major decisions made at the initial coarse level simplify this task because they reduce the number of possible options that need to be considered when decisions are made at the more detailed level.)

• The preceding planning process may be repeated at successively more detailed levels of description. [The result is a process of successive approximations (or progressive refinements) where increasingly more detailed plans gradually come to specify all features of the desired solution.]

• The final step of this planning process should then be an *implementable plan* that can be readily carried out in complete detail.

Planning and problem complexity   The utility of planning depends on the complexity of a problem. For example, simple problems may need little or no planning. Somewhat more complex problems may require only a single level of planning since one such plan may already be readily implementable. On the other hand, successively more detailed plans become increasingly helpful when one is trying to construct the solutions of more complex problems.

13.2.2   Planning examples

Lisa's plans for mailing a photograph   Section 12.5.1 discussed how Lisa approached her problem of sending a photograph to England. Her solution, outlined there, was really only a *planned* schematic solution that she had not yet actually implemented. Thus she had not yet used a knife to crop the photograph, had not yet inserted the photograph into a manila envelope together with a piece of cardboard, and had not yet determined the needed amount of postage. But she had figured out a *plan* that she could then readily implement to do all these things.

Architectural plans for a house   A very good example of planning is provided by the architectural plans needed to solve the problem of building a house. An architect typically starts by making a coarse sketch of the proposed house, then draws more detailed plans showing different views and different parts of the house, then modifies these plans after further consideration and discussions with his clients, and finally produces still more detailed plans (*blueprints*) that can actually be implemented by the contractors hired to construct the house.

Successively more refined plans are thus produced before a house can actually be constructed. As usual, these plans deal with more important features before considering more subsidiary ones. For example, the initial plan (which is coarse and specifies merely the basic shape of the house) is needed before the architect can make any more detailed plans. A more refined plan, specifying the foundation and wooden framework of the house, is then prepared before the architect worries about the walls separating individual rooms. And all these plans are made before planning for the doors, plumbing fixtures, and appropriate paints.

13.2.3 Planning and the problem-solving strategy

Applicability of the problem-solving strategy The planned solution of a problem is specified at a coarse level lacking in details. Since the general problem-solving strategy of chapter 12 is applicable at *any* level of detail, it is also useful for devising a plan for a solution. For example, in planning the construction of a problem's solution, one can still proceed by identifying obstacles or needs and then decomposing the problem into appropriate subproblems.

Schematic solutions and planning limitations Since the planned solution of a problem is coarsely described without attention to minor features, it is schematic and devoid of some detailed information. Decisions must, therefore, be made on the basis of somewhat incomplete information.

Hence there is an important difference between planning the solution of a problem and constructing its actual solution. When constructing a solution, many decisions can be made with the knowledge of the *actual* consequences of one's actions. But when planning a solution, decisions must be made with the mere knowledge of the *predicted* consequences of contemplated actions. Experts, who are very familiar with a domain, are much better than novices at anticipating the consequences of their actions. Hence experts are also better able to plan than students or other less experienced persons.

Sequencing of several subproblems When a problem is complex, an analysis of obstacles or needs can often lead to *several* subproblems that might be addressed at a particular stage. The following guidelines suggest the *sequence* in which such subproblems can usefully be considered:

1. Deal preferentially with major obstacles before dealing with minor ones. (Eliminating major obstacles, that affect many other problem features, can help in dealing with subsequent minor obstacles.)

2. On the other hand, accumulating minor obstacles may significantly hinder the solution of a problem. In this case, it may be better to remedy these minor obstacles before returning to the task of addressing more major ones.

13.2.4   Prerequisites for planning

Adequate predictions of anticipated consequences   As already mentioned, planning at a coarse level of description requires an adequate
ability to foresee the consequences of proposed actions and any ensuing difficulties, despite the fact that these actions have not actually
been implemented in detail.

Examples: Foreseeing likely consequences

Lisa's plans for mailing a photograph   Section 12.5.1 discussed Lisa's plans
for mailing a photograph to England. In making this plan, Lisa predicted that
using scissors to crop the photograph would probably lead to an uneven cut—
and then used this anticipated result to plan an alternative way of cutting by using
a knife. Note that Lisa could make this prediction only because she had often used
scissors in the past and was thus familiar with some of the likely disadvantages.

Planning for the dome problem   Figures 12.11a and 12.11b showed the
detailed solution of the dome problem, a solution implemented *without* a prior
plan for it. An expert physicist, faced with this problem, would probably start
by *planning* its solution. Such a plan would schematically indicate that a solution
should involve an application of Newton's law and an application of the energy
law—and that a combination of the results should yield the desired solution of
the problem.

An expert (unlike a novice) would be able to make such a plan because of his
or her appreciable prior familiarity with the kinds of results obtained by applying
these mechanics laws. The expert could then quickly implement this plan without the need for any other major decisions.

Planning aids   A major difficulty of planning is persons' limited
ability to predict the likely consequences of contemplated actions.
This difficulty is particularly severe if a person deals with a largely
unknown situation or has only limited experience in the relevant
domain.

Various planning aids can be used to help people visualize the consequences of proposed actions. For example, the planning aids used
by architects include pictorial sketches and scale drawings of proposed designs. They may also include the construction of small three-
dimensional models. Finally, modern computers allow computer-aided
design by providing CAD-systems that enable architects to easily visualize and modify their contemplated plans.

Utility of a planning language   Planning can also be facilitated by
qualitative language that is appropriate for describing situations without excessive detail. In particular, descriptive words or diagrams may
be better suited than mathematical equations.

Example: Use of vague language in planning

When facing a problem involving an electric current flowing through two connected wires of different diameters, expert physicists typically do their planning by saying that "The electrical resistance of each wire depends on its material and its geometry"—and only later express this statement in more precise mathematical form.

By contrast, inexperienced students' vocabulary does not include a vague word like *geometry* to denote things like length and cross-sectional area. They merely know an equation, such as $R = \rho(L/A)$, which relates the resistance R of a wire to its resistivity ρ, its length L, and its cross-sectional area A. Thus they immediately start by writing such an equation for each wire—and by writing other equations relating currents and voltages. As a result, they may easily get lost in a multitude of equations.

The preceding comments indicate at least two reasons why inexperienced students have difficulties in planning. (1) Their lack of experience in an unfamiliar domain makes it difficult for them to anticipate the likely consequences of their contemplated actions. (2) Their predominant emphasis on quantitative descriptions (such as equations) does not provide them with a qualitative language useful for planning.

13.2.5   Global and local planning

Global planning   *Global* (or *long-range*) planning aims to devise a plan for an *entire* problem-solving task. Such planning needs to consider all the successive actions needed to solve a problem. This kind of plan can then guide the detailed implementation of an entire problem-solving process.

Local planning   By contrast, *local* (or *short-range*) planning considers only some part of a problem. Such local planning is clearly easier than global planning since it needs only to predict the consequences of a few contemplated steps. Hence it is possible to do local planning even if global planning is too difficult. Furthermore, global planning can usefully be supplemented by local plans dealing with some selected or more difficult parts of a problem. (Unsophisticated students find it easier to do local planning than the global planning of an entire problem.)

13.3   SUPPORTIVE KNOWLEDGE

13.3.1   Kinds of supportive knowledge

Most problems cannot be solved without adequate amounts of supportive knowledge. This knowledge consists of the following two kinds.

1. Knowledge about the specific problem This knowledge should be provided by the prior clear description and analysis of the problem. Indeed, any deficiencies in this knowledge can have serious consequences.

2. Knowledge about the relevant domain Most significant problems (unlike mere puzzles) deal with situations encountered in real life or in particular domains of substantial interest. Hence one needs adequate declarative and procedural knowledge about the relevant domain (for example, about mechanics, medicine, electrical engineering, or some other specific domain). Furthermore, this knowledge must be in a form allowing it to be readily retrieved and used.

13.3.2 Useful knowledge about a domain

General domain knowledge It is essential to know the important concepts and principles, as well as the important methods, useful in the relevant domain. Any such knowledge must also be accompanied by applicability conditions specifying under what conditions this knowledge is valid and useful.

It is helpful if this general domain knowledge is carefully organized (for example, in hierarchical form) so that it can be readily retrieved and flexibly elaborated according to prevailing needs. It is also helpful if this knowledge can be described in multiple ways so that one can choose a description most useful for a specific problem-solving task.

Repertoire of basic routine problems Some basic problems are often relevant and can be used as building blocks for constructing the solutions of more complex problems. In particular, such basic problems include the applications of important concepts or principles in specific cases. Prior familiarity and practice should have made such basic problems so familiar that they have become *routine* (so that they can be reliably and easily implemented without much new thought). These routine problems then constitute a kind of tool chest of intellectual resources that can be called on whenever needed.

The availability of such routine basic problems is essential for dealing with complex problems. Indeed, if the mere application of every needed concept or principle would be a demanding problem requiring substantial thought, many errors would be introduced while dealing with such basic tasks. Furthermore, there would not be enough intellectual capacity left to deal with the more important decisions needed for a complex problem.

The preceding comments indicate that effective problem solving requires prior learning good enough to ensure that basic concepts and principles can be applied easily and reliably.

Analogy: Architect solving the problem of constructing a house

An architect can cope with the problem of constructing a new house because he does *not* need to think much about solving all the subsidiary problems (such as. how to install plumbing or electrical wiring, how to lay the roof, how to cast cement, and how to do carpentry.). He merely needs to call on readily available subcontractors who already know how to perform these tasks. Indeed, the architect could not do his important work if he himself found it always necessary to devote significant attention to all these subsidiary tasks.

13.4   HELPFUL FORM OF SOLUTION

Importance of good information management   Many problem-solving difficulties can be avoided if the available information about a problem is always clear and understandable.

1. The information available about a problem at any time *during* its solution should be readily apparent and comprehensible. In particular, it should be clear what has already been done and what further things still need to be done. Otherwise, one can easily get confused and may be unable to make appropriate decisions.

2. Information available about a problem *after* its solution should be sufficient so that the problem solver (and others) can readily understand what has been done and why. Such information allows the problem solver, as well as other persons, to check that the solution is actually correct. It also allows one later to modify the solution to improve it or to solve somewhat different problems.

The following means are useful for attaining the preceding goals.

Good form of a solution   The mere form (or format) of a solution may *seem* like a trivial matter of display or bookkeeping. But it is *not* trivial or unimportant since poor form can make it difficult to deal with accumulating information and may easily lead to various mistakes. The following are useful suggestions:

   • A solution should be written in a clearly legible form.
   • Equations, diagrams, and other special ingredients should be numbered for easy identification and ease of reference.
   • Titles and subtitles should be used to subdivide a long solution into clearly labeled sections.

• Preliminary and explanatory comments should be clearly distinguished from the main line of the argument.

Explanatory comments   The solution of a problem should be well documented by accompanying explanatory comments indicating what was done and why. (Otherwise neither the problem solver, nor anyone else, may afterward be able to understand the solution or to modify it when needed.) Indeed, a mere sequence of equations (or mere lines of computer code), without accompanying explanatory comments, should be carefully avoided since the solution of a problem can then become nearly incomprehensible.

Example: Lack of explanatory comments on an examination

Students have often come to me, a couple of days after an examination, to complain about their grades. I then usually ask them to explain to me what they have written on their examination. Frequently the students can *not* do this when looking back at the nearly illegible jumble of equations on their page.

If the students themselves cannot understand what they did on a problem two days previously, how can they possibly expect a professor, or anyone else, to understand it?

13.5   QUANTITATIVE AND QUALITATIVE PROBLEMS

Quantitative problems are important because they can lead to quantitative or numerical answers of any desired degree of precision. (Thus they can be used to make, or check, precise predictions entailed by scientific principles.) *Qualitative* problems, solved by qualitative reasoning, require answers that are approximate or that specify qualitative relationships among some quantities. As pointed out in section 8.4.3, such qualitative insights are also very useful in scientific work. In particular, they greatly help in discovering, inventing, designing—or in diagnosing the causes responsible for detected defects.

Both quantitative and qualitative problems are thus important. (Indeed, an inability to solve qualitative problems may indicate a lack of understanding of important ideas.) The problem-solving strategy of chapter 12 is applicable to both kinds of problems. However, there are some significant differences between them.

13.5.1   Quantitative problems

Quantitative problems, although seemingly more difficult than qualitative problems, can be relatively easy for the following reasons.

Availability of mathematical symbolism   Quantitative problems can profit from the availability of some well-developed mathematical methods (such as the methods of algebra or calculus). These provide symbolic notations that can express information about complex relationships in compact and transparent forms. Furthermore, complex reasoning processes can thereby be achieved, simply and reliably, by manipulating symbols according to well-specified rules.

Method of constraint satisfaction   Equations can also simplify problem solving by allowing use of the following method: Every equation expresses a restrictive condition (or *constraint*) satisfied by the quantities related by the equation. Similarly, several such equations specify several such constraints all of which must simultaneously be satisfied. A sufficient number of such equations can, therefore, specify so many constraints that only a single set of values of the related quantities satisfies all of them. Furthermore, algebraic methods are often sufficient to determine which particular values of the quantities satisfy all of these equations. These equations then determine *the* correct solution of the problem.

The preceding method of solving problems by *constraint satisfaction* has the following advantages (compared to methods involving more sequential reasoning). (1) The equations (or constraints) can be specified in *any* order. (2) No correctly specified equation can be harmful, even if it is not useful. (3) All relevant equations merely need to be combined at the end to yield the solution of the problem.

Parameterized problems   A *numerical* problem is one where the values of all relevant quantities are specified numerically and where the desired answer should also be in numerical form. By contrast, a *parameterized* problem is one where the values of all relevant quantities are parameters indicated by algebraic symbols. The desired answer must then be expressed in terms of these parameters. (If numerical values of these parameters are later specified in a particular case, this symbolic answer can then immediately be expressed in numerical form.)

Simple example: Numerical and parameterized problem

A problem specifies that a car travels with a constant speed of 30 miles per our, and asks how much time would be required for this car to traverse a distance of 45 miles. The desired answer is then 1.5 hours.

Alternatively, the problem might be parameterized by specifying that a car travels with a constant speed s and by asking how much time would be required for this car to traverse a distance D. In terms of these parameters, the desired time t would then be specified by the relation $t = D/s$.

This parameterized solution can readily be applied to the preceding numerical problem. In this special case the values of the parameters would be $s = 30$ miles/hour and $D = 45$ miles. Hence the numerical value of the desired time would be $t = (45 \text{ miles})/(30 \text{ miles/hour}) = 1.5$ hours.

Advantages of parameterized problems   Parameterized problems have the following significant advantages. (This is why scientists use them whenever that is possible.)

▪ *Generality of results*   The answer to any parameterized problem is a general result that can be readily specialized for any particular case where the values of the parameters are known. Hence one does *not* need to repeat the entire calculation if one wants to know the result in a case where the relevant parameters have different numerical values.

▪ *Functional dependence of answer on parameters*   The answer to such a problem indicates explicitly *how* the answer depends on various quantities in the problem. Thus one can easily arrive at important *qualitative* conclusions (for example, one might realize that the answer to a problem would be larger if some other quantity in the problem were smaller).

Example: Qualitative insights from the parameterized dome problem

The solution of the dome problem, in figures 12.11a and 12.11b, involved several parameters such as the radius R of the dome, the mass m of the man, and the strength g of the gravitational interaction. If the problem had initially specified particular numerical values of these parameters, the solution would merely have yielded a particular number for the desired height of the man above the ground. However, the solution of the parameterized problem in figure 12.11b reveals the interesting fact that this height h actually does *not* depend on the man's mass m, nor on the gravitational strength g.

▪ *Ease of calculations*   Calculations in a parameterized problem involve only algebraic symbols. Such calculations are usually much easier than calculations with cumbersome numbers. If a numerical answer is ultimately desired, one needs then only to substitute values for the known parameters at the very end (instead of doing more laborious numerical calculations throughout the entire problem). Furthermore, needless calculations can often be avoided because it can quickly become clear that some parameters may cancel and thus be irrelevant to the solution of a problem.

▪ *Ease of checking*   About the only way of checking the answer to a numerical problem is to determine whether the answer has a reasonable magnitude. But, when dealing with a parameterized problem, one can also easily check an answer by determining whether it depends on various parameters in accordance with qualitative expectations. (Indeed, this kind of check is usually most likely to reveal mistakes in a solution.)

Student difficulties with parameterized problems Some inexperienced students have difficulties dealing with parameterized equations because they have often dealt only with numerical equations in their earlier mathematics classes. Furthermore, numerical equations clearly distinguish unknown quantities (denoted by symbols like x or y) from known quantities that are mere numbers. On the other hand, parameterized equations consist entirely of various symbols—and unknown quantities may be denoted by symbols indistinguishable from those indicating known parameters. Thus students sometimes get bewildered when confronting such a multitude of undifferentiated symbols.

Aids for dealing with many symbols

To reduce confusions, it can be helpful to underline *twice* symbols denoting unknown quantities that should be found by solving a problem, to underline *once* symbols denoting unknown quantities that are of no ultimate interest (and that should thus be eliminated), and to leave *without underlines* all parameters denoting known quantities. This practice can significantly help students to distinguish the various kinds of symbols in a parameterized problem. (It has also been illustrated in the solution of the dome problem in figures 12.11a and 12.11b.)

Another difficulty is that inexperienced students often look at parameterized equations or results as mere strings of meaningless symbols. Unlike more proficient performers, they have little inclination (and little ability) to explore the significance of such parameterized equations by examining their qualitative implications (for example, by determining how a result depends on various quantities—or whether it would be larger or smaller if some other quantity were larger).

13.5.2 Qualitative problems

Qualitative problems, requiring qualitative solutions obtained by qualitative reasoning, aim mainly to reveal the important qualitative features of a situation (for example, the functional dependence of some quantity on other relevant parameters). As previously mentioned, such problems can provide important insights that are useful in scientific work. Furthermore, qualitative reasoning can often be used to discover important qualitative relationships—even when quantitative answers cannot readily be obtained.

Difficulties of qualitative problems However, qualitative problems also give rise to some special difficulties. For instance, they require *qualitative* formulations of important principles so that these can be readily applied. Mere equations are not enough. (Students may thus be handicapped by their predominant emphasis on formulas.)

In *quantitative* problems, equations provide a ready-made notation for keeping track of the changing information during problem solving. But in *qualitative* problems, one needs to devise other means for exhibiting the information available at any time during one's reasoning process. Furthermore, qualitative reasoning is sequential and thus quite different from the constraint-satisfaction process commonly used with equations in quantitative problems. For instance, the *order* of steps in a sequential reasoning process can be quite important. Indeed, at any stage an inappropriate step (even if intrinsically correct) may be harmful since it may steer one into a totally unproductive direction.

As a result, qualitative problems may sometimes be *more* difficult than quantitative problems. Thus, students may need special training to deal with qualitative problems. One can*not* expect that they will automatically profit from their prior experience with quantitative problems.

Example: Contrasting quantitative and qualitative problems

Figure 13.1 illustrates a situation where a 12–volt storage battery is connected by a wire, of resistance r, to two automobile headlights each of which has an electrical resistance R.

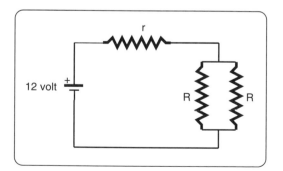

Figure 13.1
A battery connected by wires to two automobile headlights.

A *quantitative* problem might ask one to find the electric current flowing through each of these headlights. Many students find this problem fairly easy. They introduce convenient symbols to denote the current in each branch of the circuit, exploit well-known laws to write down equations connecting the currents in all these branches and the voltage drops across these branches, and then use simple algebra to solve these equations so as to find the current through each headlight.

On the other hand, a *qualitative* problem might ask the following question: If one of the headlights burns out, would the voltage drop across the other headlight increase, decrease, or remain the same? Many students find this problem appreciably more difficult than the quantitative one. Indeed, a qualitative reasoning chain leading to the answer may involve the following successive steps: (1) If one headlight burns out, its resistance becomes infinitely large so that the combined resistance of both headlights increases. (2) Then the resistance of the entire circuit, connected to the battery, increases. (3) Hence the current through this circuit, and thus also through the wire of resistance r, decreases. (4) Hence the voltage drop across this wire decreases. (5) But since the voltage drop across the entire circuit remains equal to the 12–volt voltage drop across the battery, the voltage drop across the remaining headlight must then *increase*.

13.6   WRITING AS PROBLEM SOLVING

Most of us need to engage in writing tasks of various complexity. Such tasks may involve writing letters, reports, applications for schools or jobs, and similar documents. More demanding tasks may involve writing essays, technical articles for publication, instructional materials, or entire books.

However, many people find such writing tasks difficult. Furthermore, many documents are poorly written so that they are hard to read and to understand. The main writing difficulties are ordinarily *not* language difficulties (like spelling or grammar), but more profound difficulties involving the presentation and organization of relevant ideas. For example, despite their extensive education, many graduate science students have difficulties articulating their ideas in well-organized form when they need to write the dissertation that summarizes the research leading to their Ph.D. degree.

Viewing writing as a problem-solving task   Writing can usefully be viewed as a complex problem-solving task since it is an effort undertaken to achieve particular goals. Hence the previous discussion of problem solving is also relevant to writing tasks.

Considering writing as a problem-solving task can not only facilitate the writing process, but can also make the product more interesting to the reader. This is not only true in the case of detective stories (where the usual starting point is a corpse and the goal of the associated problem is to find the perpetrator of the crime). It is also more generally true in writing tasks that aim to analyze, teach, or persuade. Indeed, by starting a written presentation with the statement of a problem to be addressed, readers become more clearly aware of the goal of their reading activities. Furthermore, they are likely to view the solution of a problem as more engaging and motivating than a dry presentation of factual information.

Applicability of problem-solving guidelines   The preceding point of view implies that the previously discussed guidelines for effective problem solving are equally applicable to writing tasks. Hence it is then very helpful to devise useful ways of decomposing a complex writing task into more manageable simpler tasks.

Appropriate planning is especially useful because it allows one to separate the task of formulating and organizing ideas from the linguistic task of expressing these ideas in good prose (with good spelling, grammar, phrasing, and style). Indeed, this linguistic task alone is often quite difficult—even if one already knows the content and sequence of the ideas that one wishes to express.

Wide importance of writing skills   Writing is important in all scientific and most other domains, is essential for communication with other people, and is also helpful for clarifying one's own ideas. Hence it seems worthwhile to indicate how our preceding discussion of problem solving can be exploited to improve writing skills. The next section outlines how a systematic problem-solving strategy, of the kind discussed in chapter 12, can be useful in guiding writing efforts.

13.7   APPLYING THE PROBLEM-SOLVING STRATEGY TO WRITING

The preceding comments suggest that the problem-solving strategy, outlined in figure 12.1, should also be helpful for writing tasks. The following paragraphs indicate more specifically how the successive phases of this strategy can be applied to a writing task.

13.7.1   Describing the writing task

Like any other problem, writing must start with a clear description of the task and should thus address the following issues listed in figure 12.2.

Goal of the writing task   Young children and inexperienced writers tend to be *author-centered*, that is, they look at the writing task largely from their own point of view. For example, they want to describe what is on their minds or to recount their own experiences. (This may perhaps be an appropriate point of view if one wants to keep a diary or write an autobiography.)

By contrast, more experienced writers tend to be *reader-centered*, that is, they keep in mind their intended readers and the effects that they wish to have on them. Thus their goals are centrally focused on their targeted audience rather than on themselves. For example, they may aim to convey information to the readers, to entertain them, to instruct them, to persuade them, to convert them, or to have other specified effects on them. But in all these cases, the author must start with a clear description of his or her desired goal.

Situation   Of course, an author must also be clear about the existing situation. For example, what knowledge does the author actually have about the topic to be discussed? What is the current knowledge of the intended readers? What are their attitudes and interests?

Conditions   Lastly, there are usually some conditions that must be heeded if the written work is to be acceptable. For example, what is an appropriate length for the written document?

13.7.2   Analyzing the writing task

The purpose of this analysis is to *do all useful preparatory work needed to facilitate the actual writing task*. As indicated in figure 12.5, this analysis should deal with the following issues:

• *Useful knowledge*   What is the knowledge to be conveyed to a reader? What are the central ideas?

• *Theoretical analysis*   What are the main components of this knowledge? How can they be organized? How can they be systematically elaborated? Which of these components are prerequisite for understanding others?

• *Analytic description*   At this point, it should be possible to describe and organize the relevant ideas in a form readily comprehensible to a reader. It is now also useful to prepare all tables and figures that may subsequently accompany the actual written document. (The writing task will then not have to be interrupted by the preparation of tables or figures, but can actually be aided by their presence.)

13.7.3 Constructing the written text

Constructing the written text involves solving the actual writing problem and can usefully follow the solution strategy of figure 12.9. Here it is important to identify the obstacles or needs that are likely to be encountered by an anticipated *reader*—and to remedy these needs by subproblems presented in a sequence that is motivating and comprehensible to such readers.

Planning   Since a writing task is ordinarily quite complex, it is wise to start the task by making a plan (or successively more detailed plans) before undertaking the actual writing task. As already mentioned, such planning can address all substantive issues concerned with the content and sequence of the ideas to be presented to the readers. The detailed writing task (the actual implementation of the preceding plans) is then enormously simplified since it can concentrate almost entirely on linguistic issues such as spelling, grammar, phrasing, and style.

In accordance with the comments made in section 13.2, writing plans are preliminary coarse versions of the intended detailed writing task. Indeed, most of the creative thinking and intellectual work (dealing with the content and organization of the ideas to be conveyed) can best be done at this planning stage—roughly at first and then gradually in more refined form.

The plans themselves are best made in the form of outlines (perhaps supplemented by some rough drawings) that focus on central issues without distracting minor details. Thus the content, sequencing, and sectioning of the desired written product can be specified in transparent form by means of phrases, titles, and occasional sentences. (Actual sentences, requiring attention to grammar and spelling, may be omitted). Most difficulties of content or logic can be identified and resolved at this planning stage. A sequence of successively more refined plans should then lead to an *implementable* plan that can be readily elaborated into detailed prose (because most significant decisions have already been made during the preceding planning).

A global plan encompassing the whole writing task may also be supplemented by more local plans that deal with only selected parts of this task. (Such local plans can be especially useful for those parts of the writing task that are expected to be particularly difficult.)

Plans in outline form are useful because they reveal the content and organization of the intended document in transparent form—and because the parts of the document can be easily rearranged and modified.

Such rearrangements and modifications become particularly easy with appropriate computer software tools [such as idea processors like *Inspiration* (Inspiration Software, 2006)].

Benefits of planning   Careful planning of a writing task provides the following advantages beyond the ones already mentioned.

1. Planning transforms a writing task into a systematic process of progressive refinements. Hence it makes it easier to become involved in a writing task, helps to avoid writer's block, and diminishes the fear produced by having to face the first blank page (or blank screen) of a lengthy writing project.

2. Planning facilitates writing with a coauthor since both writers can then jointly plan the basic content and organization of a writing project before individually getting engaged in producing detailed prose.

3. Planning can clearly reveal the basic structure of a document, to the author as well as to the reader. Hence it makes it easier for the author to modify or revise a document by rearranging its basic building blocks. It also makes it easier for a reader to organize his or her acquired knowledge and thus to remember it more readily.

4. By contrast, it is much more difficult to deal with a written document composed by merely writing prose (without significant prior planning). (a) Such a document can easily degenerate into a stream of consciousness that is difficult to refine or improve. (b) Although poor organization may be a document's major flaw, such organization is difficult to perceive or modify when it is immersed in a sea of words. A reviewer or an editor may then find it hard to disentangle organizational, grammatical, and rhetorical issues, all of which may contribute to an unsatisfactory product. (c) An author is much less inclined to accept suggestions for modifying his or her written prose than for modifying a plan. This greater reluctance to modify seemingly polished prose is understandable since this represents a larger invested effort and greater ego involvement.

Constructing the detailed text   After the preceding planning is deemed sufficiently complete, one can undertake the construction of the actual text. It is often useful to proceed section by section, refining the outline of each section before translating it into detailed prose. (Indeed, such alternation between local planning and its immediate implementation can provide some refreshing variety.) When actually writing, one can then focus predominantly on grammar, phrasing, and style—since the prior planning has already dealt with most issues of content and organization.

In writing, it is desirable to strive for fluency and clarity, but *not* for perfection. It is far preferable to seek greater perfection by relying on subsequent revisions and progressive refinements. It should be remembered that creation and criticism are *complementary* activities that can interfere with each other, although both are needed. Criticism can easily stifle creativity, and creative enthusiasm can easily cloud critical judgment. Hence creative writing and careful critiquing are best carried out alternately rather than simultaneously.

13.7.4   Assessing the written product

Any version of a written work needs to be carefully assessed, ideally from the perspective of a prospective reader. Colleagues or other outside reviewers can thus help by providing useful comments.

The assessment criteria of figure 12.12 are applicable to a written work as well as to the solution of any other problem. Hence the following questions are pertinent:

• *Goals achieved?*   Have the desired goals of the writing task been achieved?

• *Clearly comprehensible?*   Is everything in the presentation clear and unambiguous? Can all of it be readily understood by a prospective reader?

• *Internally satisfactory?*   Is the content free of inconsistencies and unmarred by needless repetitions or redundancies? Is the form of the prose satisfactory with respect to spelling, grammar, and style?

• *Externally consistent?*   Is the content of the work consistent with other known information? Is the work attuned to the perspectives of the intended audience?

• *Optimal?*   Is everything in the written work as clear and simple as possible? Is it likely to be appealing to prospective readers?

13.7.5   Revising

No written work can be regarded as finished without passing through one or more cycles of revisions that aim to improve the work so that the assessment criteria may be better satisfied. (If necessary, a revision may even go back all the way to the analysis and planning phases.)

It is useful to set a manuscript aside for some time before reading it again and revising it. The lapse of time can help to weaken one's prior mindset, to look at the work from a fresh point of view, and to perceive it more closely from the perspective of an outside reader.

13.7.6   Useful form of written work

Section 13.4 of this chapter pointed out the importance of presenting a problem solution in a good form. The same comment is also applicable to the form (or *format*) of a written work. In particular, this format should make apparent the organization of the work—its subdivision into sections and subsections (all clearly indicated by descriptive headings). It can also be helpful to use *local headings* that merely indicate the content of a particular paragraph (or of a few such paragraphs). All such headings make the work easier to read, to summarize, and to review later. (Indeed, a mere perusal of the headings alone should make apparent the information conveyed by the entire work.)

Lastly, a written work should have a large *I/W ratio* (a large ratio of ideas to words) so that a few skimpy ideas are not hidden in a morass of many words. This remark is consistent with the following advice from a classic book on good writing (Strunk and White, 2000, 23):

> *Vigorous writing is concise. A sentence should contain no unnecessary words, a paragraph no unnecessary sentences, for the same reason that a drawing should have no unnecessary lines and a machine no unnecessary parts. This requires not that the writer make all sentences short, or avoid all detail and treat subjects only in outline, but that every word tell.*

Paradoxically, this advice implies that it may take a longer time to produce a shorter written work than a longer one (because it may require more thought and planning).

13.8   EDUCATIONAL IMPLICATIONS

13.8.1   Proficient performers

Problem solving   Expert problem solvers can exploit their experience to anticipate the consequences of their actions and can thus plan effectively. When faced with a problem, they usually do substantial planning and then use this to construct a detailed solution in a relatively short time.

When constructing the solution of a problem, they usually deem it advantageous to avoid dealing with many numbers. Thus they often redescribe a problem in terms of parameters denoted by appropriate symbols, work out the solution in terms of these parameters, and replace these parameters by their numerical values only when this is needed.

Writing   Good writers may differ widely in the quality of their written products. But most of them think carefully before starting to write. They also critically assess what they produce and revise it several times.

Such writers may differ in the ways that they approach their writing tasks. For example, some may make progressively more detailed outlines and then produce detailed prose that they revise only a few times. Others may immediately start by writing coarse drafts, but then revise and refine these many times.

13.8.2   Inexperienced students

Problem solving   When solving problems, inexperienced students often do little planning. Their limited experience also makes it difficult for them to plan since they cannot readily foresee the consequences of their contemplated actions.

Students are also often handicapped because they have inadequately learned the prerequisite skills of reliably applying basic concepts and principles. Hence they often make many mistakes at this basic level. Furthermore, their need to struggle with such basic tasks makes it harder for them to think strategically about the more central aspects of a problem.

The problem solutions of inexperienced students are often disorganized and difficult to read. Mere sequences of equations, without any explanatory comments, are common. Hence these solutions are often hard to understand by the students themselves and by other persons. Mistakes in such solutions are also not readily identified.

Writing   Students' written products can be surprisingly poor (sometimes even in the case of graduate students). The defects are usually less due to grammatical or stylistic deficiencies, but more profoundly due to a lack of adequate focus and organization.

For example, students tend to tell what they have done, rather than to emphasize the information most relevant to a reader. There may be no clear argument, successive paragraphs may seem disconnected, statements may be made without adequate justification, and central points may get lost in a jungle of details.

13.8.3 Common instructional deficiencies

Problem solving As already mentioned, prevailing efforts to teach problem solving attempt do so largely by means of examples and practice. However, most of these efforts don't explicitly teach the decision-making skills required for problem solving. Furthermore, planning is usually not explicitly taught. Although students may be urged to plan, they are often not taught *how* to plan.

Another difficulty is that students are frequently asked to solve problems without having adequately learned the supportive knowledge necessary to do this. They often still struggle with simpler tasks (like applying prerequisite concepts or principles) while they need to address more complex problems. The result is cognitive overload that makes the learning of problem solving more difficult.

Lastly, there is a lack of emphasis on seemingly trivial information-management skills (such as writing legibly, organizing information effectively on a page, and providing enough explanatory comments to make one's work comprehensible). Yet, without these simple skills, students cannot effectively deal with complex tasks. Furthermore, such basic information-management skills could readily be taught if significant attention were devoted to them.

Writing Good writing skills are rarely explicitly taught (especially to students in scientific or engineering fields) despite their great importance to these students when they need to write dissertations, articles for publication, and applications for research grants or job prospects.

Even when attempts are made to teach writing skills, they are often inadequate—limited to giving students some simple writing tasks and then correcting their products by red comments on their papers. Some instructors even believe that writing skills cannot, or should not, be explicitly taught (because they should spontaneously emerge from the students themselves—or because explicit teaching might hamper students' creativity.)

The net result is that many students are left with rather poor writing skills that may only gradually improve in their later lives because of informal experiences as professional adults who must write letters, articles, grant applications, or other prose products.

13.8.4 Instructional suggestions

The preceding sections have identified some important components of problem-solving and writing skills. They have also suggested how these components could be taught explicitly and separately, learned by consistent well-supervised practice, and then integrated into proficiently usable skills.

Problem solving   Although learning a problem-solving strategy (like that of chapter 12) does not guarantee good problem solving, it does provide a systematic approach that is likely to lead to better problem solving. In particular, students can thereby be helped to decompose problems into judiciously chosen parts, to analyze problems carefully before attempting their actual solution, to make well-considered decisions so as to decompose problems into useful subproblems, and to assess their solutions carefully before judging them satisfactory. Although planning is not easy, it too can be taught more explicitly by emphasizing descriptions at different levels of detail and by helping students to use schematic problem solutions as guides facilitating the construction of more detailed solutions.

Writing   Although it is not necessary to teach all students writing skills that satisfy the literary criteria of English professors, all students (even students in scientific or technical domains) need to be taught to communicate their thoughts in clearly understandable prose. This can probably be done more explicitly and effectively than is currently the case, especially if writing is viewed as a complex problem-solving process that has much in common with systematic approaches to other kinds of problems.

13.9   SUMMARY

• Planning involves solving a problem in a coarsely described form (without attention to many details) and then using this schematic solution as a guide for constructing a more detailed solution.

• Plans can be made at progressively more detailed levels until one obtains final plans that can be readily implemented. Such plans can greatly facilitate more detailed decisions and thus simplify the solutions of complex problems.

• Problem solving is greatly facilitated by well-organized and easily retrievable supportive knowledge, including a repertoire of easily implemented basic problems (for example, applying important basic principles).

• The display of relevant information in a useful form can appreciably facilitate problem solving. Explanatory comments inserted in a solution can also greatly help the understanding of a solution and later modifications of it.

• Competence in a domain requires the ability to solve both quantitative and qualitative problems. Both kinds of problems may be equally difficult, although they have different kinds of simplifying and complicating features.

• Writing can usefully be viewed as a particular kind of complex problem solving. The problem-solving strategy discussed in chapter 12 is thus equally applicable to writing tasks. Furthermore, planning at progressively more detailed levels can be very useful to organize one's ideas before engaging in the actual task of writing well-phrased grammatical prose.

II-D Efficiency

14 Efficiency and Compiled Knowledge

The preceding chapters discussed how intellectual tasks can be performed *effectively*. As indicated in figure 2.3, this portion of the book (chapter 14) now examines how such tasks can also be performed *efficiently*—that is, with only small expenditures of valuable resources (such as time or effort). Such efficiency is important since all of us have only limited mental and other resources. For example, some tasks must be performed rapidly because the available time is short. Some tasks cannot be performed at all if too much energy and attention need to be devoted to them. Furthermore, it is clearly advantageous if tasks can be performed with facility and fluency.

To examine human efficiency more closely, the present chapter explores some of the following questions. (1) Under what conditions is efficiency especially important? (2) Is adequate efficiency necessary for effective performance? (3) Can people increase their efficiency by appropriate learning? (4) Can they increase it by replacing cumbersome thinking by more intuitive processes? (5) And *how* can they do these things?

These questions are important in all domains of human activity. But they are particularly important in scientific or other demanding domains because none of us would be able to deal with complex tasks unless we were sufficiently efficient.

Educational relevance   It is not surprising that students, who have recently learned about some unfamiliar domain, perform less efficiently than people who are highly experienced in this domain. Even competent students often work somewhat slowly and laboriously, make occasional mistakes, and may require some time to recognize and correct their errors.

On the other hand, students and most of us tend to be *naturally efficient* because we are all lazy—that is, inclined to attain our goals with a minimum amount of effort. But this *naive* efficiency can lead to carelessness, inappropriate shortcuts, a lack of attention to significant distinctions, and a focus on short-term efficiency rather than on longer-term considerations. For example, students often skip steps in algebraic calculations (although such shortcuts may ultimately lead to time wasted in looking for resulting errors). Similarly, students often start a problem without drawing a diagram of the situation (because they believe that it takes less time, and is more efficient, to plunge directly into the construction of the solution). Only after several months do some students realize that drawing diagrams, that help them to visualize the relevant situations, can ultimately save them time by avoiding many of their problem-solving difficulties.

Hence it is an educational challenge to help students to gain a more sophisticated sense of efficiency and to become *genuinely* efficient—so that they can achieve effective performance with an economical use of their available resources.

14.1 IMPORTANCE OF EFFICIENCY

14.1.1 Needs for efficiency

Efficient performance is not only intrinsically desirable, but may also be *necessary* to achieve performance dealing with the following important needs:

1. Achieving fast performance There are many situations where performance needs to be sufficiently speedy. For instance, only a limited time may be available for completing some task before a looming deadline. Similarly, when one is dealing with an emergency, very little time may be available for correcting a potentially dangerous situation.

2. Limiting required effort Only a limited amount of energy may be available for completing a task since excessive demands may cause one to become too tired or weary to continue. Furthermore, a task may not be worth doing (compared to other tasks) if it requires too much effort.

3. Performing complex tasks This may well be the most important need because we have only limited mental capacities and often must perform complex tasks involving many component tasks. If these subsidiary tasks cannot be performed efficiently (if they themselves require too much time and effort), then there may not be enough cognitive resources left to perform the centrally important parts of a task—so that the task cannot be performed at all.

Examples: Efficiency needed for complex tasks

Performing arithmetic calculations   An person could not perform substantive arithmetical calculations without the aid of an electronic calculator if the person could not perform simple additions or multiplications so efficiently that they are fast and effortless. (By contrast, a young child may barely be able to add or multiply two numbers.)

Reading   A person would not be able to read a book or technical article if the person could not decode individual words rapidly and effortlessly. Without such efficiency, the mere decoding of all the words would consume so many of the person's intellectual resources that none would be left available to understand the information conveyed in the article. (By contrast, when a young child is learning to read, it may spend all its mental efforts trying to decode individual words.)

Writing by typing   Writing an article on a computer or typewriter is possible only if typing has become so efficient that the requisite finger motions can be performed rapidly and effortlessly without any conscious attention. Only then can the writer remain focused on the central task of conveying appropriate information in readily comprehensible form.

Playing a musical instrument   One may justifiably admire the great facility with which good pianists play a Beethoven sonata, with all their attention concentrated on the artistic interpretation of the music. But the pianists can do this only because they have learned to perform effortlessly all required subsidiary tasks (such as reading a musical score, moving fingers to appropriate places on the keyboard, and rapidly playing familiar sequences of notes).

14.1.2   Improving efficiency

Since efficiency can be highly important (and since even effective performance can be inadequate unless it is sufficiently efficient), it is useful to examine some of the means by which efficiency can be achieved or improved.

Efficiency can be increased by simplifying the processes required to perform a task. Indeed, after performing a task a few times, one often realizes that the task could be performed in a simpler or more economical manner, that some shortcuts would be possible, or that there might be less cumbersome ways of dealing with the task. One can also deliberately look for such simplifications. Afterwards one can then always use the simpler ways of performing the task—and thus gain the efficiency needed to accomplish the task in less time and with less effort.

Other highly important, but less obvious, ways of improving efficiency rely predominantly on human memory and the resulting ability to learn from experience. Such ways of improving efficiency are discussed in the following sections.

14.2 COMPILING KNOWLEDGE

Efficiency for work in a particular domain can be improved by *compiling* knowledge—that is, by acquiring knowledge about the domain and remembering it in a readily usable form. The knowledge learned in this way can afterward be used again with less need to engage in deliberate thinking. Laborious thought processes can then be replaced by easier and faster recognition and retrieval processes.

For example, compiled procedural knowledge may be used to replace problem solving by resorting to remembered methods for solving similar problems. When such a familiar problem is recognized, one may then simply retrieve and apply the known methods—thereby eliminating the many decision processes that would otherwise be necessary. By dealing with familiar problems more easily and rapidly, one can thus considerably improve one's performance efficiency.

Declarative knowledge can be similarly compiled by augmenting general knowledge with specific knowledge about particular cases. Efficiency is thereby improved because one can then avoid much of the reasoning needed to apply general knowledge in a specific case. Instead, one can merely retrieve the appropriate case-specific knowledge stored in memory and apply it directly in the particular case.

A scientific example

Suppose that one is asked to find the acceleration of an object moving with some constant speed v around a circle of radius r. As mentioned in chapter 5, one does then not need to go back to the general definition of acceleration, but can merely invoke the remembered knowledge that the acceleration of such an object is directed toward the center of the circle and has a magnitude v^2/r.

Need for remembering applicability conditions Compiled case-specific knowledge must be accompanied by applicability conditions indicating when this knowledge is valid and useful. Such conditions must be stored together with the case-specific knowledge—and must then be properly retrieved at the time when this knowledge is invoked. As previously illustrated in section 5.4.3, many mistakes are likely to occur when this is *not* carefully done.

Storing general or case-specific knowledge? There arises then the following question: Is it better to remember general knowledge or compiled case-specific knowledge? The answer involves a tradeoff between the following two possibilities. (1) If one stores generally applicable knowledge, one needs to remember only relatively little knowledge.

However, one may have to engage in appreciable reasoning to apply it in any particular case. (2) If one stores case-specific knowledge, one must remember a large amount of such knowledge (and its applicability conditions) to deal with various possible situations. However, one then needs to do only little reasoning to apply this knowledge in a particular case.

The following is then a useful guideline. If general knowledge is easily applied in any specific case, it is preferable to remember the general knowledge without burdening one's memory by much compiled case-specific knowledge. But if general knowledge is *not* easily applied in common situations, it may be advantageous to remember the general knowledge as well as some case-specific knowledge.

A simple example

The *statics principle* asserts that the total force on any object must be zero if the object is at rest. Students, who remember this principle, may sometimes misapply it by forgetting the condition that it is applicable only if an object is at rest. On the other hand, the danger of misapplication does *not* exist if a student merely remembers Newton's general principle $ma = \mathbf{F}_{tot}$ which relates the acceleration $\mathbf{a}$ of any object to the total force $\mathbf{F}_{tot}$ acting on it. It is then obvious that, if an object is at rest so that its acceleration is zero, the total force on the object must also be zero.

14.3 ROUTINE PERFORMANCE

When initially performing some task, one proceeds deliberately by repeatedly deciding what to do, implementing the decision, and assessing whether the performance was satisfactory. But after the same task has been performed a few times, the task can be performed more *routinely* (that is, with less deliberate thought). The performance thus becomes more efficient and is carried out more rapidly and effortlessly.

The changed performance is due to the compiled knowledge acquired as a result of prior learning. Recognition and retrieval processes can now be used, instead of more laborious thinking, because one already knows what to do and how to do it.

What was learned? Some of the things that were learned, and that make the performance of the task easier and more efficient, include the following:

• *Decisions* have become simpler and faster. (1) Initially, one had to decide explicitly which step to perform when. But the previously acquired knowledge now allows one to simply recognize the situation in which a particular step is appropriate. (2) After the end of each step, one needed initially to decide which step to perform next. But, as a result of the previously acquired knowledge, the end of each step now automatically triggers the start of the next one. (3) Since one knows already the sequence of successive steps, one can now also anticipate what one will need to do during the next few steps.

• *Implementation* of each step has become easier because an implementation procedure is remembered from the previous performance of the task.

• *Assessing* the proper implementation of each step is also easier. Since the expected result of a step is already known, one needs merely to recognize that the result of a step matches one's expectation.

As a result of all this previously learned knowledge, the task can then be routinely performed by merely implementing a well-known procedure.

An everyday example

Suppose that a woman has given you written directions specifying how to drive to her house. You would then probably drive there by repeatedly consulting these directions and checking that you are still on track; you might get briefly confused at the junction of several roads; and you would be careful to count the specified number of traffic lights before you turn off at the street leading to your final destination.

Your behavior would probably be quite different the second or third time that you are driving to the woman's house. You might then confidently drive along by merely recognizing previously encountered landmarks; you would already know the route to follow at the junction of the several roads; and you would no longer need to count the number of traffic lights because you would simply recognize the turnoff to your final destination.

Example from a science course

Suppose that you are given a homework assignment asking you to solve a problem. You would then have to spend a considerable time deciding what to do and how to do it. But after some mistakes and inappropriate actions, you would probably figure out the correct solution.

On the other hand, suppose that you encountered a similar problem on a subsequent examination. You would then probably recognize that this is a familiar problem that you had already solved previously. Hence you would be pleased to encounter such a "simple" task on the examination. Indeed, you could then merely remember the solution method that you devised in the past and simply apply this method in the present case.

14.4   AUTOMATIC PERFORMANCE

Sufficiently repeated and consistent practice can lead to the extreme situation where routine performance becomes *automatic* (that is, to a situation where the performance can be reliably carried out without conscious awareness, even while one may be deliberately performing some other demanding task).

For example, when first learning to drive a car, most of us need to pay careful attention and perform the task quite deliberately in order to avoid accidents or to pass the examination leading to a driver's license. But, after driving for some months or years, our driving usually becomes so automatic that we can simultaneously think of other things, talk on a cell phone, argue with a passenger, dictate a letter, or deal with complicated problems (such as how to solve a mathematics problem or how to deal with a troublesome personal situation). For example, many times I have been driving while thinking about completely different things—and then suddenly become aware that I am in some appropriate place, but do *not* have the slightest memory of how I got there.

Indeed, automatic performance can be very complex, as the following amusing story illustrates.

Automatic musical performance

The Budapest string quartet was famous because of its fine interpretations of music by composers like Mozart and Beethoven. Accordingly, it also traveled widely to give concerts all over the world.

When once giving a concert before a large audience, the other musicians were highly surprised when the first violinist (by the name of Roisman) stood up, after the first movement of the quartet on the program, and started to walk back toward the dressing room. This was very unexpected since players ordinarily leave the stage only after completing an entire quartet. What had happened?

Before the performance, the musicians in the dressing room had been engaged in a game of bridge and then left in the middle of the game to go on stage. While playing the first movement of the quartet, Roisman was actually immersed in thinking about how to bid on the cards that he had been dealt. The performance proceeded perfectly—except for the fact that Roisman got distracted at the end of the first movement and, somewhat unaware of the actual context, started to leave the stage prematurely.

Playing a string quartet, in a concert performance before a large audience, is a very complex and demanding task. It involves complicated finger and bowing movements, reading a musical score, interpreting it artistically, and keeping properly coordinated with the other players. It takes any person at least ten years of experience before attaining this level of ability. Yet Roisman was doing all this automatically, without conscious awareness, while keeping his attention focused on the unrelated problem of how to bid in a game of bridge.

Possibility of mistakes   While the preceding story illustrates that complicated actions can be performed automatically without conscious thought, it also shows that the lack of deliberate thought may occasionally lead to mistakes.

An everyday example

After driving my car out of my garage, I am in the habit of automatically closing the garage door by activating the electronic control in my car. But because of lack of awareness of my actions, I later don't know whether I actually closed the door or not. Indeed, when returning home, I occasionally find that I failed to close the door.

Automatic recognition of mistakes   Even though scientific concepts are somewhat complex, familiarity with their properties allows automatic recognition of mistakes in their appropriate application. For example, a sufficiently experienced student may immediately *recognize* that the kinetic energy of a moving particle cannot possibly be negative, that the component of a vector cannot possibly have a magnitude larger than that of the vector itself, or that an object moving along a curved path cannot possibly have a zero acceleration.

Needs for automatic performance   As pointed out in section 14.1, adequate efficiency is needed to perform many important tasks. Indeed, highly automatic performance may be required to achieve fast and reliable performance without appreciable thought. The following are some examples:

• Emergency situations require rapid and appropriate actions when there is no time to think. Hence doctors or paramedics must be sufficiently well trained to perform automatically when they need to save the victim of a heart attack.

• A person writing a scientific or other professional paper must concentrate on the ideas that he or she wants to convey in good prose. Hence the person must have acquired sufficient facility that mere typing (that is, translating words in his or her mind into appropriately moved fingers on a keyboard) has become an automatic process requiring no conscious attention.

• A violinist must concentrate on the artistic interpretation of the music that he or she is playing. At the same time the violinist must also perform many required subsidiary actions (such as reading a musical score, moving each of the fingers of the left hand rapidly along any of the four strings of the violin, coordinating the motion of the right hand so that the bow presses with appropriate force on the proper string, and checking the correct intonation of the played notes). But all these actions must be performed automatically *without* any significant need for conscious thought.

The basic issue, illustrated in all these examples, is that human beings have only a limited amount of information-processing capacity. Because a significant amount of it is required for the deliberate performance of a complex task, many essential subsidiary processes need to be performed automatically *without* the need for conscious thought. Hence it is necessary that much consistent prior practice has been used to make these subsidiary processes automatic. This is one of the reasons that many years are required before someone can become highly proficient as a writer, musician, scientist, or expert in any other complex domain.

Achieving automatic performance   Only a small part of our nervous system is used for conscious processing and deliberate thinking. Most of it deals with subconscious, but important, processes. Learning can thus occur at both the conscious and subconscious levels. To learn the automatic performance of some task, one must deliberately engage in activities whereby some initially conscious actions become sufficiently well learned to be carried out subconsciously. This can be done by carrying out these same actions repeatedly and consistently under the same conditions. Automatic performance can thus be achieved by sufficient repeated and consistent practice.

The consistency of practice is highly important. One must practice doing the *same* things correctly every time without variations, and one must practice sufficiently frequently to avoid excessive forgetting between practice sessions. One may also need to practice component skills separately before practicing the performance of an entire task. These are some of the reasons why aspiring professional musicians practice so very frequently—or why science students must spend so many hours solving problems, or working in a laboratory, before they are ready to undertake independent scientific work.

How can one achieve genuinely good performance?   The preceding sections allow us to provide a partial answer to the following general question: How is it that human beings can effectively deal with some highly complex tasks despite deficient information-processing capabilities (such as limited short-term memory and attention span)? One part of the answer lies in humans' ability to think symbolically so that they can work with useful special descriptions of various situations. But the other part of the answer lies in their ability to combine deliberate thinking with subconscious processing that exploits learning and the large capacity of their long-term memory. Thus people can use their deliberate thinking to deal with the central aspects of some task. But they can perform subsidiary parts of a task routinely, without much deliberate thought, by relying on recognition processes and previously learned activities that can now be carried out without much conscious attention. Furthermore, they may have learned some subsidiary tasks so well that these have become automatic and require *no* conscious thought. A considerable part of a task can then been downloaded onto subconscious processes, thus freeing deliberate thinking for the more centrally important parts of a task.

The acquisition of all this subconscious knowledge requires a great deal of learning from prior experience—that is, a great deal of practice. This is why a person desiring to acquire proficiency in a domain needs to spend many hours (and even years) practicing. Indeed, much evidence suggests that it takes about ten years of deliberate practice for somebody to achieve genuine expertise in any particular field (Ericsson, Krampe, and Tesch-Romer, 1993; Hayes, 1985).

14.5 BENEFITS AND DANGERS OF EFFICIENT PERFORMANCE

Benefits   As discussed previously, the primary benefit of efficiency is that it increases people's ability to perform tasks rapidly and effortlessly. A secondary benefit is that the amount of practice, needed to achieve efficient performance, leads to knowledge so well consolidated as to be highly resistant to forgetting. If some forgetting does occur, earlier facility can be readily regained by some additional practice. Abilities, that have been practiced and acquired so reliably that performance has become effortless, can therefore persist for a very long time. For example, once a person has learned sufficiently well how to ride a bicycle or how to do basic algebra calculations, these skills are likely to remain available to the person even after many years.

Dangers   An obvious danger is that one may have learned to become efficient at performing a task by poor methods or in ways likely to lead to mistakes. To avoid the difficult task of overcoming deeply entrenched bad habits, one must thus be very careful in what one practices—and must make sure to practice *good* performance.

A persistent desire for efficiency can lead to deteriorating quality. Thus one's handwriting may become increasingly illegible, one's typing increasingly riddled by typographical errors, one's piano playing increasingly interspersed with wrong notes, and one's calculations increasingly marred by inadvertent errors. To avoid such kinds of sloppy performance, one must provide sufficient times when one can temporarily slow down and practice with deliberate attention to good quality.

Lastly, facility in performing some tasks may make a person reluctant to learn ultimately more efficient ways of performing them. For example, a writer who relies on his handwriting skills, and on a secretary who can type the resulting manuscripts, may be unwilling to learn how to write more efficiently by using a keyboard connected to a computer.

14.6   EDUCATIONAL IMPLICATIONS

14.6.1   Proficient performers

Experts in a field have usually acquired large amounts of knowledge that they can use routinely or even automatically. Hence they can perform efficiently and also tackle complex tasks with relative ease. However, it may have taken them much time and long experience to acquire all this knowledge. Furthermore, they are often not consciously aware of all their acquired knowledge (some of this knowledge is for them *tacit*) so that they may have difficulty communicating some of this knowledge to other people.

Experts may often simply *recognize* things that deliberately thinking students find difficult to identify. For instance, an expert physicist may read the statement of a mechanics problem and automatically visualize in his mind all the forces acting on an object. On the other hand, inexperienced students often have substantial difficulties correctly identifying all the forces on a particular object—even when they deliberately try to do this. Similarly, an expert may immediately recognize a mistake in the solution of a problem. But a student, even when realizing that something is wrong, may need considerable time to locate the responsible mistake.

14.6.2   Inexperienced students

Since inexperienced students lack the accumulated knowledge required for efficiency, they often need to proceed laboriously, with deliberate thought, to perform tasks that experts can perform quickly and almost intuitively. They may require considerable experience and practice before they can gain greater facility. Even competent students, who have learned to perform tasks correctly, are unlike experts because they usually perform these tasks more slowly, with deliberate thought, while proficient experts perform them rapidly and effortlessly. Furthermore, students often exhibit the kinds of inefficiencies mentioned at the beginning of this chapter.

14.6.3 Common instructional deficiencies

Some instructors are satisfied if their students can perform reasonably well, but are not much concerned with the efficiency of their performance. For example, they may think that it is important that students can perform tasks correctly, but that their required time is fairly irrelevant. After all, would it not be sensible to prefer a student who can answer correctly only one question on an examination—rather than another student who answers two such questions with various mistakes?

This point of view is, however, somewhat simplistic. As previously discussed, complex performance requires adequate efficiency. Hence one must make sure to provide enough practice that students learn to perform some important tasks not only correctly, but also with sufficient facility (that is, with little time and effort). For example, young students might learn how to perform simple arithmetic problems correctly by counting with the aid of the fingers on their hands. But this method would be inadequate to deal with more complex arithmetic tasks.

14.6.4 Instructional suggestions

It is particularly important to disabuse students of naive notions of efficiency that strive to save time and effort without regard to quality of performance or longer-term consequences. As mentioned at the end of the preceding chapter, it is usually much less effective to give students sage advice than to help them learn from their own experience. Thus it can be worthwhile to let students make mistakes or get into trouble by skipping steps (by failing to draw helpful diagrams or by jumping to unjustified conclusions) and then to point out that the students' actions ultimately did *increase* the time required to complete a task or did *increase* the amount of effort required to diagnose and correct the resultant mistakes.

One cannot expect students to develop highly efficient or proficient performance within the limited time of a single course. But one *can* try to provide enough time and practice so that students transcend barely tolerable efficiency to reach a level of competence allowing them to use their recently acquired knowledge with some facility. For example, students learning a foreign language should be able to speak without a constant preoccupation with grammatical rules—and students learning algebra should be able to solve algebra problems without needing to struggle with the syntax of algebraic expressions.

Striving for such a level of facile competence is well worth the requisite time invested in consistent practice. Students can thereby ensure that their acquired knowledge is not quickly forgotten—and that it can be used as a sound basis for gradually achieving genuinely efficient performance.

14.7 SUMMARY

• Efficient performance is desirable because it is fast and effortless—and also because it allows the performance of complex tasks that could not be carried out without adequately efficient performance of requisite component tasks.

• Efficiency can be achieved by compiling relevant knowledge in a form that can be readily remembered and used.

• The acquisition of compiled knowledge by previous learning enables one to use retrieval and recognition processes to perform tasks originally performed with more laborious thought. As a result, such tasks become routine so that they can be performed faster and with less effort.

• Consistently repeated practice can lead to automatic performance so that a task can be performed without conscious awareness (even while simultaneously using deliberate thought to carry out some different task).

• Because of their long experience, experts in a domain have acquired large amounts of both conscious and subconscious knowledge that they can exploit to achieve highly efficient performance.

II-E Reliability

15   Quality Assurance

The preceding chapters discussed the kinds of knowledge that enable good performance, but failed to emphasize that all such knowledge can be useful only if it can be reliably trusted to be of good quality. Hence this chapter deals with the last issue listed in figure 2.3, the reliability of acquired knowledge.

We shall be interested in exploring the following questions: (1) How can one prevent defects in knowledge or performance? (2) How can one detect such defects, diagnose the reasons for them, and ascertain why they occurred? (3) How then can one correct such defects and prevent similar defects in the future? (4) More generally, how can one deliberately examine one's own knowledge and thought processes to ensure that they are reliably effective?

All these questions are clearly important in any scientific field since one cannot use faulty or deficient knowledge to make successful predictions. They are equally important in any applied science or engineering field if one wants to design artifacts that actually work in intended ways. Lastly, since research or development projects are increasingly team efforts, it is crucial that each person can trust that the work of other people is reliable and free of mistakes.

Educational relevance   Students are often not very concerned about the quality of their work, probably because they are unduly self-confident and consider checking unnecessary or burdensome. Even on examinations, where care is clearly to their advantage, students may sometimes prominently display answers that are obviously wrong (such as molecular speeds of impossibly high magnitude). Indeed, students' mistakes are sometimes due to sheer carelessness—for example, to illegible or poorly displayed writing that can cause them to disregard relevant information.

Many students regard their mistakes as mere slips rather than as possible indications of significant deficiencies in their knowledge. Furthermore, a teacher's red marks on a paper are not impressive and don't convey the fact that even seemingly small mistakes can be fatal in the real world. For example, such mistakes can vitiate even the most laboriously designed project, can result in missing unique opportunities to run an experiment on a spacecraft, or can cause an experiment to fail or an airplane to crash. Similarly, a mere mistake in a decimal point can lead to an inappropriately specified dosage of a drug and to the resulting death of a patient.

Lastly, students often make few deliberate attempts to learn from their mistakes. As a result, they may repeatedly make the same mistake and persist for an unduly long time in some of their misconceptions.

Educational efforts should therefore deliberately motivate students to ensure the quality of their work. In particular, students should *want* to avoid deficiencies or mistakes—and should *know* how to do this.

15.1 ENSURING GOOD QUALITY

Figure 15.1 outlines a strategy useful for ensuring that performance is of good quality. This strategy includes the following main processes.

1. Preventing defects To be well prepared for undertaking a task, one must possess the needed knowledge, know the criteria specifying the desired good quality, and have means or precautions designed to prevent troublesome defects.

2. Assessing the performance One must carefully assess any completed performance in order to detect any defects that have not been prevented, to diagnose the underlying deficiencies responsible for observed defects, and to identify the likely causes leading to these defects.

3. Improving the performance The preceding assessment may then be used to correct the detected defects. Even if this is not possible, one can learn from past mistakes to improve one's knowledge and to devise improved means of preventing future performance defects.

The actions indicated in figure 15.1 are sometimes carried out spontaneously by people in everyday life. But if these actions are implemented systematically, they can ensure significantly better performance.

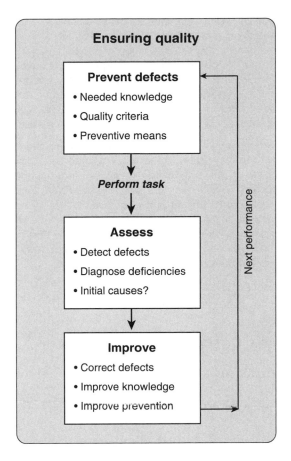

Figure 15.1
A quality-assurance strategy.

Familiar examples of quality assurance

The following examples illustrate how the actions described in figure 15.1 are commonly used in attempts to achieve good performance.

Driving a car   We know what to expect when driving a well-functioning car and are thus fairly quick to *detect* some defect when the ride seems bumpy. Stopping the car to look at it more closely, we might then diagnose that the underlying *deficiency* seems to be a flat tire. We might then suspect that the initial *cause* of the observed defect was our failure to inspect the tires before our trip. To *correct* the situation, we may then mount our spare tire. Learning from this experience, we may then also *improve* our knowledge about proper maintenance and learn that a useful *preventive measure* would be to check the condition of the tires before any long trip.

Airplane transportation   Airplane accidents can be so catastrophic that a great deal of systematic attention is paid to their prevention. For example, much time and effort are invested in good pilot training and in *preventive* airplane maintenance. If a plane crashes, thorough attempts are made to *diagnose* the *deficiencies* responsible for the crash and to identify the probable *causes* of these. Unfortunately, once a crash has occurred, it cannot be *corrected*. But every attempt is made to *improve knowledge* about the reasons for such crashes and to devise better *preventive means* to avoid similar crashes in the future.

Taking an examination   To prepare himself for an examination and *prevent* poor performance, John reviewed the relevant knowledge beforehand. When solving a problem on the examination, he arrived at a final numerical answer that seemed unreasonably large. After *detecting* this *defect*, John went over the calculations leading to his answer and *diagnosed* that one of his equations was incorrect *because* he had mistakenly applied a principle when it was not valid. John now *corrected* this defect to obtain a more sensible final result. To *prevent* similar future mistakes, he also tried to remember an explicit warning to use this principle only in those situations where it is actually valid.

The following sections examine more closely the different parts of the quality-assurance strategy of figure 15.1.

15.2   PREVENTING DEFECTS

It is far preferable to prevent defects than to correct them afterward. Indeed, an old proverb (slightly modified for modern times) asserts that "An ounce of prevention is worth a megaton of cure."

15.2.1   Needed knowledge

It is essential to have the knowledge required for any task of interest and to verify that this knowledge is effectively usable. In particular, if relevant knowledge has been acquired some time ago, one must review it to make sure that it has not been partially forgotten.

15.2.2   Quality criteria

A knowledge of appropriate criteria for judging quality is necessary for prevention as well as for remediation. Some of these criteria may be quite general, while others may pertain to a particular task of interest. Furthermore, some of these criteria may deal with the performance *process*, while others may deal with the resulting *product*.

For instance, general criteria for assessing the quality of a performance *process* might specify that this process should be systematic and targeted to achieve a clearly defined goal. They might also specify that the process should be efficient so that it does not require excessive time and effort.

Some general criteria for assessing the quality of a *product* have already been listed in figure 12.12. For example, these specify that a performance should have led to the intended goal, that the result should be clearly specified, that it should be internally satisfactory, that it should be consistent with outside knowledge, and that it should be as good as reasonably possible.

15.2.3 Preventive means

Explicit warnings about likely errors   Many mistakes can be prevented by explicit warnings about likely errors, warnings that can be remembered and thus help to prevent the occurrence of such errors. Some of these warnings may be about previously committed errors that one hopes to avoid in the future. But other warnings may concern errors that can be readily predicted (even without prior experience) because they involve failures to heed fine discriminations.

For instance, some warnings may be about errors due to inadequate specifications (such as specifying a velocity by a magnitude without mentioning its direction). Other warnings may concern the need to heed validity conditions that restrict the range of applicability of a concept or principle. Still other warnings may deal with the need to make appropriate discriminations to avoid confusions (for example, distinguishing the meaning of the word *acceleration* in science from its meaning in daily life, or discriminating between the concepts *velocity* and *acceleration*).

Clear display of information   An important, but often neglected, way of preventing defects is to ensure a clear display of the information available at any time during the performance of a task. This information may constantly change as more information accumulates during a task, but all decisions depend crucially on the information available at any stage.

To maintain a clear display of information, it is helpful to do the following: (1) Summarize all relevant information in easily legible and well-organized form. (2) Use a clear format of presentation, and subdivide long arguments into more comprehensible sections. (3) Avoid shortcuts that may make it harder to understand what was actually done and that may lead to mistakes. (Subsequent corrections may sometimes be more time-consuming than any intended time savings.)

(4) Highlight important results and label them by numbers to facilitate reference to them. (5) Include explanatory comments to make it easier to understand or modify the things that were done.

Knowing alternative methods   It is useful to know several alternative ways of performing a task (even if some of these ways may sometimes be less effective or efficient). One is then able to resort to some of these alternatives if the need arises. (For example, one may be able to make calculations on paper even if electronic calculators are malfunctioning or not available.)

Limiting dependence on other people   It is wise to avoid undue dependence on help provided by other people or "experts." Indeed, one may be completely incapacitated if such people are temporarily unavailable or fail to perform satisfactorily. Greater flexibility can be achieved if one is able to act independently in case of need (even if the results of self-reliant actions may be less good).

Anticipating difficulties   It is dangerous to assume that everything will go according to prior expectations. Thus one needs always to be prepared to deal with the *principle of maximum vexation* (or *Murphy's law*) which asserts that everything that can go wrong will probably do so. Hence it is useful to know some of the things that might fail or go awry—and also to know what one might then do to correct or circumvent the resulting difficulties.

15.3   ASSESSING PERFORMANCE

Performance can usefully be assessed both during and after the performance of a task. As previously mentioned and indicated in figure 15.1, such an assessment involves detecting defects, diagnosing the underlying deficiencies responsible for them, and identifying the likely causes leading to these deficiencies.

15.3.1   Detecting defects

Defects can be detected by noticing any deviations from expectations or from known quality criteria. It is best to detect defects *during* the process of performing a task. This can be done by closely monitoring this process at all times and promptly remedying any detected defect. In this way one can avoid an accumulation of various defects whose joint presence may make implementation of the task increasingly difficult. It is also easier to diagnose the reasons for a defect soon after it becomes apparent, rather than much later when one may no longer remember the events leading to it.

After completing a task, one needs to inspect the resulting product carefully to detect any defects that are indicated by deviations from general quality criteria (like those listed in figure 12.12) or from other more specific criteria.

People may fail to detect defects because of a biased mental set that leads them to perceive what they expect to see. Hence it is useful if a person, after completing the task, can wait some time before examining its results—because the person is then more likely to look at the results from the point of view of an outside observer. It is even better if the results can actually be checked by some other individuals since these can often perceive defects that may escape the notice of a person intimately engaged in a task.

15.3.2 Diagnosing deficiencies

When a defect has been detected, the more difficult problem is to diagnose the underlying deficiencies that are responsible for it. This problem may require some search to identify the possible deficiencies—or the formulation and checking of hypotheses suggesting what the possible deficiencies might be.

The deficiencies are often various kinds of mistakes. For example, these mistakes may be mistakes of *omission* because an important step in a method, or feature in a situation, has been forgotten or neglected. Alternatively, such mistakes may be mistakes of *commission* because a step in a method has been improperly executed or a feature in a situation has been erroneously specified.

The proper diagnosis of a deficiency facilitates subsequent improvements because these can then focus on removing the identified deficiency.

15.3.3 Identifying causes of deficiencies

Why did a particular deficiency arise—that is, what was its initial probable cause? An assessment answering this question can be very helpful in trying to prevent similar deficiencies in the future.

Many possible causes can lead to performance deficiencies. The following are merely some examples: (1) Incorrect application of a principle, or careless work, are common reasons for deficiencies. (2) Excessively many directions for specifying a method can easily lead to the omission of some steps. (3) Interruptions or distractions during a task often lead to mistakes. (4) When implementing a task, the mere intention of executing some step can be confused with its actual execution—so that the step itself remains omitted. (5) A carefully specified procedure for implementing a task may be too inflexible to deal with slightly changed circumstances or unexpected occurrences. (A more heuristic problem-solving strategy, although less well specified, may then be better suited to cope with the task.)

15.4   IMPROVING PERFORMANCE

15.4.1   Correcting defects

In many cases, one can improve one's performance by doing parts of the task again so as to correct the defects identified in the preceding assessment. When this is feasible, it should certainly be done. One is then likely to attain a result of the desired good quality.

However, identified defects cannot always be rectified because deficient performance is sometimes irremediable. For example, suppose that a scientist tries to perform an experiment and fails to notice that one wire in the apparatus is improperly connected. Then the apparatus will not work properly, all the scientist's efforts will have been wasted, and it may well be impossible to repeat the experiment for several months. As another example, suppose that an airplane crashes and 200 passengers are killed. There is then nothing that can be done to restore the plane or revive the passengers. All one can do is to try to learn from the experience so as to ensure safer airline travel for other passengers in the future.

Application to editing

You may sometimes be asked to *edit* someone else's work (that is, to check and correct it). For example, a friend may ask you to provide comments and suggestions about his or her work so that it can be improved before it is exposed to the outside world. Similarly, when an author wishes to publish an article or a book, the publisher usually asks someone else to edit the work so as to make it suitable for publication. The editor then makes various corrections and proposes some appropriate modifications.

The quality-assurance strategy of figure 15.1 suggests that an editor should specify proposed modifications that are based on explicit prior assessments. Thus it is best if the editor suggests improvements only after explicitly indicating what identified defects these are designed to remedy. This way of implementing the editing task has the following advantages: (1) Editors are then more likely to suggest modifications only for good reasons, and not merely because their own stylistic preferences differ from those of the author. (2) If authors are made aware of existing defects in their work, they themselves may be able to remedy these more effectively than an editor since they have a deeper understanding of their work and are thus also less likely to make corrections that might introduce further difficulties. (3) When authors are made explicitly aware of common kinds of defects in their work, they are more likely to learn how to avoid these in the future.

15.4.2 Improving knowledge

In all cases, whether remediable or not, it is wise to use the assessment to improve one's knowledge about what to do (or not to do) in the future. Indeed, learning from past experiences and past mistakes is a very effective way of improving one's knowledge and performance.

15.4.3 Improving prevention of deficiencies

It is always beneficial to use one's past experience to devise improved ways of preventing mistakes. For example, the prior assessment may suggest new warnings about defects to be avoided or may suggest less error-prone ways of performing similar tasks.

Written notes about experienced difficulties or misconceptions, and about the ways that were used to remedy them, can be very useful. Such notes provide the following benefits (and may even save time in the long run): (1) Writing such notes ensures a more explicit and reliable understanding of the relevant issues. (2) The writing process strengthens memory about how to avoid similar difficulties in the future. (3) Even if such a difficulty is not avoided, a person's own past notes are useful because they are readily comprehensible to the person. A look back at them can then immediately clarify the difficulty and indicate how it can be remedied.

15.5 METACOGNITION

A concern with the quality of performance leads naturally to a more general question about *metacognition* (that is, about a person's cognition about his or her own cognition). In other words, can people be explicitly aware of their own knowledge and thinking so as to improve these deliberately?

Such metacognition requires that people habitually observe their own performance, notice any deficiencies in it, and try to correct them by improving their knowledge and thinking. Such metacognition can clearly be very helpful for the following reasons: (1) People can thereby become more self-reliant and less constantly dependent on knowledge and methods transmitted by other persons. (2) The kinds of knowledge and processes devised by a person are likely to be congenial to the person and well adapted to the person's own ways of thinking. (3) Such metacognition can lead to a better recognition of one's own abilities or limitations. (4) Over extended periods of time, such metacognition can lead to substantial cumulative improvements in a person's knowledge and thinking. (5) Metacognition helps to ensure better performance quality. (6) It may also lead to greater creativity and more contributions to the knowledge of other people.

It should be apparent that metacognition is a useful intellectual skill that can be developed by focusing attention on one's own thinking and by considering explicitly cognitive issues like those discussed in the preceding chapters. Metacognition can also be enhanced by deliberate efforts to assess and improve the quality of one's own performance. Lastly, students' metacognitive abilities can be fostered by instructional approaches that not only aim to achieve good student performance, but also encourage students to become aware of the thought processes whereby such performance can be attained or improved.

15.6   EDUCATIONAL IMPLICATIONS

15.6.1   Proficient performers

Proficient persons make sure that their knowledge and skills remain usable and up to date. They frequently check their work *while* they are engaged in a task—and *afterward* carefully assess the results of their performance. Indeed, repeated checking and correcting of their work are usually integral parts of their performance.

For example, a scientist carrying out an experiment routinely checks all electrical connections before starting an experimental run and repeatedly verifies that all instruments are functioning properly during the experiment. Similarly, when making a calculation, a scientist usually does not merely manipulate symbolic equations, but also repeatedly checks that the qualitative implications of these equations are reasonable.

15.6.2 Inexperienced students

By contrast, inexperienced students often act in the ways described at the beginning of this chapter. They often *assume* that reasonably careful work will lead to good results. Because of this delusion of infallibility, they also often perceive no need to check their work. Furthermore, they often make no deliberate efforts to learn from their mistakes.

15.6.3 Common instructional deficiencies

Quality standards in many courses are often fairly lax. For example, students may get reasonably good grades despite many "minor" mistakes, even if these mistakes may lead to seriously wrong answers. Such students then merely accumulate lots of "partial credit" (even it they did not correctly implement a single task that they attempted). As a result, students often view their mistakes as mere "slips," are not discouraged from being sloppy, and don't learn that seemingly minor mistakes in real life can sometimes lead to fatal consequences.

Furthermore, students are often not explicitly taught systematic checking methods designed to reduce errors. If quality standards are too low or not enforced, students may then also have no incentives for learning such methods.

15.6.4 Instructional suggestions

It would clearly be useful to emphasize the importance of good quality and to foster in students a *desire* for good quality in their work. In particular, students would be well advised to adopt the attitude that anything done by them should be presumed to be *defective*—unless they can convince themselves otherwise. (This attitude is appropriate *not* because students are dumb, but because all human beings are error-prone.)

Students must be explicitly taught how to assess the quality of their work so that they themselves can detect and correct their mistakes. (Such teaching may be aided by a quality-assurance strategy like that shown in figure 15.1, and by some explicit assessment criteria like those in figure 12.12.)

The teaching of self-assessment can be helped by letting students assess the work of *other* students (or work deliberately constructed to

contain defects). The reason is that students are likely to be less preju-
diced and more objective when looking at the work of other persons
than when appraising their own work. Hence an examination of other
people's work can provide them with useful insights and good practice.

It is particularly useful to help students learn from their mistakes.
This can be done by exploiting each of the students' homework assignments or examinations as a learning opportunity. When grading such a
homework assignment or examination, indicate each of the detected
mistakes, but do *not* correct it. Instead, give the student immediately afterward a special assignment asking, about each of the indicated mistakes, the following two main questions (suggested by the assessment
strategy of figure 15.1): (1) What underlying deficiency is responsible
for this mistake? What was the likely cause leading to it? (2) Correct
this mistake. What can you do to improve your knowledge, and how
can you prevent a similar mistake in the future? (Students answering
these questions carefully can be rewarded by being penalized less se-
verely for their original mistakes.)

The main purpose of these questions is to engage students more
actively in their own learning than if they merely looked at an instructor's red corrections on their papers.

15.7 SUMMARY

• Even careful performance may be inadequate unless one makes deliberate efforts to ensure the good quality of everything that one does
or uses.

• Good quality can be ensured by a strategy (like that in figure 15.1)
that involves the following major steps: (1) *Preventing* defects by having
needed knowledge, heeding specified quality criteria, and devising explicit means of preventing likely mistakes. (2) *Assessing* performance
by detecting any defects, diagnosing the underlying deficiencies, and
identifying the likely causes leading to these. (3) *Improving* the performance by correcting the detected defects, improving one's knowledge,
and improving future prevention of defects.

• If consistently used, such a strategy helps one to learn from past
mistakes and can lead to systematic improvements of one's knowledge
and performance.

• Metacognition involves a person's monitoring of his or her
own performance and thought processes so as to improve them
appropriately.

• Proficient performers usually view quality monitoring and checking as integral parts of their work. But inexperienced students are often unduly self-confident and reluctant to engage in efforts needed to check their work.

15.8   GOOD PERFORMANCE AND THE INSTRUCTIONAL CHALLENGE

Good performance requires attention to all of the cognitive needs discussed in the preceding part II of the book (chapters 3 through 15). In particular, these needs include those summarized in figure 15.2: (1) The availability of both declarative and procedural knowledge, accompanied by relevant applicability conditions. (2) The ability to properly specify and interpret this knowledge—and to manage one's memory effectively. (3) The useful description and organization of all this knowledge. (4) The flexible use of this knowledge by making judicious decisions and displaying good problem-solving skills. (5) The ability

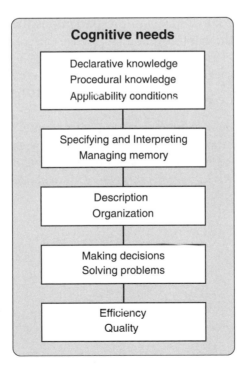

Figure 15.2
Cognitive needs for good performance.

to use knowledge efficiently while ensuring that it is of reliably good quality.

Singly, each of these cognitive needs may seem of minor importance. But collectively they are essential because they help to ensure the effective use of acquired knowledge. Indeed, the difficulties displayed by many college students in their science courses can often be traced to lacks in meeting these cognitive needs. Hence students may emerge from such courses with knowledge that is largely nominal rather than flexibly usable, that is beset by mistakes and misconceptions, and that does not provide a firm basis for further learning. Instructional efforts must, therefore, focus sufficient attention on these cognitive needs.

Preview of the following chapters   The present chapter of the book concludes part II, dealing with the cognition facilitating good performance. Hence we can now go on to explore the other cognitive and educational issues mentioned at the end of chapter 1.

In particular, the next two chapters (chapters 16 and 17) examine some of the prior knowledge and preconceptions that students bring to instruction. Although this initial knowledge can sometimes facilitate the learning of scientific subjects, it may often be unduly naive and lead to substantial learning obstacles that need to be overcome. Instructional efforts must thus pay proper attention to such preexisting student knowledge.

All the subsequent chapters (starting with chapter 18) then discuss the following central instructional challenge: *How can a better understanding of the preceding cognitive issues be exploited to develop instruction that can help students learn good performance in scientific or similar complex domains?*

III   PRIOR KNOWLEDGE

16   Unfamiliar Knowledge Domains

A person's prior knowledge can greatly influence the ease with which the person can learn unfamiliar knowledge in some other domain. An important special case is that where a student, who is familiar with everyday knowledge, has to learn the knowledge needed in a scientific or similar such domain. The existence of the student's prior knowledge may then sometimes help, but often also hinder, the learning of the unfamiliar knowledge.

Indeed, the learning difficulties can be substantial since they may involve not only specific factual and procedural knowledge, but also the overarching cognitive framework in which such knowledge is embedded. This framework specifies the primary goal of interest in a particular domain and the requirements needed to attain this goal. All the knowledge in such a domain is thus explicitly or implicitly devised to help attain its primary goal and its corresponding requirements.

This present chapter explores the following general questions: (1) What kinds of difficulties are encountered when one is trying to learn about an unfamiliar knowledge domain? (2) What is the primary goal of science, and how does it differ from the primary goals everyday life? (3) What are the corresponding requirements of these goals, and how do they differ between science and everyday life? (4) What are some of the differences between scientists' and students' conceptions of science? (5) How do these differing conceptions affect students' learning of science?

The next chapter will then illustrate in greater detail how a particular subject (mechanics), that has historically been studied by scientists within the scientific framework, has led to concepts and principles significantly different from those developed more naturalistically within the framework of everyday life. It will then become apparent how such differences can cause many learning difficulties for students.

Educational relevance   The preceding questions are obviously important for science education and for efforts to improve such education. Indeed, many students need to take science courses, and such students often have difficulties learning the relevant scientific subjects. For example, students commonly focus on learning factual information—while their teachers may aim to teach them how to apply basic scientific principles and how to use these to solve scientifically significant problems. Furthermore, students often exhibit various scientific misconceptions that are persistent and difficult to change. Teachers of such students thus face a great number of practical instructional challenges.

16.1   PRIOR KNOWLEDGE AND NEW LEARNING

16.1.1   Learning and knowledge restructuring

When people try to learn something, they don't approach the learning process with blank minds, but come with all kinds of preexisting knowledge. Thus they have a prior knowledge structure that must be modified. This prior knowledge may either help or hinder the new learning, but cannot be ignored because it may have important effects.

Analogy: Remodeling a house

Learning is more analogous to remodeling an existing house than to building a new house on bare ground. For example, when remodeling a house, some modifications may be fairly easy because some needed structures are already in place. However, other modifications may be difficult (or even impossible) because previously existing structures may interfere—or may even completely prevent such modifications from being made.

16.1.2   Different knowledge domains

There exist many different knowledge domains suited for the performance of different kinds of tasks. For example, the *everyday domain* is well suited for the tasks commonly encountered in everyday life, *science* is well suited for the tasks of predicting and explaining many observable phenomena, *mathematics* is well suited for calculations and logical reasoning tasks, and the *law* is well suited for the handling of legal documents and litigations. There exist also many more specialized domains (such as physics, chemistry, biology, geology, psychology, engineering, medicine, accounting, business, and real estate).

Topical knowledge about a domain   Every such domain contains a great deal of *topical* knowledge about the topics and tasks of particular interest in this domain. If one wants to learn about an unfamiliar domain, one must thus learn much of the topical knowledge of this domain. For example, if one wants to learn physics, one must learn much factual knowledge about physics, many of the special concepts and principles of physics, and the special methods needed to apply these.

Cognitive framework of a domain   The topical knowledge about a domain is embedded in a more general *cognitive framework*. This framework specifies the primary *goals* in this domain, the requirements needed to attain these goals, and the beliefs prevalent in the domain. If one wants to learn about a domain, one must thus not only learn its topical knowledge, but must also acquire more general knowledge about its broader cognitive framework. (This general knowledge may be called *metaknowledge* since it is higher-level knowledge about more specific knowledge.)

For example, topical knowledge of mathematics involves knowledge of the concepts, principles, and reasoning methods of mathematics. But *metaknowledge* of mathematics is more general knowledge about the goals of mathematics and the requirements needed to attain these goals (for example, the criteria for judging the validity of mathematical proofs).

Knowledge of a domain's cognitive framework has pervasive consequences. For example, it specifies what is deemed important or valid in the domain, what kinds of topical knowledge are useful, and what sorts of performance are considered desirable.

Coexistence of different frameworks   Different cognitive frameworks may coexist without mutual interference—if they are properly used for different purposes or in different contexts. Familiar examples are the differing cognitive frameworks of everyday life, of science, of the law, of the arts, and of religion. However, difficulties may arise if these frameworks are indiscriminately commingled.

Seemingly incompatible frameworks

Seemingly incompatible cognitive frameworks may sometimes coexist in the same person. For example, a scientific framework (which is highly rational, innovative, and empirically grounded) may coexist with political or religious beliefs that are largely ideological and deeply rooted in historical traditions. (Even if such different frameworks are concerned with explanations or predictions, they may judge their validity by very different criteria.)

The coexistence of seemingly incompatible cognitive frameworks in the same person is not unduly surprising. Human beings have only a veneer of rationality on top of a largely non-rational base, they may deal with different concerns in different ways, and there are no intrinsic human requirements for any over-arching consistency. Hence people can be so compartmentalized that they may use quite different ways of thinking in different domains.

16.1.3   Learning about unfamiliar domains

Learning about an unfamiliar domain is particularly difficult. Indeed, one must then not only learn new concepts and factual knowledge, but needs then also to modify preexisting knowledge so as to adopt a new cognitive framework and learn new ways of thinking. The following learning difficulties are then commonly encountered:

1. Importing ways of thinking, effective and efficient in the previously familiar domain, into the unfamiliar domain where they are inadequate.

2. Trying to devise new ways of thinking that can overcome perceived inadequacies and may be better adapted to the new domain. However, without sufficient learning from people who are familiar with the new domain, persons may devise ways of thinking that are ineffective or inefficient.

16.1.4   Applications to the learning of science

Many students (from elementary school all the way up to college or graduate school) need to learn scientific subjects—and many students find this difficult. This is a common and important case where students need to go from the familiar domain of everyday life into an unfamiliar domain (the domain of science).

At first blush one might think that these domains are not very different since "the whole of science is nothing more than a refinement of everyday thinking" (Einstein, 1982, 290). But this refinement, extending over several centuries, has been very substantial and has resulted in a scientific domain that is significantly different from everyday life.

Accordingly, the next several sections compare the scientific cognitive framework with the everyday framework that is familiar to most students. In particular, these sections compare the central goals and corresponding requirements of these two domains, identify their salient differences, and examine some of the implications for learning and instruction.

16.2 EVERYDAY AND SCIENTIFIC DOMAINS

Everyday life is a *naturalistic* domain—one that developed as a result of natural evolutionary processes, mostly without explicitly formulated goals or systematic methods designed to attain these goals. By contrast, science is an *artificial* (or humanly designed) domain that is focused on a highly explicit goal and has been deliberately constructed by special people ("scientists") in efforts to attain this goal.

These significant differences have important implications that are examined more closely in the following paragraphs.

16.2.1 Contrasting goals

Primary goals of everyday life   The primary goals of everyday life, although *implicit* and rarely explicitly formulated, are roughly the following: To lead a pleasant life and to cope satisfactorily with the issues encountered in it. Such coping requires also the ability to explain observable phenomena adequately so as to make sense of the world, and the ability to make predictions so as to anticipate adequately the results of one's actions.

Primary goal of science   On the other hand, science has the following highly *explicit* primary goal: To discover compact theoretical knowledge that enables the prediction or explanation of the maximum number of observable phenomena on the basis of a minimum number of basic premises. (Figure 16.1 illustrates schematically this correspondence between theoretical knowledge and observable phenomena.) Einstein (1982, p. 293) describes this goal in the following words:

> The aim of science is, on the one hand, a comprehension, as complete as possible, of the connection between the sense experiences in their totality, and, on the other hand, the accomplishment of this aim by the use of a minimum of primary concepts and relations.

Hence, science requires the creation of compact knowledge that is specified sufficiently precisely to allow unambiguous and testable predictions of many observable phenomena. Furthermore, the consistent implementation of this requirement is believed to lead to increasing progress toward the scientific goal.

Relation between pure and applied science

Goal of an applied science   The preceding comments specify the primary goal of a pure science. By contrast, the primary goal of an applied science (like engineering or medicine) is to acquire knowledge that enables the design of

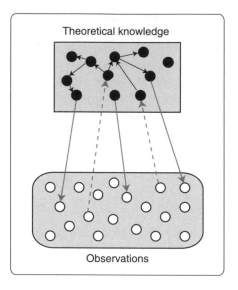

Figure 16.1
Correspondence between theoretical knowledge and observations.

practical means for achieving desired human goals. Such design requires adequate abilities to predict the consequences of contemplated actions. Hence the intellectual goal of pure science is a necessary subgoal (or requirement) for an applied science.

There is a strong mutual interaction between pure and applied sciences, for the following reasons.

Pure sciences help applied sciences Pure sciences provide knowledge and methods that are highly useful for applied sciences. Furthermore, pure sciences often suggest various practical applications.

Applied sciences help pure sciences Applied sciences often provide excellent tests of theoretical knowledge since the ability to design practical applications requires highly successful predictions. In their attempts to design practical applications, applied sciences may also encounter poorly understood phenomena that need to be explained by pure science. Lastly, applied sciences often develop devices and instruments that are highly useful for purely scientific investigations.

16.2.2 Contrasting requirements

Correspondingly different requirements are needed to attain the differing goals of everyday life or of science.

Requirements of everyday life As previously mentioned, we aim to make our lives adequately pleasant (although we can't always expect

to achieve happiness). Similarly, we aim to make our everyday performance satisfactory (although not necessarily perfect). In other words,
we aim to *satisfice* (to make situations satisfactory), but don't ordinarily
strive to *optimize* (to make situations as good as possible). For example,
rather than striving for perfection, we often strive for efficiency (performance requiring relatively little effort, time, or money) to keep life reasonably pleasant.

Requirements of science By contrast, science explicitly aims to
predict and explain the *maximum* number of observable phenomena
on the basis of a *minimum* number of fundamental premises. Science
thus strives for the best possible performance within its limited domain. The scientific goal of *optimal* performance is thus more ambitious
than the everyday goal of *satisfactory* performance. Correspondingly,
the achievement of the scientific goal requires significantly more deliberate care and effort.

16.2.3   Examination of the scientific goal

A closer examination of the scientific goal (and of the words used in
its specification) leads to a better understanding of some of its implications and requirements.

Theoretical knowledge   As already mentioned, theoretical knowledge
is compact knowledge that is specifically devised to enable extensive
predictions and explanations of observable phenomena. This theoretical knowledge can be freely invented. The *only* criterion of its validity
is its predictive and explanatory power. Hence scientific theoretical
knowledge does *not* need to agree with common sense, with any philosophical or ideological preconceptions, with our own predilections, or
with the opinions of any authorities.

A theory is *not* necessarily unique. Thus there may be more than one
theory capable of predicting or explaining a certain range of observable
phenomena. In this case, the better theory is the one that can successfully predict or explain a *larger* range of phenomena. (If two theories
can equally well predict the *same* range of phenomena on the basis of
an equally small number of basic premises, then the better theory is the
one that is simpler.)

Observations   Observations are *reliable* sense perceptions (for example, perceptions achieved by seeing, hearing, or feeling). Reliability is
an important criterion that can be checked by agreement between

different observers or by reproducibility (that is, by repeated consistent observations at different times). Thus one can guard against perceptions that are due to hallucinations or fantasies.

Various devices can be used to increase the reliability of observations. For example, the perception of hot or cold is much less reliable than the visual observation of a *thermometer* designed to measure temperature. Similarly, the visual observation of astronomical event may often be less reliable than the visual inspection of a *photograph* of that event.

Observations versus theoretical statements   It is important to distinguish clearly between observations and theoretical statements. For example, reliable observations remain the same, even if their theoretical interpretations change.

For instance, people may say that they "*see*" a virus when they are looking at the screen of an electron microscope. But they are actually only looking at the shadow produced by an electron beam that passed through some sample. This shadow might actually be produced by something other than a virus—and only careful theoretical interpretations, consistent with other observations, can lead to the claim that the electron microscope provides information about a virus.

Example contrasting observable and theoretical statements

Does the statement "a box is lying on the table" describe an observation? This statement seems true since different people looking at the table all agree that they see a box lying on the table. Furthermore, after a photograph has been taken of the situation, all these people agree that the photograph shows a box lying on the table.

But suppose that someone throws a ping-pong ball at the box and that the ball goes through the box without bouncing back. These people would then properly still believe their prior observations, but would no longer say that a box is lying on the table. Why?

The statement "I *see* a box lying on the table" *does* describe an observation. But the statement "A box *is* lying on the table" does *not* refer to a sense perception. It is a *theoretical statement* predicting that anybody looking at the table (or a photograph of it) would see a box—and that objects thrown at it would be deflected. The actual observations agree with the first of these predictions, but not with the second. Thus this theoretical statement is *false*, and another theory is needed to account for the actual observations. (Such an alternative theoretical interpretation might be that beams of laser light are creating a *hologram* of a box lying on a table.)

Predictions   Predictions and explanations involve inferences of the kind discussed in section 7.3.2. In particular, scientific predictions must clearly specify how fundamental theoretical premises and legitimate reasoning methods imply the predicted phenomena.

Predictions (unlike forecasts) need *not* necessarily refer to future events. For example, one might use scientific knowledge to predict that a solar eclipse should have been observed in Greece in the year 328 BC. (This prediction might be verified by ascertaining whether written documents from that time did record observations of such an eclipse.)

Explanations Explanations must clearly specify the premises on which they are based. To explain some phenomena, one must thus identify appropriate theoretical premises and show how logical inferences from these can lead to the prediction of these phenomena. (Pure mathematics does *not* deal with observable phenomena, but is a knowledge domain that merely involves basic postulates about abstract entities and the relations among them. Hence explanations in mathematics involve purely *logical proofs* showing that certain properties can be logically predicted from these postulates.)

Understanding Although the word *understand* is somewhat vague, scientists commonly say that they *understand* a subject to the extent that they can make many relevant inferences (such as predictions and explanations).

16.3 CONTRASTING SCIENTIFIC AND EVERYDAY COGNITIONS

Although the basic requirements for good performance (usability, effectiveness, flexibility, efficiency, and reliability) are similar in science and in everyday life, they need to be more exacting in science to achieve the more ambitious scientific goals. Hence the correspondingly needed kinds of knowledge and thought processes differ in some significant ways. The following paragraphs focus on the issues listed in figure 2.3 (and discussed in the preceding chapters) in order to examine the significant differences in greater detail. An understanding of these differences can also help teachers to understand why students often run into difficulties when they try to import everyday thinking into scientific domains.

16.3.1 Usability of knowledge

Kinds of knowledge (science) *Declarative scientific knowledge* includes reliable and accurate factual knowledge about many observable phenomena, including many not commonly observed in everyday life (for example, atomic or astronomical phenomena). This declarative knowledge also includes compact theoretical knowledge that is explicitly formulated for its high predictive and explanatory power. The basic components of this knowledge are clearly specified concepts unambiguously connected to observations. Such concepts are scientifically relevant only if they are useful for purposes of prediction or explanation—and they must be sufficiently precisely specified to lead to unambiguous predictions. However, these concepts or principles do *not* need to agree with common sense, with any ideological preconceptions, or with the opinions of authority figures.

Procedural scientific knowledge includes deliberately designed and precisely specified methods (like those of logic, algebra, or calculus) that enable correct long inference chains starting from compact theoretical knowledge. Such procedural knowledge includes also more approximate qualitative methods facilitating search (such as methods needed for discovering, inventing, diagnosing, and problem solving).

Applicability conditions (especially validity conditions) are explicitly specified for all observational and theoretical knowledge. These applicability conditions enable important discriminations and help to avoid the dangers of excessive (or inadequate) generalizations.

Types of knowledge (everyday)

Declarative everyday knowledge includes informal factual knowledge about numerous phenomena observable in everyday life. A large amount of such knowledge is accumulated as a result of our daily experiences. However, this knowledge is usually not carefully checked to assess its reliability or scope. Furthermore, this knowledge involves concepts that are ordinarily only vaguely specified by comparisons with prototypical cases, by analogies, or by recognition processes. Ambiguity or imprecision is often tolerable, and can be resolved by *ad hoc* modifications or by negotiations with other people. The knowledge abstracted from experience also includes some general beliefs or principles, but their realm of applicability is limited and not clearly specified.

Procedural everyday knowledge includes informal methods and guidelines for performing various tasks. However, there is no need for long reasoning chains since it is often sufficient to rely on large amounts of accumulated knowledge.

Applicability conditions are vaguely recognized, but are usually *not* explicitly specified. Occasional difficulties caused by knowledge misapplications can often be adequately corrected when they occur.

Specifying and interpreting (science) To attain the goal of optimal predictive and explanatory power, scientific concepts and principles must be precisely specified and unambiguously interpreted in any specific case. Such precision can often be achieved by *operational* (*procedural*) specifications that connect concepts clearly to actual observations.

Specifying and interpreting (everyday)

Concepts in everyday life need only to be *adequately* specified. Thus, concepts are often specified by analogies to particular cases—or by paraphrases (such as dictionary definitions) that merely relate them to somewhat different concepts. Ambiguities can be reasonably well tolerated and fine discriminations are often not needed. (For example, words like *force, energy, momentum*, or *power* are often used interchangeably, although they have distinct meanings in physics.) Connotations, which may be misleading in science, can sometimes also be used for aesthetic reasons (such as in poetry). They may also be deliberately exploited in politics or advertising to persuade people about things that are untrue or that could not withstand more critical examination.

16.3.2   Effectiveness of knowledge

Methods and inferences (science)   Scientific work often relies on explicit methods whose implementation is carefully checked. Well-formulated inference methods (provided by logic or mathematics) are necessary to ensure correct long reasoning chains leading from compact theoretical knowledge to the predictions or explanations of diverse phenomena. In addition, more informal methods, exploiting induction and analogies, help to make discoveries or generate hypotheses.

Methods and inferences (everyday)

Explicit methods are occasionally also used in everyday life (for example, procedures for cooking recipes or instructions for assembling furniture). However, such methods often need not be precisely specified. Since everyday life usually relies on large amounts of compiled knowledge, long inference chains are rarely needed. Furthermore, inferences based on analogy or induction are often adequate for many purposes.

Useful forms of knowledge (science)   Multiple descriptions are commonly used in science to reveal existing relationships and to facilitate different kinds of tasks. These descriptions aim at different precisions and may use different symbolic representations (such as verbal, mathematical, or pictorial descriptions). Precise quantitative or mathematical descriptions are commonly used for clear specifications of relationships and for correctly implementing long reasoning chains. More qualitative descriptions are used for discovering, diagnosing, planning, or implementing progressive refinements.

Scientific knowledge is deliberately organized so that it is highly coherent and globally consistent. A hierarchical organization facilitates these properties since it helps selective retrieval, checking of consistency, and extensibility of the knowledge. It also helps to achieve *parsimony*—that is, it allows a limited knowledge of basic principles to deal with much larger amounts of knowledge.

Useful forms of knowledge (everyday)

Qualitative descriptions are usually adequate in daily life. They rely largely on verbal descriptions, occasionally supplemented by some pictures.

Everyday knowledge is voluminous and largely organized in the form of a large associative network (like that illustrated in figure 9.3). Local consistency of the knowledge in particular contexts is usually adequate, without the need for global consistency of the entire knowledge.

16.3.3   Flexibility

Making decisions (science)   Decisions in science often need to be made systematically and carefully, although they may be based on heuristic guidelines similar to those in everyday life.

Making decisions (everyday)

Although decisions in everyday life can sometimes be more complex than those in science, they are often made far less systematically.

Solving problems (science)   Systematic problem-solving methods are often used in the natural sciences. Although these methods involve heuristic decisions, they can exploit a body of reliable well-organized scientific knowledge. The solution of any problem must be explicit, verifiable by other people, and well justified in terms of accepted scientific knowledge. The criteria specifying the correctness of a solution are usually very clear, and the results can frequently be tested by experimental observations.

Solving problems (everyday)

Problem solving in everyday life tends to be less systematic, may be based on unreliable knowledge, and is occasionally approached by trial and error. There is often no strong need to justify the problem-solving methods or the validity of a generated solution, and the criteria for judging successful solutions are sometimes poorly specified. (Yet, many problems in everyday life are more complex and difficult than those in the natural sciences, especially if these problems involve people and interpersonal relations.)

16.3.4 Efficiency and reliability

Efficiency (science) Deliberate efforts aim to make some processes highly efficient so that they can be used as component processes facilitating the performance of complex tasks. Efficiency is also commonly judged by its long-term consequences.

Efficiency (everyday)

People tend to be naturally efficient since they want to minimize the amount of time and effort needed to attain desired goals. However, they are usually focused on short-term efficiency rather than on the longer-term consequences of their actions.

Ensuring quality (science) Quality assurance is extremely important in science which aims to achieve *optimal* predictive and explanatory abilities. Hence scientific endeavors are judged according to explicit quality criteria (ultimately based on the ability to predict or explain observable phenomena—or less directly based on agreement with well established scientific principles). Continuing efforts are also made to improve the reliability and efficiency of scientific processes, with significant attention paid to their long-term consequences.

The validity of scientific knowledge is repeatedly checked and is ensured in the following ways: (1) Since scientific knowledge is highly cumulative, new knowledge or applications presume the validity of existing knowledge. Hence any deficiencies of existing knowledge are quickly detected. (2) There exist strong social incentives that ensure high quality. For example, confirmations of results expected from existing knowledge don't elicit much attention, but discoveries of discrepancies or of unexpected results are highly rewarded by prizes or international prestige.

Ensuring quality (everyday)

Although quality assurance is also important in everyday life, adequate quality is usually sufficient. Furthermore, commonly used quality criteria are diverse and somewhat vague, often based on agreement with common sense, with prevailing beliefs or religious tenets, with ideological or philosophical preconceptions, with majority opinions, or with the views of "experts" or other authority figures.

16.3.5 Comparison of science and everyday life

The preceding differences between the scientific and everyday domains are significant and important, but do *not* imply that all everyday knowledge and thought processes are discarded in the scientific domain. Furthermore, some everyday knowledge *can* successfully be refined into scientific knowledge.

However, the following issues must always be kept in mind when one is trying to work in a scientific domain: One constantly needs to heed the important scientific requirements; to realize that these are different from everyday requirements because of the distinctly different goals of science; to appreciate that some of these differences may be considerable (as illustrated by the comments in the preceding sections); and to recognize that learning to work in a scientific domain may therefore be a demanding task. Thus one may need to abandon or refine familiar everyday knowledge and thought processes that are inadequate or potentially deleterious in the scientific domain—and may need to learn new knowledge and ways of thinking that can meet the scientific requirements more effectively.

16.4 SCIENTISTS' AND STUDENTS' CONCEPTIONS OF SCIENCE

16.4.1 Scientists' or teachers' conceptions

Scientists (and good science teachers) are usually well aware of the scientific cognitive framework and abide by it. Thus they focus on the primary scientific goals of prediction and explanation—and are familiar with the requirements needed to attain these goals. Accordingly, good science teachers emphasize the abilities to reason clearly, to predict and explain, to make inferences, and to solve problems.

16.4.2 Students' conceptions

Similarity to everyday conceptions Inexperienced students commonly approach science with the familiar cognitive framework of everyday life. Thus they predominantly try to learn factual information. They tend to specify concepts as loosely as in daily life, adopt everyday conceptions of explanation, and are often satisfied with arguments not based on scientific principles.

Naive or misleading conceptions of science In addition, students often approach the learning of science with naive or misleading conceptions about science. (Some of these conceptions may even be reinforced by their prior school experiences). For example, many students view science as a valuable collection of facts and formulas. Hence their main aim is to memorize facts and formulas, rather than to learn thought processes enabling them to predict and explain. They also may focus predominantly on scientific tools (such as formulas, symbolic manipulations, and laboratory instruments) and thus may lose sight of the ulterior scientific goals.

The kinds of homework and tests given during instruction may also be misleading. For example, they may suggest that any problem should, like a homework exercise, be solvable in no more than ten minutes. (Students often don't realize that real problems may require days or months of thought.) Similarly, students often come to rely on teachers to check their work—and don't learn that they alone need ultimately be responsible for the good quality of their work.

16.4.3   Discrepancies between teacher and student conceptions

Science teachers and students may not be aware of their differing conceptions about science. These different conceptions may lead them to pursue inappropriate goals in science courses and can cause significant misunderstandings. The next paragraphs mention several examples.

What is the meaning of "construct"?   The following are some observations of students in a course on Euclidean geometry (Schoenfeld, 1983; Schoenfeld, 1985, chapter 1). The students were asked to construct a circle that is tangent to a straight line at a specified point— and that is also tangent to another intersecting straight line. Many students started working with ruler and compass in attempts to draw such a circle—and continued working in this way for an appreciable time without ever abandoning their purely empirical way of approaching this task.

However, this approach (no matter how long continued and how precisely executed) could never lead to the solution of the specified problem. The reason is that mathematicians' meaning of *construction* in geometry is highly idealized and differs from the everyday meaning of that word. In mathematical language, *constructing* some entity means *showing how* (using basic postulates and theorems of geometry) one could construct this entity precisely by using merely a straightedge and a compass.

A mathematical construction task is thus really a purely intellectual task requiring a proof showing that something *can* logically be done in a specified way. An actual drawing may possibly help to *suggest* such a proof. But no amount of actual drawing, no matter how meticulous, can ever provide such a proof. If students are not aware of the mathematical cognitive framework, they can thus easily be led to pursue inappropriate goals.

What is an explanation?   The following is a common occurrence in a basic physics course. The students have previously learned how to describe motion—and have recently also learned Newton's law $ma = \mathbf{F}_{tot}$ which relates the acceleration $\mathbf{a}$ of any object to the total force $\mathbf{F}_{tot}$ acting on the object. This law has been discussed and illustrated. It has also been pointed out that this law is the cornerstone of Newtonian mechanics because it relates motions and interactions—and thus provides the basis for very many predictions and explanations.

The teacher now asks a student to consider a pendulum with a bob weighing 2 pounds. At the instant when this swinging pendulum is vertical (with the bob at its lowest position and moving fastest), what is the force exerted by the string supporting the bob? In particular, is this force equal to, larger than, or smaller than 2 pounds? The following is a typical conversation that now ensues:

Student: *"2 pounds."*
Teacher: *"Why?"*
Student: *"Because the string must support a weight of 2 pounds."*
Teacher: *"Why is that?"*
Student (after some thought):   *"Because the upward force on the bob by the string has to balance the 2-pound downward gravitational force on the bob."*

Here the student has several times been asked to explain *why* his answer is correct. Yet, he seems oblivious of the scientific requirement that an explanation must involve logical reasoning from well-accepted scientific premises. Instead, the first time the student simply considers it *obvious* that the force exerted by the supporting string should be 2 pounds. When pressed further, he provides an explanation by stating that "the forces must balance." However, this is merely a common-sense notion that is *false* in this case (and is *always* false unless an object is at rest or moving with constant velocity).

This example is interesting for the following reasons. Although the student has recently learned Newton's law, a scientific principle of great predictive power, it does not occur to him that invocation of this law should provide a satisfactory scientific explanation. If the student had done this, he would have realized that, since the bob is moving along a circle with a velocity of constantly changing direction, the acceleration of the bob is *not* zero. Hence Newton's law $ma = \mathbf{F}_{tot}$ implies that the total force on the bob can*not* be zero—that is, that the forces on the bob *don't* balance. (Indeed, since the bob's acceleration is directed upward at the instant when the string is vertical, the upward force on the bob by the string must be *larger* than the downward gravitational force by the earth.) Thus all of the student's answers were not only scientifically unjustified, but also incorrect.

What is the meaning of "understanding"?   Some years ago, I suspected that students, entering a basic physics course requiring a prerequisite knowledge of calculus, did not even have an adequate knowledge of arithmetic and elementary algebra. I warned students that I would give them a test assessing their competence in these elementary subjects and provided them with a sample test. Yet only about half of the students passed the actual performance test. Indeed, one of these students failed to pass *four* successive alternative versions of this test. When I suggested to him that he was ill prepared, he felt offended because he thought that he knew these elementary subjects quite well.

A couple of months later, this student came to my office to tell me that he realized that he and I seemed to mean different things by *understanding*. *He* had always thought that he understood arithmetic (or any other subject) if he was familiar with it and had worked with it. But *I* seemed to mean that understanding some knowledge involved the ability to use it for solving various problems.

This was a profound insight on the part of this student. From his everyday perspective, he had thought that *understanding* meant familiarity with factual knowledge. Accordingly, he had felt offended when I suggested that he lacked an adequate understanding of arithmetic. But from my scientific perspective, *understanding* a subject involved the ability to use it to make diverse inferences, to solve problems, and to predict or explain.

Note that such differing conceptions of *understanding* have important implications for learning. If a student believes that *understanding* implies mere familiarity with factual knowledge, then the student will be satisfied and stop learning without striving to attain any reasoning abilities.

What is calculus?   During the last couple of decades, mathematicians have undertaken several projects designed to improve the teaching of calculus. The main aim has been to replace the primary emphasis on mathematical formalism with a broader concern focused on teaching students to think in terms of calculus concepts, to use verbal and graphical descriptions in addition to mathematical manipulations, and to let students apply mathematical thinking to some realistic problems.

However, quite a few students have been unhappy with this new approach (Culotta, 1992). Their own conceptions about calculus don't agree with their mathematics teachers' conceptions of the important things to be taught. The students believe that they are not learning "real math", complain about the fact that there are no answers in the back of the book, and long for straightforward bite-sized exercises instead of more substantial problems. As one student wrote on a course evaluation, "I wish I had to memorize more. I'm sick of real-life models."

It is clear that students' preexisting cognitive frameworks, derived from everyday notions or from their experiences in prior courses, can significantly impede efforts of educational innovation.

What is to be learned? Many science instructors attempt to help students acquire coherent scientific knowledge that interrelates various facts and that can be used to infer other useful information. Such instructors don't merely teach students various facts or formulas, but try to help them learn how these can be obtained from more basic knowledge. However, students are often *not* interested in acquiring such coherent knowledge, but are mostly focused on learning facts and formulas. This attitude is well illustrated by the following student statement, quoted in an article by Hammer (1994, 159):

> *I feel that proving the formula is not really necessary for me, it doesn't matter if I can prove it or not, as long as I know that someone has proven it before...here I am paying 15,000 dollars a year...I'm not going to derive this thing for them; they're going to derive it for me and explain to me how it works.*

16.5   EDUCATIONAL IMPLICATIONS

16.5.1   Proficient performers

Most scientists are familiar with the scientific cognitive framework and act in accordance with it. They have attained their proficient performance as a result of much intellectual effort and consistent discipline. Indeed, any good scientist (even if not eminent) has spent ten or more years dedicated to the pursuit of scientific goals and deliberately practicing ways of thinking of the kind discussed in the preceding chapters (Ericsson, Krampe, and Tesch-Romer, 1993; Ericsson and Charness, 1994).

Good scientists have thus been using the scientific framework so habitually that their knowledge of it has become largely tacit. Many such scientists are, therefore, no longer consciously aware of the implications of this scientific framework and don't fully realize that students may find it unfamiliar or strange. Hence they also often teach specialized scientific knowledge without much explication of the cognitive framework in which it is embedded.

16.5.2 Inexperienced students

Many students approach scientific subjects with inadequate or misleading notions about the cognitive framework of science. They often have no clear understanding of scientific goals or of the requirements for attaining these goals. They lack an awareness of the significant differences between the cognitive framework of science and that of everyday life. Thus they tend to import knowledge and thinking familiar from everyday life into the scientific domain where such knowledge and thinking may be inadequate or inappropriate.

Even when students become more clearly aware of scientific goals and requirements, they may find it difficult to abide by them since they need then to transcend deeply entrenched familiar conceptions. Indeed, appreciable discipline is required to consistently pursue new goals and engage in new ways of thinking.

As a result, many students strive to acquire factual knowledge, to memorize formulas, to learn procedures or symbol-manipulation skills—and do not focus primarily on learning flexible reasoning skills needed to predict or explain. Similarly, students are often satisfied with vaguely specified concepts, with lacks of significant discriminations, and with incoherent organizations of acquired scientific knowledge. For example, they may state scientific concepts or principles that they cannot properly interpret in specific instances. They often lack systematic methods of implementing long inference chains or of solving problems. Furthermore, they may pay little attention to the quality of their work. They don't consistently assess and revise it—and often view their mistakes as mere "slips."

16.5.3 Common instructional deficiencies

Most science teachers aim primarily to teach the specialized scientific knowledge of a particular discipline, but don't do much to help students learn about the cognitive scientific framework subsuming this specialized knowledge. Thus students are often left with a myopic perspective that focuses predominantly on factual knowledge and particular methods, rather than on significant scientific goals. Students' motivation for learning can thereby also be reduced.

A lack of explication of ulterior scientific goals can also lead to significant divergences between students' and teachers' expectations. For example, a teacher may want to stress reasoning and problem-solving abilities, while students are intent on learning formulas. As already pointed out, students may thus be led to oppose useful educational improvements because these may not correspond to the students' naive notions about what they should learn.

16.5.4 Instructional suggestions

Students' understanding of the scientific framework can have a pervasive impact on their learning of particular scientific knowledge. Hence it is necessary to make students explicitly aware of this scientific framework and of some of its implications.

It is useful to explicate (and repeatedly remind students of) the primary scientific goals of prediction and explanation—and to point out some of the corresponding requirements to attain these goals. When any specific scientific knowledge is taught, it is always useful to indicate how it contributes to the scientific goals. (Indeed, this can sometimes motivate learning that might otherwise seem somewhat abstruse.) Students may also be asked to identify in what ways everyday kinds of knowledge and thinking are *not* adequate to attain the scientific goals in particular situations.

Furthermore, scientific goals and requirements can always be kept at the forefront of all learning. For example, textbooks and homework assignments usually present many exercises and practice problems. Most of these, no matter how simple, are actually exercises in prediction or explanation. Hence it might be advantageous to phrase them explicitly in this way—namely to present a situation and then always ask students to predict something or to explain something.

16.6 SUMMARY

• Dealing with an unfamiliar knowledge domain (like science) requires not only learning new knowledge about special topics, but also learning about the subsuming cognitive framework (that is, learning about the primary goals of this new domain and about the requirements needed to attain these goals).

• The primary goals of everyday life strive for adequately pleasant and successful functioning in daily life. On the other hand, the primary goals of science focus on achieving optimal abilities to predict and explain observable phenomena.

• These differing primary goals imply significantly different cognitive requirements in everyday life (the domain familiar to students) and in science.

• Hence scientists (or science teachers) and inexperienced students sometimes have conflicting conceptions about science and about the learning of science.

• An explication of these differing conceptions leads to a better understanding of the kinds of difficulties commonly encountered by students trying to learn scientific subjects—and can also suggest improved instructional approaches.

17 Naive Scientific Knowledge

The preceding chapter compared the cognitive frameworks of science and of everyday life. This chapter illustrates these comments more concretely in a particular case and indicates some of their educational implications.

People have always needed to deal with their environment and, to cope with it, have tried to explain and predict their observations of it. Working within the framework of everyday life, they have thus developed knowledge that overlaps some scientific knowledge, but does *not* aim to attain the explicit scientific goal of optimal prediction and explanation—and does *not* abide by the scientific requirements needed to attain this goal. This everyday scientific knowledge (which may be called *naive* or *informal* scientific knowledge) is also the knowledge that most students commonly bring to their study of science in schools.

Historically, such naive science has been the origin of most modern science. Many scientists, working within the scientific framework and explicitly pursuing its requirements, have over many years refined such naive science into the present-day *formal* science. This formal science is significantly different from naive science, and is also much more successful in predicting and explaining many phenomena. On the other hand, students' prior knowledge of naive science can greatly affect their learning of formal science—occasionally helping such learning, but often interfering with it.

This chapter exemplifies these remarks in the particular case of the science of *mechanics* which is concerned with the prediction and explanation of motion. In this context, we shall examine the following questions: (1) What are some of the salient characteristics of naive scientific knowledge—and how do they differ from those of formal scientific knowledge? (2) For example, what are some naive conceptions of motion? (3) What are some naive notions about the causes of motion and about forces? (4) How are such naive notions refined in the formal science of mechanics? (5) What are some of the student difficulties that result from the differences between their familiar naive science and the formal science that they are trying to learn?

Educational relevance   Many students need to study mechanics in their basic physics or engineering courses, especially since this subject is an essential prerequisite for many more advanced courses. Most students also experience many difficulties when trying to learn this subject. One common source of confusions arises because naive knowledge about motion and forces is so prevalent in our daily lives. As a result, many students exhibit misconceptions and mistakes that are difficult to remedy and that are remarkably persistent. The teaching of mechanics thus represents a challenge for many instructors (although this challenge is fairly typical of that encountered in trying to teach many other science courses).

17.1   CHARACTERISTICS OF NAIVE SCIENTIFIC KNOWLEDGE

Naive scientific knowledge is derived from personal observations and similar observations made by other people. It has gradually evolved and become shared throughout our society because, by allowing some predictions and explanations, it facilitates people's daily functioning and helps their survival. Historically, modern scientific knowledge gradually emerged from such naive knowledge and became extensively refined during the last few centuries. Hence present-day *formal* scientific knowledge has become significantly different from the naive scientific knowledge that existed at earlier times, that is still widespread in our daily lives, and that is common among many students. Indeed, many naive scientific conceptions prevalent today are similar to conceptions prevailing at earlier times before they became refined by modern scientific work.

Differences between naive and formal science   The differences between naive and formal scientific knowledge are largely consequences of their development within different cognitive frameworks. In formal scientific domains, this framework (discussed in the preceding chapter) specifies a highly explicit and deliberately pursued goal—devising compact knowledge in which a minimum number of basic premises enables *optimal* prediction and explanation of the maximum number of observable phenomena. Furthermore, highly systematic efforts, extending over many generations, have succeeded in making this knowledge more precise and in extending the range of observable phenomena encompassed by it.

Although naive scientific knowledge deals with some scientifically relevant topics, it did evolve within the framework of everyday life. It strives merely for knowledge enabling *adequate* predictions or explanations of commonly encountered phenomena, does *not* try to satisfy the stringent requirements of formal science, and does *not* aim for coherent knowledge of great accuracy and wide scope. Accordingly, naive scientific knowledge has some of the following characteristics that are similar to those of everyday knowledge.

Content of naive scientific knowledge Naive scientific knowledge is based on observations that may be unreliable because they have often neither been refined nor repeatedly tested. The concepts used in naive science are only vaguely defined, and their proper interpretation is often not clearly specified. Thus these concepts may be ambiguous, may not be clearly related to observable phenomena, and may occasionally even be inconsistent with some observations. Since these concepts may fail to make significant discriminations, they can also lead to inappropriate generalizations.

Procedural knowledge in naive science is largely informal and rarely uses well-explicated methods (like those common in logic or mathematics). Inference chains are usually fairly short, relying on induction or analogies based on large amounts of accumulated knowledge (rather than on long deductive inference chains derived from relatively few fundamental premises).

The limits of validity of naive scientific knowledge are often not clearly specified. Furthermore, the validity criteria are not stringent and may be based on agreement with common sense or tradition, without requiring great predictive or explanatory power.

Form of naive scientific knowledge Naive scientific knowledge is largely qualitative and uses mostly verbal descriptions. Quantitative mathematical descriptions or methods are rarely used.

Naive scientific knowledge consists of loosely related bits of knowledge that may even be mutually inconsistent. The whole knowledge, in the form of an associative network, can thus be somewhat fragmentary, lack global coherence, and have only limited applicability (DiSessa, 1988).

Quality assurance   There are no systematic attempts to check the quality of naive scientific knowledge—and no deliberate efforts to broaden its range of validity. As already mentioned, the prevailing quality criteria are diverse and vague. For example, they can be based on common sense or traditions, on personal experience or philosophical preconceptions, on ideological or religious beliefs, or on the opinions of authorities or presumed experts.

17.2   STUDENTS' PRIOR KNOWLEDGE ABOUT SCIENCE

When students need to learn a scientific subject, they bring with them some preexisting knowledge that is similar to the naive scientific knowledge prevalent in everyday life, but that also includes an admixture of more specialized scientific knowledge acquired in schools. However, this school-derived scientific knowledge is often limited and superficial, sometimes consisting more of scientific vocabulary than of substantive scientific knowledge. Furthermore, *school science* (scientific knowledge taught in schools) may sometimes differ from genuine science. For example, some teachers or textbooks may be simplistic, misleading, or obsolete in their approach—and may occasionally even convey significant errors or misconceptions.

17.2.1   Kinds of prior student knowledge about science

Students don't come to instruction with blank minds, but with significant prior knowledge. In particular, their prior knowledge about science includes both scientific *topical* knowledge (knowledge about various topics of scientific interest) and scientific *metaknowledge* (general knowledge about scientific goals and requirements). Both these kinds of knowledge may differ significantly from genuine scientific knowledge. Thus students' knowledge about specific scientific topics may be naive and differ from actual scientific knowledge about these topics. More profoundly, students' knowledge about the scientific cognitive framework may also be deficient or faulty.

Consequences of prior knowledge   Such prior student knowledge may appreciably help or hinder the acquisition of new knowledge. It may *help* when the familiar prior knowledge has features similar to those of the new knowledge to be acquired. But it may *hinder* when the prior knowledge is significantly different from the new knowledge, for then this preexisting knowledge may need to be modified or replaced—and this need can give rise to confusions and to learning difficulties that are hard to overcome.

17.2.2 Naive knowledge about scientific topics

The preceding chapter already discussed some of the difficulties caused by deficient scientific metaknowledge (that is, by deficient or lacking general knowledge about scientific goals and requirements). By contrast, we now examine some of the difficulties caused by students' prior knowledge about specific scientific topics.

Naive scientific knowledge (whose evolution and characteristics were briefly discussed in the preceding sections) includes various naive notions differing significantly from the concepts and principles of more systematically developed formal science. Such naive notions can easily persist in everyday life where they may seem congenial and adequate—and where no stringent criteria are imposed on the predictions and explanations of observable phenomena.

For example, such naive notions may be consistent with unreliable observations, or they may be inconsistent with careful observations, or both of the preceding situations may be true. Naive notions can also persist because of deficient discriminations. For example, inadequate discriminations may lead to faulty generalizations. Conversely, distinctions between irrelevant features may obscure a greater range of validity.

17.2.3 Naive scientific knowledge in particular domains

The preceding general comments about naive scientific knowledge can be made more concrete by illustrating them in the specific scientific domain of *mechanics*. There are several reasons for choosing this particular domain. (1) Naive scientific notions are especially prevalent in mechanics since moving objects are commonly observed in everyday life. (2) A discussion of these notions can, therefore, also be comprehensible to persons without a significant knowledge of physics. (3) Basic mechanics is a prerequisite for most scientific work and often causes many learning difficulties. (4) Students' naive notions about mechanics have been extensively investigated. (See, for example, McCloskey, 1983; McDermott, 1984; Halloun and Hestenes, 1985a, 1985b).

The following three sections illustrate that students need to modify or transcend very many naive conceptions in order to learn a scientific subject like mechanics.

17.3 NAIVE CONCEPTIONS ABOUT MOTION

17.3.1 Inadequately specified conception of motion

In everyday life or naive science, the word *motion* is poorly specified—and often implicitly refers to motion relative to us on the ground.

Scientific conception of motion   By contrast, the scientific concept of *motion* is clearly defined and more general. Indeed, in physics *position* is a *relative* concept—that is, a concept that must always be specified relative to some other things. (These things are said to constitute a *reference frame.*) Correspondingly, the *motion* of an object (the *change* of its position) must also be specified relative to some reference frame.

Motion is thus a purely *relative* concept, and the reference frame can be chosen in *any* convenient way. For example, the reference frame might be the ground, a train moving relative to the ground, a rotating merry-go-round, or anything else. Specific concepts describing motion (concepts like *velocity* and *acceleration*) must then always be described relative to some specified reference frame.

Since this general scientific conception of motion does not correspond to students' more naive notion, it can easily cause confusions and misunderstandings.

Students' misunderstanding of the scientific concept of motion

In physics classes, I always explained that motion is a relative concept and gave several examples. (For instance, a mother, sitting in a train that is moving relative to the ground, also moves relative to the ground. The baby, lying in the mother's lap, does *not* move relative to the mother. But a house on the ground *does* move relative to the mother.) After all these examples, I asked students the question "Does the sun move relative to us on the earth"? Many of the students claimed that the answer is *no.* After all, they had previously learned in school that Copernicus and Galileo made the important discovery that it is the earth that moves around the stationary sun.

Note that these students merely seemed to have accepted the statements of these authorities and of the teachers that had told them about these great men. Despite the many prior examples illustrating that motion is a relative concept, they were unwilling to accept that it is scientifically equally correct to say that "The sun moves relative to the earth" or that "The earth moves relative to the sun." Not only are both statements perfectly consistent, but each implies the other. (However, it is much *simpler* to describe the motion of the earth and of the planets relative to the sun.)

17.3.2   Undifferentiated motion concepts

In everyday life (and in naive science), motion is described in terms of several concepts that do *not* reflect significant discriminations useful in science.

Speed   In everyday life, an object's motion is most commonly described by its *speed*, a concept that describes how rapidly the distance traversed by the object changes with time. (This description pays no attention to any changes in the *direction* of the object's motion.)

Velocity   In physics, motion is more precisely described by the concept *velocity* which specifies the rate of change of an object's *position* (rather than merely the rate of change of its traversed *distance*). This velocity is characterized not only by its *magnitude* (that is, by the object's speed), but also by the object's *direction* of motion. Thus there is an important distinction between an object's *velocity* and its *speed*. (For example, a car moving around a curve with *constant* speed has a *changing* velocity since the *direction* of its motion changes as it moves around the curve.)

Acceleration   In everyday life and in naive science, the word *acceleration* is used to describe the rate of change of an object's *speed*. For example, this naive acceleration may be used to specify how rapidly the speed of a car changes from zero to 60 miles/hour. On the other hand, a car moving around a curve with a *constant* speed is *not* considered to be accelerating.

By contrast, in physics the same word *acceleration* is used to describe a more general concept, namely, the rate of change of an object's *velocity*. This scientific acceleration (previously discussed in chapter 5) thus describes *any* change of velocity, irrespective of whether this change involves a change of its magnitude (of its *speed*) or of its direction. (For example, according to this definition, a car moving around a curve with constant speed *is* accelerating since the *direction* of its velocity is changing.)

17.3.3   Discrimination difficulties

Different concepts denoted by same name   The preceding scientifically defined concepts involve important discriminations between the meanings of the same words (like *velocity* or *acceleration*) when used in everyday life or in science. They also involve discriminations between changes of magnitude, changes of direction, or changes of both. Thus it is not surprising that students often fail to make these discriminations and become confused.

Lack of discrimination between velocity and acceleration Another important distinction is that between *velocity* and *acceleration*. Indeed, both concepts describe motion, but they describe different aspects of motion. (Velocity describes a change of *position*, while acceleration describes a change of *velocity*.) But in everyday life the word *motion* is often used indiscriminately without attention to this distinction. Hence students also often fail to heed this distinction.

For example, even after having learned about these scientific concepts, many students claim that "If the velocity of an object is zero, then the object is not moving so that its acceleration must be zero." For instance, when a stone is thrown vertically upward, its velocity is zero when it reaches its highest point. Many students then claim that the stone's acceleration at this instant is also zero. (This is *not* correct. Although the stone's velocity at this instant is zero, it is still changing since it is directed downward and slightly larger at a slightly later time.)

A similar situation, previously discussed in section 5.4.4, involves a pendulum swinging back and forth. The velocity of the bob is then zero at the instant when it reaches the extreme end of its swing. Many students claim that the bob's acceleration at this instant must then also be zero. (This is again *not* correct. Although the bob's velocity at this instant is zero, it is still changing since it is slightly different slightly later when the bob moves again downward along its circular path.)

Another example is provided by the following frequently asked naive question: "Why does the moon not fall toward the earth since it is affected by the gravitational force directed toward the earth?" This question arises because of the poorly specified meanings of words like *fall* or *move*. It is certainly true that the moon, traveling in a circular orbit around the earth, does *not* move toward the earth (that it does not travel with a *velocity* directed toward the earth). But its *acceleration is* directed toward the earth. Indeed, it is because of this acceleration that the direction of the moon's velocity changes in such a way that the moon moves around a circular orbit rather than along a straight path.

17.4 NAIVE NOTIONS ABOUT THE CAUSES OF MOTION

What causes objects to move? From a naive or everyday point of view this question is answered in several possible ways.

No cause is necessary One possible naive notion is that no cause is necessary because the world is just this way. In other words, objects naturally move in particular ways under certain conditions, and no special cause needs to be invoked to account for this behavior. (For example, objects near the surface of the earth naturally fall to the ground—and no further explanation is necessary.)

Scientific conception of inertia

In formal science, a somewhat similar (but more sophisticated) idea is expressed in terms of the *inertia law*, one of the fundamental principles of Newtonian physics. This law asserts that motion can be especially simply described relative to some special reference frames called *inertial frames*. [Such a frame may consist of the distant stars or (approximately) of objects fixed on the surface of the earth]. The natural situation (in the absence of any perturbing influences) is then one where an object moves with *constant velocity* (that is, with constant speed along a straight line). In other words, the inertia law asserts that any *non-interacting* object (that is, any object uninfluenced by other objects) moves with *constant* velocity relative to an inertial frame.

The notion of cause then arises only to explain *how* the motion of an object deviates from constant velocity if this object *is* affected by the presence of other objects.

Cause specified by undefined words Naive students often specify a cause for motion by a word that is somehow associated with motion and that they have somewhere heard or read. For example, students may say that an object moves because it has some *momentum, energy,* or *force* (where all these words may be used indiscriminately). Somehow the word itself specifies the cause, and no further explanation is needed.

Similarly, some students may say that objects fall to the ground because of *gravity*. Somehow *gravity* is just something (otherwise unspecified) that exists and that causes objects to fall downward.

Contrast with scientific concepts

Although words like *force, momentum,* and *energy* are actually used in physics, they have there well-specified and distinct meanings.

According to physics, objects fall to the ground because they interact with the neighboring earth. (This particular kind of interaction is called *gravitational*, is widely prevalent throughout our universe, and has some quite specific properties.)

Cause is some motive power within an object   Another naive scientific notion, common among students, is that motion is due to some motive power residing within an object. This motive power may be designated by various names, often used interchangeably (names such as *inertia*, *momentum*, or *force*). Thus a student may say that an object moves because it has inertia or because of the force in it. (This motive power may perhaps be suggested by an analogy to animals who move because something within them causes them to move).

This motive power is also related to the observed persistence of motion. For example, students know that, after a cart on a horizontal floor has been given a push, it keeps moving for a while afterward. Students may then say that the persistence of the cart's motion is due to its *inertia* or *momentum*. (Although it is not clear what the students mean by these words, their use of the word *inertia* is compatible with the inertia law of physics.)

Students may go on to explain the slowing down of the cart by saying that its momentum is gradually lost. (Naively, the slow loss of the cart's momentum seems perhaps analogous to the weakening of an animal's motive power because of fatigue, a gradual loss of its available energy.)

When students are asked to predict the path of a stone thrown horizontally from a cliff, some say that that path is similar to path 1 or to path 3 in figure 17.1. The students' naive notion seems to be that the stone's *momentum* initially keeps the stone moving horizontally in the way that it was launched. After a while, however, this initial momen-

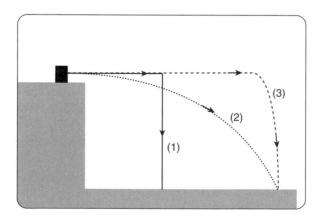

Figure 17.1
Path of a stone thrown horizontally from a cliff.

tum is lost and the stone then falls down vertically like all other objects. (The stone's actual path is indicated by the curved path 2 in figure 17.1.)

Figure 17.2 shows a curved copper tube lying on a horizontal table. When a marble is shot into the end A of this tube, what is the path of this marble after it emerges from the other end B of the tube? Many students predict that this is the curved path 1. Apparently they believe that the marble's curved motion inside the tube leads it to acquire some corresponding circular momentum that persists and causes it to continue around a curved path after leaving the tube. (The actual path of the emerging marble is the straight path 2 in figure 17.2.)

The preceding examples illustrate the kinds of naive ideas that students commonly bring to instruction. As we have seen, some of these ideas are not totally wrong from a scientific perspective. But many of them are vague, have ill-specified domains of validity, and often lead to predictions inconsistent with actual observations.

Scientific descriptions of these examples

Naive ideas, like those exhibited by many students, have historically been prevalent before being developed into modern science. However, modern physics deals with motion in simpler and more consistent ways leading to correct predictions.

For example, if a cart is moving along a horizontal smooth floor, the interactions of the cart with the floor are so small that they have approximately negligible effects on the horizontal motion of the cart. The inertia law, stated at the beginning of this section, then predicts properly that the cart will continue moving with constant velocity. However, since the floor is not perfectly smooth, the small interactions of the cart with the floor cause the velocity of the cart not to

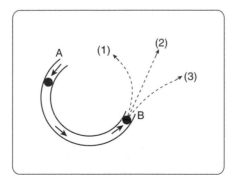

Figure 17.2
Path of a marble emerging from a curved tube.

remain constant. Hence the speed of the cart gradually decreases so that it slows down.

After a stone is thrown horizontally from a cliff, it still interacts with the neighboring earth and thus does *not* travel with constant velocity along a horizontal straight line. Instead, its gravitational interaction with the earth causes the stone to have a downward acceleration so that its velocity is constantly bent toward the downward direction. The result is then a curved path like that illustrated by path 2 in figure 17.1.

After the marble emerges from the horizontal curved tube shown in figure 17.2, it no longer interacts with this tube. Hence the inertia law predicts that the marble should simply continue moving with the velocity that it had when it emerged from the tube—so that it should continue moving along the straight path 2. (It is completely irrelevant that the marble *previously* moved along a curved path, while forced to do so by its interaction with the curved tube.)

17.5   FORCE AS A CAUSE OF MOTION

The notion of *force* is commonly invoked in everyday life or naive science. But this word can have various vague meanings and can be associated with different properties.

17.5.1   Naive uses of the word "force"

Force as something inside an object   Students sometimes think of force as a property residing inside an object. For example, they may say that "A bullet shot from a gun keeps moving because of the force given to it when the gun was fired." Similarly, in daily life one may sometimes say that a particular individual is a *forceful person*. Here again *force* is somehow conceptualized as a property inside the person, a property which enables the person to influence other people so as to move them to action.

Force as a push or pull   In daily life, a force is often considered as a push or pull—as something analogous to the exertion of a muscular effort. This conception does *not* envisage a force as something within an object, but as something describing the influence of one object on another.

Scientific conception: Force as a concept describing interactions

The concept *force*, as used in physics, has some similarity to the notion of a push or pull. Like a push or pull, it can be characterized by a magnitude and a direction, but it is *not* necessarily associated with any muscular effort. It is merely a particular concept used to describe an interaction between objects.

To be specific, an object A is said to *interact* with another object B if the behavior of A is influenced by the presence of B. According to this scientific conception, a force must always be specified by indicating the interacting objects. For example, one can speak about the "force exerted on A by B" or the "force exerted on B by A."

An interaction between two objects is *mutual*—if A is influenced by B, then B is also influenced by A. However, the *magnitude* of the influence on the two objects may be different and depends on an object property called its *mass*. More precisely, this mutuality of interactions is expressed by the fact that (according to the scientific definition of force) the force on A by B has the same magnitude as the force on B by A, but has the opposite direction.

Force is connected with effort The naive conception of force as a push or pull suggests that some effort is required to produce a force—or that only a person or animal can produce a force. For example, if a book lies on a table, does the table exert a force on the book? Some students say that the table does *not* exert a force on the book, perhaps because there is no visible indication of any effort exerted by the table.

Scientific description of the force on the book

From a *physics* point of view, the book interacts with the table since it is clearly affected by the presence of the table. (Indeed, if the table were removed, the book would fall to the floor.) Thus a physicist would certainly say that the table *does* exert a force on the book.

Throwing or dropping a stone Another example, connected with human effort, is illustrated in figure 17.3 where a man, standing on the ground, has a stone in his hand and throws it horizontally to the right. Most students then properly believe that the stone subsequently follows a trajectory like that indicated by path 3 in figure 17.3.

Consider now a different situation where the man in figure 17.3, *while running to the right*, simply releases the stone held in his hand. Many students then say that the subsequent trajectory of the stone

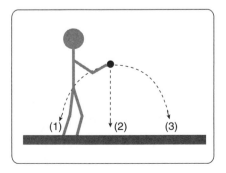

Figure 17.3
Path of a stone after leaving a man's hand.

relative to the ground is like that indicated by path 2 (that is, the stone simply falls vertically to the ground). However, this prediction is *wrong*.

The two preceding situations seem perhaps different to the students since the ball is *thrown* in the first situation (where the man needed to exert muscular effort to do this) and since the ball is merely *released* in the second situation.

Scientific description: Initial velocity is the same in both cases

From a physics point of view, both of the preceding situations are very similar. Irrespective of whether the stone is thrown horizontally, or is merely released by the running man, it starts its trajectory with some horizontal velocity relative to the ground. Hence its subsequent motion relative to the ground must be similar and resemble path 3.

Force is needed to produce motion   Students often believe that the natural situation, in the absence of perturbing influences, is one where an object is at rest. Hence motion must be produced by some applied force.

This naive belief is contradicted by the scientific inertia law. It is also inconsistent with the students' own expectation that a cart continues to move for an appreciable time after it has been given an initial push. Furthermore, this naive belief prevents some students from believing that a bullet fired from a rifle can keep moving a long distance without some force that continues pushing it along after it has left the rifle.

Partial scientific justification of students' belief

The students' belief is not totally unjustified. Most objects commonly encountered in daily life interact with many other objects (for example, with the neighboring earth, with the surface of the ground, with other touching objects, and with the surrounding air). Under these conditions, some applied force may indeed be required to keep an object moving despite its many interactions with other things (despite "friction"). The physics inertia law, which specifies only the behavior of an object *not* interacting with anything else, is thus rarely exemplified in daily life. Its validity becomes readily apparent only in some special conditions (for example, in outer space where heavenly bodies are very far from other objects, in the case of electrons moving in a vacuum, or (approximately) in the case of objects sliding on a very smooth ice surface).

17.5.2   Relation between force and motion

Motion is along the direction of the force   A common everyday notion is that an object moves with a velocity along the direction of the force acting on it. This is generally *not* true. (For example, when a baseball

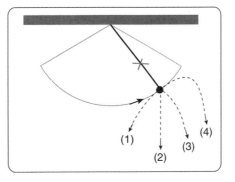

Figure 17.4
Path of a pendulum bob after the string has been cut.

is moving along a curved trajectory through the air, the only significant force on the ball is the downward gravitational force exerted on
it by the earth. But the baseball does *not* move in the downward
direction.)

As another example, figure 17.4 illustrates a pendulum whose string
is suddenly cut while the pendulum bob is moving along its upward
swing. When students are asked to predict the subsequent motion of
the bob, many say that the bob then falls down along path 2 (straight
down from the position that it had at the instant when the string was
cut). The students properly believe that, after the string is cut, the only
force acting on the bob is the downward gravitational force by the
earth. Hence they conclude that the resulting motion of the bob must
then also be straight downward. However, this prediction is *not* correct.

Physics relation between acceleration and force

The inertia law of physics asserts that any non-interacting object moves with
constant velocity (that is, with *zero* acceleration). Hence the interaction of an object with other objects manifests itself by a *nonzero* acceleration of the object.
This acceleration **a** can then be specified by a relation of the form

$$m\mathbf{a} = \mathbf{F}_{tot} \tag{17.1}$$

where the quantity $\mathbf{F}_{tot}$ on the right side specifies how the acceleration of the
object depends on the distance of this object from all other objects and on the
properties of all these objects. This quantity $\mathbf{F}_{tot}$ is called *the total force on the
object* and is merely a quantity that describes the effect of the object's interactions with all other objects. (Some other quantities can also be used to describe these interactions and are used, instead of force, in more sophisticated
applications of mechanics.)

The *total* force on an object can actually be determined by considering this object interacting *separately* with every other object—and is simply the vector sum of the individual forces on the object by every other object.

The mass m of the object has been included in the relation (17.1) so that equal magnitudes of the forces between any *two* interacting objects yield the proper relationship between the magnitudes of their accelerations.

The relation (17.1), called *Newton's law*, specifies how an object's acceleration **a** (describing the object's *motion*) is related to the total force $\mathbf{F}_{tot}$ (describing the *interactions* of the object with all other objects). Hence this relation provides great predictive power and is the basis of the entire classical science of mechanics. It only needs to be supplemented by detailed knowledge about a few special interactions (such as gravitational, electric, and contact interactions).

As the preceding comments indicate, the naive notion that a force produces a *velocity* along the direction of the force is *not* correct. In science, this notion is replaced by Newton's law (17.1) which specifies that a force produces an *acceleration* along the direction of the force. Hence the velocity is only *indirectly* affected.

Scientific answer to the pendulum problem of figure 17.4

After the pendulum's string in figure 17.4 has been cut, the remaining downward gravitational force on the bob produces a corresponding downward *acceleration* of the bob. Hence the bob initially keeps moving with the slightly upward velocity that it had when the string was cut, but this velocity is gradually bent downward as a result of the downward gravitational acceleration. Hence the bob moves along a trajectory similar to path 4 in figure 17.4.

Forces balance   Students commonly have the notion that forces must balance. For example, figure 17.5a illustrates a 2-pound block sus-

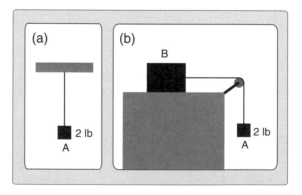

Figure 17.5
A two-pound block A suspended from a string. (a) String hanging from the ceiling. (b) String passing over a pulley and attached to a sliding block B.

pended from the ceiling by a string. Many students then say (correctly) that the force exerted by the string must be 2 pounds since the upward force on the block by the string must balance the downward gravitational force of 2 pounds on the block.

In figure 17.5b, the same 2-pound block A is suspended by a string that passes over a pulley. The other end of the string is attached to a heavier block B which then slides along a horizontal table. Here again students often say that force exerted by the string must be 2 pounds since the upward force on block A by the string must balance the downward gravitational force of 2 pounds on this block. But this prediction is *wrong*.

Scientific predictions for the situations in figure 17.5

When several forces act on an object they do *not* necessarily balance—that is, the resultant total force on the object is *not* necessarily zero. Instead, Newton's law (17.1) asserts that this total force is always related to the object's acceleration.

In figure 17.5a, where the 2-pound block A hangs from the string and is at rest, the block's acceleration is zero. Hence the total force on this block must also be zero. Thus the magnitude of the upward force on block A by the string must be equal to the magnitude of the downward gravitational force on this block by the earth—that is, it must be equal to the 2-pound weight of the block.

But in figure 17.5b the 2-pound block A is *not* at rest, but descending with increasing speed while pulling the block B along the surface of the table. Hence the block A moves with an acceleration along the downward direction. According to Newton's law, the *total* force on block A must then also be directed downward. Thus the magnitude of the upward force on block A by the string must be *smaller* than the magnitude of the downward gravitational force on this block by the earth—that is, it must be smaller than the 2-pound weight of the block.

17.6   EDUCATIONAL IMPLICATIONS

17.6.1   Proficient performers

Present-day physicists have thoroughly assimilated the formal science of mechanics. This science, based on Isaac Newton's work about three centuries ago, transcends all earlier naive notions with a more precise description of motion (of the kind discussed in chapter 5) and with the fundamental insight that the acceleration of any object is related to its interactions with all other objects. This relation is quantitatively expressed by Newton's law $m\mathbf{a} = \mathbf{F}_{tot}$ which relates the acceleration $\mathbf{a}$ of any object to the *total* force $\mathbf{F}_{tot}$ on the object (that is, to the vector sum of all the individual forces on the object). Each such force is merely a convenient concept describing how the interaction of this object with some other object depends on the properties of these objects and the distance between them.

There are actually only a few kinds of such forces (such as long-range forces like gravity and some short-range forces due to touching objects) and their properties are well known. Hence a knowledge of Newton's law, and of the properties of these forces, leads to very many correct predictions and to wide-ranging applications in physics, astronomy, engineering, and other fields.

Contemporary physicists are very familiar with this modern scientific knowledge of mechanics and have used it for many years. Hence much of this knowledge has to them become so intuitive that they invoke it spontaneously without much deliberate thought. Thus they have often forgotten many of their earlier naive notions—and may sometimes find it surprising that students (and people in everyday life) may resort to such notions.

17.6.2 Inexperienced students

From a *logical* point of view, scientific mechanics (based on very few explicit basic concepts and principles) is actually much simpler and much more correctly predictive than the multitude of naive notions of the kind mentioned in the preceding three sections. But this scientific mechanics is significantly different from the many more primitive notions prevalent among students and in everyday life. From a *psychological* point of view, it is then scarcely surprising that many students find the learning of scientific mechanics difficult.

Furthermore, naive scientific notions are not only consistent with the everyday cognitive framework, but have often been intuitively used since early in a person's life (Bloom and Weisberg, 2007). These naive notions are usually adequate and efficient in daily life. Their inadequacies within the scientific framework are thus not readily recognized by students to whom this framework seems foreign. Hence students are prone to import their naive conceptions into the study of science and don't find it easy to replace them with scientific concepts and logical ways of thinking that are different from those common in everyday life.

Persistence of naive scientific notions   As the preceding three sections indicate, inexperienced students (even those who have successfully completed an introductory physics course) have difficulties transcending their preexisting naive notions and ways of thinking. Indeed, their naive scientific notions can persist for a long time and are difficult to change. For instance, even after scientific instruction, students commonly revert to naive notions of the kind mentioned in the preceding sections. (For example, they may claim that a force is required to produce motion or that the velocity of an object is directed along the direction of the force exerted on it).

The persistence of naive scientific notions about motion has been consistently observed in many countries and seems to be largely independent of the instructors who teach science courses. (See Halloun and Hestenes, 1985a; also the other references listed for this chapter.) Indeed, some special tests have been devised to assess how well physics courses help students to transcend their naive notions about mechanics (Hestenes and Wells, 1992; Hestenes, Wells, and Swackhamer, 1992).

Wide prevalence of persisting naive notions   Naive notions about mechanics are probably particularly difficult to change since phenomena involving motion or forces have been acquired since early childhood and are very familiar from everyday life (Planinic et al., 2006). But naive notions in other domains of physics are also quite common [for example, in electricity (McDermott and Shaffer, 1992) or optics (Goldberg and McDermott, 1987)]. Indeed, many studies have been carried out to identify students' naive physics notions (McDermott and Redish, 1999).

Naive scientific conceptions are also commonly seen among students in scientific domains *outside* of physics, for example, in chemistry or biology (Duit, 2006; OISE/UT, 1998). Naive conceptions in geology may perhaps be somewhat easier to change (Muthukrishna et al., 1993)), probably because geological phenomena are of less concern in everyday life.

Prior *scientific* notions can also cause difficulties in more advanced scientific fields. Thus physics students, who are trying to learn quantum mechanics, suffer from specific misconceptions caused by their prior knowledge of classical mechanics and may find it difficult to assimilate the more modern conceptions of quantum mechanics (Singh, 2001; Singh, Belloni, and Christian, 2006).

Student difficulties not due to prior notions   Not all student difficulties are due to their preexisting naive notions. As in the case of the concept *acceleration* discussed in chapter 5, many difficulties are also due to students' failures to heed fine discriminations. For example, students may fail to distinguish *velocity* and *acceleration*, often fail to identify *all* the forces acting on a particular object, or may determine the total force by adding all these forces as numbers rather than as vectors.

17.6.3   Common instructional deficiencies

Some instructors simply attempt to teach "correct" scientific knowledge and behave as if their task were to fill students' blank minds with new knowledge. But the learning process is more complex. Students don't have blank minds, but *do* have preexisting naive knowledge whose existence cannot be ignored since it can cause significant learning difficulties.

As a result of such instruction, students often emerge from science courses with persisting prior naive knowledge. Many students are thus left with all kinds of naive conceptions and scientific misconceptions, even after ostensibly completing science courses with good grades (Halloun and Hestenes, 1985a).

17.6.4   Instructional suggestions

The following are some suggestions that can help to remedy such deficiencies.

Explicate inadequacies of students' prior knowledge   Make students aware that their existing knowledge may be beset by inconsistencies and may also be inadequate to predict or explain some observable phenomena. Hence address explicitly the challenge of improving this knowledge so as to make it scientifically more satisfactory—a challenge that may require significant changes in students' preexisting conceptions (Posner et al., 1982).

Motivate and explicate the knowledge to be learned   Remind students that the goal of science is to devise compact knowledge enabling the prediction and explanation of many observable phenomena. Emphasize that this is not only an intellectually challenging goal, but also one with many practical implications. Then constantly point out the increasing predictive power that students acquire as the result of their learning and the wide utility of their new knowledge.

Ensure that students acquire coherently organized scientific knowledge
Don't attempt to replace previous naive knowledge elements piecemeal with scientifically correct knowledge elements. (This would merely re-

place prior fragmentary knowledge with new fragmentary knowledge, a process that is both difficult and unlikely to lead to good performance). Instead, try to replace naive prior knowledge with new scientific knowledge that is coherent, well organized, and compact (based on only a few central concepts and principles that can be readily elaborated).

Start from simple rather than from familiar situations   It is useful to introduce new knowledge by starting from a consideration of *simple* rather than familiar situations (for example, by first considering the motion of objects in outer space, rather than in daily life where objects usually interact with many other things). This can have the following advantages: (1) It illustrates a widely used scientific method (namely, dealing with simple cases to elucidate more complex ones). (2) It avoids starting from familiar situations that may be beset by various naive scientific conceptions that are hard to overcome. (3) By going from simpler to more complex situations, students can be automatically led to elucidate the features responsible for naive familiar conceptions (for example, the very many interactions often present in daily life).

Explicitly compare new and prior knowledge   Point out the similarities and differences between newly acquired scientific knowledge and preexisting student knowledge. Emphasize the importance of heeding the differences in order to avoid mistakes and confusions. Also point out discriminations in applicability conditions (for example, that prior knowledge may not be entirely wrong, but may merely be of limited scope).

Ensure students' ability to use scientific knowledge properly   Give students adequate practice in properly interpreting and using newly acquired scientific knowledge in concrete instances. Such practice is essential so that students can consolidate their new knowledge, recognize its utility, and feel comfortable with it. In particular, confront students with situations that reveal the inadequacies of their prior knowledge. As far as possible, let them themselves detect their errors, diagnose the nature of these errors, try to identify the causes leading to them, and correct such errors by the proper application of their newly acquired scientific knowledge.

Deliberate instructional attempts to help students transcend their naive prior notions are described in some of the references (Minstrell, 1989; Mazur, 1997).

17.7 SUMMARY

• Knowledge about scientifically relevant topics has naturally evolved to enable predictions and explanations that are *satisfactory* for coping with everyday life. But this naive scientific knowledge is significantly different from formal scientific knowledge that has been deliberately devised to achieve *optimal* predictive and explanatory power.

• Naive scientific knowledge, like much of everyday knowledge, consists of an accumulation of loosely specified concepts and methods. It can be adequately useful in daily life, but may be inconsistent with reliable observations.

• The contrast between naive science and actual science can be well illustrated by comparing everyday ideas about motion with the science of mechanics, which has systematically refined such ideas into a coherent form enabling far greater predictive power.

• Students, who are attempting to learn science, find it difficult to modify or transcend their preexisting naive scientific conceptions. Hence such conceptions often persist for a long time and cause many confusions.

• To be effective, science instruction must be explicitly aware of students' naive prior notions. But such naive conceptions cannot merely be replaced by miscellaneous conceptions of greater scientific validity. They must be transcended by *coherent* scientific knowledge that is recognized to be more valid and useful—and that can be applied in a variety of specific situations.

IV   LEARNING AND TEACHING

18 Developing Instruction

The preceding chapters examined the knowledge and thought processes that enable good performance—and also discussed the prior knowledge commonly possessed by inexperienced students. Hence we are now prepared to deal with the following central problem: *How can one develop instruction for helping students learn the knowledge and thinking needed in scientific or similar complex domains?*

This problem addresses an educationally ambitious goal that is difficult to achieve. To make some progress toward this goal, the present chapter explores the following questions: (1) Can this major problem be approached in ways similar to the kinds of problems discussed in the preceding chapters? (2) How can this complex problem be decomposed into simpler problems that can be addressed separately? (3) What then would be a systematic instructional development process that could be discussed more fully in the subsequent chapters?

Educational relevance Since the present chapter (as well as all later ones) are centrally concerned with learning and teaching, they are clearly pertinent to all educational efforts. Hence these chapters, unlike earlier ones, will no longer need a concluding section to point out their educational relevance.

18.1 INSTRUCTIONAL DEVELOPMENT AS A PROBLEM-SOLVING TASK

Learning and instruction To identify the issues involved in instructional development, it may be useful to recall figure 1.1, reproduced here in figure 18.1. This figure indicates a specific person S (the *student*) who is transformed from an initial state S_i to a final state S_f where S can perform tasks that S could not do before. This transformation process is called *learning*. A process deliberately undertaken to facilitate such

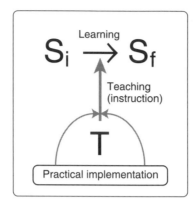

Figure 18.1
Learning and teaching.

learning is called *teaching* (or *instruction*) and may be implemented by
interaction with a teaching system T consisting of a human teacher,
books, computers, and other components.

   Goal of instructional development   Instruction aims to attain the goal
of endowing a student with new performance capabilities. Like any
other goal-directed task, instruction can thus be viewed as a problem.
Indeed, it is a complex problem requiring one to identify and implement many carefully chosen kinds of actions leading to the desired
goal.

   The development of instruction is of primary interest in many different situations (for example, when one is trying to teach an individual
student, or aiming to teach a class of students, or attempting to write a
textbook or other instructional materials). Since the development of instruction can be regarded as a problem-solving process, the discussion
of problem solving in chapters 11 through 13 is highly relevant. Hence
the following pages will exploit the problem-solving knowledge previously discussed in those chapters.

   Theoretical view of instruction   The preceding comments dealt with
observable performance. From a more theoretical point of view, such
performance is the result of underlying knowledge and associated
thought processes. Instruction can then be regarded as involving a
transformation (or modification) of a student's knowledge and thinking. Correspondingly, instructional development can be viewed as a

complex problem with the goal of *helping a student to modify his or her knowledge structure so as to enable the desired performance.*

Comments on this formulation of the instructional goal

The preceding goal has been carefully phrased to emphasize the following features.

Helping the student   The word *helping* has been used to point out the indirectness of instructional interventions. One cannot directly change a student's knowledge (for example, one cannot directly modify a student's brain, or use a syringe to inject new knowledge into a student, or load new software into a student as if he or she were a computer). Instead, one must rely on the student's own processing and can only *help* the student to engage in processing that leads to desirable learning.

Modifying knowledge   One can only *modify* a student's knowledge since a student always possesses some preexisting knowledge. (Thus instruction is more closely analogous to remodeling an existing house than to building a new one from scratch.) The existence of such prior knowledge can facilitate, as well as hinder, a student's learning.

Knowledge structure   The words *knowledge structure* emphasize that a person's knowledge does not consist of a mere compilation of knowledge elements, but involves a well-organized structure of such elements.

Implications   Instructional development (the process of producing instruction) requires complex problem solving similar to that needed to produce other complex functioning systems (such as machines, automobiles, or computer programs). The process of developing instruction can therefore *not* be expected to be simpler than that needed for projects in such other domains.

18.2   STAGES OF INSTRUCTIONAL DEVELOPMENT

General development process   The process of developing *any* product can usefully be decomposed into the following three successive stages:

1. Designing an effective product with desired features and functioning. The result is a product *design* (a completely specified plan) that may be assessed to determine its adequacy.

2. Producing such a product   The result is then a prototypical product that can be assessed to determine whether it has the desired features and functionality.

3. Deploying the product so that it can be made available to many people. The outcome is then a widely distributed product whose efficacy and practical utility can be suitably assessed.

Examples of development processes

Developing an airline transportation system In this case, one needs (1) to design a properly functioning airplane by exploiting an adequate understanding of aerodynamics, (2) to construct at least one prototype plane capable of functioning reliably when handled by skilled pilots and mechanics, and (3) to deploy such planes to create a practical airline transportation system available to numerous passengers under realistic conditions of uncertain weather and only moderately competent personnel.

Developing a drug for a particular disease In this case one needs (1) to exploit available medical knowledge in order to design a drug with an appropriate chemical structure and mode of functioning, (2) to synthesize the actual drug and assess its efficacy under carefully controlled conditions, and (3) to deploy such drugs to create a practical delivery system that can produce many of these drugs in suitable factories, distribute them in pharmacies and hospitals, and train physicians to use them properly.

Instructional development process The preceding comments imply that instructional development can be similarly decomposed into the following three stages:

1. Designing an effective learning process that leads to the desired performance. This learning process should indicate the content and sequence of the suggested learning steps—and may be helpful to a learner even in the absence of any outside instructor. (The specified learning process can then be assessed to determine whether it is adequately complete and free of deficiencies.)

2. Producing instruction that helps a student to engage in the specified learning process. Such instruction (implemented by a teacher or other means) needs to provide a student with adequate guidance, support, and feedback. The result should be prototypical instruction that is successful for teaching some students under favorable conditions. (Such prototypical instruction can then be assessed to determine its efficacy.)

3. Deploying instruction for teaching many diverse students in realistic settings. This involves designing and implementing practical means of instructional delivery that can be adapted to students of various backgrounds and abilities, that can provide needed instructional materials, and that can train competent teachers. (The efficacy and usefulness of such instructional delivery must then be suitably assessed.)

These three stages of instructional development are summarized in figure 18.2. (In figure 18.1 they correspond, respectively, to the horizontal arrow, to the vertical arrow, and to the curved arrows at the bottom.)

Stages of instructional development

(1) Designing an effective learning process

(2) Producing instruction to foster learning

(3) Deploying practical instruction

Figure 18.2
Stages of instructional development.

Comments about instructional development All aspects of instructional development involve complex problem solving. Devising an instructional prototype may perhaps require more creative thinking, but implementing practical instructional delivery may sometimes be equally challenging. Successful prototype instruction is a necessary prerequisite for practical instruction addressed to many diverse students. After all, if instruction does not work reliably under favorable conditions (with a motivated student assisted by excellent teachers), it cannot be expected to work with many students under realistically practical circumstances. On the other hand, even successful teaching of a few students is usually *not* sufficient to show that such teaching will be successful for many diverse students under practical conditions.

Separating the instructional development process into the previously mentioned three successive stages is helpful because it decomposes a complex process into more easily manageable parts. On the other hand, there are no sharply defined boundaries separating these stages, nor is their sequence rigidly fixed. (For example, if practical implementation difficulties arise, one may need to go back and modify the prototype design to facilitate its practical implementation.) Nevertheless, it is useful to discuss these stages of instructional development separately, as is done in the next three chapters. It is also helpful to keep in mind that the same specified learning process may sometimes be implemented by different instructional methods.

18.3 OVERVIEW OF INSTRUCTIONAL DEVELOPMENT

Importance of instructional development The task of developing effective instruction is *practically* important for anyone teaching a course and (perhaps even more so) for anyone writing a textbook or producing other instructional materials. The ability to develop effective instruction provides also a severe test of *theoretical* ideas about the underlying kinds of knowledge, thinking, and learning needed for complex tasks.

Addressing the stages of instructional development   Each stage of the instructional development process has a well-defined goal that may be attained by appropriate problem solving. The basic problem-solving strategy, outlined in figure 12.1 and discussed in chapters 12 and 13, is thus applicable to every stage (whether initially planning or designing, or subsequently implementing in detail). This strategy, applied to instructional development, is summarized in figure 18.3 and its successive phases are briefly outlined in the next few paragraphs.

• *Describing the problem*   The strategy starts with an effort to formulate a clear description of the particular instructional problem. Thus one needs to describe the *initial situation*, the particular instructional *goal*, and any *conditions* affecting the proposed solution process.

• *Analyzing the problem*   This second phase of the strategy tries to identify pertinent useful knowledge, analyzes the instructional problem with the aid of this knowledge, and then tries to arrive at analytic problem description likely to facilitate the solution of the problem.

• *Constructing the solution of the instructional problem*   This is the most important and difficult phase since it may require many complex decisions. Hence the following chapters discuss this phase in appreciable detail.

If a task is complex, it is helpful to engage in progressively more refined planning that leads to a *complete plan* (or *design*) which can then be implemented to lead to the desired product. When a development process is decomposed into successive stages with distinct goals, each of these stages can then be designed before it is actually implemented.

For example, the problem-solving process of figure 18.3 can be applied to each of the stages of the instructional development process outlined in figure 18.2. In the first of these stages, the solution of the instructional problem should then yield a design of an effective learning process; in the second stage, it should yield a design (and subsequent implementation) of instruction to foster learning; and in the third stage it should yield a design (and subsequent implementation) for deploying instruction under practically realistic conditions.

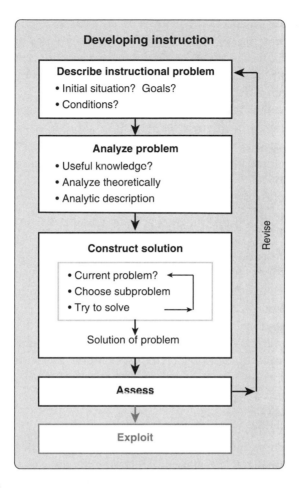

Figure 18.3
Problem-solving strategy for developing instruction.

Utility of design for complex tasks

It is useful to plan any complex task before attempting its implementation. For example, engineers fully plan (or *design*) a plane before mechanics can actually construct it. Architects create the design of house before giving it to the carpenters and masons who actually build the house. Company executives design the structure of a company before actually hiring the personnel to fill the positions in the company organization.

• *Assessing* This phase of the strategy aims to assess the proposed solution of the instructional problem. If this solution has merely led to a design, one can assess whether it is adequately complete, clearly formulated, and free of deficiencies. If the design has actually been implemented, one can assess its actual efficacy in achieving the desired results. Any observed deficiencies can then be remedied by subsequent revisions.

• *Exploiting*   This last phase of the strategy is not obligatory, but can facilitate future work. It involves reflecting about the solution of an instructional problem to exploit what one has learned from it (such as new ideas or methods potentially useful for future instructional purposes).

Preview of the following chapters   An instructional development process, like the one outlined in the preceding paragraphs, does not necessarily *guarantee* good instruction. Indeed, there is no such thing as some uniquely good instruction. But some instructional development projects may be far better than others (for example, because they lead to more effective or efficient learning by students, or to greater ease of implementation).

Better instruction is more likely to be achieved by a systematic and carefully considered development process of the kind outlined in this chapter. Hence the following chapters examine in greater detail the three stages of this instructional development process.

18.4   SUMMARY

• The development of instruction can conveniently be decomposed into the following three stages: (1) Designing an effective learning process. (2) Producing instruction to foster learning by well-chosen instructional methods. (3) Deploying practical instruction for many diverse students by appropriate means of instructional delivery.

• Each of the preceding stages involves complex problem solving that can be facilitated by the problem-solving strategy discussed in chapter 12 and illustrated in figure 18.3.

• It is useful to carefully design each stage of instructional development before attempting its actual implementation.

• The three stages of instructional development are discussed more fully in the next three chapters.

19 Designing the Learning Process: Goals

This chapter begins to discuss the design of an effective learning process (the first stage of the instructional development process outlined in chapter 18). The instructional problem at this stage is primarily concerned with the process whereby a student can usefully learn some new knowledge. The present chapter indicates how this process can be analyzed so as to arrive at a well-formulated learning goal. The next chapter outlines the means whereby the learning process may be achieved. The subsequent chapters will then discuss how the learning process can actually be implemented by suitable instruction.

In following the problem-solving strategy outlined in figure 18.3, we shall aim to describe and analyze the learning problem from a cognitive point of view. This analysis should help to specify clearly *what* should be learned so that the next chapter can examine *how* it may be learned.

19.1 DESCRIBING THE LEARNING PROBLEM

The consideration of a learning problem must start with its clear specification. In particular, this requires answering the following questions outlined in figure 19.1: (1) What is known about a student in the initial situation before new learning? (2) What is the desired performance expected of a student after learning? (3) What are the conditions affecting the learning process?

The answers to these questions need to be clearly specified in terms of observable features. (More theoretical considerations, about underlying knowledge or thought processes, are best left to the later analysis of the problem.)

Description of a learning problem

- Initial situation

- Goal: Desired performance

- Learning conditions

Figure 19.1
Describing the learning problem.

19.1.1   Initial situation

Who is the student?   The situation is relatively simple when dealing with a particular student with well-known characteristics, but is more complex if one is dealing with a *group* of students. In this latter case one must try to identify the characteristics of a *typical* student—and then indicate the range of variability in the characteristics of different students in the group.

If the differences among students are sufficiently small, adaptations to various students can be achieved by minor adjustments in the learning process. Otherwise, different learning approaches may be needed.

Initial student performance abilities   What are the student's abilities before new learning? Specifically, what kinds of tasks can the student perform, and how well can the student perform them? What kinds of tasks can the student *not* perform? Under what *conditions* can the student perform these tasks? For example, can the student perform these only when explicitly prompted to do so—or does the student perform them spontaneously whenever they are appropriate?

The preceding questions are most reliably answered by actual assessments—by suitable performance tests given to the students. It is dangerous to *assume* that students have certain abilities merely because they have ostensibly studied relevant subjects, or because they received good grades in courses where such performance abilities were presumably taught. All too often students may only have acquired some nominal knowledge that they can talk about, but cannot actually apply.

Courses taken by students in the past may even be detrimental. They can lead students to a misleading sense of confidence when they are faced with material that appears well known to them, but that they don't really know how to use. Such students are often uninterested in learning knowledge that *seems* familiar, but that they don't actually possess.

Students' prior notions   It is also useful to ascertain (by questionnaires or interviews) students' prior conceptions about the domain that they are expected to study. Do they have faulty or misleading conceptions that need to be corrected or transcended if new learning is to be successful?

Other student characteristics   Lastly, it can helpful to elucidate some other information about the students. For example, what is their background and prior experience? What are some of their interests and attitudes? What are their work habits? All such information can be useful to motivate students and to tailor instruction to their individual characteristics.

19.1.2   Learning goals

Operational specification of goals   The desired student performance on particular kinds of tasks needs to be clearly specified. This specification should focus on *observable* performance and should avoid words like *know*, *appreciate*, or *understand* which are so vague as to be almost meaningless.

This specification of goals should be *operational*: it should specify what one actually would need to *do* to determine how well the desired performance has been achieved. For example, if one wants to use a word like *understand*, then one needs to specify what one would need to *do* to determine whether a student has achieved understanding. Similarly, a *syllabus* that merely lists topics to be covered in a course is of little utility—unless it specifies what students should actually be able to *do* after they have studied any such topic.

It is useful to specify actual methods and instruments that may ultimately be used to assess a student's performance after the instruction. For example, one may specify some typical questions on final assessment tests, as well as methods or scoring schemes for interpreting the results of such tests.

Utility of operational goal specifications   An operational specification of instructional goals is useful for several reasons. (1) Such a specification describes the intended instructional goals in a clear and concrete fashion. (2) When kept in mind during the design process, it helps to ensure that the proposed design is adequate to attain these goals. (3) It helps to avoid the temptation of introducing seemingly interesting topics or comments that don't really contribute to the achievement of the instructional goals, but may merely distract or overload the students. (4) It provides clear criteria that both teachers and students can later use to assess how well the learning goals have been achieved or whether further learning is still needed.

Adequacy of performance specifications   The specification of the performance, expected of students after their learning, must be adequately precise. What *kinds* of tasks should a student then be able to perform? Also, what is the desired *quality* of the expected performance? For example, is the expected performance merely nominal (so that the student can talk about a topic and answer some simple questions about it), or is it actual performance of some significant tasks?

What is the level of competence to be achieved by the student? Is it minimally adequate performance, competent performance, or proficient performance? Is a student expected to achieve performance that is effective, flexible, and efficient? (Proficient expert-like performance can, however, be expected only after many months or years of experience.)

One may need to be judiciously discriminating in the specification of desired competence levels for different skills. Thus one may aim for reliably competent performance on some tasks, but may be content with tolerable performance on some less important tasks.

Performance conditions   Under what conditions should the desired performance be exhibited? Is it only when the student is explicitly prompted, or is it whenever such performance would be appropriate? Also, is the desired performance to be achieved only immediately after the instruction, or is it to be still part of a student's capabilities some months or years after the instruction?

Are the learning goals sensible?   Learning goals may be desirable but not sensible. For example, a certain course may aim to endow students with some highly desirable knowledge and skills. But, given the limited preparation of the students, this aim might realistically not be achievable during the available time. An instructor would then be well advised to aim for more modest goals.

Instructors frequently feel compelled (sometimes because of outside requirements) to "cover" a certain number of topics in a course. This urge to cover topics can be stressful to both teachers and students, and can also lead to learning that is so superficial that it doesn't provide a base for further learning. The urge to *cover* thus needs to be critically examined. As the physicist Victor Weisskopf once said, the aim of instruction should not be to *cover* a subject, but to *uncover* it (to reveal and clarify it).

Lastly, one has to be careful that specified learning goals are actually useful for the attainment of ultimately important goals. For example, if the ultimate goal is to prepare science students to become good researchers, how useful is it to teach courses that focus predominantly on mathematical arguments, but fail to emphasize the qualitative thinking useful in research?

19.1.3   Learning conditions

There are ordinarily some conditions that affect the learning process and that must be heeded when designing this process.

Constraints and available resources   A learning task is usually constrained by various limitations, such as (1) the time available for learning, (2) the abilities and prior preparation of the students, (3) the help available to students, and (4) the available money, space, computational facilities, and other resources.

On the other hand, student learning may be facilitated by available human resources (teachers and other students) and learning aids (books and computers).

Learning may also be significantly affected by the context in which it occurs. For example, this context may include one or more of the following: (1) lecture halls for large numbers of students, (2) smaller classrooms for fewer students, (3) seminar rooms permitting closer interaction between a teacher and individual students, and (4) laboratory space with special equipment.

Interaction between conditions and goals   The learning conditions may sometimes interact with the learning goals. For example, existing constraints (such as limited student preparation or limited available time) may require an adjustment of the learning goals so as to make them more realistically attainable.

19.2   ANALYZING THE LEARNING PROBLEM

The strategy of figure 18.3 suggests that, after a learning problem has been clearly described, it should be analyzed more theoretically with

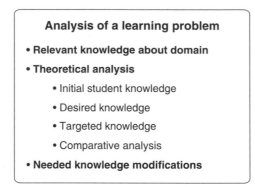

Figure 19.2
Analyzing the learning problem.

specific attention paid to the relevant kinds of knowledge and thinking. Such an analysis of the learning problem is centrally important
for instructional development. This analysis can usefully examine the
issues that are indicated in figure 19.2 and elaborated in the following
paragraphs.

19.2.1   Relevant domain knowledge

Analyzing a learning problem requires a thorough knowledge of the
pertinent domain. For example, if an instructor wants to facilitate
the learning of a particular field of science or mathematics, an essential
prerequisite is a sufficiently deep knowledge of this field and adequate
working experience with it. Indeed, an instructor's knowledge and experience should extend appreciably *beyond* the narrow boundaries of
what students are expected to learn.

19.2.2   Analysis of initial student knowledge

Importance of preexisting knowledge   The description of the learning
problem specifies a student's abilities before the intended learning. This
information needs then to be analyzed more closely to identify the underlying knowledge and thought processes responsible for the student's
prior abilities.

Any student (other than a newborn baby) comes to new learning
with some preexisting knowledge. Chapter 17 already indicated that

such prior knowledge is not easily modified—and that its existence may either help or hinder the acquisition of new knowledge. Adequate information about this prior knowledge is, therefore, important to facilitate new learning.

Model of a student's prior knowledge Sources of information, that can be useful for elucidating a student's prior knowledge, may include (1) the student's responses in an interview or on some diagnostic performance tests, (2) information about the student's background and educational history, and (3) previous research or interviews with students having a similar background and history.

These sources of information can allow one to formulate a *model* specifying the student's knowledge before any new learning. (A *model* is a simple theory that aims to predict and explain a limited range of observations.) Such a model should at least partially predict the student's initial behavior and performance. For example, it may indicate the content of the student's knowledge (including knowledge that is vague, faulty, naive, or misleading); the ways that this knowledge is described and the kinds of descriptions familiar to the student; and the organization of the student's knowledge and its organizational deficiencies. The model may also indicate whether the student tends to make important discriminations, to attribute clear meanings to the words that he or she uses, to think logically, to check his or her work, and so forth.

Example: Model of a novice student's knowledge about motion

The scientific description of motion requires some important discriminations. A model of inexperienced students' knowledge about motion would thus lead to the expectation that students would commonly *fail* to make such discriminations. Actual observations, of the kind mentioned in chapter 17, also agree with such expectations. Hence a model of an inexperienced student would predict that such a student would be likely to confound velocity with speed, to claim that an object moving with constant speed along a curved path has no acceleration, to confuse velocity and acceleration, to believe that the acceleration of an object must be zero if its velocity is zero, and so forth.

Lastly, it is helpful to have some information about the student's *meta*knowledge about the domain to be studied (for example, about the student's ideas about the goals and requirements in a scientific domain). As pointed out in chapter 16, these ideas can greatly affect how students focus their attention—and must ultimately be transcended if the students are unduly naive.

All such information is helpful to devise an effective learning process. Even a primitive model of a student's initial knowledge and performance can be useful (and is certainly better than no such model at all).

19.2.3   Analysis of desired knowledge

Relevant knowledge   What knowledge is useful for achieving the desired student performance? In addressing this question, one needs to focus on all relevant aspects of this desired knowledge (for example, declarative and procedural knowledge, the description and organization of this knowledge, and the thought processes enabling the effective use of this knowledge).

Task analyses   It is helpful to start by considering various tasks that a student will be expected to perform after learning (for example, tasks of the kind specified in the previously suggested final assessment tests). One can then try to identify the underlying kinds of knowledge and thinking that are needed to perform these tasks. For example, this can be done by purely theoretical analyses, by detailed observations of proficient performers engaged in these tasks, and sometimes also by observing oneself performing such tasks.

Although such observations may be somewhat time-consuming, they help to make the relevant tasks highly concrete. They may also reveal tacit knowledge outside the range of conscious awareness of some expert performers.

Observation methods   To make such observations systematically, one can ask a person to talk out loud about his or her thinking while the person is performing a task (without any interruptions by the observer, except for possible reminders to keep working and talking). The person's verbal statements can be tape-recorded and later transcribed. Together with the person's written work, they constitute a *protocol* that can subsequently be analyzed in detail to elucidate the person's knowledge and thinking.

The preceding method, called *protocol analysis*, has been fruitfully used in psychological investigations aiming to identify human thought processes in complex tasks (Van Someren, Barnard, and Sandberg, 1994; Ericsson and Simon, 1984). The person's talking does not seem to interfere unduly with his or her natural thinking.

Although the method does *not* reveal everything going on in the mind of the person working on a task, it reveals much more than is ordinarily apparent. Furthermore, after the person has finished the task (so that interruptions no longer disturb his or her natural thinking during the task), the observer may also ask the person to explain further some of his or her previous thought processes.

This method of analyzing think-aloud protocols does not need to be used as carefully for practical instructional applications as for purely psychological work. Nevertheless, when used judiciously, it can be useful—especially when the relevant tasks are complex.

Knowledge analysis   Particular task analyses, like those just described, allow a more general *knowledge analysis* that can specify the underlying knowledge useful for *all* the desired kinds of tasks in the relevant domain. Such a knowledge analysis is more compact and general than the analysis of a particular task. (For instance, the *same* underlying knowledge may be used repeatedly to deal with somewhat different tasks.)

Knowledge analysis versus task analyses

For example, task analyses might reveal how mathematicians solve particular algebra problems. But it may then be possible to identify the underlying knowledge and thinking required for solving *all* such problems involving linear equations.

As another example, task analyses might reveal how persons drive along particular routes. But it may be of greater interest to identify the knowledge required to drive along *all* such routes (such as knowledge about steering, braking, heeding traffic signs, driving uphill and downhill, and so forth).

19.2.4   Analysis of targeted performance

Limited utility of observing proficient performers   Observations of the kind mentioned in the preceding paragraphs can certainly help to elucidate the knowledge useful for achieving the desired performance. But although such observations of proficient performers can be suggestive, they can also be misleading for the following reasons. Proficient performers have, by virtue of their extensive experience, acquired much tacit knowledge and have often learned to perform many tasks routinely or automatically without much deliberate thought. Moreover, as pointed out in section 2.6 and experimentally illustrated in section 5.4.6, "experts" don't always perform well.

Model of targeted performance   Novice students cannot realistically be expected to achieve, in a limited time, good performance in the way that proficient performers do. The actual learning goal must thus be performance that is well adapted for carrying out the desired kinds of tasks—and is also well adapted to the capabilities of the students. This performance, which may be called the *targeted performance*, is performance of the kind that students might realistically be expected to acquire as a result of short-term learning. Such targeted performance may often achieve fairly good performance by deliberate thinking, while experts might use automatic recognition processes. Targeted performance thus aims to achieve good performance like a competent novice, rather than like a proficient expert.

A model of targeted performance (and corresponding *targeted knowledge*) is thus really a theoretical *prescriptive* model that aims to specify the knowledge and thinking that *should* allow inexperienced students to achieve good performance. It is not a *descriptive* model specifying what experts *actually do* (although it may be partly suggested by observations of such experts). Instead, a model of targeted performance may be partly based on some theoretical analyses and hypotheses.

Assessing models of targeted performance   How can one determine whether a theoretical model of targeted performance is satisfactory? One way is by assessing the extent to which instruction, based on this model, is actually successful in achieving sufficiently good student performance. Another more direct way is by assessing whether some agent (human or computer), acting in accordance with the model, does actually achieve competent performance.

For example, one may try to program a computer so that it performs tasks in accordance with the proposed model. If the computer succeeds in achieving competent performance, then this provides evidence that the model is satisfactory. [For example, Klahr and Carver (1988) tested in this way a model specifying effective human debugging of computer programs.]

Alternatively, one may test a model with humans. (After all, persons are special computers with natural-language and pattern-recognition capabilities far exceeding those of silicon-based computers.) Thus persons (who have no prior acquaintance with the knowledge required to perform the pertinent tasks) may be asked to act like robots by simply following detailed directions specified according to a proposed model of targeted performance. If these robot-like persons succeed in achieving competent performance, then this provides evidence that the model is satisfactory. [For example, Heller and Reif (1984) tested in this way a model specifying effective human methods for describing mechanics problems.]

Example: Testing a simple theoretical model of targeted performance

A model, specifying the knowledge and processes needed for driving to the airport, might explicate corresponding step-by-step directions. To test this model, one might ask a man (who is totally unfamiliar with the region) to drive a car while a passenger sitting next to him reads aloud the directions specified by the model. If the driver then actually arrives at the airport, the model would be judged satisfactory. But if the driver gets lost without reaching the airport, or gets stuck without knowing what to do next, then the model would be deemed inadequate and would need to be revised.

Models of targeted performance must satisfy such adequacy tests. Indeed, if a model of targeted performance is *not* sufficient to lead to satisfactory performance, then the test clearly indicates either that the model fails to specify some essential knowledge or that it contains erroneous knowledge. It would certainly be undesirable to design instruction that would teach faulty knowledge. Hence it is necessary to discard or modify a model of targeted performance if there are indications that it is *not* sufficient to produce satisfactory results.

Utility of good models of targeted performance   A good model of targeted performance clearly specifies what students should learn and is thus centrally important for designing instruction. For instance, in discussing some successful instructional innovations, Collins, Brown, and Newman (1989) cite three specific instructional cases. The first of these taught students how to read effectively with good comprehension (Palincsar and Brown, 1984), the second taught children how to write more effectively (Scardamalia and Bereiter, 1985), and the third taught strategies for solving mathematics problems (Schoenfeld, 1985). All these successful teaching efforts, as well as the one that aimed to teach debugging skills in computer programming (Klahr and Carver, 1988), were based on explicit models of the knowledge and thinking useful for performing the relevant tasks—and then engaged in deliberate efforts to teach this knowledge.

Explicit teaching in the coaching of athletes

When teaching high-level athletic skills, good coaches commonly try to identify the component skills needed for good performance, then teach these explicitly, and finally integrate these so that their students can use them jointly. But such careful analyses of good performance (and explicit teaching of component skills) are probably more common in athletic domains than in more intellectual fields.

Needs addressed by a model of targeted performance   A model of targeted performance strives to achieve good performance by specifying knowledge and thought processes that are appropriate for the intended students. Thus it needs to consider the characteristics of good performance mentioned in section 2.2 and tries to endow students with knowledge and thinking of the kind discussed in chapters 3 through 15.

19.3   COMPARATIVE ANALYSIS

After the preceding analyses, it becomes possible to compare the features of the student's initial knowledge and those of the targeted knowledge.

19.3.1   Relevant features

This comparison can focus on all the relevant cognitive needs listed in figure 15.2. For example, in what respects does the student's initial declarative and procedural knowledge differ from that of the targeted declarative and procedural knowledge? In what respects does the description and organization of the student's initial knowledge differ from that of the targeted knowledge? In what ways do the student's initial thought processes differ from those of the targeted thought processes?

Assessment of differences   The detected differences can be summarized by answering the following questions:

• What desired features are lacking in the student's initial knowledge? (These features need then to be acquired as a result of the instruction.)

• What undesirable features are present in the student's initial knowledge? (These features need then to be removed or modified as a result of the instruction.)

• What desired features are already present in the student's initial knowledge? (These features should be preserved or exploited in the instruction.)

19.3.2   Needed knowledge modifications

The answers to the preceding questions help to identify the knowledge modifications needed to transform the student's knowledge into the targeted knowledge. The needed knowledge modifications may thus be of the following kinds:

• Some new knowledge features may need to be acquired (either imported from outside sources or generated by the student).

• Some existing knowledge features may need to be removed or inactivated so that they will no longer be used.

• Some existing knowledge features may need to be modified (for example, removed and replaced by some newly acquired knowledge features). (A knowledge feature in the preceding list may indicate *any* knowledge feature, such as an element of declarative or procedural knowledge, a form of description or organization, or a particular thought process.)

The preceding analysis is useful for the following reasons: (1) It helps to specify clearly what needs to be taught. (2) It helps to avoid unwarranted assumptions that students might learn some things spontaneously without any instruction. (3) It can ultimately also be useful for diagnosing why certain performance deficiencies occur *after* ostensible learning.

19.3.3   Analytic specification of a learning problem

The goal of the analyzed learning problem can now be specified in the following compact and useful way:

The goal of learning is to achieve the knowledge modifications identified by the analysis of the learning problem.

19.4   SUMMARY

• To describe a learning problem, one needs to specify a student's initial performance capabilities, the student's finally desired performance capabilities, and any conditions affecting the learning process.

• A subsequent analysis may be used to identify the underlying knowledge responsible for a student's initial performance *before* learning. Similarly, the analysis needs to examine the tasks that a student should be able to perform *after* the learning and the knowledge that the student can use to perform such tasks.

• One needs to formulate a model of the targeted knowledge and thinking skills whereby a student can achieve the desired performance at a level of competence consistent with the constraints of limited abilities and limited available time.

• A comparative analysis of a student's initial knowledge and targeted knowledge allows one to determine what modifications of the student's knowledge need to be achieved by the contemplated learning.

20 Designing the Learning Process: Means

The analysis in the preceding chapter clarified the goals of the intended learning by specifying *what* should be learned, namely the desired modifications of a student's prior knowledge. This chapter tries to specify *how* such learning may be achieved by appropriate means (learning activities) that can produce the desired modifications of the student's existing knowledge.

Accordingly, we shall explore the following questions: (1) How can one simplify the learning process by decomposing it into successive subprocesses and sequencing these appropriately? (2) How can one facilitate learning by managing memory without overloading it? (3) How can one help learning by exploiting a careful organization of the relevant knowledge? (4) How can one ensure that newly acquired knowledge is usable and reliable? (5) Finally, how can one assess the extent to which a suggested learning process is effective in achieving its goals?

20.1 DECOMPOSING AND SEQUENCING THE LEARNING PROCESS

A learning process can be facilitated by decomposing it into successive subprocesses (or *segments*) of manageable size, each of which aims to construct a part of the desired knowledge structure. (For example, such a learning segment might correspond to a lecture or a section in a textbook.) The learning of each segment can then be addressed separately.

Judicious decisions must be made about how these segments should be sequenced. As usual, such decisions can be made by assessing the options available at any stage and choosing the seemingly most useful option. The basic guideline is *prior preparation* (that is, earlier learning should facilitate later learning). In judging the utilities of various options, one thus needs to assess the extent to which the consequences of an option (of a contemplated learning step) are likely to prepare the student for subsequent learning.

Such judgments of utility often involve tradeoffs between short-term and long-term utilities of learning steps. Thus it is ordinarily most useful to focus on an important learning step likely to have many beneficial consequences for further learning. However, sometimes it may be more useful to address a minor step that deals with more immediate concerns hindering further progress. For example, one may sometimes be led to choose a step that is likely to overcome an apparent learning obstacle—despite the fact that some other steps might ultimately be more important for subsequent learning.

20.1.1   Sequencing for explicit preparation

Judicious sequencing of learning segments can prepare a student *explicitly* for later learning (thus reducing the student's coping difficulties in the future). Such sequencing can help the student to acquire prerequisite or facilitating knowledge at an earlier stage.

Examples: Explicit preparatory knowledge

Such preparatory knowledge might include knowledge about algebra or vectors, about helpful symbolic representations, knowledge about forms of organization useful for dealing with new knowledge, procedural knowledge about useful problem-solving methods, or knowledge about helpful ways of checking one's work.

20.1.2   Sequencing for implicit preparation

Learning segments can also be sequenced so as to prepare a student *implicitly* for later learning. This can be done by letting the student initially deal with *simpler* or more familiar tasks. During this process, the student can *implicitly* learn knowledge that facilitates later learning for dealing with more difficult tasks.

Examples: Implicit preparation by simpler cases

Simpler cases   Simpler cases may be special cases that are simpler than more general cases. They may also be analogous cases that are simpler than the cases of ultimate interest. Furthermore, qualitatively described situations may be simpler than situations described in quantitative detail.

Simpler versus more familiar cases   Simpler cases provide good preparation. But familiar cases, that may *seem* simpler because of prior acquaintance with them, are *not* necessarily simpler. For example, (as mentioned in chapter 17) the familiar motions of objects observed in everyday life are actually quite complex because such objects interact almost always with many other things (such as with the surrounding air or with supporting surfaces). On the other hand, the *unfamiliar* motions of objects in outer space, or of objects moving in a vacuum, are much simpler since such objcects interact with almost nothing else. Hence such simple, but unfamiliar, motions can provide a better starting point for elucidating the basic principles of mechanics.

20.1.3 Successive approximations

It is particularly useful to decompose a learning process by successive approximations (by subdividing the process into smaller steps that progressively get the student's knowledge to approach the desired one). This has the following advantages: (1) It provides a systematic way of decomposing the learning process into easily managed smaller steps that progressively refine a student's knowledge until it becomes the knowledge ultimately needed for the desired performance. (2) Earlier steps in this process prepare for later steps since familiarity with earlier knowledge provides practice that facilitates the acquisition of later knowledge.

The preceding guidelines are also summarized in figure 20.1.

Guidelines for effective learning

- **Decompose and sequence**
    - Sequencing for explicit preparation
    - Sequencing for implicit preparation
    - Using successive approximations
- **Facilitate the learning process**
    - Active processing
    - Effective encoding
    - Managing cognitive load
- **Exploit useful organization**
    - Overviews and previews
    - Constructing a knowledge cluster
    - Constructing related clusters
    - Facilitating knowledge transfer
- **Ensure usability**
- **Ensure reliability**

Figure 20.1
Guidelines for designing an effective learning process.

20.2 ENCODING NEW KNOWLEDGE

20.2.1 Active processing

Learning requires active processing by the learners since they must effectively encode new information and integrate it with their preexisting knowledge. For example, one cannot learn when one is asleep or unconscious. Nor can one passively sit while acquiring new knowledge by injections from a syringe or by swallowing some miraculous pills. In particular, mere reading or listening lead usually to little useful learning. It is much better if learners are actively engaged by actually *doing* something with any newly acquired or modified knowledge—and by taking appreciable responsibility for their own learning (instead of depending excessively on help from teachers).

Effective learning thus requires active engagement by students (a requirement often not met in many classrooms).

20.2.2 Effective encoding

The retention and retrieval of learned knowledge is largely dependent on the strength and form of its encoding. There are several ways of ensuring that this encoding leads to readily remembered knowledge and skills.

Strong encoding by practice Practice is essential to ensure that acquired knowledge and skills are properly remembered. Such practice provides the active processing that is needed for strong encoding of the knowledge in long-term memory—and thus also helps the retention of this knowledge so that it can be readily remembered at later times.

Effective practice must be deliberate and consistent. As discussed in section 6.2.2, *massed* practice (a large amount of practice compressed into a short time) leads to rapid forgetting. It is far better to spread practice over a longer period of time since such *distributed* practice (involving repeated partial forgetting and relearning) leads to knowledge that is retained over much longer periods of time. (For example, cramming before examinations is a poor way of learning.)

Reliable encoding by many connections New knowledge can be more easily remembered if it is related to other existing knowledge by many connecting links (since these then provide more available paths by which the new knowledge can be retrieved). Thus it is helpful to use or describe new knowledge in several different ways.

Useful descriptions   Newly acquired knowledge can be more easily remembered if it is described in a useful form. For example, knowledge encoded in pictorial form (so that it can be readily visualized) is often more easily remembered than the same knowledge encoded in purely verbal form.

Careful descriptions can also help to avoid confusions by identifying important discriminations. Furthermore, they can reduce retrieval difficulties due to the kinds of interference effects discussed in section 6.2.2.

It is useful to describe newly learned knowledge in multiple forms (for example, in verbal, pictorial, and mathematically symbolic forms—or in qualitative as well as in more precise quantitative ways). The newly acquired knowledge can then be more readily remembered—and can also be more easily adapted to the performance of different kinds of tasks.

Useful descriptions can often be most easily learned by successive approximations. Thus one can start with simple, approximate, or qualitative descriptions—and then gradually refine these by making them more precise and quantitative. In this way, one can also learn how to translate between such different forms of description.

20.3   MANAGING COGNITIVE LOAD

Learning to construct a modified knowledge structure may require some complex processing. Hence the difficulties, involved in coping with the needed processing, should not be excessive.

20.3.1   Cognitive load

The *cognitive load* involved in a task is the cognitive effort (or amount of information processing) required by a person to perform this task. If the cognitive load needed for learning becomes excessive, little or no learning can occur. Hence the cognitive load at any stage of a learning process must be kept within reasonable bounds.

This does *not* mean that that the cognitive load should always be as small as possible, for at least two reasons. (1) Learning would be *inefficient* because the entire learning process would then consist numerous small steps—and would thus become unduly fragmented and long. (2)

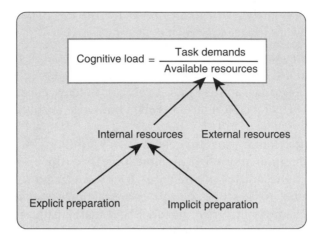

Figure 20.2
Factors affecting cognitive load.

Learning might then also become so *boring* that the learner's attention could not be maintained and would drift—thereby reducing the active processing needed for effective learning.

A learning process should thus be designed so that the cognitive load is always of *reasonable* magnitude—neither so large as to be overwhelming, nor so small that learning becomes inefficient or boring.

The cognitive load involved in performing a task depends on the task demands compared to the resources available for performing this task. As schematically indicated in figure 20.2, this cognitive load is larger if the task demands are larger, but is smaller if more resources are available for performing the task.

Example: Cognitive load involved in a multiplication task

The task of multiplying two large numbers requires several calculations to be performed in appropriate sequence. But the cognitive load involved in this task is much reduced if a person has available appropriate *internal* resources (such as a knowledge of the multiplication tables and of the procedure for long multiplication) or has available some *external* resources (such as paper on which to write or an electronic calculator).

In general, the cognitive load involved in a learning task can be reduced either by *de*creasing the intrinsic task demands or by *in*creasing the resources available to the person. The following paragraphs indicate some of the ways that a student's cognitive load during learning can be reduced to manageable levels.

20.3.2   Reducing cognitive load by reducing task demands

One way of decreasing task demands is by reducing the *magnitude* of a required knowledge modification. This can be done by *not* asking a student to acquire simultaneously all relevant knowledge about a topic. Instead, one may ask the student to acquire some partial knowledge that can later be expanded to help the student obtain more complete knowledge.

Another way of decreasing task demands is by reducing the required *quality* of an initial knowledge modification. Thus one can start by imposing only approximate or qualitative requirements—and only later try to refine performance so that it becomes more precise and quantitative.

Such a more gradual approach, proceeding by successive approximations, provides the following advantages. (1) The student is not overwhelmed by having to deal with too much new knowledge at one time. (2) Some basic new knowledge becomes thereby more immediately available, more readily interpretable, and more easily remembered. (3) Students find it more motivating to acquire some knowledge that they can immediately use. (4) The use of some partial knowledge provides helpful practice facilitating the acquisition of further knowledge.

Examples: Reducing excessive cognitive load

Learning vector concepts   Textbooks for introductory college physics often start with a chapter dealing with vectors. After defining vectors, this first chapter typically discusses how vectors can be added and subtracted, how they can be described by their numerical components, and how they can be multiplied in two different ways to obtain their *dot product* or *cross product*. Much of this information is then not used until much later.

An alternative approach (exemplified in Reif, 1995) is to introduce vector concepts gradually so that new concepts can be assimilated in stages and then used immediately. Thus the first chapter might merely define vectors and discuss how they can be added or subtracted. A later chapter might then discuss how vectors can be described by their numerical components—and could immediately show how this description is useful for dealing with projectile motions. Still later, another chapter might introduce the dot product of vectors and immediately show how it is useful in discussing the physics concept of *work*. And even later still, another chapter might introduce the cross product of vectors and show how it is useful for discussing rotational motion.

Difficulties in learning a drawing program   When I recently tried to learn Freehand (a drawing program that I wanted to use on my computer), I was faced with an instructions manual that spent no less that the first 50 pages discussing the various features of this program, its available commands, and its many different kinds of palettes—all before it indicated how I might draw a single line!

The cognitive load for me was excessive. I could not remember all this information and found this a difficult way to learn. I kept wishing for a more gradual approach that would allow me to practice actually *drawing* at least some things while trying to learn other related information.

Learning complex computer applications   Commercially available computer programs can be very useful for accomplishing a wide variety of tasks (such as writing, drawing diagrams, modifying photographs, or making video presentations). But they have also become increasingly complex as computer programmers have sought to include ever more features in them (to an almost pathological extent called *featuritis*). Although these features may sometimes be useful, they also greatly increase the difficulty of learning or using these computer programs.

One way of remedying these difficulties would be to accompany such programs by better instructions manuals. After first providing an overview of the functions and capabilities provided by such a program, the first part of such a manual would specify only the most important features needed to use the program for relatively simple tasks. This part alone might be sufficient to satisfy some users. But to help users interested in performing more complex tasks, some of the topics discussed in this part would refer to other parts where these topics are elaborated in greater detail. If carefully designed, such a hierarchically structured manual would be less likely to overload the potential users of the program and would also make the program better suited to users of differing degrees of sophistication.

20.3.3   Reducing cognitive load by appropriate resources

Reducing cognitive load by increasing internal resources   Cognitive load can be significantly decreased by increasing a student's internal knowledge resources. This can be done by prior learning that provides a student with helpful or prerequisite knowledge (for example, with a knowledge of some useful descriptions or of some helpful mathematics).

Reducing cognitive load by increasing external resources   Students can also be helped by external resources that assist the students while they are trying to learn. Such assistance can provide students with various helpful devices (such as charts, pages summarizing important information, workbooks, and calculators). Alternatively, students may be asked to perform only part of a task while a teacher (or other external agent) performs the rest of it. The gradual removal of assistive external resources can then ultimately lead to independent performance by the students. (Such external resources thus play a role analogous to that of training wheels that are provided to children who are trying to learn how to ride a bicycle.)

20.4 EXPLOITING USEFUL ORGANIZATION

Knowledge is not just an amorphous collection of miscellaneous items, but an organized structure (more similar to a house than to a pile of stones). Its organization makes it clear how its components fit together and how they can be assembled. As previously mentioned, the process of learning some knowledge is somewhat similar to the process of building or remodeling a house. In all such cases a preexisting organization, and an awareness of the planned organization, help to build further parts of the structure. For example, when building a house, one first assembles the major components (such as the foundation, walls, and roof). These can then be exploited to support other components or to facilitate the assembly of subsidiary components (like interior partitions and doors).

Learners find it difficult to acquire and retain new knowledge unless they can connect it to appropriate knowledge previously possessed by them. This is why it is hard to learn previously unfamiliar knowledge or to learn it unsystematically without adequate guidance (for example, to learn it merely by practical experience, by independent discovery, or by trying to solve various problems). On the other hand, *after* one has acquired a well-organized coherent knowledge structure, this can greatly facilitate the acquisition of further knowledge as a result of practical experience, discovery, problem solving, or independent exploration (Kirschner, Sweller, and Clark, 2006).

Learners thus need to acquire an effective organization of their knowledge. Hence students should be helped to organize their knowledge in a useful form, to maintain their knowledge in well-organized form at all stages during the learning process, and to modify this organization by successive approximations so as to obtain an effective organization of their final knowledge. (Such an organization may be similar to the hierarchical organization discussed in section 9.5.)

Persistent attention to the organization of knowledge provides the following advantages. (1) Well-organized knowledge can be more readily remembered and retrieved for various purposes. (2) It is much easier to learn well-organized knowledge than to acquire knowledge piecemeal (and then either leave it in a disorganized form or try to organize it all at once at the very end). (3) As a student's knowledge is gradually extended and reorganized, the student gets valuable practice in using well-organized knowledge. (4) When students participate in reorganizing their knowledge, they become more actively engaged and thus learn more effectively. (5) Students thereby also get to appreciate the benefits of a good knowledge organization and learn how to exploit such an organization.

As illustrated in the following paragraphs, attention to the organization of knowledge can also suggest useful ways of sequencing the acquisition of further knowledge.

20.4.1   Overarching knowledge

If students can embed new knowledge in some overarching knowledge, they are provided with the rudiments of a more comprehensive knowledge organization and become better prepared for subsequent learning.

Orienting overviews   When starting the discussion of a major topic, it is useful to provide students with an overview of its main parts and of the issues to be examined. Such an overview can be sketchy and lacking in details, so that it can make sense to unsophisticated students. However, it can be sufficient to let these students know what to expect and to provide them with a more meaningful learning context.

Preparatory previews   More generally, students can be prepared for later learning if they are provided with a preview of somewhat broader knowledge, including knowledge to be learned later. For example, when starting with a simple discussion of some topic, one can also briefly mention the finally desired knowledge about the topic. This kind of preparatory preview requires little time or effort by the students, but can make them initially aware of the existence of more complete knowledge.

This helps to embed a student's learning task in a broader and more meaningful context, and can also help to avoid misconceptions about the range of applicability of newly learned knowledge. For instance, while it is useful to discuss simple situations first, the resulting danger is that students then often invoke them inappropriately afterward (because these situations are then more familiar and have also a beguiling simplicity).

Examples of preparatory previews

Basic mechanics principles   Some discussions of mechanics start with *statics*, the simple situation where objects are at rest and where the total force on any object is zero. However, a preparatory preview can then mention that more generally, when objects are *not* at rest, the total force is *not* zero. This preview may help students later to avoid the misconception that the total force on an object is always zero.

Ohm's law in electricity   An important principle asserts that the electric current I in an circuit element is proportional to the potential drop V across this element. This principle is summarized by Ohm's law $V = RI$ (where R is the electrical resistance characterizing the element). However, when this law is introduced, it is useful to point out immediately that this law is only valid if Coulomb electric forces alone are responsible for the current. This preparatory preview can help to avoid subsequent confusions that lead students later to apply this law indiscriminately in the presence of electric forces produced by changing magnetic fields.

20.4.2   Constructing a knowledge cluster

As discussed in section 9.5, knowledge can be made more coherent by organizing it into clusters where some central knowledge subsumes associated subordinate knowledge. This result can be achieved in the following two ways:

1. If some central knowledge is already available, elaborate it progressively to obtain associated knowledge subsumed by it (see figure 20.3).

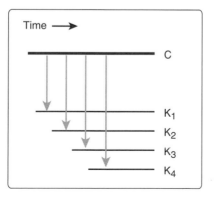

Figure 20.3
Schematic diagram indicating some central knowledge C successively elaborated into the subordinate knowledge elements $K_1, K_2, \ldots$.

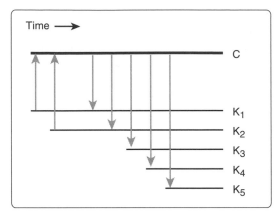

Figure 20.4
Schematic diagram indicating the knowledge elements K_1 and K_2 used to identify some central knowledge C. This can then be elaborated into all the knowledge elements $K_1, K_2, K_3, K_4, \ldots$.

2. If some central knowledge is *not* available, use available special cases to identify subsuming central knowledge and then elaborate it further (see figure 20.4).

The following examples illustrate these two processes more concretely.

Example 1: Elaborating available central knowledge

Interaction is a concept widely useful in science. (One says that *A* interacts with *B* if its behavior is affected by the presence of *B*.) This concept of interaction is also familiar from everyday life. For instance, the interaction between a child and its mother is apparent if the child's behavior depends on whether the mother is present or not.

As schematically indicated in figure 20.3, one can then use the familiar concept of interaction as a central concept to start learning about mechanics—and then gradually elaborate this concept to deal with progressively more complex interactions. Thus one can begin by discussing the interaction of one object with another, and then the interaction of one object with several other objects. One can then also introduce some specific concepts useful for describing interactions (for example, concepts such as *force*, *work*, and *potential energy*). Furthermore, one can discuss various kinds of interactions (such as elastic, gravitational, electric, and magnetic interactions). One can then also realize that the entire science of mechanics deals with the relation between motion and interactions. The concept of interaction thus comes ultimately to encompass much of physics.

Furthermore, in learning mechanics, the concept *interaction* is a much better starting point than the concept *force* which, although commonly used in everyday life, has various misleading connotations and is also less generally useful in physics.

Example 2: Using special cases to identify and elaborate central knowledge

When a topic is largely unfamiliar to a student, it is often helpful to start by discussing various examples and simple situations. As schematically indicated in figure 20.4, one can thus be led to identify some *general* principle that is applicable in all these situations and thus more widely relevant. After that, one can apply this principle to many other particular situations and also let the students themselves apply it to such situations.

For instance, when starting to study mechanics, one can first discuss the motion of a single object that is moving in outer space where it interacts with nothing else. Then one can discuss the motion of an object interacting with *one* other object—and can try to formulate some principles that apply to this simple situation. Then one can discuss the motion of an object interacting with *two or more* other objects—and extend the previous principles to this more complex situation (see, for example, Reif, 1995). After this, one has actually obtained general mechanics knowledge applicable to *all* situations—and this knowledge can then be elaborated and applied to a vast range of particular situations.

20.4.3 Constructing related knowledge clusters

Another way of exploiting knowledge organization during learning arises when the knowledge to be acquired consists of several parts. One can then fully elaborate one part, then fully elaborate a second part, then a third part, and so on. However, the ensuing disadvantage is that a student gets fully immersed in an earlier part without any awareness of the other parts. Not only can this be unmotivating, but students may then mistakenly come to believe that the knowledge acquired at an earlier time is more broadly applicable than is actually the case.

A better way of proceeding involves first outlining, *without* appreciable details, an overview of all parts of the relevant knowledge. Then one can successively elaborate in detail the knowledge subsumed by the first of these parts, then the knowledge subsumed by the second of these parts, and so forth until one has elaborated the knowledge of all these parts. (Figure 20.5 illustrates this process schematically.)

The preceding process makes immediately apparent (without complicating details) the organization of the *entire* relevant knowledge. Thus it provides a preview of the structure within which the more detailed knowledge can be embedded. Throughout the learning process, the students can then remain aware of the entire context—without the danger that the trees might obscure the forest.

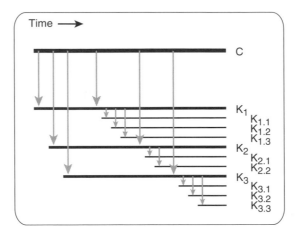

Figure 20.5
Schematic diagram indicating some central knowledge C subsuming the subordinate kinds of knowledge K_1, K_2, and K_3. These can then be elaborated into further knowledge elements subsumed by each.

Examples: Outlining related topics before their elaboration

States of matter   When discussing the states of matter, one can discuss in detail first the solid state, then the liquid state, and then the gaseous state.

However, it is better to start by outlining briefly the salient characteristics of solids, gases, and liquids. Afterward, one can then discuss separately, in greater detail, first the highly ordered solid state, then the highly disordered gaseous state, and finally the intermediate liquid state.

Different kinds of motion   It is simplest to start by discussing motion with constant velocity, but this often leads students to make some unwarranted assumptions about motions in more complex cases.

Hence it is better to start by pointing out various possible kinds of motions. After that, one can first consider in detail the simplest case—that of motion with constant velocity (such as a car moving with constant speed along a straight road). Then one can consider in detail the special case of motion with constant acceleration (such as a thrown baseball flying though the air). Then one can discuss in detail less special situations (such as the motion of planets in circular or elliptical orbits).

20.4.4   Facilitating knowledge transfer

Knowledge transfer is the ability to use knowledge in a domain beyond the one in which is was initially acquired or used. Such knowledge transfer can be much facilitated by appropriate forms of knowledge organization or description.

Transfer by analogy   It may be possible to organize knowledge so as to make apparent analogies indicating a correspondence between familiar knowledge elements and some new knowledge elements. Such analogies can then be exploited to make inferences about new knowledge dealing with unfamiliar topics.

Such knowledge extensions by analogy can be useful and suggestive, but are *not* necessarily correct. Indeed, an analogy may not make clear which new knowledge elements do (or do not) correspond to original knowledge elements—or make clear the nature of this correspondence. Hence inferences based on such analogies may not be valid.

Transfer by generalization   It may be possible to organize some knowledge in a more general form that is applicable to a larger number of specific instances. If the range of applicability of the generalized knowledge is specified, it then becomes clear how seemingly different instances are related. Hence it also becomes possible to make reliably *valid* inferences about situations that are identified as particular instances of the general knowledge.

Examples of knowledge transfer

Projectile motion   One can learn about the motions of various objects near the surface of the earth (for example, falling stones or baseballs flying through the air). Afterward, one may possibly realize that the motion of an electron between two electrically charged parallel plates is analogous. (In this analogy, the constant gravitational force on the projectile near the earth corresponds to the constant electrical force on the electron.) Hence the mathematical discussions of these motions should be similar.

Alternatively, one can learn about the *general* case of motion of an object under the influence of a *constant* force (one that is constant in magnitude and direction). One such instance is then the motion of a projectile subject to the approximately constant gravitational force near the earth. Another such instance is the motion of an electron affected by the constant electrical force between electrically charged plates. The discussions of these motions must then be clearly identical.

Planetary motion   One can learn about the motion of a planet (such as the earth) around the sun. Later, one may then realize that the motion of an electron around the nucleus of an atom is analogous. (In this analogy, the electron corresponds to the planet, the heavier nucleus corresponds to the sun, and the electrical force on the electron by the nucleus corresponds to the gravitational force on the planet by the sun.) This analogy then suggests that the motion of an electron around the nucleus should be similar to the motion of a planet around the sun.

Alternatively, one can learn about the *general* case of motion of an object under the influence of a force which is directed toward a much heavier object (and whose magnitude depends on its distance r from the heavier object like $1/r^2$). One such instance is then the motion of a planet influenced by the gravitational force due to the sun. Another such instance is the motion of an electron influenced by the electrical force due to the nucleus. Both of these motions (from the point of view of classical mechanics) must then be identical.

20.5   ENSURING THE UTILITY OF ACQUIRED KNOWLEDGE

Any newly acquired knowledge should be useful for performing some significant tasks. Thus, students should not be content to have learned some knowledge (or to have apparently completed the study of some topic) unless they have acquired the cognitive resources needed to use it appropriately.

As indicated in figure 2.3 or 15.2, the students themselves (with the assistance of instructors) should thus make sure that they can properly interpret their acquired knowledge in various specific cases, can describe it in different ways, and have organized it so that it can be readily remembered. The students should also be able to infer various implications, to implement properly any newly learned methods, to solve some unfamiliar problems, and to assess whether their own performance is satisfactory. If significant deficiencies are apparent, students need to engage in further learning to ensure that their acquired knowledge is actually useful.

Limitations and learning priorities   Sufficient time is required to learn knowledge well enough that it can be used effectively. Thus one must also recognize that a learner's available time may be limited. However, not all knowledge needs to be learned equally well. Francis Bacon once said that "Some books are to be tasted, others to be swallowed, and some few to be chewed and digested." A similar comment can be made about learning different kinds of knowledge. Thus students may have to decide on sensible priorities—and instructors should help them to make such decisions.

For example, some knowledge may have to be learned only well enough that one is aware of its existence—and knows where one can go to learn more if the need arises. Similarly, some knowledge may be too demanding to be adequately learned when it is first encountered; it may then be better to postpone further learning until one has had more experience and attained greater maturity. However, mere tidbits of knowledge are never enough for any serious work.

Any domain requires at least a core of knowledge that can flexibly be used and that can serve as a solid base for further learning. If students don't acquire such a useful core of knowledge, their learning efforts are likely to be largely wasted and to result merely in superficial knowledge that is quickly forgotten.

Advantages of ensuring utility   Several advantages are achieved by ensuring that newly acquired knowledge is actually useful. (1) Learning is more motivating to students if the resulting knowledge can be used in some meaningful ways. (2) The use of newly acquired knowledge leads to more active processing by students—and thus helps them to better encode and remember that knowledge. (3) It is easier to learn partially useful knowledge that can be gradually improved than to acquire a large amount of inert knowledge that one must then learn to use at the end. Such gradual learning can also appreciably reduce the cognitive difficulties encountered at any stage. (4) Earlier use provides students with practice that can help them to diagnose difficulties and to facilitate subsequent learning.

20.6   ENSURING THE RELIABILITY OF ACQUIRED KNOWLEDGE

Several things can be done to ensure that acquired knowledge remains correct and is not quickly forgotten.

Quality assessments   Repeatedly checking the quality of acquired knowledge is very important, especially since this quality can deteriorate as a result of forgetting or careless use. (A desire for speed and efficiency can easily lead to such carelessness.) It is certainly essential to assess the quality of acquired knowledge at the end of a learning segment and to make sure that this knowledge can be used appropriately. Furthermore, it is highly desirable that students themselves learn how to assess the quality of their own knowledge and do this even without external encouragement. It is also possible to teach some checking skills explicitly (Klahr and Carver, 1995).

Periodic reviews   As already mentioned, effective encoding of newly acquired knowledge can greatly help to ensure that this knowledge is remembered and that it can be properly retrieved. But since memories gradually decay, acquired knowledge may not remain permanently accessible. Hence memory can usefully be refreshed by periodic reviews and by practice in applying previously acquired knowledge. Such reviews can also check the correctness of the knowledge and remedy any detected deficiencies. Furthermore, they can help to integrate available knowledge so that recently acquired knowledge can be used in conjunction with previously existing knowledge.

20.7 ASSESSING A LEARNING DESIGN

After an effective learning process has been designed, it can be partially assessed. However, a more complete assessment is possible only after this learning process has actually been implemented (by instruction of the kind discussed in the next chapter).

Theoretical assessment   Some aspects of a learning design can, and should, be assessed shortly after its completion. It is important to answer the following questions: Does the designed learning process seem adequate to lead to the desired final performance? Does it fail to deal with some important features? Does it include unnecessary or redundant features that could readily be omitted (and might thereby facilitate the learning task)? Are there any gaps that fail to deal with issues required for subsequent learning? Do any steps impose learning demands that transcend students' expected capabilities?

Frequently, some of these questions cannot be satisfactorily answered. The designed learning process needs then to be appropriately revised. Indeed, the examination of a proposed design may often reveal enough deficiencies that several successive revisions may be necessary before the design of an effective learning process seems satisfactory.

Experimental assessment   If possible, a proposed learning design should be experimentally tested by trying to implement it with one or more individual students. In this case, one must try to interact with the students in such a well controlled way that they actually do engage in the specified learning process. One can then observe where the students experience difficulties, and all such difficulties may suggest appropriate revisions of the learning design.

Preliminary nature of these assessments   As already mentioned, all such assessments and revisions should be considered preliminary—to be subsequently extended and improved after effective instructional interactions have been explicitly specified and implemented. However, assessments of a proposed learning design are important because any uncorrected flaws in such design are likely to undermine the efficacy of any instruction based on it.

20.8   ACHIEVING GENUINELY GOOD PERFORMANCE

Many people merely strive to achieve adequately good performance and then make no further learning efforts. Attempts to achieve *genuinely good performance* require, however, much more practice and dedication. Such practice does not consist of mere repetitions of newly acquired skills, but must be *deliberate practice* devoting systematic efforts to improve one's performance.

Deliberate practice   In particular, such deliberate practice (consistently carried out over long periods of time) involves the following kinds of activities: (1) Constantly observing one's performance while trying to improve it. (2) Explicitly identifying any detected performance deficiences, trying to remedy each individually, and thus attempting to achieve improved performance without any such deficiencies. (3) Devoting full attention to all such improvement efforts, while avoiding any distractions. (4) Focusing on important details, and working on them carefully and slowly, before trying to achieve speedier performance. (5) Analyzing how better performance might be achieved— and trying to profit from any useful criticisms or feedback obtained from teachers or other people.

Such deliberate practice is essential to achieve genuinely good performance in any domain—irrespective of whether this involves science or mathematics, writing skills, musical performance, or athletic prowess (Ericsson, Krampe, and Tesch-Romer, 1993; Ericsson and Charness, 1994). Indeed, people in most such fields require about ten years of deliberate practice before they can become genuine experts.

20.9   SUMMARY

• The design of an effective learning process builds on a prior analysis (like that in chapter 19) that identifies the desired knowledge modifications.

• The design of the learning process can be helped by the following guidelines: (1) Decompose and sequence the learning process to provide explicit or implicit preparation. (2) Facilitate learning by active processing and careful managing of cognitive load. (3) Exploit a useful knowledge organization to provide overarching knowledge, to construct and elaborate knowledge clusters, and to facilitate knowledge transfer. (4) Ensure that the resulting knowledge is useful and reliable.

• The design of a learning process can be theoretically assessed by checking whether it seems adequate to lead to the desired performance. It may also be assessed experimentally by trying to use the design to teach some individual students.

• Genuinely good performance (surpassing the kind of adequately good performance pursued by many people) can only be achieved by deliberate practice extending over a long time—and may ultimately lead to genuine expertise in a particular field.

21 Producing Instruction to Foster Learning

The preceding chapters aimed to specify an effective learning process. Although such a specification may aid the learning of some people, it alone is ordinarily insufficient to help students to learn. Hence we now turn to the second stage of the instructional development process—the problem of teaching by instruction that can help students to engage in effective learning.

Following the general development process outlined in figure 18.3, we shall explore the following questions indicated in figure 21.1: (1) How can one describe an instructional problem? (2) How can one analyze it to identify important instructional needs? (3) How can one devise useful means facilitating students' learning? (4) How can one assess the merits of a suggested instructional approach?

21.1 DESCRIBING THE INSTRUCTIONAL PROBLEM

We assume that the prior work, needed to specify an effective learning process, has been completed so that one can address its instructional implications.

21.1.1 Specification of the problem

Situation This chapter considers the relatively simple situation where a teacher is dealing with a single student—or with a small number of similar students who can be adequately handled by a single teacher interacting with them. (If one cannot deal satisfactorily with this simple situation, it is unlikely that one will be able to deal with more numerous students.)

Although there is no sharp distinction between this situation and one where it is necessary to teach larger numbers of students, the

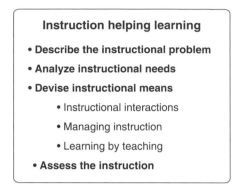

Figure 21.1
Instruction to promote learning.

distinction is important because of the greater complexity of the latter situation. Hence we postpone until the next chapters a discussion of practically important cases where one must deal with more than about twenty diverse students, where several teachers may be involved, where the same teaching effort may often need to be repeated many times, and where it may become cost-effective to create teaching aids (such as textbooks, workbooks, or computer programs) that can be used repeatedly with different groups of students.

Instructional goal   The goal of the instructional problem is to *devise methods and teaching interactions that can help to ensure that students engage in effective learning.*

21.1.2   Importance of this instructional goal

Although the preceding goal seems simple and is easily stated, it is difficult to achieve. Indeed, students often fail to learn the knowledge and activities that were apparently taught. When students do *not* perform satisfactorily after some instruction, it is then difficult to know whether the instruction did not specify an effective learning process or whether the students did not actually engage in this process.

As an example, suppose that an instructor tried to teach students a useful method for solving certain kinds of problems, explicated this method in some detail, demonstrated it, led students through it in class, and then asked students to apply it in order to solve some further problems. However, when the students themselves tried to solve these problems, they did *not* follow the recommended method but reverted to an unsystematic approach previously familiar to them. Although the taught method may be effective, the instruction was then *not* adequate to ensure that students actually learned to use it.

Effective teaching must thus manage the instructional interactions sufficiently well that students actually engage in a suggested learning process. Coaches trying to train persons to become good athletes, or teachers aiming to train persons to become good musical performers, commonly supervise individual students closely enough to ensure such effective learning. They guide a student to perform in effective ways, monitor him or her carefully while practicing, and provide corrective feedback so that the student is sure to learn good skills (without acquiring bad habits that may be difficult to break or lead to injuries). The following is a somewhat amusing example of such effective supervision.

An unconventional example of effective music instruction

When the famous violinist Jascha Heifetz was a child, he was initially taught by his father. For the reasons just mentioned, the latter thought that carefully supervised practice was so important that he was always present when Jascha practiced—and locked up the violin to prevent Jascha from practicing in his absence (Benoist, 1978). Although such thoroughly supervised individual learning supervision may perhaps seem excessive, it is clear that it had no deleterious effects on Jascha Heifetz's subsequent career.

21.1.3 Explicating learning goals to students

It is helpful to explicate an instructional goal as a learning goal for the students. Learning can then be viewed by students as a problem-solving task (Bereiter and Scardamalia, 1989) or as a collaborative problem-solving task carried out by students jointly with a teacher. This point of view provides the following advantages: (1) The student can then have a clear goal in mind while learning. Furthermore, the learning process can follow a systematic problem-solving strategy of the kind discussed in section 12.1. (2) Both the students and the teacher have then clearer criteria for determining students' progress toward the specified learning goal. (3) Students can be actively engaged by questions inviting them to contribute to the problem-solving process. (4) The teacher becomes less of a superior omniscient person, but more like someone who may also learn from the students. (5) Even if the teacher must transmit some information and students cannot significantly participate in this process, the teacher can demonstrate problem-solving that leads to a well-specified learning goal. (6) Teachers are then also less likely to resort to unmotivated ways of learning that don't reflect the ways of thinking of real learners or problem solvers.

Examples of unmotivated or unrealistic learning

Mathematics   The instructor writes a complicated algebraic expression on the blackboard and then proceeds to manipulate this expression until he arrives at a useful result. But where does this initial expression come from? Why would anyone ever think of such an expression?

The instructor has here used a *method of revelation* that is unsatisfying to the students and that does not teach them how working mathematicians really think.

Physics   It is fairly common to tell students that there once was a great man, called Isaac Newton, who formulated three laws of motion that students should now use. But how would one ever *discover* such laws?

A teacher could, however, start with the clearly motivated problem of discovering principles useful for predicting the motions of objects. The teacher could then show how (irrespective of the actual historical development) some simple observations and plausible hypotheses lead naturally to Newton's laws. In this process, the students would learn better how scientific laws are discovered, how to express Newton's laws in modern form, how to interpret them properly, and thus also how to avoid some common misconceptions.

21.2   ANALYZING INSTRUCTIONAL NEEDS

Any task is ordinarily carried out by a series of successive steps, each of which addresses the following three essential needs: (1) deciding what to do, (2) implementing this decision, and (3) assessing whether the implementation was satisfactory (and correcting it otherwise).

For example, in the simple case where a task involves writing a sentence, one needs (1) to decide what one wants to say, (2) to implement this decision by writing appropriate prose, and (3) to assess whether the written sentence does convey the intended message.

In the particular case of a learning task, an experienced student might possibly engage in all the appropriate actions to implement the learning process independently. But most students need assistance from an outside agent (such as a teacher) who can help ensure that they engage in the appropriate actions. To address the previously listed three essential needs, the teacher should then provide the following kinds of assistance:

1. Assistance in deciding what to do can be provided by *guidance* from the teacher (who can direct a student to carry out some specific actions).

2. Assistance in carrying out the chosen actions can be provided by *support* from the teacher (who may help the student in implementing the chosen actions).

3. Assistance in assessing the student's implementation of these actions can be provided by *feedback* from the teacher (who can monitor the student's performance and provide corrective information to the student).

To facilitate learning, interactions between a student and a teacher must then provide appropriate *guidance*, *support*, and *feedback*. (The word *coaching* is commonly used for instruction providing these three forms of assistance.) These assistance processes may be provided either explicitly by verbal instructions or implicitly by demonstration. However, all such assistance must gradually be reduced (or *faded*) so that the student ultimately learns to perform well independently.

The preceding remarks suggest how the instructional problem may be solved by providing appropriate learning assistance. The next several sections discuss how to assist learning by helpful instructional interactions and by careful management of students' learning process.

21.3   HELPFUL INSTRUCTIONAL INTERACTIONS

As we have seen, the instructional problem can be addressed by combining the design of an effective learning process with instructional interactions ensuring that students engage in this process. The following paragraphs discuss ways of doing this by appropriate guidance, support, and feedback.

21.3.1   Guidance

Explicit guidance   The guidance given to students may be both explicit and *direct*. The following are some examples: (1) A teacher may give students explicit directions or advice specifying what they should do. (2) The teacher may provide needed information. (3) The teacher may answer questions asked by the students.

The guidance given to students may also be explicit, but more *indirect*. The following are some examples: (1) A teacher may ask questions to focus the students' attention appropriately or to make them think more deeply. (2) A teacher may provide students with specific hints.

Implicit guidance The guidance given to students may also be much less explicit. For example, a teacher may demonstrate (or *model*) how to perform particular tasks, or may try to serve as a role model that students can imitate.

Implicit guidance can also be provided by appropriately structuring the learning context. For example, a teacher may select or restrict the resources (books, calculators, and other tools) available to the students. Alternatively, the teacher may provide students with special tools (for example, with special software such as outline processors that facilitate hierarchical thinking).

More generally, implicit guidance can be provided by limiting the number of options available to a student. For instance, this can be done by restricting the commands available in a computer interface (for example, by initially eliminating complex commands from a word processor that students need to learn). It can also be done by limiting what a student can possibly do next, and thus enforcing a particular sequence of steps.

Timeliness and individuality Guidance is *prompt* if it is immediately provided to a student whenever it is needed. Alternatively, guidance is delayed if it is provided only at times specified by the instructional system (for example, at the next class meeting or at the instructor's next office hour). Prompt guidance is usually more effective because it is more likely to be heeded and can prevent students from going off in inappropriate directions.

Individualized guidance is adapted to the current needs of a specific student. By contrast, generic guidance is designed for a typical student in a group or class. Individualized guidance is more useful, but can only be provided with greater difficulty or at greater costs.

21.3.2 Support

Explicit support Explicit support can be used to provide a student with direct assistance while the student is learning to perform a task. Such support can also be called *scaffolding* by analogy to the scaffolds that help support a building during construction, but are ultimately removed to leave a freestanding structure. (Another analogy is suggested by the *training wheels* that help a child learn to ride a bicycle, but are discarded after the child has become proficient enough to ride without any outside assistance.)

Such explicit support can assist the student during learning by providing help when the student is stumbling, correcting mistakes while they occur, and preventing the student from getting stuck without knowing what to do.

Another form of explicit support can be realized if a teacher takes over the implementation of a part of a task while the student does the rest. After sufficient learning by the student, the support can then be reduced by letting the student progressively take over more of the task until he or she is able to perform the entire task independently.

Implicit support Support can also be provided more implicitly (for example, by encouragement reassuring students that they know enough to perform a task independently).

Timeliness and individuality Support is *prompt* if it is provided while a student is actually engaged in a learning task. Support is less timely if it is merely provided by advice before the student engages in a learning task, or by some retrospective comments afterward.

Individualized support, provided to a student according to his or her particular abilities and needs, can be most effective. However, in instruction dealing with numerous students, the support given to individual students is commonly much more *generic* and reflects merely the presumed needs of a typical student.

21.3.3 Feedback

Explicit feedback An instructor may give students explicit feedback by (1) observing students so as to provide them with information about their performance and about any detected deficiencies, (2) providing students information about likely reasons for their deficiencies, and (3) providing suggestions for improving the students' performance and for correcting their deficiencies. (Such suggestions can be given explicitly, or somewhat less explicitly by asking well-chosen thought-provoking questions.)

Implicit feedback Implicit feedback can be particularly effective if it is *intrinsic*—that is, if it is provided by a student's work itself (rather than by an instructor). Any performance deficiencies become then directly apparent to the student without a teacher's intervention. For example, it is very apparent to students that their computer programs don't run because of some faulty syntax, or that their laboratory experiments don't yield the desired kinds of results. A student can then not simply blame an instructor for being pedantic if the instructor gives the student a poor grade because of some missing semicolons in the student's computer program. The actual failure of a program to run is far more convincing than an instructor's red marks on a paper.

Timeliness and individuality   Feedback is *prompt* if it is given to a student immediately after the student's actions. Such prompt feedback has the advantages that it is more comprehensible since the student's actions are then still fresh in his or her mind—and since the student can then immediately correct any deficiencies. By contrast, when a corrected homework assignment is returned to students a week after they turned it in, the feedback to the students is much delayed. Indeed, by that time students may have lost any interest in that homework—and may have forgotten what they did or why they did it.

Individualized feedback, based on an individual student's actions and observed ways of thinking, can clearly be more effective than more generic feedback based on the observed performance of a class of students. (Of course, well-designed generic feedback may also incorporate some adaptation to the needs of individual students.)

21.4 MANAGING INSTRUCTION

Instruction must be carefully managed to achieve the instructional goal of ensuring that students engage in an effective learning process. Such management can be achieved by using the instructional interactions discussed in the preceding section and by assisting students in some of the ways discussed in the following paragraphs.

21.4.1 Decomposition of the learning task

The most basic way of assisting students' learning is by decomposing instruction (and the corresponding learning task) into manageable segments. Each such segment (such as a section of a book or session of a class) can usefully consist of the following three phases.

Initial phase of an instructional segment   This initial short phase (largely outlined by the teacher) should provide a motivating context for the contemplated learning problem. Thus it may (1) identify the students' current (and presently lacking) abilities and knowledge, (2) specify the goal of the instructional segment (the desired abilities and correspondingly needed knowledge), and (3) outline a sketchy plan indicating how this goal might usefully be pursued.

Central phase of a segment In this central phase, students need to undertake the task of attaining the specified learning goal. In collaboration with the teacher, they then need to engage in the lengthy process of identifying and elaborating newly needed knowledge, ensuring that they can interpret it properly, describing and organizing it in useful ways, applying it to solve pertinent problems, and getting enough practice to make certain that their newly acquired knowledge is effectively usable.

Final phase of a segment An instructional segment should be completed by assessing whether students have acquired the desired capabilities and knowledge. Such an assessment can be provided by well-designed tests—and subsequent reviews needed to ensure that students have reliably acquired the desired knowledge and capabilities. (Otherwise, it is unwise to let the students go on since they would then build their subsequent work on a house of cards and be beset by cumulatively increasing learning difficulties).

21.4.2 Levels of instructional management

Instruction can be managed by providing various levels of supervision and assistance to students.

Limited feasibility of managing instruction The level of instructional management may be limited by practical considerations and available resources, particularly when there is a need to deal with many students. For example, students commonly receive very little individual guidance, support, and feedback in the large classes prevalent in many high schools and most colleges.

Students in such classes often spend much of their time listening to lectures or reading textbooks (and few attempts are made to ensure that the transmission of all this information actually leads to effective learning). Students often get more actively involved in their learning only when they work on their homework assignments. But since such homework is done at home without supervision, students can easily engage in inefficient or ineffective activities—and may thus practice poor activities or engage in fruitless floundering. Furthermore, feedback to the students is often minimal and long-delayed, usually consisting of little more than some red marks on homework papers that are returned at a later time.

Under these conditions, it is difficult to teach more effective ways of thinking or better problem-solving processes. Even if such processes are explicitly explained and demonstrated, students (in the absence of good supervision) often don't use them but revert to old thinking patterns. Effective teaching may thus become difficult or impossible under these circumstances, even when using good instructional materials and methods.

Limited desirability of managing instruction Even if tight instructional management is possible, it may not always be desirable. For example, in some cases it may be preferable to give students greater freedom to pursue their own learning inclinations and thereby also to foster greater independence. However, it is illusory to believe that effective learning will occur if students are merely given free reins without appreciable guidance (Kirschner, Sweller, and Clark, 2006).

Weaning from instructional assistance Whenever students are provided with instructional assistance, it is ultimately necessary to wean them appropriately so that they are able to perform independently. This can be done by *fading* the instructional assistance—that is, by reducing it gradually so that students become progressively better able to function on their own. In addition, it is useful to help students to acquire better skills of independent learning so that they can continue to learn without external assistance and may require less instructional support in future learning activities.

21.4.3 Individual tutoring

The highest level of instructional management can be achieved when an individual student is taught by a particular teacher or *tutor*. In this case, the tutor has a great amount of control about the timing and sequence of the information presented to the student—and also about all the activities carried out by the student with this information. Furthermore, the tutor can at all times provide the student with appropriate guidance, support, and feedback. A tutor who has a good knowledge about the subject matter to be taught (and also about the pedagogy involved in teaching and learning processes) is then in a very good position to supervise the student so as to produce successful learning. It is then not surprising that individual tutoring seems to be the most effective teaching method (Bloom, 1984).

Kinds of tutoring activities   If a tutor has engaged in sufficient preparation to design an effective learning process, he or she can help a student to learn by engaging in the following activities suggested by the needs for good performance (as discussed in chapters 3 through 15):

• The tutor can explicate the learning problem by clarifying what the student presently knows or does not know, by specifying a learning goal, and by suggesting a possible plan for attaining this goal.

• The tutor can help the student to encode new knowledge by (1) focusing the student's attention appropriately, (2) helping the student to encode pertinent declarative and procedural knowledge, (3) helping the student to specify and interpret this knowledge while ensuring important discriminations, and (4) strengthening this acquired knowledge by adequate practice.

• The tutor can help to consolidate all this knowledge by helping the student to (1) describe this knowledge in multiple ways, (2) integrate this knowledge with other preexisting knowledge, (3) organize all this knowledge in useful forms facilitating retrieval, and (4) use this knowledge to solve problems of various complexity.

• The tutor can help the student to (1) improve performance efficiency by suitable practice, (2) detect and correct any performance deficiencies, and (3) thus assess and revise newly acquired knowledge.

• The tutor can gradually reduce the instructional assistance and thus promote more independent performance by the student.

• Finally, the tutor can monitor whether the student maintains good performance over longer periods of time and can help to refresh the student's knowledge when necessary.

Such instructional assistance can be very useful to a student trying to learn scientific or other complex knowledge—or to a student trying to achieve good proficiency. This is why (as mentioned in section 21.1.2) individual coaching is used in efforts to train good athletes or musical performers. However, it is also clear that individual tutoring can practically *not* be provided to most students because it would be prohibitively expensive to supply an individual tutor for every student—and because enough good tutors would not be available.

21.4.4   Minimalist instruction

While individual tutoring provides tight control over the instructional process, the opposite extreme of loose control may be appropriate in some other situations. This is especially the case when the skills to be learned are not particularly demanding (such as the skills needed to use a word-processing program) and when one is dealing with students who have become fairly good independent learners. In such situations, it may be easier and less costly to avoid complex instructional management. It may also be better not to burden such learners with unnecessarily voluminous textbooks or instructions manuals (that they often don't read anyhow). Furthermore, it may be more motivating for such people if they can immediately start doing useful tasks and gradually learn more while engaged in them.

Instruction may then merely introduce students to some centrally important parts of some new knowledge, illustrate it briefly, and then let students use and elaborate this knowledge further while actually trying to perform some meaningful (and initially simplified) tasks. Additional help may then be provided only when students encounter difficulties or have further questions. This instructional approach has some of the following advantages beyond those already mentioned: (1) It can lead to effective learning, and good retention of newly acquired knowledge, since it gets students actively engaged in their own learning. (2) It makes students better prepared to learn independently in their later lives where instructors are not always readily available. (3) It ensures that the knowledge acquired by students is actually usable for performing significant tasks.

Some of these advantages can, in fact, be realized in practice. For example, *minimalist instruction* has been advocated and effectively used for teaching computer software applications like word processors (Carroll, 1990). Bulky instructions manuals are then replaced by much sparser basic instructions that users can quickly begin to apply for useful work—while also gradually learning more complex or efficient commands. When judiciously used, such minimalist instruction may sometimes also be useful for teaching some scientific knowledge.

21.5   LEARNING BY TEACHING

21.5.1   Efficacy of teaching for learning

Many people report that they really learned a subject only after they themselves had taught it. Indeed, when they were asked to teach, they could no longer remain in the more passive roles that they had originally assumed as students. Instead, they themselves had to systematize and organize all their knowledge before they could explain and teach it to others.

Hence students' learning can be fostered not only when they are being taught, but also when they themselves assume the roles of instructors engaged in teaching other people.

Benefits of teaching When students teach, they themselves need to acquire the relevant knowledge. They must also explicate this knowl edge in greater detail so that they can explain it to other people. Furthermore, they need to organize this knowledge appropriately so that they can decide what is centrally important and what is more peripheral, they need to demonstrate how this knowledge can be used to implement some significant tasks, and they need to assess and correct the work of other people. As a result of all these activities, the students need to become actively engaged in dealing with the relevant knowledge and thinking—and all such active engagement leads to better learning.

The preceding considerations suggest that effective learning can be enhanced by deliberately letting students engage in teaching. The following paragraphs indicate some ways that this can usefully be done.

21.5.2 Deliberate explaining

Explaining is an important part of teaching and can, even by itself, be instructionally useful.

Self-explanations and learning from examples In real life, many of us learn from examples (for instance, by observing what other people do). It is also common in instruction to illustrate important ideas or methods by concrete examples so that students can learn from them. But what students *actually* learn from them depends greatly on what they do while studying such an example. If they merely read an example without much thought, they are likely to learn very little. But if they read it while trying to understand what it illustrates (for instance, if they try to explain to themselves what is being done and why), then they may learn a great deal.

Investigations have shown that, when some students read examples of problem solutions, they do not extract much generally applicable knowledge. Instead, they tend to deal with other problems by relying largely on remembered examples. On the other hand, when better students read an example of a problem solution, they try to explain it to themselves by identifying the basic principles that were applied, by figuring out how they were applied, by monitoring their own understanding, and by correcting their misunderstandings (Chi et al., 1989, 1994).

Observations of students studying examples can thus reveal much about their knowledge and ways of learning. Furthermore, it is apparent that students can learn significantly from examples if they are encouraged to explain these to themselves.

Difficulties of learning from examples   On the other hand, learning from examples may *not* be an easy task. For instance, if the solution of a problem consists largely of a sequence of statements or equations without additional documentation, it may be difficult to figure out *what* was actually done. It may even be harder to figure out *why* this was done (how somebody *decided* what to do, what options were considered, and why a particular one was selected while others were discarded). Furthermore, inductive reasoning may be needed to extract general knowledge from a particular example—and such reasoning can easily lead to faulty generalizations and misleading knowledge. Hence it is probably better if a student does not need to learn significantly *new* knowledge from examples, but can use such examples mostly to explore or refine previously acquired knowledge.

Explaining to other people   Students can also usefully learn by explaining to other people. For example, it is useful if students are asked to explain clearly *how* they solved a problem, to explain what they did and why. As pointed out in section 13.4, such a written explanation also provides the documentation needed to ensure that a solution can be understood by other people.

Finally, students can be helped to learn if they are placed in a position (such as learning cooperatively in a group) where they need to explain knowledge and methods to some other students.

21.5.3   Reciprocal teaching

Actual teaching can be more instructive than mere explaining. In particular, reciprocal teaching is a systematic method in which a teacher and a student alternately reverse roles (so that the student assumes the role of the teacher and the teacher assumes the role of the student).

Reciprocal teaching of reading skills   The reciprocal-teaching method was first applied to teach seventh-grade students how to read with good comprehension (Palincsar and Brown, 1984; Brown and Palincsar, 1989). In this work, Brown and Palincsar started by formulating a model of good reading. This model, partly suggested by what good readers seem to do, specified a reading strategy involving the following four repeatedly used basic processes: (1) summarizing what has been read, (2) asking relevant questions, (3) clarifying what has been read, and (4) predicting what is likely to come next. (Note that these processes correspond to basic cognitive needs listed in figure 2.3. Thus process 1 involves specifying, processes 2 and 3 involve interpreting, and process 4 involves making inferences.)

• *Implementation of the method* To implement the method, the teacher begins by pointing out the importance of these processes. Then the student and the teacher both silently read a short prose passage. After this reading, the teacher demonstrates the reading strategy by summarizing what they have read, asking some questions about it, trying to clarify it, and predicting what would come next. (Throughout all of this, the teacher invites the student to participate as much as possible.) Afterward, the teacher and student read another passage and switch roles so that it is now up to the student to summarize, to ask questions, to clarify, and predict. (The teacher may help the student to engage in these activities.) The role reversals are then repeated many times while the teacher gradually reduces the assistance provided to the students.

• *Efficacy of the method* The preceding reciprocal-teaching method proved highly effective. Indeed, after about twenty such teaching sessions, students' scores on a reading-comprehension test improved from about 15 percent to 85 percent (Palincsar and Brown, 1984). Even after a lapse of six months, the students' performance score on such a reading test was still 60 percent (and could be restored to the 85 percent level after one day of reciprocal-teaching training).

Generalized form of reciprocal teaching A colleague and I (Reif and Scott, 1999) were interested in formulating the reciprocal-teaching method in a more general and explicit form so that it might also be implemented with the aid of a computer playing the role of the teacher. Furthermore, we wanted to apply the method to help college students deal with physics problems.

• *General formulation of the method* As previously mentioned, the performance of a task requires repeated application of the following functions: *deciding* what to do, *implementing* the decision, and *assessing* whether the results are satisfactory. Our general formulation of the reciprocal-teaching method involves an explicit separation of these functions between a teacher and a student (as indicated in figure

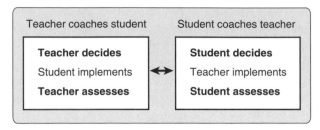

Figure 21.2
Reciprocal teaching with alternating coaching by a teacher and student.

21.2). The student can then repeatedly see each function demonstrated by the teacher before he or she needs to perform it. In this way, the student learns to pay attention to each of these functions and to practice each separately (but within a realistic total context).

• *Application to problem solving in physics*   The solution of any mechanics problem requires one to draw a diagram specifying the motion (by velocity and acceleration) of every relevant object and also specifying *all* the interactions of this object (described by *all* the forces exerted on this object by other objects). Many students have remarkably much difficulty in performing this task because they often fail to describe properly an object's motion, omit mention of some forces, or ascribe the wrong properties to them.

We were able to specify an explicit procedure leading to the correct description of an object's motion and of all forces on it. However, even when we tried to teach and demonstrate this procedure, students often failed to implement it properly. Hence we attempted to teach this procedure more effectively by using the general reciprocal-teaching method of figure 21.2. In this method the teacher describes a problem and first acts as the teacher. In this role, (1) the teacher (following the recommended procedure) tells the student which step to address; (2) the student then implements this step; (3) the teacher, assessing the student's performance, provides appropriate feedback and asks the student to correct any detected mistakes. The roles are then reversed with a different problem so that the student assumes the role of teacher. Thus (1) the student tells the teacher what to do (and the student is warned if he or she does not follow the steps of the recommended procedure); (2) the teacher then implements the specified step (but may sometimes deliberately make common kinds of mistakes); (3) the student needs to detect and correct any such mistakes.

• *Computer implementation of the method*   We could also implement this method by letting a properly programmed computer play the role of the teacher. The advantage was that such a computer (which we called a PAL, a *P*ersonal *A*ssistant for *L*earning) could then provide individual instructional supervision to every student in a large class. This implementation test of the method proved fairly successful, with an efficacy approaching that which could be provided by individual human tutors (Reif and Scott, 1999).

Other forms of learning by teaching   Methods, where students assume teaching roles, can be extended to deal with more numerous students. For example, methods (like *peer teaching* and *collaborative learning*) will be discussed in the following chapters dealing with practical educational delivery.

21.5.4   Self-teaching

Self-teaching involves deliberate learning without any outside assistance. The ability to teach oneself independently is a valuable skill since people in our rapidly changing world often need to learn new knowledge and skills without the benefit of any available teachers.

This chapter's previous comments about learning and instruction are equally applicable to efforts undertaken to learn independently, but the learner must then also assume the functions of an instructor. The difficulties of independent learning are particularly pronounced if one tries to learn about an unfamiliar domain without the guidance of any textbook or other learning guides. In this case, one starts out with only vague ideas about what needs to be learned and is thus unable to plan appropriately. Hence one is forced to immerse oneself in the learning process while only progressively discovering useful sources of knowledge—and only gradually perceiving what is more or less important, how to organize one's accumulating knowledge, and how to assess one's own performance.

Independent learning is appreciably simpler if appropriate textbooks or other teaching aids are available, but the task is still demanding. It requires appreciable self-discipline to engage in active learning rather than mere reading. Even in the absence of any teacher, one must identify important new concepts, make sure that one can interpret them properly in various situations, actually implement newly learned methods, solve problems suggested by self-posed questions, and test oneself repeatedly to check one's understanding before proceeding further.

When independent learners do not understand something or get confused, they are also unable to seek help from some readily available teacher. Such learners must thus attempt to figure things out by themselves, may possibly consult some other books, or may try to consider some simple examples that can help to clarify the issues.

Independent learning (self-teaching) can thus be a difficult task. However, if it is done well, independent learning can be quite effective, especially since it requires much active individual engagement in the learning task. Indeed, it might be quite useful to teach students better skills of independent learning. Such skills would help students to deal with situations where externally provided instruction is poor or inadequate—and would also provide students with excellent preparation for their future lives.

21.6   ASSESSING INSTRUCTION

Any instructional effort should be suitably assessed to determine its efficacy. Such an assessment tests both the design of the learning process and the instructional means used for its implementation.

21.6.1   Kinds of assessments

Comparative student assessments   Students' learning in many courses is usually assessed by giving students tests comparing their performance—and then assigning them grades on the basis of their relative standing in the course. This practice is called *grading by the curve* if some specified fractions of the students are then given appropriate grades (such as A, B, C, D, or F).

This kind of assessment is of little interest unless one really wants to compare the performance of one student relative to another (for example, to decide whether one should hire one student rather than another). Such comparative assessments provide, however, little or no information about the actual competence of the students or about the effectiveness of the instruction.

For example, if you need surgery, would you rather want to know how the surgeon ranked in his class compared to other students, or how good he is at performing the pertinent kind of surgery? Might a student, who received a grade of A in a class at one school, not have received a grade of C in a similar class at another school? Might not 20 percent of the students in a class have received grades of A—although not a single student in the class actually achieved proficient performance? As an extreme example, would an instructor ever dare to give failing grades to *all* the students in a class if none achieved an acceptable level of competence?

Performance assessments   It is usually of far greater interest to assess students' actual (rather than relative) performance capabilities. Thus a *summative assessment* (one carried out at the end of an instructional effort to ascertain its instructional efficacy) may use suitable tests to answer the following questions: What performance abilities have students achieved (compared to their abilities before the instruction)? Also, how well have these abilities been achieved by various students?

Are performance improvements due to instruction?

Such assessments must rule out the possibility that students might have acquired improved abilities *without* any instruction (for example, simply because of the passage of time or because of other experiences in their lives). For this reason, one may also have to compare these students with a similar group of students who spent the same amount of time *without* experiencing the same instruction.

Even a careful summative assessment of instructional efficacy has some important limitations. In particular, it provides no information about the reasons why instruction may have been effective in some ways and less effective in some other ways—or how the instruction might be improved. For example, suppose that an instructional effort were successful in raising the fraction of students successful in passing the final performance test in a class from 60 percent to 80 percent. Although one might be pleased by this success, one would then still not know the answers to the following crucially important questions: Why were 20 percent of the students still unable to perform satisfactorily? And what would one need to do to improve the instruction?

Diagnostic performance assessments   The preceding limitations can be overcome by assessments that are more diagnostic so that they can provide detailed information on what parts of the instruction work or don't work—and why. Such assessments are then more *formative* (that is, focused on understanding how instruction might be improved). Indeed, such assessments are essential to improve instructional designs and implementations.

21.6.2 Implementing diagnostic assessments

Advances in any scientific or engineering field depend crucially on detailed assessments to determine what kinds of knowledge and methods are effective or not—and to ascertain the underlying reasons for successes or failures. Progress in educational knowledge and practice requires similarly detailed assessments. Thus it is useful to answer the following questions:

- What knowledge and capabilities have students attained as a result of some instruction? How well have these been attained?
- What are the reasons why some kinds of knowledge and capabilities have *not* been attained?
- What learning difficulties have been experienced by the students? And what teaching difficulties have been encountered by instructors?
- How could instruction be improved?

The following paragraphs indicate some ways of obtaining such detailed information.

Detailed observations of individual students   Observations of individual students provide the most effective way of ascertaining how students think and of identifying their learning difficulties. But, while such observations can be realized in one-to-one interactions between a student and an individual tutor, they are more difficult to achieve in large classes. However, they are not impossible in such settings if an instructor invites a few students to visit him or her individually so that they may receive personal help or express their reactions to the class. Under these conditions the instructor may then observe a student while he or she works on a problem or answers some questions.

Although such a situation may not be fully equivalent to a laboratory investigation of a student's thought processes, it can still yield much more detailed information than is ordinarily available to an instructor in a class. For example, it can reveal how well students can apply newly learned concepts and what misconceptions they exhibit. Furthermore, the instructor can then also informally try out some new instructional ideas.

Diagnostic tests   Observations of a few individual students are not only difficult to implement and time-consuming, but may also be misleading since they may not be representative of the larger number of students in a class. Hence it is also useful to design tests and questionnaires that can easily be given to many students. However, the questions on any such test must be *diagnostic* (that is, they must be designed in such a way that an inappropriate answer clearly indicates the particular kind of knowledge deficiency exhibited by a student). Students' written answers or problem solutions may also be much more informative about students' thinking than their answers on multiple-choice tests.

Complementarity of individual observations and group tests The preceding two assessment methods can profitably be used jointly because they provide mutually supportive information.

Individual student observations can provide detailed information about students' thinking and learning difficulties, information that no group test alone can elucidate. However, this information may not be representative of all students (although it can be useful in designing well-focused questions for use in a group test).

Conversely, students' responses on a group test may indicate confusions or difficulties exhibited by many students. But the underlying reasons for these difficulties can sometimes be revealed only by more detailed observations of individual students.

The utility of the information obtained from any such assessments must ultimately be judged by the extent to which it helps to produce more effective and efficient instruction.

21.6.3 Assessing long-term learning

Learning assessments, that are carried out at the end of a course or shortly thereafter, are rather unrealistic because they don't determine students' knowledge or capabilities retained after a longer time (when students may need these for subsequent courses or for work in real life). Hence it is useful to augment such short-term assessments with longer-term assessments carried out more than a month after the end of instruction.

Such assessments (implemented at that later time by tests somewhat similar to those given at the end of instruction) can help to determine longer-term retention of acquired knowledge and abilities. Hence they can also reveal whether knowledge exhibited at the end of instruction was solidly incorporated in a student's mind or merely the ephemeral manifestation of last-minute cramming.

The effectiveness of earlier learning can also be assessed after a much longer time, when much knowledge may seemingly have been forgotten. For example, to assess how much knowledge has been retained, one can determine how long a time of renewed learning is required to restore a student's knowledge to its earlier level.

21.6.4   Interaction between assessing and learning

Assessment methods can have a great effect on learning and teaching. Indeed, students commonly try to learn skills that are actually assessed or graded, but pay little attention to anything else. For example, even if an instructor in a class emphasizes problem-solving and reasoning skills, the students are unlikely to learn such skills if the instructor's examinations require predominantly the recall of factual knowledge.

The following is an important implication: *Educational innovations striving to attain different learning goals are unlikely to succeed if assessment methods are not correspondingly modified.*

21.6.5   Revising and exploiting

Efforts to assess instruction invariably reveal various deficiencies that need to be corrected by suitable revisions. In fact, *repeated* revisions may often be necessary. Although the need for such revisions may sometimes seem discouraging, experienced teachers or instructional designers recognize that successive revisions are required for performing most complex tasks. For example, note the many successively produced versions of commercial software applications (like word processors, spreadsheets, and others)! There is no reason to expect that the development of good instruction is any simpler than that of such software programs.

Furthermore, any complex development process (such as that required to write a book or create instruction for a course) is so lengthy that a person involved in it may be changing during that time— learning new things and modifying his or her ways of thinking. Thus it can easily happen that things that seemed satisfactory at the beginning of a development process may seem flawed or misguided at the end. It is then ultimately necessary to know when to stop revising, to acknowledge that perfection is an unattainable goal, and to realize that "the best can be the enemy of the good."

On the other hand, life does not ordinarily end at the completion of an instructional development process. Hence it is highly useful to identify and remember the lessons learned during such a process so that they can be exploited for future instructional purposes.

21.7 SUMMARY

• After an effective learning process has been designed, it is necessary to solve the instructional problem of ensuring that students actually engage in such learning.

• This problem can be addressed by suitable interactions with an instructional system that assists students by providing appropriate guidance, support, and feedback.

• All such instructional assistance must gradually be reduced to ensure that students learn to perform independently.

• Instruction must decompose the instructional process into manageable segments leading to reliable modifications of a student's knowledge.

• Individual tutoring (which allows the highest level of control over the instructional process) is probably the most effective teaching method, but is practically available only to very few students.

• Students' learning can be significantly helped if they themselves try to explain what they know or do, or to teach other persons. In particular, reciprocal teaching is a highly successful method where students and instructors alternately assume the teaching role.

• Instruction can be improved by careful assessments of its efficacy. Such assessments should try to ascertain what capabilities students actually attained and why they experienced particular learning difficulties.

• Such assessments can be achieved by combining detailed observations of some individual students with diagnostic tests given to larger numbers of students.

V IMPLEMENTING PRACTICAL INSTRUCTION

Instructional delivery (the deployment of instruction) aims to devise practical ways of providing effective instruction to many diverse students. There is no sharp distinction between the task of providing instruction to many students and the simpler task of teaching a small number of students. Indeed, *all* these tasks require efforts like those discussed in chapters 18 through 21 (namely, designing an effective learning process and devising instruction ensuring that students engage in effective learning). But the practical problem of delivering such instruction to many students involves additional difficulties and challenges of the kind outlined in the following paragraphs.

22.1   THE INSTRUCTIONAL DELIVERY PROBLEM

22.1.1   Coping with diversity

Numerous situations require the teaching of many students who have diverse backgrounds and abilities and whose individual characteristics are not well known. Since it is realistically impossible to deal with every individual student, one can then try to ascertain the existing communalities and significant differences among the targeted students. Fortunately, the communalities are often found to be appreciably larger than the differences. (For example, students in different countries with different educational systems often exhibit similar kinds of learning difficulties.)

Hence one attempts to design (and, if possible, test) instruction for a *typical* student—and then to build in some variability so that this instruction can be adapted to diverse individual students. In this way, one can try to accommodate students with somewhat different abilities and differing prior knowledge.

Examples: Dealing with diversity in other domains

Manufacturing clothing   All men have similar body structures with two legs, but differ significantly in their heights and girths. Hence clothing manufacturers try to accommodate everybody by producing pants of similar shapes, but with somewhat different lengths of pant legs and different sizes of waists.

Producing antibiotics   The design of antibiotics is based on an understanding of processes that are effective in killing certain bacteria. But since people are somewhat different, particular antibiotics may not be effective for some people (or may even produce dangerous reactions). To deal with such individual differences, it is then useful to produce somewhat different antibiotics of the same type.

22.1.2   Typical constraints

Practical instruction addressed to many students is often beset by many constraints imposed by limited resources and the social context.

Limited availability of teaching talent   The number and availability of teachers is usually limited. Furthermore, the *quality* of available teaching talent is often far from ideal, and the training of teachers may be inadequate.

Limited time   Courses are instructional periods of limited length, commonly extending over a few weeks or months during which students are supposed to learn the desired knowledge and skills. The number of contact hours during which students can interact with their teachers is usually quite small. Furthermore, students often must spread their available time over many different courses, as well as over their personal lives.

Spatial separation   Students commonly must travel to the place where instruction can be provided to them. Since students often live far apart, there also exist difficulties impeding mutual communication or cooperative work.

Limited physical resources   Limitations of money and space may limit access to laboratories or computers. It may sometimes even be difficult to have access to seminar rooms or laboratory space in schools that have been predominantly equipped with lecture halls.

22.1.3   Advantages of large numbers of students

On the other hand, the existence of large numbers of students makes it possible to exploit instructional approaches that would otherwise not be feasible or cost-effective. In particular, the production of good text-books, of specialized computer software, or of other instructional materials can be very costly and require considerable time. Such large initial investments of time and effort become possible only if they can subsequently be amortized by repeated and widespread use by many students.

22.1.4 Choice of instructional delivery methods

Various methods have been devised to deal with the complexities of delivering instruction to many diverse students. Each such method may involve human teachers as well as various artifacts (such as books, computers, and classrooms). The same basic instructional design may also be implemented by different methods; however, some of these may be more effective than others in achieving the desired instructional goals.

Particular advantages and disadvantages   Each instructional delivery method has some particular advantages and disadvantages (or limitations). Hence an appropriate choice of instructional delivery methods is helped by explicitly identifying the advantages and disadvantages of each. Effective and efficient learning is thus facilitated by the following guideline: *Strive to use an optimal combination of delivery methods so as to exploit their particular advantages and minimize their disadvantages.*

Although this guideline may seem sensible, it is often not followed. Indeed, it is more difficult to choose an optimal combination of means than to simply select a particular one. For example, a particular delivery method (such as teaching by lectures) may be chosen merely because it is traditional or the easiest to implement. Similarly, some other delivery method (such as instruction aided by computers) may be chosen primarily because it seems novel or fashionable.

Important characteristics of a delivery method   In considering the utility of a particular delivery method, it is helpful to examine the following questions:

• What are the particular advantages and disadvantages (or limitations) of the method?

• To what extent does it actively engage students in their own learning?

• Does it provide adequate amounts of guidance, support, and feedback?

• How explicit and effective is the learning assistance provided to students? Can it be flexibly adapted to the needs of individual students?

• How easily can the method be modified or revised?

• How costly is the delivery method? Is this cost justified by the utility of this method compared to that of some alternative methods?

Review of common delivery methods   The following sections review briefly some traditional, but still widely used, instructional delivery methods and point out their salient characteristics. The next chapter then examines a number of more innovative methods.

22.2 LECTURES

Lectures provide a time-honored way whereby a teacher can talk to numerous students at the same time and thus transmit information to them. Hence lectures are commonly used in many settings (such as high schools, colleges, universities, and professional schools). For example, they are frequently the primary means of dealing with large introductory college courses.

22.2.1 Advantages of lectures

Efficacy of transmitting information   Lectures allow a well-organized presentation of some relevant knowledge. They also provide a relatively easy way whereby a teacher can provide information to large numbers of students assembled at the same time in a single large room. Numerous students can be handled at the same time (more than 500 in some basic college classes). Hence lecturing is a rather inexpensive educational method (certainly very much cheaper, and more readily implemented, than individual tutoring would be).

A knowledgeable teacher needs only a relatively small amount of time to prepare a lecture. Furthermore, a lecturing teacher can be observed while talking and can also demonstrate particular ways of thinking. (He or she can at least make clear how to pronounce technical words previously unfamiliar to the students.) The quality of a lecture, and its potential utility to students, may however depend greatly on the abilities of a particular lecturer.

It is also fairly easy to augment a lecture by slides, by demonstrations of actual experiments, and by movies or video discs showing interesting phenomena. All such means can help to transcend mere words by more direct observations of the real world.

Ease of modification Lectures can be readily modified if new needs arise, if somewhat different kinds of students have to be addressed, or if newly discovered knowledge needs to be communicated. Hence lectures can flexibly be changed to avoid obsolescence or to explore alternative modes of presentation.

Minor possibilities for guidance and feedback Lectures offer some (although very few) opportunities for guidance and feedback to students. For example, a lecturer may provide some general learning advice to the assembled students—or can answer an occasional question posed by a student who is not intimidated by the surrounding crowd and is bold enough to speak up in the middle of a lecture.

22.2.2 Disadvantages of lectures

Lack of active student engagement Students sitting in a lecture are mostly passive listeners and may do very little of the active processing required for learning. Indeed, they may possibly think about totally unrelated things (or sometimes even read a newspaper). Furthermore, students' attention can easily drift, especially since it is difficult to maintain attention for as long as an hour.

As pointed out in the preceding paragraph, lectures also provide students with little instructional guidance, support, and feedback. Thus it may well be true that "a lecture is a method whereby information can be transferred from the notebook of a professor to the notebook of a student, without passing through the mind of either."

Illusory learning A teacher may easily be led to believe that students learn much more from lectures than is actually the case. Unfortunately, the mere transmission of information often does *not* lead to significant learning if sufficient guidance, support, and feedback are lacking.

For example, as previously mentioned, one advantage of lectures is the possibility of including instructive demonstrations. But investigations have revealed that, although such demonstrations may be entertaining, students learn very little by watching them. Significant learning occurs only when students are forced to become more actively engaged (for example, when they are asked to predict the outcome of a demonstrated experiment) (Crouch et al., 2004).

Unsuitability for transmitting complex ideas   Lectures are poorly suited to convey complex arguments or derivations that require substantial thought and effort to be understood. There just is not enough time for a listener to comprehend or think about complex ideas before the lecturer has already gone on to discuss other things.

Similarly, if a student fails to understand what the teacher tried to convey during the first ten minutes of a lecture, the student may be unable to understand the rest of the lecture—and may be merely forced into a desperate attempt to take down meaningless notes.

Poor adaptation to individual student needs   Lectures are unresponsive to the needs of different students. They proceed at the same rate, regardless of a student's individual abilities or prior preparation. Also, they are available only at fixed locations and fixed times, irrespective of a student's health problems or other emergencies. If students miss some lectures, about the only thing they can do is to borrow some other students' notes of these lectures.

22.3   TEXTBOOKS

Textbooks, exploiting the well-developed technology of the printing press, provide a widely used means of instruction. Their goal, like that of lectures, is to transmit useful information in a form that can be readily assimilated by students.

22.3.1   Advantages of textbooks

Effective distribution   Textbooks can be widely distributed and used to transmit information in a packaged form that is flexibly available to a student at any time or place. This information can be well organized and repeatedly reviewed before a textbook is printed. Furthermore, a textbook can include pictures as well as words.

Permanence and flexibility   Unlike a lecture, a textbook is a durable item. It can be studied and reviewed by a student as often as needed to assimilate the presented ideas. It can be available to a student at any time or place and can be used by the student for as long as desired. Furthermore, it can be loaned or given to other students. Except for possible obsolescence, a textbook is also long lasting.

Useful adjuncts to many instructional methods   Good textbooks alone can be used for independent study. However, textbooks are often most helpful when used in conjunction with other instructional methods (such as lectures or discussions) that provide direct contact with human teachers.

22.3.2 Disadvantages of textbooks

Educational limitations Although textbooks are designed to transmit much information, students may merely engage in passive reading (especially since a textbook provides them with little or no feedback about their comprehension). Hence students may actually learn much less than expected. It is true that some textbooks may also include a few questions or problems. But these are of little utility unless students actually try to answer them and receive appropriate feedback about their attempts to do this.

A particular textbook may also not be well adapted to the needs and abilities of different students. It may then be necessary to resort to several different textbooks or to provide students with supplementary educational materials.

Costs of production or modification Considerable costs (of time, effort, and money) are required to produce a textbook. (These costs must then be amortized by repeated and widespread use by many students who pay for these books.) Furthermore, once produced, textbooks are difficult to modify or revise. Modifications can ordinarily be done only, at considerable cost, by issuing a new edition after a substantial lapse of time.

22.4 HOMEWORK ASSIGNMENTS

To remedy the lack of active student involvement when listening to lectures or reading textbooks, students are often given assignments on which to work by themselves when they are at home. Such homework assignments give students an opportunity to apply and practice the knowledge previously communicated to them.

22.4.1 Advantages of homework

Practice and self-assessment Well-designed homework assignments guide students to engage actively in useful practice to apply their recently acquired knowledge. Students can thereby strengthen and consolidate their knowledge. Furthermore, they can determine whether they can actually use this knowledge, they can detect misconceptions or other difficulties, and may have an opportunity to remedy these.

Individual feedback   If completed homework assignments are afterward reviewed and "graded", students can receive individual feedback about their performance and about any detected deficiencies in their knowledge. Indeed, when students have learned most of their knowledge from lectures or textbooks, this may be the students' *only* opportunity to receive individual feedback about the quality of their acquired knowledge.

Relatively cheap production   Considerable care is required to produce good homework assignments that can help students to learn. However, once such assignments have been produced, they can be used repeatedly with different groups of students. Producing homework assignments is thus a relatively inexpensive process. What can be much more laborious and expensive is the task of correcting students' individual homework assignments and of providing each student with useful comments. (However, this task can sometimes be delegated to teaching assistants or other helpers.)

22.4.2   Disadvantages of homework

The limitations of homework assignments are due mostly to the lack of direct interaction between a student and a teacher.

Lack of assistance while working   Students don't receive any guidance or feedback *while* they actually do their work at home. Thus students may spend appreciable amounts of time floundering—or practicing activities that are ineffective or inappropriate.

Long-delayed feedback   The individual feedback given to students, when their corrected homework assignments are returned to them, is usually received several days after the students completed their work. By this time the students may have largely forgotten what they did, or why they did it. Hence this feedback may have lost much of its efficacy in helping students to learn.

Inadequacy of feedback   The individual feedback given to students is often not very informative, but largely limited to a few red marks or corrections indicated on the students' papers. Furthermore, the task of correcting homework assignments is often not performed with great care (for example, relegated to some teaching assistants).

22.5 SMALL INSTRUCTIONAL GROUPS

All of the preceding instructional methods are practical enough to be used with large numbers of students, but none of them provides the amounts of guidance, support, and feedback that are desirable to promote effective learning. Neither do they provide instructional assistance of the kind potentially available from a good individual tutor (like the one mentioned in section 21.4.3). However, it is possible to ameliorate the situation by sometimes assembling students in small groups where they can interact with a human teacher. The following paragraphs list some such opportunities.

Office hours and course centers Students may, when they wish, be able to go to scheduled office hours of the instructor (or of some teaching assistants) so that they can ask questions and get some individual help.

It is also possible to set up a "course center" where teaching assistants may be available for consultation at fixed times. There, students may then obtain some individual help from a teaching assistant (or possibly from some other students who have also come to the course center). In all these arrangements, students may then be able to get some help *on demand* (that is, at times requested by them).

Seminars or discussion groups Seminars or discussion groups (consisting of fewer than about 25 students) may be scheduled at regular times to accompany large lectures. Such a seminar may be led by a teacher (the main instructor or a teaching assistant) who is then able to interact somewhat with individual students, to address some of their questions, and to discuss their homework assignments.

Such a small seminar provides several advantages: (1) The students can, to some extent, be actively involved in thinking and exploring pertinent questions. (2) There also exist at least some opportunities for individual guidance and feedback to students. (3) Such seminars can be readily modified according to changing needs.

Of course, the instructional efficacy of such a seminar depends crucially on the competence of the presiding teacher. Furthermore, only a limited amount of *individual* guidance and feedback can be given to any one student.

Laboratories Laboratories (commonly used in some science or engineering courses) are somewhat similar to seminars, but provide students with the opportunity and equipment needed to engage in realistic work. Thus students can perform experiments or observe actual phenomena related to more abstract concepts studied in a course. Students in such a laboratory setting can then work independently, or together with other students, while having access to help provided by a laboratory instructor.

While well-designed laboratories can be valuable, they may often degenerate into routine cookbook exercises performed by students who merely implement procedures specified by a laboratory manual—and learn very little in the process. However, even in introductory science courses it is possible to ask the students themselves to design some experiments, to plan the methods for carrying them out, to implement these methods, and then to analyze the results (Reif and St. John, 1979). Indeed, laboratories can be structured as investigative learning environments where students can explore new phenomena, test hypotheses, and solve realistic problems (Etkina, Murthy, and Zou, 2006). Such laboratories may then actually provide useful learning experiences and help to teach scientifically useful ways of thinking.

22.6   ASSESSMENT OF INSTRUCTIONAL DELIVERY

Practical instructional delivery needs to be carefully assessed to determine its efficacy and efficiency. The assessment methods needed to do this are largely the same as the ones discussed in the preceding chapter dealing with instruction intended for smaller numbers of students.

22.6.1   Needs for summative assessments

When instructional-delivery projects have been completed, they often require *summative assessments* to determine the resulting effects. Such assessments aim to answer the following kinds of questions: How effective has been an effort undertaken to improve a course or other instructional project? Has money, that was provided by a school or outside agency (like the National Science Foundation), been usefully spent? Has a particular course, that was taught this year after some improvement efforts, actually been more effective than the same course taught in the preceding year? Is a particular course, taught at one school or with one instructional method, more or less effective than the same kind of course taught at another school or with a different instructional method?

Lack of common measurement standards   All such questions share the difficulty that their answers require common measurement standards. Otherwise, one cannot compare the instructional effectiveness of a course at one time with that of the same course at another time, nor compare the effectiveness of a course taught under some conditions with that of the course taught under different conditions.

However, such common measurement standards are often not available. For example, different assessment tests may be given at different times. Similarly, different instructors in a course may use assessment tests that are ostensibly similar, but may grade these tests according to different criteria. Meaningful comparisons are thus difficult to achieve.

As a result it is possible to devise different innovative curricula, but have no reliable measures of their efficacy. The lack of common measurement standards also makes it difficult to achieve cumulative improvements since educational efforts (like innovative efforts in the fashion industry) are then largely judged on the basis of personal opinions. Furthermore instructors, like most other people, are prone to self-deception about the success of their own efforts.

Inadequacy of simplistic solutions   One might think that the preceding difficulties could be overcome simply by giving the *same* assessment test to two groups of students that one wishes to compare. However, this would not be a trustworthy method unless neither the students nor the instructors know about the questions on this test before it is actually given. For example, if the same test is given in two successive courses, students in the later course may have obtained prior knowledge about the particular questions on the test. Similarly, if the same test is given simultaneously in two courses, the instructors in these courses may (consciously or not) have used their knowledge of the test to teach the students so as to prepare them explicitly for this particular test.

Possibilities of improved performance assessments   In principle, the preceding measurement difficulties might be overcome by clearly specifying the particular capabilities to be assessed. One could then prepare an appreciable number of test questions, of equivalent difficulty, for assessing each capability. The performance test could then be constructed by picking, *at random*, one of these questions for each capability to be assessed.

Neither the students, nor the instructors, would then know beforehand the specific questions included on the performance test. (They would know about the *capabilities* to be assessed, but not the specific questions on the test.) Thus neither the students nor the instructors would know how to prepare for the *specific* questions asked on the test. This kind of test could then be used as a common measuring standard for assessing performance at different times or in different courses.

Randomized controlled assessments The preceding kind of process, for assessing instructional effectiveness, would be somewhat similar to the randomized controlled trials used in medical research to assess the efficacy of different drugs or treatment options. Such well-controlled randomized assessment processes have ordinarily *not* been used to ascertain the efficacy of courses or other instructional projects.

However, the U.S. Department of Education recently proposed to use this approach for assessing teaching methods developed for secondary school mathematics (Bhattcharjee, 2005). Applicants, in grants programs for improving the teaching of elementary high-school algebra, would thus be required to assess more carefully the extent to which their innovative teaching methods are actually effective. To do this, they would be asked to use randomized controlled trials and quasi-experimental designs (with an experimental group receiving the innovative instruction and a control group receiving the conventional instruction).

Such randomized controlled assessments might provide more reliable evaluations of instructional effectiveness and of educationally innovative projects. They might also diminish somewhat the prevalence of unjustified claims of superior instructional efficacy. But, as in medicine, they would *not* eliminate the need for other assessment methods (Riehl, 2006).

22.6.2 Importance of detailed diagnostic assessments

Important unanswered questions Although summative assessments of educational effectiveness are useful, they fail to answer the following kinds of centrally important questions:

- Why have some students failed to achieve some desired capabilities?
  - What difficulties have been encountered by students and teachers?
  - How could instruction be improved?

Methods for answering such questions   Such questions can only be answered by more detailed investigations of the following kinds:

1. Observing some individual students closely while they work. (As mentioned in section 21.6.2, this can be done in large classes by selecting a few students, observing them closely while they talk out loud about their thinking, and subsequently reviewing their work with them.)

2. Giving larger groups of students diagnostic tests that are constructed so that particular answers provide clear indications of specific deficiencies of students' knowledge.

The first of these methods provides the most detailed information about students' knowledge and thinking, but may be unrepresentative of larger number of students. The second of these methods is more representative of all the students, but provides less detailed information. Hence it is most useful to use *both* of these methods in combination.

The implementation each of these methods requires thought, work, and time. But the detailed information that they provide can reveal the kinds of knowledge and thinking that students lack or use inappropriately—and the resulting understanding can greatly help to devise improved instructional approaches.

22.7   SUMMARY

• All instruction requires the design of effective learning processes and of instruction ensuring that students engage in such learning. But the teaching of large numbers of students also requires particular attention to useful means of instructional delivery.

• Traditional, but still widely used, instructional delivery methods involve predominantly lectures, textbooks, homework assignments, seminars, and laboratories.

• Lectures provide an easy and inexpensive way of transmitting information to many students at the same time—and can also be readily modified. But they don't promote effective learning since they keep students in the passive roles of mere listeners and can provide very little guidance or feedback.

• Textbooks provide an effective and durable means of distributing knowledge and can be flexibly used by students at any time or place. But they can easily lead to passive reading and can provide only limited amounts of feedback.

- Homework assignments allow students to practice and apply newly learned knowledge or skills. But the instructors' reviews of such assignments provide students only with minimal and long-delayed feedback.
- The assessment of instructional delivery methods is often hindered by the lack of common measurement standards. Randomized controlled assessments could help. However, more detailed diagnostic assessments are necessary to elucidate the reasons for observed learning difficulties and to devise ways of improving the instruction.

23   Innovative Instructional Methods

Excellent instruction might be provided by private tutors (with a good knowledge about particular subjects—and also about teaching and learning) who could provide every student with individual guidance, support, and feedback. Some more innovative instructional methods, that have gradually come to be used in recent years, try to come somewhat closer to this ideal situation (which is unattainable because of resource limitations). But every such method is an imperfect compromise that has some desirable features, but lacks some others.

Most of these innovative instructional methods share some of the following characteristics: (1) They are not merely focused on the transmission of information, but are also concerned with actual student learning. (2) They tend to be interactive so as to promote active student engagement. (3) They are inclined to exploit electronic technology and sometimes also pay attention to cognitive issues (Bruer, 1993; Bransford, Brown, and Cocking, 2000).

The following paragraphs provide an overview of some of these methods so that readers may be aware of their existence and might use them when they seem useful. (The indicated references provide more detailed information.)

23.1   MODIFIED LECTURE FORMS

23.1.1   Interactive lectures with peer instruction

Changed structure of a lecture   To improve student learning, Mazur has used *peer instruction*, a method that modifies lectures in the following ways (Mazur, 1997). The instructor divides a lecture into short segments (of about 15 minutes) each of which focuses on some particular topic. At the end of each such segment, the instructor asks a probing question designed to ascertain the students' understanding of the ideas that have just been presented. (This question is usually of the multiple-choice variety and of a difficulty likely to elicit wrong answers by about half the students.) The students in the class are then given one or two minutes to formulate their individual answers and to report these to the instructor. (For example, the students can do this by raising a card showing one of the letters A, B, C, . . . indicating their proposed answer.)

The students are then urged to discuss their answers with another student sitting near them—and to explain their reasoning so as to persuade the other student that it is correct. After this discussion, which may last two to four minutes, the instructor ends the discussion, polls the students again for their answers (which may have changed as a result of the preceding discussion), explains the correct answer and the reasoning leading to it, and then moves on to the next topic. (To compensate for the time taken up by such peer discussions, the students may be asked to do some reading about relevant topics *before* the class.)

Use of class response systems   Such interactive lectures can be facilitated by commercially available response systems that allow students in a class to ask questions or to respond electronically to questions posed by an instructor. An electronic display on the instructor's desk can then immediately indicate the answer given by each student—and also cumulatively show how many students gave each kind of answer. Such electronic systems, available from several manufacturers (Class response systems, 2005), can help to implement interactive lectures like those devised by Mazur or other people (Meltzer and Manivannan, 2002).

Advantages of such interactive lectures   These modified lectures provide the following benefits: (1) They make a lecture less tedious by breaking it into parts small enough to maintain the students' attention. (2) All students need to answer some questions and to discuss their answers with other students. Hence students become actively engaged in trying to understand presented ideas and are thus more likely to learn from the lecture. (3) By posing a well-formulated question and almost immediately ascertaining the students' answers, the instructor gets prompt feedback about how well the students have understood the presented ideas—and can then also quickly try to remedy any perceived difficulties or misunderstandings.

Such lectures don't overcome all the disadvantages of lecturing. However, they can be fairly readily implemented and there is good evidence that they can substantially improve students' learning (Crouch and Mazur, 2001).

23.1.2 Structured lectures focusing on central knowledge

Students are often overburdened by lengthy textbooks, or by so much information conveyed in a short time, that they are left with miscellaneous bits of knowledge rather than with some coherent knowledge that they can remember and use. To ameliorate this difficulty, Lisa Scott and I experimented in one course with lectures emphasizing the structure of the conveyed knowledge. When the instructor introduces a topic in such a lecture, he or she discusses it briefly and summarizes it in the form of some centrally important knowledge. The instructor then illustrates how this knowledge can be elaborated and used—and also asks the students to use it themselves in one or two simple cases.

During the lecture, the students are also given a couple of summary sheets that explicate, in well-organized form, the central knowledge subsuming the discussed topics. (These sheets may also include a couple of examples illustrating some elaborations or applications of this knowledge.) The students are then asked to solve all subsequent homework problems by elaborating and using the central knowledge identified on these summary sheets (without invoking any formulas listed in the textbook).

Such structured lectures are thus deliberately designed to make highly explicit the central knowledge conveyed by a lecture. They aim to leave students with a small core of well-organized knowledge that they might be readily able to remember, elaborate, and use. (Because we were able to try such structured lectures in only a single course, we could not assess their general efficacy.)

23.1.3 Lectures replaced by workshops

Instead of emphasizing the coherence of newly acquired knowledge, another innovation seeks mainly to ensure that such knowledge is meaningfully connected to actual observations. To this end, Laws has developed a course where all lectures are replaced by two-hour workshops that combine a large number of activities in a laboratory setting (Laws, 1997). These activities may include discussions with instructors and classmates, qualitative observations, data gathering, assisted derivations of equations, problem solving, using spreadsheets and computer-based laboratory tools, and other such activities.

Such workshops have the virtue of keeping students very actively engaged. But it is difficult to compare students' resultant learning with that in other innovative courses.

23.2 COOPERATIVE LEARNING

In adult life, we ordinarily have no access to any designated teachers, but learn a great deal by interactions with colleagues, peers, and other individuals. Thus one may well ask why students could not learn more by interacting with their fellow-students. Such peer interactions could remedy the shortage of available teaching talent—for example, the common situation where a single adult teacher needs to deal with a large number of students in a class. Furthermore, students could thereby become better prepared for their subsequent lives where they will most often need to learn from other people like themselves.

Description of cooperative learning Cooperative (or collaborative) learning is an instructional method whereby students learn from each other. *In principle*, the method can be implemented by letting students work collaboratively in a group. The students would then have opportunities to work together so as to share ideas, to formulate and pose questions, to clarify their ideas, to discuss, and to critique each other. *In practice*, the situation is more complex because none of the preceding effects may automatically ensue by merely assembling students in a group and telling them to collaborate. Indeed, some careful design is required to ensure that students in a group actually engage in fruitful collaboration.

Guidelines for creating cooperative learning groups Most students are used to work independently or competitively, rather than collaboratively. Merely asking students to work cooperatively does, therefore, usually *not* lead to the desired results. However, the task of setting up well-functioning cooperative learning groups is facilitated by heeding the following guidelines (Johnson, Johnson, and Holubec, 1993; Johnson and Johnson, 1994).

• *Fostering positive interdependence* Structure groups so that each group member's efforts are required for the functioning of the entire group—as well as for the individual's own success.

• *Mutually helpful interactions* Foster interactions whereby students promote each other's success by helping, supporting, and encouraging each other. Such mutual assistance should be both academic (so that students help each other learn and deal with intellectual tasks) and personal (so that students feel that others care for them).

• *Individual and group accountability* Devise performance assessments that incorporate two levels of accountability. (1) The group must be accountable for achieving its goals. (2) Each member of the group must be held accountable for contributing his or her share of the work and for achieving appropriate individual competence.

• *Teaching needed interpersonal skills* Teach social and interpersonal skills just as deliberately as more intellectual academic skills. Indeed, working collaboratively in any context requires adequate skills of leadership, communication, trust building, and conflict management. Such skills are often not automatically acquired unless sufficient attention is paid to them.

• *Group self-assessments* Ensure that groups deliberately examine their own performance to ascertain how well they achieve their goals and maintain effective working relationships. In this way groups can determine what member actions to modify, what group behaviors to change, and how to improve their own functioning.

Implementations of cooperative learning With some attention to the preceding guidelines, cooperative learning may be useful in many situations. It can be more readily implemented if groups are structured by assigning specific roles to different students in a group. For example, one student may be assigned the role of decision maker who suggests plans of action, another one assigned the role of implementer who works out details and keeps records, another one assigned the role of critic who questions plans and detects errors, and so forth. Furthermore, students can be asked to implement some specified instructional strategies.

For instance, cooperative groups, with students in prescribed roles, have been used to teach problem solving in physics (Heller, Keith, and Anderson, 1992; Heller and Hollabaugh, 1992). The previously described reciprocal-teaching strategy, with its clearly specified roles of instructor and student, is also well suited to be used with cooperative groups of students (Brown and Palincsar, 1989).

Advantages of cooperative learning Cooperative learning makes it possible to exploit the available teaching abilities of other students and thus to profit, in an inexpensive way, from ordinarily unused teaching resources. It also prepares students for the kinds of collaborative activities and learning often needed in business enterprises and professional life.

Students in a group become actively involved with each other. They may ask each other questions, help each other, criticize each other, and defend their points of view when these are challenged. Thus they may learn from each other and also teach each other. All these activities require active processing helpful for learning. Furthermore, as pointed out in section 21.5, teaching provides also an excellent way of learning.

Fellow students, who themselves have learned something only in the recent past, sometimes have a better understanding of the learning difficulties encountered by other students than instructors with their long-familiar knowledge acquired years ago. Hence students can sometimes explain things better, and in more comprehensible language, than can teachers who are more remote from the students' experiences.

Lastly, working with other students in a group may help to make learning more motivating and engaging than listening to a lecture or reading a textbook.

Limitations of cooperative learning   Cooperative learning can easily become a situation where "the blind lead the blind." Fellow students, who act as teachers, have much less subject-matter knowledge and much less experience than mature instructors. Furthermore, they have thought much less about cognitive issues that are relevant to teaching and learning. Hence they can ordinarily provide other students with much less useful guidance, support, and feedback than that available from good instructors.

In addition, students commonly also lack some of the interpersonal social skills that adults have acquired as a result their long experience interacting with other people. As a result, cooperative groups can also be beset by personality conflicts that might be avoided by more mature people.

Jigsaw methods   As already mentioned, one shortcoming of cooperative learning is that no student in a group has special expertise about the topic to be studied. This deficiency can be partly overcome by the *jigsaw method* (so called because it involves rearranging students as in a jigsaw puzzle). This is a particular cooperative learning method (Aronson and Patnoe, 1997) in which some students are specifically required to learn about a particular topic so that they can teach it to other students.

To implement the method, students in every group meet to decide who among them will study one of the assigned topics in greater depth. All the students (from different groups), who have agreed to study a particular one of these topics, then meet together in their own special group to study this topic, to become knowledgeable about it, and sometimes also to prepare instructional materials useful for teaching others. After all these special groups have completed their work, the students reassemble in their original groups. Each of these groups then contains a student who has become particularly expert about a particular one of the assigned topics. Hence this student is now well prepared to help teach the other students in the original group. As a result, all the students in this group are then in a much better position to learn cooperatively about the assigned topics.

Jigsaw methods can engage students to think more explicitly about teaching and also about a specific topic to be taught. Furthermore, all students are then helped with their learning by being provided with more knowledgeable fellow students who are better prepared to teach.

23.3 PACKAGED INSTRUCTION

Instruction does not necessarily require contact with human teachers, but can exploit means of packaging instruction in forms that can be made directly available to students and widely distributed. Textbooks are a familiar way of packaging and distributing instruction in this way. Such textbooks can be quite effective in conveying information, but are limited in their ability to produce learning because they may fail to engage students in more than passive reading. However, instruction can also be packaged in more interactive ways of the kind described in the following paragraphs, ways that exploit familiar printing methods or more modern computer technologies.

23.3.1 Workbooks or tutorials

Printed instructional materials can be made more interactive by including questions that students need to answer—and by also indicating somewhere the correct answers so as to provide students with appropriate feedback. The questions in such instructional materials (commonly called *workbooks* or *tutorials*) are usually of the multiple-choice kind so that correctness of the answers can be readily judged.

Students who are given such tutorials can then learn from them without necessarily requiring the aid of a human teacher. Thus a student can try to answer the questions in the tutorial, can check his or her answers by comparing them with those provided in the tutorial, and can then try to correct any detected mistakes or misconceptions by referring to other information available in the tutorial or in a textbook.

Although such printed tutorials have often been used to teach factual information or simple skills, they need *not* be restricted to such mundane teaching efforts. With good instructional design, they can also be used to teach more sophisticated abilities.

Design of tutorial questions   Questions can be carefully sequenced according to a model of effective learning. For example, investigations of common student difficulties and mistakes can provide the basis for asking searching questions probing students' understanding. Incorrect answers can help to diagnose students' difficulties or misconceptions— and can then be used to guide students to a place in the tutorial where their difficulties can be specifically addressed. For instance, well-designed tutorials of this kind have been used to help students learn difficult physics concepts (McDermott, Shaffer, et al., 2002; Van Heuvelen, 2004).

Use of multiple-choice questions   Such questions provide the advantage of great simplicity in judging answers, but don't allow more complex individually generated student responses. Furthermore, they may assess the ability to *recognize* correct answers rather than the ability to *generate* them. However, careful design can minimize these limitations and make such questions quite challenging.

For example, one may not only ask students to identify which of several proposed answers is correct, but can also ask more difficult questions of the following kind: (1) Which of several proposed answers is *not* correct. (2) Identify *all* of the proposed answers that are correct (or *all* of the answers that are *not* correct). (3) After a student has selected a particular answer, one may also ask the student to select an appropriate reason justifying *why* his or her chosen answer is correct.

Example of a multiple-choice question with justification

A student is asked to consider a three-pound book lying on a table and is then asked whether the force exerted on the book by the table is larger than, smaller than, or equal to 3 pounds. After giving the correct answer (3 pounds), the student may then be asked whether this is so because of Newton's second law relating acceleration to total force, because of Newton's third law relating mutual forces, or because of neither. (Many students display a major misconception by claiming, incorrectly, that the reason is the third law asserting that mutual forces have the same magnitude).

Multiple-choice questions also have some distinct advantages for learning. By explicating alternatives, they can help to make clear important discriminations that can help students to avoid confusions. Furthermore, they can make apparent some of the options that students need to consider when making decisions in problem solving or when trying to identify mistakes in their own work.

23.3.2 Self-paced courses

Structure of a self-paced course An instructor in a self-paced (or "Keller-plan") course eliminates all (or most) lectures. Instead, the instructor provides students with a detailed study guide that advises students what, and how, to study with the aid of a textbook or other instructional materials (such as printed tutorials). The students can also have access to teaching assistants who can help them when necessary.

The study guide decomposes the material to be studied into well-specified segments (with an approximate study time of a week or so). Whenever a student has completed his or her study of such a segment, the student must take a competence test assessing his or her performance in dealing with the studied topics. If the student's performance on this test is satisfactory, the student may go on to the next segment. Otherwise, the student needs to study some more (and perhaps get some help from available human tutors or teaching assistants) after which the student may take another version of this competence test. This process is repeated as often as needed until the student can demonstrate satisfactory competence. (In practice, no more than about four versions of a test are necessary to allow every student to pass the test and then go on.)

Advantages of self-paced courses The primary advantage of a self-paced course is its great flexibility. Thus students can take a test whenever they feel ready—and may take as much time as they need to study any topic. The only requirement is sensible pacing so that the student can complete studying all the required segments (and passing the corresponding competence tests) during the time allocated to the entire course. A student, who completes all these competence tests satisfactorily, gets a passing grade in the course. (A final examination at the end of the course may also be used to assess a student's more cumulative and integrated understanding—and may contribute to the student's final grade in the course.)

A self-paced course also provides other flexibilities. For example, students can study at times most convenient to them, may spend as much or as little time as they need, may take a little time off when they are sick or overburdened by other courses, may not need to go to classes at any fixed times, and may even be geographically remote some of the time. Some students can also profit from a self-paced course if they are less prepared than most and thus need more study time. Similarly, they can use a self-paced course to acquire some prerequisite knowledge without interfering with their other scheduled courses.

A self-paced course also guarantees that students have achieved at least a satisfactory degree of competence in their studies. This is because all the completed competence tests ensure that every student has been able to perform adequately some significant tasks. By contrast, in ordinary courses without such clearly assessed competence tests, a student may emerge with a passing grade merely by accumulating lots of "partial credit", but may be unable to perform any task reliably without mistakes.

Self-paced courses also help to prepare students for later life where they will need do study independently without outside assistance. When self-paced courses have been implemented, they have proved quite successful (Green, 1971; Taveggia, 1976; Kulik, Kulik, and Cophen, 1979).

Disadvantages of self-paced courses   The teaching efficacy of a self-paced course depends crucially on the quality of the available instructional materials (textbooks, study guides, and tutorials) since neither lectures nor other regularly scheduled teaching sessions are provided. Since mere access to a textbook is usually inadequate, there is thus an essential need to provide students with sufficiently good study guides and other forms of packaged instruction.

Because many students lack self-discipline, procrastination can easily lead them not to complete all the requirements by the end of a self-paced course. (They can thereby disrupt the logistical arrangements of the course and thus also harm other students.) However, this problem can be remedied by imposing a few deadlines and some incentives for completing required work within a reasonable time.

The role of the instructor in a self-paced course is changed from that of a lecturer to that of a person writing study guides, preparing competence tests, and managing the course logistics. Some instructors find these tasks more time consuming and less ego-gratifying than lecturing. This is probably the main reason why self-paced courses have not been more widely used.

23.3.3   Distance learning

The preceding example of self-paced courses illustrates that personal contact with a supervising teacher is not necessary for students' learning. This is particularly true in the case of adult students (students in colleges, universities, or professional fields) who have acquired greater learning skills and more self-discipline than younger students. In this case, it is possible to rely more on instruction, packaged in various forms, to reach students located at a distance and spread out over a large area. One can then also achieve appreciable economies by reducing the expenses needed to build more schools, create new campuses, and pay the salaries of numerous teachers.

An outstanding example of this kind of *distance learning* is the Open University of Great Britain (Open University, 2005). This university was established around 1970 to provide higher education to many individuals who would otherwise have no access to conventional universities because they cannot afford these financially, are located remotely from them, are working part-time, are disabled, or for other reasons. The Open University has currently an enrollment of around 150,000 undergraduate students, more than 30,000 postgraduate students, and some 11,000 students working toward higher degrees. About 70 percent of all students are in full-time employment, and more than 50,000 students are sponsored by their employers for their studies. More than 25,000 of the Open University students live outside of Great Britain.

To reach this many students, the Open University uses a style of teaching called *supported open learning* whereby students study mostly independently with the aid of packaged instructional materials that are supplemented by some human assistance. The regular faculty of the Open University have no direct contact with students, but are largely engaged in the production of instructional materials that are packaged in the form of books, study guides, radio or television programs, audio or video discs, home-experiment kits, and instruction delivered over the Internet. (The faculty members also engage in some research that is similar to that carried out at other universities.) All these instructional materials are widely available to the students. There are also regional centers with some teaching staff who can be consulted personally or by telephone conferences.

Students thus learn largely on their own time by reading, working on various course activities, and writing assignments that they send in to be corrected. In addition, some students get together at particular places during the summer months for seminars or laboratory work where they can have contacts with other students and some teaching staff.

The Open University is now ranked among the top British universities for the quality of its teaching. Most of its courses are also available throughout Europe. It has come to accommodate a large population of people previously excluded from access to higher education. Furthermore, it serves the needs of teachers, engineers, and other professionals who must repeatedly update their skills.

23.4 TECHNOLOGY-SUPPORTED INSTRUCTION

Instruction can be packaged in particularly useful forms by exploiting modern information technologies such as computers, compact discs (CDs or DVDs), the Internet, video technologies, and various other media.

23.4.1 Computer-assisted instruction

Computers are well suited for instructional purposes because they provide a dynamic medium that can not only convey information in visual and auditory forms, but can also flexibly interact with users so as to respond to their actions. Because computers have also become increasingly powerful, cheap, and widespread, there now exist increasingly many opportunities to use computers for educational purposes.

With properly designed software, a computer can play the role of an individual tutor available to a student at any convenient time. Because computers can be interactive, they can simulate human tutors, but can be provided at very much lower costs. People have been trying to exploit these potentialities for quite a few years, but only recently have they come to be more fully realized.

Producing an instructional computer program is much more complex than writing a textbook since it requires programming software that is highly interactive and can deal appropriately with diverse student responses. The simplest forms of computer-assisted instruction have been somewhat similar to printed tutorials by using multiple-choice questions and preprogrammed responses to anticipate student answers. Even such relatively simple computer tutors can provide significant benefits by engaging students more actively in their learning, by exploiting dynamic visual displays, by providing students with prompt good feedback, and by maintaining the students' attention better than a printed page (Larkin and Chabay, 1992).

When using computer technology, designers and teachers are sometimes tempted to exploit predominantly its abilities to provide multiple colors, vivid animations, and interesting sound effects. However, these things may be distracting to students without providing them with significant educational benefits. Hence it is necessary to remain focused on centrally important educational goals.

Adequate attention certainly needs to be devoted to good design of the human-computer interface. Such design is not merely desirable for aesthetic reasons to achieve a pleasing appearance of the computer display. It also can fulfill important psychological functions by visually clarifying the structure of the knowledge to be conveyed and by keeping a student's attention properly focused on the most relevant elements of a display. However, the instructional efficacy of a computer tutor depends primarily on a good cognitive analysis of the knowledge and skills required for good performance—and on the use of effective instructional strategies.

For example, section 21.5.3 mentioned PALs (Personal Assistants for Learning), computer tutors designed to help students learn how to apply basic principles of Newtonian mechanics (Reif and Scott, 1999). These tutors were based on an analysis of the thinking needed to describe motion and identify forces—and on an investigation of common student difficulties in implementing these tasks. Furthermore, the computer tutor explicitly used the reciprocal-teaching strategy whose efficacy had been well established by psychological research in other domains.

Systematic instructional efforts can also lead to the use of computers as integral parts of an entire course. For example, at the University of Illinois they have been used to provide computer-assisted instruction, simulated laboratory experiments, and logistical support in a large introductory chemistry course (Smith, 1998; Smith and Stovall, 1996).

23.4.2   Intelligent tutoring systems

Computer tutors can be made appreciably more effective, although more complex, by using the techniques of artificial intelligence (AI). Such tutors can then exhibit more human-like intelligence and are called *cognitive tutors* or *intelligent tutoring systems*. Unlike simpler computer tutors, where all questions and available responses have originally been preprogrammed, such intelligent tutors behave more like human experts who have an actual knowledge of the subject matter and can use it flexibly to solve various problems. Thus they can also use this knowledge to observe each student's work, to diagnose a student's particular difficulties, and to provide appropriate individualized help.

Intelligent computer tutors of this kind have been used to teach subjects such as computer programming, plane geometry, and algebra (Anderson, Corbett, Koedinger, and Pelletier, 1995). Such a computer tutor incorporates a cognitive model of the knowledge that is needed to solve problems in the domain of interest. The tutor then uses this *domain model* to monitor a student working through a problem and to constantly compare the student's work with the actions that would be generated by the computer with the aid of its own domain knowledge. By tracing the student's work in this way, the computer tutor can know what the student is doing or thinking at any time—and what help may be needed. Hence the tutor can provide advice and hints that are individualized to the student's particular approach to a problem.

In addition, the computer tutor can use the student's responses and errors to construct, and constantly update, a model of the student's knowledge at any time. The tutor can then use this *student model* to provide feedback that is well adapted to a student at a particular stage, to individualize suitably the selection of problems given to the student, to sequence these problems effectively, and to pace the student appropriately through a curriculum.

A student can then always obtain timely feedback from the computer tutor, with substantial cognitive and motivational benefits. For example, in a study investigating the efficacy of a computer tutor designed to teach the Lisp programming language, immediate feedback led to learning times that were three times shorter than learning times with more delayed kinds of feedback. The tutor also led to substantial learning improvements. For example, after the instruction, students completed programming problems in one-third the time required by comparable students taught by conventional classroom instruction—and scored 25 percent higher on subsequent performance tests (Corbett and Anderson, 1991).

More recently, intelligent computer tutors have also been practically deployed in urban schools to teach basic algebra. These algebra tutors have been quite effective and have led (on national tests designed by the National Council of Teachers of Mathematics) to about twice as good scores as those achieved by students in conventional comparison classes. Students, taught with the aid of these computer tutors, also scored about 15 percent better on standardized tests of basic algebra skills (Koedinger, Anderson, Hadley, and Mark, 1997; Corbett, Koedinger, and Hadley, 2001).

The use of such intelligent computer tutors in actual classrooms can also have other beneficial effects. For example, teachers serve more as collaborators in learning and have more time to provide students with individualized help. Furthermore, students appear to be more motivated, to have more fun, and to feel less embarrassed by their mistakes.

23.4.3   Computer simulations

Since computers can dynamically display all kinds of situations, they can also be useful to simulate phenomena or processes that would be difficult or impossible to observe directly (Gould, Tobochnik, and Christian, 2006).

Visualizing abstract concepts   Many theoretical concepts are used in science to help predict or explain observable phenomena. (For example, such concepts include electric or magnetic fields, wave functions or energy levels in quantum mechanics, and many others.) Since such concepts are highly abstract, it is very helpful if they can be visualized so that one can more readily think about them. Computers can be very useful for producing readily observable displays that portray such abstract concepts and can simulate their dynamic behavior in the course of time. (For example, one may thus simulate the electric and magnetic fields produced by an accelerating electron.)

Simulating phenomena that cannot readily be observed directly   Many phenomena, that are difficult or impossible to be observed directly, may usefully be simulated on a computer display. For example, the simplest (and theoretically easiest) motion is that of an object in outer space where it interacts with nothing else. But any object commonly observed in everyday life interacts with many other things (or is affected by *friction*) so that it moves in quite different ways. A computer can, however, easily simulate the motion of objects unaffected by friction and can thus also be useful in helping to learn basic principles of mechanics (White, 1993).

Objects observed in everyday life do not move with extremely high speeds close to the speed of light. (Relativity theory is most relevant for such objects.) Similarly, objects observed in everyday life are very much larger than atoms. (Quantum mechanics is most directly relevant for objects of atomic size.) But computers *can* readily simulate the behavior of objects moving with very high speeds or of objects of atomic size. Hence such simulations can be very useful for students who are trying to learn relativity theory or quantum mechanics.

Simulated experiments   Experiments performed in a laboratory can be quite time-consuming and sometimes potentially dangerous. But some such experiments can also be simulated on a computer. A student can then perform more such experiments in a given time—and also learn more about the design and interpretation of such experiments (rather than about more routine manipulations). Furthermore, some such simulated experiments can be excellent preparation for the implementation of actual experiments (e.g., Smith, 1998).

23.5   POTENTIAL BENEFITS OF EDUCATIONAL TECHNOLOGY

A discussion of educational delivery would be incomplete without pointing out some of the potential benefits provided by the use of increasingly available electronic technology.

23.5.1   Advantages of technology-supported education

Multimedia capabilities   Computers have become increasingly powerful, small, and generally available. Alone (or combined with other electronic display or communication technologies), they provide unique abilities to communicate information by sight and sound—and to do this dynamically rather than just statically. Furthermore, they can be highly interactive, responding appropriately to various kinds of user inputs.

Computer tutors   As mentioned in section 23.4, properly programmed computers can act as private tutors who are able to provide individualized instruction to any particular student. Thus they can provide prompt individual guidance, support, and feedback to every student—the kind of individual learning assistance that is important for effective learning, but that is usually absent in instruction prevalent in large classes or in many introductory college courses. Even if such a computer tutor is less effective than a good human tutor might be, it may still be much better than the absence of any tutorial assistance.

The instruction packaged in such electronic form can be addressed directly to individual students, without necessarily requiring human teachers as intermediaries. Thus the task of training teachers can become somewhat less essential. The very presence of computer tutors, used by students in a class, can also help to train teachers and to foster educational improvements. Indeed, teachers can thereby be made aware of new kinds of knowledge and new teaching methods—and also become forced to deal with students exposed to such new knowledge and methods.

Better exploitation of human talent   The use of educational technology can free human talent to do what it can do best. For example, computer tutors and other forms of packaged instruction can help students deal with somewhat routine tasks (such as with learning new factual knowledge, applying such knowledge in relatively simple situations, or practicing unfamiliar methods or skills).

On the other hand, such packaged instruction often does *not* have the flexibility or judgment possessed by good human teachers. But, if more routine teaching tasks can be relegated to computers or other forms of packaged instruction, the time thus liberated can be used by human teaching talent to do what it can do best (for example, to answer more wide-ranging questions asked by students, to explain some things in greater depth, to observe students more closely to diagnose their difficulties, to provide useful advice, or to serve as human role models).

Flexible instructional delivery   Modern technology (such as computers, electronic communication, and the Internet) allows more flexible instructional delivery than traditional methods that rely on lectures and classes supervised by human teachers. For example, it makes possible *distance learning* whereby students can learn while not attending classes at a particular place or while not having face-to-face contact with teachers. It also can help students to learn even if they are sick and unable to attend classes—and it facilitates learning by adults who are fully employed or who need to update their training.

Improved learning environments Educational technology can also help to provide environments that are more congenial, and more conducive to learning, than traditional teacher-supervised classes. (1) Such technologically supported environments can be less intimidating or judgmental than ordinary classrooms—and can also be far more patient. (2) They can provide instruction at any time or place convenient to a student—and are thus also readily available for frequent reviews. (3) They can provide excellent practice environments by simulations, by displays that focus selective attention on the most relevant features of a situation, and by access to rich databases, spreadsheets, and other information-processing tools.

23.5.2 Possibilities of significantly better education

The world's best teachers are few in number and are *not* available to most students. Furthermore, most teachers have only limited expertise, time, and resources needed to prepare, test, and revise instructional approaches. Hence the vast majority of students do *not* have access to the best possible teaching.

On the other hand, technology provides powerful means of delivering and distributing education—means that have (to some extent) already been widely exploited in the past with highly significant results. The following are some examples.

Instructional improvements realized by some past technologies

Printing technologies Before the invention of the printing press, education was accomplished mostly by oral communication and by means of hand-written documents. Printing technology made possible the wide distribution of books and the existence of large book collections in libraries. Hence we now take it for granted that much education relies on the availability of textbooks that students can study to learn—and that instructors can use to assist their teaching efforts.

A personal example may help to illustrate some significant aspects of the resultant situation. When I was student in high school, I was somewhat bored. One reason was that a public library, not far from my home, allowed a poor boy like me to borrow (at no cost) books by people like Bertrand Russell and other such authors. The ideas discussed in these books seemed to me far more stimulating than many of the topics discussed in school.

Although it is perhaps not surprising that the school environment seemed somewhat dull to me, I was really unjustified in my sense of disappointment. There are very few people as intellectually outstanding as Bertrand Russell—and one could not possibly recruit these as high-school teachers. Such people could, however, expound their ideas in books. Printing technology could then make these ideas readily accessible to everybody in the world—and could thus help to educate even poor boys like myself. (Indeed, if computer technology had been available at an earlier time, Bertrand Russell might have packaged his ideas in a more interactive form that could simulate conversations with him.)

Sound-recording technologies   In past times, students interested in learning to play a musical instrument had to rely mostly on locally available music teachers. But the development of recording technology (the phonograph and more modern compact discs) has markedly changed the situation. Nowadays, such recording technology allows all students to hear artistic interpretations of music by the world's best musical performers. Hence a student's musical education is no longer limited by access to local musical talent, but can easily profit from the best talent available anywhere in the world.

Educational potentialities afforded by modern technology   The preceding examples indicate that presently available information technology provides the possibility of providing most students with much improved education. Indeed, it might be possible to assemble groups of highly talented persons, some of whom have outstanding expertise in particular subject-matter fields—and others who have equally high expertise in education, psychology, computational technology, and other relevant domains. Such a group of persons might then devote consistent effort and appreciable time to produce well-designed instruction packaged so that it can be interactive and widely distributed. Since such instruction would be in highly explicit forms, it could also be fairly readily assessed and improved. Subsequent repeated revisions could then lead to cumulative further improvements. The initial large investments of talent and efforts could then be amortized by repeated and widespread use of the produced instruction.

In principle, the talent and effort thus invested in education could far surpass that presently available to most students—with major beneficial effects. In fact, there are some indications of incipient efforts to exploit the educational potentialities of modern technologies. (Examples, discussed in the preceding section, might be the Open University of Great Britain and the use of intelligent computer tutors deployed to teach mathematics in high schools.) However, such efforts are still far from achieving their possible impact. Some of the reasons are mentioned in the following paragraphs.

Economic and social factors impeding the possibilities   Our present educational system is largely labor intensive. Teachers at many different places teach similar courses, and often do so repeatedly year after year. The situation is somewhat similar to that of the cottage industries that were prevalent a few centuries ago. For example, many women, at different places, were then repeatedly knitting sweaters that were subsequently used by people in nearby locations.

The advent of knitting machines and other textile technology changed the situation into one that became much more capital intensive. The widespread and repeated investment in human labor then became replaced by large initial capital investments in machinery and factories that were capable of producing good clothing on a large scale, clothing that could be widely distributed to people far from the place of manufacture. The large initial investments could then be recouped by the wide distribution of the resulting products.

Indeed, most modern industry has become capital-intensive in this way. Furthermore, the large initial investments in talent and technology allow the manufacture of products of far better quality than might otherwise have been possible by any labor-intensive cottage industry.

For example, any one of us can presently buy, at very low cost, an electronic calculator capable of easily making calculations that are far more complex than those possible by calculations on paper or by the mechanical calculators available thirty years ago. The development of such electronic calculators has required large amounts of special scientific knowledge, great technological talent, special facilities for preparing highly pure materials, and the creation of the semiconductor industry. No cottage industry could ever have assembled all these resources needed to produce our cheaply available electronic calculators!

Efforts to improve education by exploiting the potentialities of modern technology will probably also require large initial investments of talent, time, and money. Hence they are unlikely to make significant progress if educational institutions do not shift from their current labor-intensive practices to more capital-intensive ways. But since such shifts (like those from cottage industries to modern industries) require appreciable periods of time, they are unlikely to be realized in the near future.

23.5.3 Limitations and dangers of educational technology

Educational technology, like all other technology, can be used or misused. Technological means of providing instruction cannot be expected to have the flexibility, judgment, and wisdom of good human teachers. Hence educational technology should not be used merely to replace human teachers, but to exploit these as creators of educational materials and for other tasks where their unique talents can be most useful.

Furthermore, technology can easily be exploited to deal with information in fairly mindless ways (for example, to display, retrieve, or transmit information—rather than to facilitate more complex thinking or learning). Efforts to improve education should thus not merely exploit the facilities provided by information technologies, but should keep central attention focused on important thinking and learning processes.

23.6   SUMMARY

- Innovative instructional delivery methods are less concerned with the mere transmission of information, but tend to be more interactive and to exploit modern technologies.
- When using interactive lectures with peer instruction, the instructor periodically interrupts a lecture to ask questions, the students display their answers after some mutual consultation, and the instructor immediately discusses these answers.
- In cooperative learning students work in carefully structured collaborative groups so that they can become more actively involved and also learn by teaching others. However, none of the students then benefits by learning from persons with special expertise. This difficulty can be partially overcome by using jigsaw methods.
- Instruction can be packaged in workbooks or tutorials so that it can be used by students for learning without a human teacher. Such packaging allows the use of self-paced courses and also of distance learning.
- Modern information technologies can be used to provide computer-assisted instruction, to construct intelligent computer tutors with nearly human capabilities, and to produce simulations of phenomena or concepts difficult to observe.
- Such modern technology could potentially provide much better education to many students by investing excellent talent in instructional development efforts that could be widely exported in interactive forms. However, such investments would require that more capital-intensive approaches replace current labor-intensive educational practices.

24 Some Educational Challenges

There exist many educational problems and challenges. Before ending this book, it seems appropriate to mention a few such educational challenges that seem to me particularly relevant to the issues discussed in the preceding pages. If such challenges were addressed, they could yield significant practical benefits.

24.1 PROVIDING MORE INDIVIDUAL LEARNING ASSISTANCE

Common lack of individual guidance and feedback   The need to educate large numbers of students is commonly addressed by using classes in which one teacher deals with many students. Under these conditions it is difficult or impossible to provide appreciable individual guidance and feedback to any particular student. This is a serious limitation. For example, even well-designed instruction can easily fail if students don't actually engage in the activities specified by the instruction. Indeed, without adequate individual supervision, how can one ensure that students actually engage in suggested learning tasks and perform them properly?

For example, when trying to teach students better methods for performing some tasks, instruction may provide excellent advice about *what* to do and *how* to do it. But, when students are left largely on their own, they often don't follow this advice or implement it incorrectly. Instead, they commonly engage in unsystematic activities or revert to previously familiar poor habits. Hence even the best instruction can remain ineffective without adequate supervision of an individual student's learning process.

Potentialities of computer tutors   Although it is impossible to provide every student with an individual tutor who can supervise the student's work, it *would* be possible to provide every student with a computer that is programmed to provide good individual guidance, support, and feedback. By simulating a good private human tutor, such a computer could then also be available to the student at any convenient time and place.

Section 23.4.2 already mentioned such computer tutors, deployed in high-school classrooms, who are helping students to learn basic algebra (Corbett, Koedinger and Hadley, 2001). But even simpler and more easily produced computer programs (without the techniques of artificial intelligence) could be helpful for teaching some important topics or skills. The main requirement is that such computer tutors should be based on a careful analysis of the needed thought and learning processes—and that they should incorporate good instructional design. For example, the PALs (*Personal Assistants for Learning*), mentioned in section 21.5.3, were intended as possible prototypes of such computer tutors (Reif and Scott, 1999).

Potential benefits   A more extensive use of such relatively simple, but well-designed, computer tutors could provide the following significant benefits:

1. Every student, even in a large class, could be provided with much better individual guidance, support, and feedback. Many students' learning could thus be substantially improved. (Although a computer tutor might not be as good as a well-qualified private human tutor, it might still provide much better individual learning assistance than most students currently receive in their classes.)

2. The availability of such computer tutors could help to liberate the time of human teachers to deal with more complex instructional tasks beyond the scope of such computer tutors.

3. The presence of good computer tutors could also make teachers more aware of some different or better instructional methods—and could thus contribute to teacher training.

4. Such computer tutors might also help to improve cooperative student learning by helping some students to become more knowledgeable about particular topics or skills—so that they would be better prepared to assist the learning of their fellow students.

24.2   TEACHING GENERAL THINKING AND LEARNING SKILLS

Most educational efforts aim to teach the knowledge and methods that are useful in some particular domain. However, it also seems possible to address the more ambitious goal of teaching students some *general* thinking and learning skills that are widely useful in many domains.

Examples of general skills   One example of a relatively simple, but important general skill, is that needed to ensure the quality of one's performance (for example, by assessing whether one's solution of a problem is actually correct). This skill requires some of the thought processes discussed in section 12.6 and in chapter 15. These processes are actually quite general. Many of the processes useful for checking the quality of one's work are equally pertinent whether checking one's work on a problem in mathematics, a problem in physics or chemistry, a problem in biology or engineering, or even a writing task in English composition.

Similarly, chapters 4 and 5 discussed the issues relevant for learning how to specify and interpret a previously unfamiliar scientific concept. Chapter 9 discussed how knowledge can be effectively organized to make it easier to remember and to retrieve when needed. Chapters 12 and 13 discussed useful problem-solving methods. The issues discussed in all these chapters are again quite general, equally applicable to work in mathematics, physics, chemistry, biology, or engineering.

Utility of general skills   The preceding examples indicate that some widely applicable general skills can facilitate work and learning in all such fields. Each such general skill must ordinarily be supplemented by more specific skills useful in a particular domain. (For example, when trying to solve problems in mechanics, general problem-solving skills need to be augmented by more special problem-solving skills applicable in mechanics.) But the general skills provide useful starting points and are particularly helpful when one is trying to learn about new topics or to undertake unfamiliar tasks.

A knowledge of such general thinking or learning skills can thus be very useful. Indeed, experts in a particular field often exhibit flexibility in tackling diverse tasks because they have previously acquired a good knowledge of such general thinking and learning skills.

Hence it would be very useful to teach students explicitly some important general thinking and learning skills. (1) Such general skills would be valuable to students in their later lives because students would thereby become better independent learners (able to continue learning on their own, even without formal instruction). (2) Subsequent instructional efforts could also be reduced and simplified because they could presuppose students who have become more competent learners. (3) Teaching could be made more efficient since there would be less need to teach similar thinking skills repeatedly in different courses.

Teaching of general thinking skills The effective teaching of such general thinking skills would be a major educational challenge, but does not seem to be impossible. For example, in some rather primitive work a long time ago, we could show that students could be taught a general skill of learning new physics concepts—and could then transfer this skill to learn an unfamiliar concept in accounting (Larkin and Reif, 1976; Reif, Larkin and Brackett, 1976).

To teach some general thinking skills, it would be useful to identify a few such widely applicable skills (like the previously mentioned skills of quality assurance, concept interpretation, knowledge organization, and problem solving)—and to teach explicitly some of the most important processes needed to implement each such skill. After that, it would be necessary to illustrate the *same* general skill, and practice its application, in a variety of *different* specific cases. Ideally, this should be done in several courses dealing with different subjects. (For example, a student should repeatedly practice applying the *same* general skill of quality assurance in a mathematics course, in a physics course, in a chemistry course, and in writing tasks assigned in a history course). The explicit learning of a general skill, and its instantiation in a variety of special contexts, could thus allow students to learn a general skill that they could subsequently flexibly use in diverse situations.

Indeed, some investigators (Etkina et al., 2006) recently attempted to devise explicit methods to teach some general scientific abilities to students enrolled in a basic college physics course. For example, such abilities included describing physical processes in multiple ways, relating qualitative and quantitative explanations, examining limiting cases in order to improve problem-solving abilities, designing and carrying out an experimental investigation, and communicating effectively the methods and results. In many cases, these teaching efforts were successful and suggest that further attempts to teach generally useful thinking skills might be very useful.

Efforts addressing the teaching of such general capabilities could be more readily implemented if instructors in different fields had sufficient common interests and expertise in cognitive or educational issues.

Unfortunately, instructors in today's colleges or universities ordinarily share few such common interests outside their specific professional disciplines.

24.3   MORE SCIENTIFIC APPROACHES TO EDUCATION

Historical development of scientific fields   Most presently important fields of scientific endeavor started originally as arts or crafts, as areas of scholarship or philosophical argumentation, or as socially valued professions. At some time, this early stage was then transcended because of particular scientific advances, newer technological developments, and the influx of more analytic kinds of talent. As a result, these fields developed into successful pure or applied sciences that led to important accomplishments with far-reaching implications.

For example, in fields like physics or chemistry, the transformation into successful sciences happened more than about two centuries ago. In fields like metallurgy, biology, and medicine, the transformation occurred not much more than fifty years ago. For example, medicine has become a fairly well developed applied science exploiting relatively recent developments in physics, chemistry, biology, and many technological fields.

Education still seems to be at a fairly early stage of development and is often pursued as an art or craft, as a profession, or as a field of philosophical argumentation. But the last fifty years have seen significant advances in the cognitive sciences (which have led to a better understanding of thought and learning processes) and major progress in information technologies (such as computers, video technologies, and communication). These scientific and technological advances offer potential opportunities for new approaches to education and significant improvements in it. Indeed, indications of such newer approaches are reflected in some of the preceding pages—and in some of the references listed in this and the preceding chapters (for example, Bruer, 1993; Bransford, Brown and Cocking, 1999). Thus there now seem to exist realistic opportunities to transform education into somewhat more of an effective applied science.

Challenge of an applied science of education   Exploiting these existing opportunities represents a major challenge. The challenge is *not* just that of systematically developing more effective ways of teaching. Education involves more than teaching—in the same way that agriculture involves more than farming or that medicine involves more than medical practice. An applied science tries to build on basic insights about underlying mechanisms, insights often provided by pure sciences. Thus agriculture transcends farming because it tries to exploit insights from plant biology, genetics, chemistry, and other sciences—subjects that are not of particular interest to many practicing farmers. Similarly (after the 1910 Flexner report), medicine came to be pursued with a greater emphasis on underlying basic sciences such as biochemistry and physiology—fields that, before then, were not part of the knowledge of most medical practitioners.

A successful applied science of education needs similarly to build on a broader base that transcends the interests and experiences of many educational practitioners (such as teachers in classrooms)—although some of their contributions may be very valuable. It needs to exploit a wider range of basic issues concerned with thinking and learning (issues explored in the cognitive sciences), social issues, and issues in information technology. For example, the relevant issues encompass not merely those discussed in discipline-oriented journals (such as the *Journal for Research in Mathematics Education*, the *American Journal of Physics*, or the *Journal of Engineering Education*), but also some issues in journals concerned with cognition and learning (such as *Cognition and Instruction* or the *Journal of the Learning Sciences*).

It certainly would be helpful if there were respected reports (somewhat similar to the 1910 Flexner report on medicine) that advocated somewhat more scientific approaches to education and if there were some universities that assumed leadership in this direction (as Johns Hopkins University did in medicine). Indeed, there have appeared some recent articles proposing a more scientific approach to education (Handelsman et al., 2004; Heron and Meltzer, 2005; Wieman and Perkins, 2005), but these proposals seem to focus predominantly on improved teaching and better modes of instructional delivery rather than on more basic issues.

Requirements for addressing the challenge   There is no assurance that we shall ever attain an applied science of education that is as successful as modern medicine. But the following things would help to move education in that direction: (1) having some respected universities committed to pursue this goal, (2) attracting more good analytical talent to education (talent of the kind that currently goes into fields such as physics or molecular biology, and (3) providing better training to educational practitioners (college or university professors and teachers at all levels) so that they are more knowledgeable about cognitive issues and educationally useful technologies—and thus can approach their educational tasks in more analytical and effective ways.

All these things are difficult to achieve (especially since they would require changing some prevailing beliefs and institutional practices). But if consistently pursued, even small steps in such directions might have significant effects in the foreseeable future.

24.4 MORE SIGNIFICANT EDUCATIONAL ROLE OF UNIVERSITIES

Universities' views of education In principle, the important functions of a university involve research (the advancement of knowledge), education, and public service. In practice, these functions are viewed rather differently. Thus universities commonly pursue excellence in research, but are content with adequacy in education.

For example, most universities view education primarily as a service function, *not* as a significant intellectual field to be advanced. (Schools of education play ordinarily no significant roles in the educational functions of the larger university.) The following medical analogy may perhaps clarify this distinction. A community hospital views medicine as a service function by trying to provide good medical care to various patients. By contrast, Harvard Medical School views medicine primarily as an important science to be advanced. As part of the process of advancing this science, it also delivers excellent care to patients in university hospitals, using these as laboratories for testing new medical ideas and as arenas for training new medical personnel.

Prevailing norms reflect these differing university views about education. For example, faculty promotions, honors, and visiting professorships are commonly awarded on the basis of research accomplishments in well-established disciplines—but not because of good teaching performance, educational accomplishments, or the authoring of excellent textbooks. The following personal anecdote may be instructive.

A revealing personal anecdote

Many years ago I talked to the dean of the University of California at Berkeley shortly before I went on a sabbatical leave. He told me that he was impressed by all the educational work that I had done during the preceding few years (for example, I had written two well-regarded textbooks and also instituted a new science course for nonscience majors). He then added that I ought now to get back to more physics research.

It has sometimes been said that the university does not reward educational activities because they are difficult to evaluate. The dean's statement clearly indicated that this is *not* the case. He explicitly recognized that my educational work had been good. It was not a question of *evaluation*, but of *valuation*. Educational work at the university is not *valued* as much as research in other fields. Otherwise, would it not be odd to acknowledge that somebody has done good work in a particular area, and then to advise him to do something else?

Of course, the dean's advice was sound because he recognized the university's differing norms (excellence in research and adequacy in education). He seemed to believe that I had transgressed these norms by doing more in education than these norms specified—and was thus endangering my university career.

Universities' educational deficiencies and paradoxes Universities could potentially play a major role in promoting more scientific approaches to education. They contain some of the world's most talented people (and some of their departments are centrally concerned with cognitive issues and information technology). But most of these talented people don't think much about education, even if they are involved in teaching.

Many undergraduates, who come to a college or university, are for the first time confronted with demanding intellectual tasks of the kind involved in science, engineering, mathematics, or other fields. They are then also asked to engage in serious problem solving and writing tasks. Yet, these undergraduates are often still immature and have poorly developed learning skills. Hence there arises the following paradox: Precisely at the time when students need to acquire some complex intellectual skills, their instructors have thought little about the relevant thinking and learning processes.

Of course, these instructors are ordinarily very knowledgeable about the subject matter of their field of expertise. But they have not thought much beyond this, have little or no training outside their discipline, and ordinarily merely teach in the way that they themselves have been taught. Paradoxically, the highly educated university professors in a university's teaching faculty have ordinarily received no training relevant to teaching and are thus largely ignorant of pertinent educational, psychological, or social issues. Thus they act very much like farmers (or other practitioners of some craft) who rely predominantly on common sense, tradition, and personal experience—but have little understanding of the underlying issues affecting the practices in which they are engaged.

How might universities play a more significant educational role? As the preceding comments indicate, it would be advantageous if universities were more interested in advancing education as an intellectually significant applied science. This would also entail direct practical benefits to the universities' own educational functions. A university might then be in a position more similar to that of a good medical school that advances the science of medicine while also providing first-rate medical care.

Such a fostering of education would require the kind of leadership that is nowadays often lacking in universities. Nevertheless, the following modest suggestions might be helpful if universities were inclined to move in such a direction.

It could be useful to set up some interdisciplinary university programs that are focused on education and on the training of students who are interested in educational careers. These programs would involve the collaboration of some faculty members from particular disciplines with other faculty who have suitable expertise in the cognitive sciences and information technologies. (There currently exist a few programs with approximately such characteristics.)

Better preparation of university faculty members could help them to become somewhat more knowledgeable about the thinking and learning processes involved in their discipline—and thus better able to deal with the students whom they need to teach. It might also be helpful to arrange a few seminars that existing faculty could attend to help them think somewhat more about the cognitive and educational issues pertinent to their teaching activities.

The norms of the university might also be made more flexible so as to allow some specialization of functions. The excellence of an institution does *not* require that every member of the institution be equally excellent in *all* functions provided by the institution. Indeed, such a requirement can be unrealistic and unattainable. For example, a modern physics department consists of theoretical and experimental physicists. A particular physicist is rarely equally competent in both theory and experiment, but if each is excellent in his or her own field (and understands the work of others sufficiently to communicate with them), then the department as a whole will be excellent. Similarly, requiring every individual faculty member to be judged on the basis of his or her performance in research, education, and community service usually results only in various levels of adequacy in each of these areas. But requiring every faculty member to be *excellent* in at least one of these areas would ensure an excellent university faculty—even if some faculty are excellent in research but less so in education, or if some faculty are excellent in education and less so in research. It would then be only important that the faculty members talk to each other and respect each other's work.

Making all faculty somewhat more knowledgeable about educational issues could not only promote better education, but also have the following two advantages. (1) It might lead to somewhat better interactions among faculty members in different disciplines since faculty could then share some common intellectual interests in education (rather than being largely limited to talking about academic politics). (2) It also would make it easier to pursue a goal like that mentioned at the end of section 24.2—to teach the same general thinking and learning skills in courses dealing with different subject-matter disciplines.

Lastly, university science departments could then also contribute more effectively to the training of K–12 science teachers and thus help to remedy present deficiencies in science education at these levels. For example, science and education faculty members at the University of Colorado recently started a joint program to recruit and train undergraduate science students as *learning assistants* (Otero et al., 2006). Not only have these helped to improve science courses at the University, but some of these learning assistance have become motivated to pursue future careers as science teachers at lower levels.

24.5 SUMMARY

• At the end of this book, it seems appropriate to point out a few educational challenges relevant to the cognitive issues discussed in the preceding pages.

• Even relatively simple (but carefully designed) computer programs could lead to computer tutors able to provide many students with more of the individual guidance and feedback that is needed for effective learning, but that is commonly lacking in large classes.

• Students could be taught some widely useful general thinking and learning skills. They would then be much better prepared to deal with their future courses and the demands of their future lives.

• Recent advances in the cognitive sciences and information technologies provide an opportunity for transforming education into more of an effective applied science. However, this would require an influx of good new talent and the kind of university leadership that helped to foster a more scientific medicine after the 1910 Flexner report.

• Universities currently view education largely as a service function, and not as a significant field to be advanced (not as a field like medicine, engineering, or another applied science). A changed perspective could not only further more scientific approaches to education, but also increase the efficacy of the universities' own educational functions.

References

Preface

Calaprice, A. (Ed.). (2000). *The expanded quotable Einstein*. Princeton, NJ: Princeton University Press.

Einstein, A. (1954). *Ideas and opinions*. New York: Crown.

Halloun, I. A., and Hestenes, D. (1985). The initial knowledge state of college students. *American Journal of Physics, 53*, 1043–1055.

Handelsman, J., Ebert-May, D., Beichner, R., Bruns, P., Chang, A., DeHaan, R., Gentile, J., Lauffer, S., Stewart, J., Tilgham, S. M., and Wood, W. B. (2004). Scientific teaching. *Science, 304*, 521–522.

Heron, P. R. L., and Meltzer, D. E. (2005). The future of physics education research: Intellectual challenges and practical concerns. *American Journal of Physics, 73*, 390–394.

PER. (2005). *Physical Review Special Topics-Physics Education Research*. ⟨http://prst-per.aps.org/⟩.

Reif, F. (1965). *Fundamentals of statistical and thermal physics*. New York: McGraw-Hill.

1 Performance, Learning, and Teaching

Einstein, A. (1954). *Ideas and opinions*. New York: Crown.

2 Intellectual Performance

Feynman, R. P. (1985). *"Surely you're joking, Mr. Feynman!" Adventures of a curious character*. New York: Norton.

Halloun, I. A., and Hestenes, D. (1985). The initial knowledge state of college students. *American Journal of Physics, 53*, 1043–1055.

4   Specifying and Interpreting Concepts

Halloun, I. A., and Hestenes, D. (1985). The initial knowledge state of college students. *American Journal of Physics, 53*, 1043–1055.

Heller, J. I., and Reif, F. (1984). Prescribing effective human problem-solving processes: Problem description in physics. *Cognition and Instruction, 1*, 177–216.

Wason, P. C., and Johnson-Laird, P. N. (1972). *Psychology of reasoning: Structure and Content.* Cambridge, MA: Harvard University Press.

5   Interpreting Scientific Concepts

Halloun, I. A., and Hestenes, D. (1985). The initial knowledge state of college students. *American Journal of Physics, 53*, 1043–1055.

Labudde, P., Reif, F., and Quinn, L. (1988). Facilitation of scientific concept learning by interpretation procedures and diagnosis. *International Journal of Science Education, 10*, 81–98.

Reif, F., and Allen, S. (1992). Cognition for interpreting scientific concepts: A study of acceleration. *Cognition and Instruction, 9*, 1–44.

Shaffer, P. S., and McDermott, L. C. (1994). Personal communication.

Schaffer, P. S., and McDermott, L. C. (2005). A research-based approach to improving student understanding of the vector nature of kinematical concepts. *American Journal of Physics, 73*, 921–931.

6   Managing Memory

Anderson, J. R. (2000). *Learning and memory: An integrated approach* (2nd ed.). New York: Wiley. [Memory processes are discussed in chapters 6, 7, and 8.]

Miller, G. A. (1956). The magical number seven, plus or minus two: Some limits on our capacity to process information. *Psychological Review, 63*, 81–87.

7   Methods and Inferences

Etkina, E., Murthy, S., and Zou, X. (2006). Using introductory labs to engage students in experimental design. *American Journal of Physics, 74*, 979–986.

Eylon, B., and Reif, F. (1984). Effects of knowledge organization on task performance. *Cognition and Instruction, 1*, 5–44.

Reason, J. (1990). *Human error.* Cambridge: Cambridge University Press. [See especially chapter 3.]

Reif, F., and St. John, M. (1979). Teaching physicists' thinking skills in the laboratory. *American Journal of Physics, 47*, 950–957.

8 Describing Knowledge

Bernstein, J. (1979, December 3). *The New Yorker*, p. 84.

Biederman, I., and Shiffrar, M. M. (1987). Sexing day-old chicks: A case study and expert systems analysis of a difficult perceptual-learning task. *Journal of Experimental Psychology: Learning, Memory, and Cognition, 13*, 640–645.

Einstein, A. (1954). *Ideas and opinions*. New York: Crown.

Feynman, R. P. (1965). The development of the space-time view of quantum electrodynamics. In *Nobel lectures, Physics 1963–1970*, Amsterdam: Elsevier (1972). 1965 Nobel lecture, pp. 155–178. [Also available at ⟨http://nobelprize.org/nobel_prizes/physics/laureates/1965/feynman-lecture.html⟩.]

Gleick, J. (1992). *Genius: The life and science of Richard Feynman*. New York: Pantheon Books.

Hadamard, J. (1954). *The psychology of invention in the mathematical field*. New York: Dover. (Original work published by Princeton University Press, 1945.)

Hestenes, D., and Wells, M. (1992). A mechanics baseline test. *The Physics Teacher, 30*, 159–166.

Hestenes, D., Wells, M., and Swackhamer, G. (1992). Force concept inventory. *The Physics Teacher, 30*, 141–158.

Hughes-Hallett, D., Gleason, A. M., and McCallum, W. G. (2003). *Calculus* (3rd ed.). New York: Wiley.

Kaiser, D. (2005). *Drawing theories apart: The dispersion of Feynman diagrams in postwar physics*. Chicago: University of Chicago Press.

Kane, G. (2005). Picturing particle processes. *Science, 309*, 2000–2001. [Brief descriptive review of Kaiser's book.]

Larkin, J. H., and Simon, H. A. (1987). Why a diagram is (sometimes) worth 10,000 words. *Cognitive Science, 11*(1), 65–100.

Mazur, E. (1997). *Peer instruction: A user's manual*. Upper Saddle River, NJ: Prentice Hall.

Ohanian, H. C. (1985). *Physics*. New York: Norton.

9 Organizing Knowledge

Bagno, E., and Eylon, B. (1997). From problem solving to a knowledge structure: An example from the domain of electromagnetism. *American Journal of Physics, 65*, 726–736.

Eylon, B., and Reif, F. (1984). Effects of knowledge organization on task performance. *Cognition and Instruction, 1*, 5–44.

Ohanian, H. C. (1985). *Physics.* New York: Norton.

Poincaré, H. (1902). *La science et l'hypothèse.* Paris: Flammarion. [The quotation, translated by me, is near the beginning of chapter 9. An English translation of this book, titled *Science and hypothesis,* was published in New York by Dover Publications in 1952.]

10   Making Decisions

Dawes, R. M. (1988). *Rational choice in an uncertain world.* Orlando, FL: Harcourt Brace.

Dijksterhuis, A., Bos, M. W., Nordgren, L. F., and Baaren, R. B. (2006). On making the right choice: The deliberation-without-attention effect. *Science, 311,* 1005–1007.

Gigerenzer, G. (2007). *Gut feelings: The intelligence of the unconscious.* New York: Viking Penguin. [Discusses why intuitive judgments and simple rules of thumb may often be quicker and more effective than more elaborate decision processes.]

Gigerenzer, G., Todd, P., and the ABC Research Group (1999). *Simple heuristics that make us smart.* New York: Oxford University Press.

Groopman, J. (2007). *How doctors think.* New York: Houghton Mifflin. [This book, written by a physician, describes how doctors make decisions and gives examples of common forms of biased thinking.]

Hertwig, R., Barron, G., Weber, E. U., and Erev, I. (2004). Decisions from experience and the effect of rare events in risky choice. *Psychological Science, 15,* 534–539. [Investigation of a common source of bias in decision making.]

Kahneman, D., Slovic, P., and Tversky, A. (Eds.) (1982). *Judgment under uncertainty: Heuristics and biases.* Cambridge: Cambridge University Press.

Klein, G. (1998). *Sources of power: How people make decisions.* Cambridge, MA: MIT Press.

Plous, Scott. (1993). *The psychology of judgment and decision making.* New York: McGraw-Hill. [A good summary of psychological research on decision making and of common biases involved in such decisions.]

Schwartz, B. (2004). *The paradox of choice.* New York: Harper Collins. [The availability of more options can complicate decisions and may make things worse.]

Simon, H. A. (1956). Rational choice and the structure of environments. *Psychology Review, 63,* 129–138.

Tenner, E. (1997). *Why things bite back: Technnology and the revenge of unintended consequences.* New York: Vintage Books.

Thomas, W. I., and Thomas, D. S. (1928). *The child in America.* New York: Knopf.

11 Introduction to Problem Solving

Woods, D. R., Hrymak, A. N., Marshall, R. R., Wood, P. E., Crowe, C. M., Hoffman, T. W., Wright, J. D., Taylor, P. A., Woodhouse, K. A., and Bouchard, C. G. K. (1997). Developing problem solving skills: The McMaster problem solving program. *Journal of Engineering Education, 86*, 75–91.

12 Systematic Problem Solving

Chi, M. T. H., Feltovich, P. J., and Glaser, R. (1981). Categorization and representation of physics problems by experts and novices. *Cognitive Science, 5*, 121–152.

Heller, J. I., and Reif, F. (1984). Prescribing effective human problem-solving processes: Problem description in physics. *Cognition and Instruction, 1*, 177–216.

Hsu, L., Brew E., Foster T. M., and Harper, K. A. (2004). Resource letter RPS-1: Research in problem solving. *American Journal of Physics, 72*, 1147–1156. [This is a good recent source of references on problem solving.]

Newell, A., and Simon, H. A. (1972). *Human problem solving.* Englewood Cliffs, NJ: Prentice Hall.

Sabella, M. S., and Redish, E. F. (2007). Knowledge organization and activation in physics problem solving. *American Journal of Physics, 78*, 1017–1029.

Schoenfeld, A. H. (1985). *Mathematical problem solving.* Orlando, FL: Academic Press.

Silver, E. A. (Ed.), (1985). *Teaching and learning mathematical problem solving: Multiple research perspectives.* Hillsdale, NJ: Lawrence Erlbaum.

13 Dealing with Complex Problems

Inspiration Software, Inc. (2006). *Inspiration 8.0.* Portland, OR. ⟨http://www.inspiration.com⟩ [This is a software application facilitating the processing of ideas rather than words, and can be very helpful in planning tasks by the use of outlines or diagrams.]

Strunk, W., and White, E. B. (2000). *The elements of style* (4th ed.). Needham Heights, MA: Allyn & Bacon. [This is a classic little book on good writing.]

14 Efficiency and Compiled Knowledge

Ericsson, K. A., Krampe, R. T., and Tesch-Romer, C. (1993). The role of deliberate practice in the acquisition of expert performance. *Psychological Review, 100*, 363–406.

Hayes, J. R. (1985). Three problems in teaching general skills. In S. F. Chipman, J. W. Segal, and R. Glaser (Eds.), *Thinking and learning skills.* Vol. 2: *Research and open questions* (pp. 391–405). Hillsdale, NJ: Lawrence Erlbaum.

Schneider, W. (1985). Training high-performance skills: Fallacies and guidelines. *Human Factors, 27,* 285–300. [A good paper summarizing training methods facilitating automatic performance.]

Schneider, W., and Shiffrin, R. M. (1977). Controlled and automatic human information processing: I. Detection, search, and attention. *Psychological Review, 84,* 1–66.

Shiffrin, R. M., and Schneider, W. (1977). Controlled and automatic human information processing: II. Perceptual learning, automatic attending, and a general theory. *Psychological Review, 84,* 127–190.

15 Quality Assurance

Brown, A. L. (1978). Knowing when and how to remember: A problem of metacognition. In R. Glaser (Ed.), *Advances in instructional psychology* (vol. 1). Hillsdale, NJ: Lawrence Erlbaum.

Dörner, D. (1996). *The logic of failure: Recognizing and avoiding error in complex situations.* Cambridge, MA: Perseus Books. [This book discusses the use of computer simulations to study people dealing with complex problems and to identify people's inadequacies in coping with them.]

Reason, J. (1990). *Human error.* Cambridge: Cambridge University Press. [Chapters 6 and 8 are particularly relevant.]

16 Unfamiliar Knowledge Domains

Culotta, E. (1992). The calculus of education reform. *Science, 255,* 1060–1062.

De Corte, E., Op't Eynde, P., and Verschaffel, L. (2002). "Knowing what to believe": The relevance of students' mathematical beliefs for mathematics education. In B. K. Hofer and P. R. Pintrich (Eds.), *Personal epistemology: The psychology of beliefs about knowledge and knowing* (pp. 297–320). Mahwah, NJ: Lawrence Erlbaum.

Einstein, A. (1982). *Ideas and opinions.* New York, NY: Crown.

Ericsson, K. A., and Charness, N. (1994). Expert performance: Its structure and acquisition. *American Psychologist, 49,* 725–745.

Ericsson, K. A., Krampe, R. T., and Tesch-Romer, C. (1993). The role of deliberate practice in the acquisition of expert performance. *Psychological Review, 100,* 363–406.

Hammer, D. (1994). Epistemological beliefs in introductory physics. *Cognition and Instruction, 12,* 151–183.

Hofer, B. K., and Pintrich, P. R. (Eds.) (2002). *Personal epistemology: The psychology of beliefs about knowledge and knowing.* Mahwah, NJ: Lawrence Erlbaum.

Redish, E. F., Saul, J. M., and Steinberg, R. N. (1998). Student expectations in introductory physics. *American Journal of Physics, 66*, 212–224. [A survey probing students' expectations, how these differ from experts' expectations, and how they even seem to deteriorate as a result of prevailing instruction.]

Reif, F., and Larkin, J. H. (1991). Cognition in scientific and everyday domains: Comparison and learning implications. *Journal of Research in Science Teaching, 28*, 733–760.

Schoenfeld, A. H. (1983). Beyond the purely cognitive: Belief systems, social cognitions, and metacognitions as driving forces in intellectual performance. *Cognitive Science, 7*, 329–363.

Schoenfeld, A. H. (1985). *Mathematical problem solving*. Orlando, FL: Academic Press.

Schommer, M. (1990). Effects of beliefs about the nature of knowledge on comprehension. *Journal of Educational Psychology, 82*, 498–504.

17   Naive Scientific Knowledge

Bloom, P., and Weisberg, D. S. (2007). Childhood origins of adult resistance to science. *Science, 316*, 996–997.

diSessa, A. (1988). Knowledge in pieces. In G. Forman and P. B. Pufall (Eds.), *Constructivism in the computer age* (pp. 49–70). Hillsdale, NJ: Lawrence Erlbaum.

Duit, R. (2006). *Bibliography-STCSE: Students' and teachers' conceptions and science Education.* ⟨http://www.ipn.uni-kiel.de/aktuell/stcse/stcse.html⟩ [A large bibiliography of publications dealing with differing conceptions.]

Goldberg, F. M., and McDermott, L. C. (1987). An investigation of student understanding of the real image formed by a converging lens or concave mirror. *American Journal of Physics, 55*, 108–119.

Halloun, I. A., and Hestenes, D. (1985a). The initial knowledge state of college students. *American Journal of Physics, 53*, 1043–1055. [Persistence of naive scientific notions about mechanics after ostensibly good instruction.]

Halloun, I. A., and Hestenes, D. (1985b). Common sense concepts about motion. *American Journal of Physics, 53*, 1056–1065.

Hammer, D. (2000). Student resources for learning introductory physics. *American Journal of Physics, 68*, S52–S59.

Hestenes, D., and Wells, M. (1992). A mechanics baseline test. *The Physics Teacher, 30*, 159–166. [A test used to assess students' abilities to distinguish scientific mechanics concepts from more naive scientific notions.]

Hestenes, D., Wells, M., and Swackhamer, G. (1992). Force concept inventory. *The Physics Teacher, 30*, 141–158. [Another test used to assess students' abilities to distinguish scientific mechanics concepts from more naive scientific notions.]

Mazur, E. (1997). *Peer instruction: A user's manual.* Upper Saddle River, NJ: Prentice Hall.

McCloskey, M. (1983, April). Intuitive physics. *Scientific American, 248*, 122–130.

McDermott, L. C. (1984, July). Research on conceptual understanding in mechanics. *Physics Today, 37*, 24–32. [Students' naive conception about mechanics.]

McDermott, L. C., and Redish, E. F. (1999). Resource letter: PER-1, Physics Education Research. *American Journal of Physics, 67*, 755–767.

McDermott, L. C., and Shaffer, P. S. (1992). Research as a guide for curriculum development: An example from introductory electricity. Part I: Investigation of student understanding. *American Journal of Physics, 60*, 994–1003.

Minstrell, J. A. (1989). Teaching science for understanding. In L. B. Resnick and L. E. Klopfer (Eds.), *Toward the thinking curriculum: Current cognitive research* (pp. 129–149). Alexandria, VA: Association for Supervision and Curriculum Development.

Minstrell, J., and Stimpson, V. (1996). A classroom environment for learning: Guiding students' reconstruction of understanding and reasoning. In L. Schauble and R. Glaser (Eds.), *Innovations in Learning: New environments for education* (pp. 172–202). Mahwah, NJ: Lawrence Erlbaum.

Muthukrishna, N., Carnine, D., Grossen, B., and Miller, S. (1993). Children's alternative frameworks: Should they be directly addressed in science instruction? *Journal of Research in Science Teaching, 30*, 233–248. [Naive geology notions addressed in instruction.]

Ontario Institute for Studies in Education, University of Toronto (OISE/UT). (1998). *Biology misconceptions.* ⟨http://tortoise.oise.utoronto.ca/~science/biomisc.htm⟩.

Planinic, M., Boone, W. J., Krsnik, R., and Beilfuss, M. L. (2006). Exploring alternative conceptions from Newtonian dynamics and simple DC circuits: Links between item difficulty and item confidence. *Journal of Research in Science Teaching, 43*, 150–171.

Posner, G. J., Strike, K. A., Hewson, P. W., and Gertzog, W. A. (1982). Accommodation of a scientific conception: Toward a theory of conceptual change. *Science Education, 66*, 211–227.

Singh, C. (2001). Student understanding of quantum mechanics. *American Journal of Physics, 69*, 885–895.

Singh, C., Belloni, M., and Christian, M. (2006, August). *Physics Today, 59* (8), 43–49.

19 Designing the Learning Process: Goals

Brown, A. L., and Palincsar, A. S. (1989). Guided cooperative learning and individual knowledge acquisition. In L. B. Resnick (Ed.), *Knowing, learning, and instruction: Essays in honor of Robert Glaser* (pp. 393–451). Hillsdale, NJ: Lawrence Erlbaum.

Collins, A., Brown, J. S., and Newman, S. E. (1989). Cognitive apprenticeship: Teaching the crafts of reading, writing, and mathematics. In L. B. Resnick (Ed.), *Knowing, learning, and instruction: Essays in honor of Robert Glaser* (pp. 453–494). Hillsdale, NJ: Lawrence Erlbaum.

Ericsson, K. A., and Simon, H. A. (1984). *Protocol analysis of verbal data.* Cambridge, MA: MIT Press.

Heller, J. I., and Reif, F. (1984). Prescribing effective human problem-solving processes: Problem description in physics. *Cognition and Instruction, 1,* 177–216.

Klahr, D., and Carver, S. M. (1988). Cognitive objectives in a LOGO debugging curriculum: Instruction, learning, and transfer. *Cognitive Psychology, 20,* 352–404.

Palincsar, A. L., and Brown, A. L. (1984). Reciprocal teaching of comprehension-fostering and comprehension-monitoring activities. *Cognition and Instruction, 1,* 117–175.

Scardamalia, M., and Bereiter, C. (1985). Fostering the development of self-regulation in children's knowledge processing. In S. F. Chipman, J. W. Segal, and R. Glaser (Eds.), *Thinking and learning skills: Research and open questions* (pp. 563–577). Hillsdale, NJ: Lawrence Erlbaum.

Schoenfeld, A. H. (1985). *Mathematical problem solving.* Orlando, FL: Academic Press.

Van Someren, M. W., Barnard, Y. F., and Sandberg, J. A. C. (1994). *The think aloud method: A practical guide to modelling cognitive processes.* New York: Academic Press.

20 Designing the Learning Process: Means

Ericsson, K. A., and Charness, N. (1994). Expert performance: Its structure and acquisition. *American Psychologist, 49,* 725–727.

Ericsson, K. A., Krampe, R. T., and Tesch-Romer, C. (1993). The role of deliberate practice in the acquisition of expert performance. *Psychological Review, 100,* 363–406.

Kirschner, P. A., Sweller, J., and Clark, R. E. (2006). Why minimal guidance during instruction does not work: An analysis of the failure of constructivist, discovery, problem-based, experiential, and inquiry-based teaching. *Educational Psychologist, 41*(2), 75–86.

Klahr, D., and Carver, S. M. (1988). Cognitive objectives in a LOGO debugging curriculum: Instruction, learning, and transfer. *Cognitive Psychology, 20,* 352–404.

Reif, F. (1995). *Understanding basic mechanics.* New York: Wiley.

Singley, K., and Anderson, J. R. (1989). *The transfer of cognitive skill.* Cambridge, MA: Harvard University Press.

Ward, M., and Sweller, J. (1990). Structuring effective worked examples. *Cognition and Instruction, 7,* 1–39. [Devising examples with attention to cognitive load.]

21   Producing Instruction to Foster Learning

Bain, K. (2004). *What the best college teachers do.* Cambridge, MA: Harvard University Press. [Instructional suggestions based on detailed observations of very good teachers.]

Benoist, A. (1978). *The accompanist: An autobiography of Andre Benoist.* Neptune, NJ: Paganiniana.

Bereiter, C., and Scardamalia, M. (1989). Intentional learning as a goal of instruction. In L. B. Resnick (Ed.), *Knowing, learning, and instruction: Essays in honor of Robert Glaser* (pp. 361–392). Hillsdale, NJ: Lawrence Erlbaum.

Bloom, B. S. (1984). The 2 sigma problem: The search for methods of group instruction as effective as one-to-one tutoring. *Educational Researcher, 13,* 4–16.

Brown, A. L., and Palincsar, A. S. (1989). Guided cooperative learning and individual knowledge acquisition. In L. B. Resnick (Ed.), *Knowing, learning, and instruction: Essays in honor of Robert Glaser* (pp. 393–451). Hillsdale, NJ: Lawrence Erlbaum.

Carroll, J. M. (1990). *The Nurnberg funnel: Designing minimalist instruction for practical computer skill.* Cambridge, MA: MIT Press.

Chi, M. T. H., Bassok, M., Lewis, M. W., Reimann, P., and Glaser, R. (1989). Self-explanations: How students study and use examples in learning to solve problems. *Cognitive Science, 13,* 145–182.

Chi, M. T. H., Leeuw, N., Chiu, M. H., and LaVancher, C. (1994). Eliciting self-explanations improves understanding. *Cognitive Science, 18,* 439–477.

Kirschner, P. A., Sweller, J., and Clark, R. E. (2006). Why minimal guidance during instruction does not work: An analysis of the failure of constructivist, discovery, problem-based, experiential, and inquiry-based teaching. *Educational Psychologist, 41*(2), 75–86.

Palincsar, A. L., and Brown, A. L. (1984). Reciprocal teaching of comprehension-fostering and comprehension-monitoring activities. *Cognition and Instruction, 1,* 117–175.

Reif, F., and Scott, L. A. (1999). Teaching scientific thinking skills: Students and computers coaching each other. *American Journal of Physics, 67*, 819–831.

22 Traditional Instructional Methods

Bhattacharjcc, Y. (2005). Can randomized trials answer the question of what works? *Science, 307*, 1861–1863.

Crouch, C. H., Fagen, A. P., Callan, J. P., and Mazur, E. (2004). Classroom demonstrations: Learning tools or entertainment? *American Journal of Physics, 72*, 835–838.

Etkina, E., Murthy, S., and Zou, X. (2006). Using introductory labs to engage students in experimental design. *American Journal of Physics, 74*, 979–986.

Reif, F., and St. John, M. (1979). Teaching physicists' thinking skills in the laboratory. *American Journal of Physics, 47*, 950–957.

Riehl, C. (2006, June/July). Feeling better: A comparison of medical research and education research. *Educational Researcher, 35*(5), 24–29.

23 Innovative Instructional Methods

Anderson, J. R., Corbett, A. T., Koedinger, K. R., and Pelletier, R. (1995). Cognitive tutors: Lessons learned. *Journal of the Learning Sciences, 4*, 167–207.

Aronson, E., and Patnoe, S. (1997). *The jigsaw classroom: Building cooperation in the classroom* (2nd ed.). New York: Addison Wesley Longman. [See also Elliot Aronson's related Web site ⟨http://www.jigsaw.org⟩.]

Bransford, J. D., Brown, A. L., Cocking, R. R. (Eds.). (2000). *How people learn: Brain, mind, experience, and school* (expanded ed.). Washington, DC: National Academy Press. [A good review of modern educational approaches. Chapter 9 deals with technology to support learning.]

Brown, A. L., and Palincsar, A. S. (1989). Guided cooperative learning and individual knowledge acquisition. In In L. B. Resnick (Ed.), *Knowing, learning, and instruction: Essays in honor of Robert Glaser* (pp. 393–451). Hillsdale, NJ: Lawrence Erlbaum.

Bruer, J. T. (1993). *Schools for learning: A science of learning in the classroom.* Cambridge, MA: MIT Press. [A good review of some cognitively based educational approaches.]

Class response systems. (2005). Classtalk, ⟨http://www.bedu.com/ICC.html⟩; InterWrite PRS Personal Response System, ⟨http://www.gtcocalcomp.com/interwriteprs.html⟩; TI Navigator, ⟨http://education.ti.com/us/product/tech/navigator/features/features.html⟩; H-ITT Classroom response system, ⟨http://www.h-itt.com⟩.

Corbett, A. T., and Anderson, J. R. (1991). Feedback control and learning to program with the CMU Lisp Tutor. Paper presented at the annual meeting of the American Educational Research Association, Chicago, IL.

Corbett, A. T., Koedinger, K. R., and Hadley, W. H. (2001). Cognitive Tutors: From the research classroom to all classrooms. In P. S. Goodman (Ed.), *Technology enhanced learning: Opportunities for change* (pp. 235–263). Mahwah, NJ: Lawrence Erlbaum.

Crouch, C. H., and Mazur, E. (2001). Peer instruction: Ten years of experience and results. *American Journal of Physics, 69,* 970–977.

Gould, H., Tobochnik, J., and Christian, W. (2006). *Introduction to computer simulation methods.* Boston: Addison-Wesley.

Green, B. A. (1971). Physics teaching by the Keller plan at MIT. *American Journal of Physics, 39,* 764.

Heller, P., and Hollabaugh, M. (1992). Teaching problem solving through cooperative grouping. Part 2: Designing problems and structuring groups. *American Journal of Physics, 60,* 637–644.

Heller, P., Keith, R., and Anderson, S. (1992). Teaching problem solving through cooperative grouping. Part 1: Group versus individual problem solving. *American Journal of Physics, 60,* 627–636.

Johnson, D. W., and Johnson, H. (1991). *Learning together and alone: Cooperation, competition, and individualization* (3rd ed.). Englewood Cliffs, NJ: Prentice Hall.

Johnson, R. T., and Johnson, D. W. (1994). An overview of cooperative learning. In J. Thousand, A. Villa, and A. Nevin (Eds.), *Creativity and collaborative learning.* Baltimore, MD: Brookes Press.

Johnson, D. W., Johnson, R. I., and Holubec, E. J. (1993). *Cooperation in the classroom* (6th ed.). Edina, MN: Interaction Book.

Koedinger, K. R., Anderson, J. R., Hadley, W. H., and Mark, M. A. (1997). Intelligent tutoring goes to school in the big city. *International Journal of Artificial Intelligence in Education, 8,* 30–43.

Kulik, J. A., Kulik, C. L., and Cophen, P. A. (1979). A meta-analysis of outcome studies of Keller's personalized system of instruction. *American Psychologist, 34,* 307–318.

Larkin, J. H., and Chabay, R. W. (Eds.). (1992). *Computer-assisted instruction and intelligent tutoring systems: Shared issues and complementary approaches.* Hillsdale, NJ: Lawrence Erlbaum.

Laws, P. W. (1997). Millikan Lecture 1996: Promoting active learning based on physics education research in introductory physics courses. *American Journal of Physics, 65,* 14–21.

Linn, M. C. (1995). Designing computer learning environments for engineering and computer science: The scaffolded knowledge integration framework. *Journal of Science Education and Technology, 4*(2), 103–126.

Mazur, E. (1997). *Peer instruction: A user's manual.* Upper Saddle River, NJ: Prentice Hall.

McDermott, L. C., Shaffer, P. S., and Physics Education Group at the University of Washington. (2002). *Tutorials in introductory physics.* Upper Saddle River, NJ: Prentice Hall.

Meltzer, D. E., and Manivannan, K. (2002). Transforming the lecture-hall environment: The fully interactive physics lecture. *American Journal of Physics, 70*, 639–654.

Open University of Great Britain (2005). ⟨www.open.ac.uk⟩.

Reif, F., and Scott, L. A. (1999). Teaching scientific thinking skills: Students and computers coaching each other. *American Journal of Physics, 67*, 819–831.

Resnick, L. B. (1987). *Education and learning to think.* Washington, DC: National Academy Press.

Smith, S. G. (1998). Integrating computers into the first-year chemistry laboratory. *Journal of Chemical Education, 75*, 1080–1090.

Smith, S., and Stovall, I. (1996). Networked instructional chemistry: Using technology to teach chemistry. *Journal of Chemical Education, 73*, 911.

Taveggia, T. C. (1976). Personalized instruction: A summary of comparative research, 1967–1974. *American Journal of Physics, 44*, 1028–1033.

Van Heuvelen, A. (2004). *Active physics.* Palo Alto, CA: Addison-Wesley.

White, B. Y. (1993). Thinker tools: Causal models, conceptual change, and science education. *Cognition and Instruction, 10*, 1–100.

24 Some Educational Challenges

Bransford, J. D., Brown, A. L., Cocking, R. R. (Eds.). (2000). *How people learn: Brain, mind, experience, and school* (expanded ed.). Washington, DC: National Academy Press.

Bruer, J. T. (1993). *Schools for learning: A science of learning in the classroom.* Cambridge, MA: MIT Press.

Corbett, A. T., Koedinger, K. R., and Hadley, W. H. (2001). Cognitive tutors: From the research classroom to all classrooms. In P. S. Goodman (Ed.), *Technology enhanced learning: Opportunities for change* (pp. 235–263). Mahwah, NJ: Lawrence Erlbaum.

Etkina, E., Van Heuvelen, A., White-Brahmia, S., Brookes, D. T., Gentile, M., Murthy, S., Rosengrant, D., and Warren, A. (2006). Scientific abilities and their assessment. *Physical Review Special Topics-Physics Education Research 2*, 020103. ⟨http://prst-per.aps.org/pdf/PRSTPER/v2/i2/e020103⟩.

Handelsman, J., Ebert-May, D., Beichner, R., Bruns, P., Chang, A., DeHaan, R., Gentile, J., Lauffer, S., Stewart, J., Tilgham, S. M., and Wood, W. B. (2004). Scientific teaching. *Science, 304*, 521–522.

Heron, P. R. L., and Meltzer, D. E. (2005). The future of physics education research: Intellectual challenges and practical concerns. *American Journal of Physics, 73*, 390–394.

Larkin, J. H., and Reif, F. (1976). Analysis and teaching of a general skill for studying scientific text. *Journal of Educational Psychology, 68*, 431–440.

Otero, V., Finkelstein, N., McCray, R., and Pollock, S. (2006). Who is responsible for preparing science teachers? *Science, 313*, 445–446.

Reif, F., Larkin, J. H., and Brackett, G. C. (1976). Teaching general learning and problem-solving skills. *American Journal of Physics, 44*, 212–217.

Reif, F., and Scott, L. A. (1999). Teaching scientific thinking skills: Students and computers coaching each other. *American Journal of Physics, 67*, 819–831.

Wieman, C., and Perkins, K. (November 2005). Transforming physics education. *Physics Today*, 36–41.

Index